The Secret Relationship Between Blacks and Jews

Volume One

Prepared by
The Historical Research Department
The Nation of Islam
P.O. Box 81051
Springfield, MA, U.S.A. 01138

Fifth printing, 2005

Published by The Nation of Islam
Chicago, Illinois U.S.A.

Printed in the Nation of Islam

The Secret Relationship Between Blacks and Jews

Volume One

Blacks and Jews have recently begun to question their relationship and its strategic role in their individual development. This report is an examination of documented historical evidence and is intended to provide an historical perspective for intellectual debate of this crucial social matter.

This report was prepared by
The Historical Research Department of

The Nation of Islam

1991

ALL PRAISE IS DUE TO ALLAH

Note on Sources

The information contained herein has been compiled primarily from Jewish historical literature. Every effort has been made to present evidence from the most respected of the Jewish authorities and whose works appear in established historical journals or are published by authoritative Jewish publishing houses. A substantial body of evidence that supports the findings herein was excluded by the editors and deemed to be from sources considered anti-Semitic and / or anti-Jewish.

Footnote Abbreviations

The following abbreviations will be substituted for often-cited reference material.

AJA – American Jewish Archives (Cincinnati: Hebrew Union College)
AJHQ – American Jewish Historical Quarterly changed from *PAJHS*—Publications of the American Jewish Historical Society—at vol. 51, September 1961.
EAJA – Herbert I. Bloom, *The Economic Activities of the Jews of Amsterdam in the Seventeenth and Eighteenth Centuries* (Port Washington, NY / London: Kennikat Press, 1937)
EHJ – Salo W. Baron, Arcadius Kahan, and Nachum Gross, eds., *Economic History of the Jews* (New York: Schocken Books, 1975)
EJ – *Encyclopaedia Judaica* (Jerusalem: Keter Publishing House, Ltd., 1971)
Emmanuel HJNA – Isaac S. and Susan A. Emmanuel, *History of the Jews of the Netherland Antilles* (Cincinnati: American Jewish Archives, 1973)
Karp, JEA(1,2,3) – Abraham J. Karp, ed., *The Jewish Experience in America: Selected Studies from the Publications of the American Jewish Historical Society,* 3 vols. (Waltham, MA: American Jewish Historical Society, 1969)
MCAJ(1,2,3) – Jacob Rader Marcus, *The Colonial American Jew: 1492-1776,* 3 vols. (Detroit: Wayne State University Press, 1970)
JRM/Docs. – Jacob Rader Marcus, *American Jewry: Documents of the Eighteenth Century* (Cincinnati: Hebrew College Union Press, 1959)
MEAJ(1,2) – Jacob Rader Marcus, *Early American Jewry,* 2 vols. (Philadelphia: Jewish Publication Society of America, 1951)
JRM/Essays – Jacob Rader Marcus, ed., *Essays in American Jewish History* (American Jewish Archives, KTAV Publishing House, 1975)
JRM/Memoirs(1,2,3) – Jacob Rader Marcus, *Memoirs of American Jews 1775-1865,* 3 vols. (New York: KTAV Publishing House, 1974)
MUSJ(1,2) – Jacob Rader Marcus, *United States Jewry, 1776-1985* (Detroit: Wayne State University Press, 1989)
PAJHS – Publications of the American Jewish Historical Society changed to (*AJHQ*) American Jewish Historical Quarterly, vol. 51, September 1961.

Table of Contents

cannot legalize "slavery" = RICO

slavery - prisoners of war
- punishment for crime
upon being duly convicted

Editors' Note

This study is structured as a presentation of historical evidence concerning the relationship of one people with another. The facts, as established by highly respected scholars of the Jewish community, are here exposed and linked by as sparse a narrative as is journalistically permitted. It is not the mission of this study to interpret the data to an extent greater than is required to present these facts clearly. The facts, we believe, speak for themselves. Statements will be presented and then verified by references, which are fully cited in the footnotes. Some statements may seem redundant only because we have made every attempt to include the words of every Jewish scholar who has commented on the subject at hand. We have made every effort to be fair and just in the presentation of this data and hereby invite all analysis to the contrary.

The terms *buy, own* and *sell,* and variations thereof, in connection with the commerce in Black people, will be used with reservation and primarily for the convenience of the reader. In no way should the reader infer sanction of these activities—which are wholly illegal and immoral crimes against humanity—by the use of the terminology of legitimate commercial transactions. Also, the term *slave* refers to the African men, women and children who were forcibly entrapped in dehumanizing conditions for the profit of others. We do not accept such a term as descriptive of their character or nature, only of their circumstance.

And finally, the subject at hand is a controversial one and should be approached with great sensitivity. Those who would use this material as a basis for the violation of the human rights of another are abusing the knowledge herein. The wise will benefit to see this as an opportunity to develop a more equitable relationship between the families of man.

Introduction

Throughout history Jews have faced charges of economic exploitation of Gentile communities around the world. Indeed, no single group of people has faced blanket expulsion in so many places around the world as frequently as have the Jews. The pattern and the charges are familiar: monopolization, usury, "sharp practices," selling of "cheap" goods, frequent bankruptcies, etc. All such claims seem to preface the expulsion orders and are vigorously denied both by those charged and by the Jewish writers of history.

But this is not the only charge that is made against Jews. Jews have been conclusively linked to the greatest criminal endeavor ever undertaken against an entire race of people—a crime against humanity: the Black African Holocaust. They were participants in the kidnapping and forcible exportation of millions of Black African citizens into a wretched and inhuman life of bondage for the financial benefit of Jews. The effects of this unspeakable tragedy are still being felt among the peoples of the world at this very hour.

Deep within the recesses of the Jewish historical record is the irrefutable evidence that the most prominent of the Jewish pilgrim fathers used kidnapped Black Africans disproportionately more than any other ethnic or religious group in New World history and participated in every aspect of the international slave trade. The immense wealth of Jews, as with most of the white colonial fathers, was acquired by the brutal subjugation of Black Africans purely on the basis of skin color—a concept unfamiliar to Moses. Now, compiled for the first time, the Jewish sources reveal the extent of their complicity in Black slavery in the most graphic of terms.

Until now, the facts herein were known only to a few. Most have always assumed that the relationship between Blacks and Jews has been mutually supportive, friendly and fruitful—two suffering people bonding to overcome hatred and bigotry to achieve success. But history tells an altogether different story. This report will focus on the hidden history of Blacks and Jews from the Jewish historical record. Rabbi Henry Cohen, author of the book *Justice Justice*, makes a telling point:

> [T]he parallels between the Nazi terror and the American slave trade are more startling than we may realize. When Negroes were brought from the heart of Africa to the American South, one-third died enroute to the African coast and one-third died in the suffocating prisons on board ship. Once here, families were purposely broken up; husbands, wives, and children forced to go their separate ways. Must we be reminded of the death toll in the suffocating boxcars bound for Auschwitz or of the tearing of children from their mothers' arms.[1]

Still true

Furthermore, in Roberta Strauss Feuerlicht's *The Fate of the Jews: A People Torn Between Israeli Power and Jewish Ethics*, she confronts the reality of her people's western development:

> [W]hether so many [Southern] Jews would have achieved so high a level of social, political, economic and intellectual status and recognition, without the presence of the lowly and degraded slave, is indeed dubious. How ironic that the distinctions bestowed upon [Jewish] men like Judah P. Benjamin were in some measure dependent upon the sufferings of the Negro slaves they bought and sold with such equanimity.[2]

It is a relationship that is not fully known—one that needs further analysis. Hidden and misunderstood, it is indeed time to reopen the files to review and reconsider *The Secret Relationship Between Blacks and Jews.*

---

[1]Rabbi Henry Cohen, *Justice, Justice: A Jewish View of the Black Revolution* (New York: Union of American Hebrew Congregations, 1968), p. 48.

[2]Roberta Strauss Feuerlicht, *The Fate of the Jews: A People Torn Between Israeli Power and Jewish Ethics* (New York: Times Books, 1983), pp. 187-88, note 5.

Jews and the African Slave Trade

Throughout the history of the practice, Jews have been involved in the purchase and sale of human beings. This fact is confirmed by their own scholars and historians. In his book *A History of the Jews*, Solomon Grayzel states that "Jews were among the most important slave dealers" in European society.[3] Lady Magnus writes that in the Middle Ages, "The principal purchasers of slaves were found among the Jews....[T]hey seemed to be always and everywhere at hand to buy, and to have the means equally ready to pay."[4] Henry L. Feingold stated that "Jews who were frequently found at the heart of commerce could not have failed to contribute a proportionate share to the [slave] trade directly or indirectly. In 1460, when Jews were the masters of the nautical sciences in Portugal, that nation was importing 700-800 slaves yearly."[5]

The success of these medieval merchants was enhanced by their supreme linguistic abilities. They spoke Arabic, Persian, Roman, Frankish, Spanish and Slavonic and "displayed a business acumen far in advance of the times."[6]

---

[3]Solomon Grayzel, *A History of the Jew: From Babylonian Exile to the End of World War II* (Philadelphia: Jewish Publication Society of America, 1948), p. 312.

[4]Lady Magnus, *Outlines of Jewish History*, revised by M. Friedlander (Philadelphia: Jewish Publication Society of America, 1890), p. 107; *Jewish Encyclopaedia*, vol. 11 (New York and London: Funk and Wagnalls, 1905 - 1916), p. 402: "At the time of Pope Gregory the Great (590-604) Jews had become the chief traders in this class of traffic."

[5]Henry L. Feingold, *Zion in America: The Jewish Experience from Colonial Times to the Present* (New York: Twayne Publishing, 1974), pp. 42-43.

[6]Marcus Arkin, author of *Aspects of Jewish Economic History* (Philadelphia: Jewish Publication Society of America, 1975), pp. 44-45, reveals that in some European provinces, Jewish traders "appear to have held almost a monopoly of international commerce – so much so that the words 'Judaeus' and 'mercator' appear as synonyms in Carolingian documents." See S. D. Goitein, *Jewish Letters of Medieval Traders* (New Jersey: Princeton University Press, 1973), pp. 6, 16, 17, 18. Also, Magnus, *Outlines of Jewish History*, p. 152, confirms the same. Notice the juxtaposition of the first two sentences of the Magnus passage:

> They accepted the state of things, and so long as they were let alone, commerce, too, became in Jewish hands a dignified, a useful, and an honourable calling. They dealt in slaves, as was the necessity of the time, and these slaves were the better off for having Jewish masters; their trading fleets sailed on the Mediterranean, and their ready-tongued travellers brought the products of the East to the markets of the West. But gradually all this sort of commerce became impossible....Then, by force of feeling as well as by law, the slave trade was put down.

The Jews' participation in the slave trade, particularly their trafficking in non-Jewish slaves, incited the moral indignation of Europe's Gentile population. The Europeans reacted by taxing the Jews and some were expelled from their host countries for this activity.[7] The expulsion of Jews by European governments was not unusual, with most of the complaints centered around economic exploitation, monopolizing, or "sharp practice." By 1500, with the exception of certain parts of Italy, Western Europe had closed its doors to Jewish people.[8] The following listing is a partial record of the countries and dates of the Jews' expulsion from various European communities.[9]

Mainz, 1012
France, 1182
Upper Bavaria, 1276
England, 1290
France, 1306
France, 1322
Saxony, 1349
Hungary, 1360
Belgium, 1370
Slovakia, 1380
France, 1394
Austria, 1420
Lyons, 1420
Cologne, 1424
Mainz, 1438
Augsburg, 1439
Upper Bavaria, 1442
Netherlands, 1444
Brandenburg, 1446
Mainz, 1462
Mainz, 1483
Warsaw, 1483
Spain, 1492
Italy, 1492
Lithuania, 1495
Portugal, 1496
Naples, 1496
Navarre, 1498
Nuremberg, 1498
Brandenburg, 1510
Prussia, 1510
Genoa, 1515
Naples, 1533
Italy, 1540
Naples, 1541
Prague, 1541
Genoa, 1550
Bavaria, 1551
Prague, 1557
Papal States, 1569
Hungary, 1582
Hamburg, 1649
Vienna, 1669
Slovakia, 1744
Bohemia/Moravia, 1744
Moscow, 1891

Over the next centuries the centers of Jewish development moved into the Western Hemisphere, where land and commercial opportunities provided the incentives for immigration. The open and ungoverned territory and the docile and vulnerable indigenous population were an irresistible attraction to the "maligned race." They acquired great wealth in their Caribbean

---

The *Universal Jewish Encyclopaedia*, vol. 9, p. 565, states that, for the same reason, the Jews were "especially adapted" to the slave trade.

[7]*EJ*, vol. 14, pp. 1660-64; *EHJ*, pp. 271-72. According to Magnus (p. 106), however, "Selling people into slavery has a dreadful sound, but in those days it was not quite so dreadful a thing, nor even so avoidable a one, as it would be in these. Great tracts of cultivated land were constantly being laid waste; what was to be done with the vanquished dwellers thereon?" S. D. Goitein, *A Mediterranean Society, The Jewish Communities of the Arab World as Portrayed in the Documents of the Cairo Geniza*, vol. 1 (Berkeley: University of California Press, 1967), p. 147, reasons similarly.

[8]Yosef Hayim Yerushalmi, "Between Amsterdam and New Amsterdam: The Place of Curaçao and the Caribbean in Early Modern Jewish History," *PAJHS*, vol. 72 (1982-83), p. 173; Lee Anne Durham Seminario, *The History of the Blacks, The Jews and the Moors in Spain* (Madrid, 1975), pp. 40-42.

[9]Richard Siegel and Carl Rheins, eds., *The Jewish Almanac* (New York: Bantam Books, 1980), pp. 127-29.

and South American enterprises and eventually moved into the American Northeast, which became the economic focal point. It started with the forced expulsion of the Jews from the Spanish empire and with the early explorer and "discoverer" of America, Christopher Columbus.

Columbus, Jews and the Slave Trade

> *"Not jewels, but Jews, were the real financial basis of the first expedition of Columbus."*[10]

On August 2, 1492, more than 300,000 Jews were expelled from Spain,[11] ending their five-century involvement in the Black hostage trade in that region. In fact, the Spanish Jews amassed large fortunes dealing in Christian slaves and became quite prominent within Spain's hierarchy.[12] They had obtained the most important offices and positions of trust in the cabinets and counting houses of the rulers and had maintained great influence over the regional trade, causing many to believe that the Jews exercised an unhealthy domination over the economy of the region.[13] The rulers were convinced enough to order all Jews to either convert to Christianity or leave Spain.

The Marranos: The Secret Jews

The Marranos were those compulsorily converted Jews and their descendants who outwardly became Christians but secretly continued to meet in the synagogue, celebrated feast days and observed the Jewish Sabbath. The name *marrano* may be derived

---

[10]George Cohen, *The Jew in the Making of America* (Boston: Knights of Columbus, Stratford Co., 1924), p. 33.

[11]Seymour B. Liebman, *The Jews in New Spain: Faith, Flame, and the Inquisition* (Coral Gables, Florida: University of Miami Press, 1970), p. 32: The actual number is in dispute. Some authorities have said that 160,000 families were expelled, while others have said 800,000 individuals; few have estimated over one million.

[12]Harry L. Golden and Martin Rywell, *Jews in American History: Their Contribution to the United States of America* (Charlotte: Henry Lewis Martin Co., 1950), p. 5; Feuerlicht, p. 39: "The golden age of Jewry in Spain owed some of its wealth to an international network of Jewish slave traders. Bohemian Jews purchased Slavonians and sold them to Spanish Jews for resale to the Moors." Also, *Jewish Encyclopaedia*, vol. 11, p. 402.

[13]M. Kayserling, *Christopher Columbus and the Participation of the Jews in the Spanish and Portuguese Discoveries* (New York: Hermon Press, 1894), pp. 28, 29, 30, 31, 83.

from the old Castilian *marrano* (swine) or perhaps from the Arabic *mahran* (forbidden). In 1350, Spain began a series of conversion drives to convert all Jews in Spain to Christianity (see the section entitled "The Spanish Inquisition"), and in unprecedented numbers—and with little resistance—the Jews converted.[14] This rush to mass conversion, an event unparalleled in Jewish history, is perhaps best summed up by Cecil Roth: "It was not difficult for insincere, temporizing Jews to become insincere temporizing Christians."[15]

The "Marranos," also called *conversos* (the converted), or *nefiti* (the neophytes), or "New Christians," were simply charged with not being Catholic. The same applied to the Muslims, who were expelled in like manner and in greater numbers than the Jews.[16] Some fifty thousand Jews chose to convert rather than leave their land and their riches.[17]

Contrary to popular notions, those who left were not refugees searching for religious freedom, but entrepreneurs looking for economic opportunities. When they fled, they brought with them few Torah scrolls and even fewer copies of the Jewish holy book Talmud. When asked what he thought most Marranos knew of Judaism after their flight from Spain and Portugal, Roth answered in one word—"Nothing."[18]

The majority fled south and eastward to North Africa and to centers like Salonika, Constantinople, Aleppo and Damascus[19]; while others sought and found refuge in the Netherlands, where they "established synagogues, schools, cemeteries and a high level of wealth and culture."[20] Most escaped "with considerable sums of money."[21] Though scattered throughout the globe by political,

---

[14]Max I. Dimont, *The Jews In America: The Roots, History, and Destiny of American Jews* (New York: Simon and Schuster, 1978), p. 23.

[15]Dimont, p. 24.

[16]Dimont, p. 27.

[17]Dimont, p. 27. Liebman, *The Jews in New Spain*, p. 32: Father Mariana, a Jesuit, stated: "Many persons [condemned] the resolution adopted by...Ferdinand in expelling so profitable and opulent a people, acquainted with every mode of collecting wealth."

[18]Dimont, p. 28.

[19]Simeon J. Maslin, "1732 and 1982 in Curaçao," *AJHQ*, vol. 72 (December 1982), p. 158. According to Lee Anne Durham Seminario, *The History of the Blacks, The Jews and the Moors in Spain* (Madrid, 1975), p. 17, Jews were familiar with North Africa:

> There are some Catalonian and Majorcan maps of the fourteenth century, drawn from the knowledge gleaned from Jewish merchants who could travel with relative freedom in North Africa, and showing, with surprising accuracy, the routes from the Mediterranean to the land of the Negroes in Guinea and the western Sudan.

[20]Maslin, p. 160.

[21]Dr. M. Kayserling, "The Colonization of America by the Jews," *PAJHS*, vol. 2 (1894), p. 75.

economic and religious circumstances, they would reunite later in an unholy coalition of kidnappers and slave makers.

The day after the Spanish expulsion, Christopher Columbus, whose actual name was Cristobol Colon, took a group of Jewish refugees with him to the New World.[22] Queen Isabella signed both the expulsion decree and Columbus' voyage order the very same day. But it was not the queen or the king who funded the voyage. George Cohen, among many Jewish historians, proclaims that wealthy Jews financed the expeditions of Columbus, and adds that the story of Isabella's jewels "is not founded on facts," but rather it was an invention "intended to glorify the Queen."[23]

Three Marranos—Luis de Santangel (or Santangelo),[24] a wealthy merchant, Gabriel Sanchez,[25] the royal treasurer, and his assistant Juan Cabrero,—influenced Queen Isabella to help them finance the voyage. Cabrero and Santangel invested 17,000 ducats, which would be well over $100,000 today.[26] Alfonso de la Caballeria and Diego de Deza also provided funds; Abraham Ben Samuel Zacuto provided astronomy and navigation equipment and Isaac Abravanel also assisted. Six prominent Jews accompanied

---

[22]Max J. Kohler, "Luis De Santangel and Columbus," *PAJHS*, vol. 10 (1902), p. 162: Columbus himself, in his journal, calls attention to the "coincidence" of his first voyage of discovery and the expulsion of the Jews from Spain, in the following passage: "So, after having expelled the Jews from your dominions, your Highness, in the same month of January, ordered me to proceed with a sufficient armament, to the said regions of India." For further clarification see Kayserling, *Christopher Columbus,* p. 85 and p. 85 note.

[23]G. Cohen, *Jew in the Making of America,* p. 37; Kayserling, *Christopher Columbus,* p. 74, states the same: "This story...has recently been relegated to the realm of fable."

[24]Cecil Roth, *History of the Marranos* (Philadelphia: Jewish Publication Society of America, 1932), pp. 272-73: "The first royal grant to export grain and horses to America was made in favor of Luis de Santangel, who may thus be reckoned the founder of two of the greatest American industries." Kohler, "Columbus," p. 159: "In Emilio Castelar's 'Life of Columbus,' *Century Magazine,* vol. 44 (July, 1892), p. 364, an interesting passage concerning Columbus' indebtedness to the Jews reads as follows: 'It is a historical fact that one day Ferdinand V, on his way from Aragon to Castile, and needing some ready cash, as often happened, owing to the impoverishment of those kingdoms, halted his horse at the door of Santangelo's house in Calatayud, and, dismounting, entered and obtained a considerable sum from the latter's inexhaustible private coffers.'" Also, Kayserling, *Christopher Columbus,* shows that this same Luis de Santangel, who was then chancellor of the royal household and comptroller general of Aragon, personally advanced nearly all this money (pp. 55-79). He says (p. 75): At that time "neither Ferdinand nor Isabella, had at their disposal enough money to equip a fleet." See Kohler, "Columbus," p. 160.

[25]Roth, *Marranos,* p. 272: "Gabriel Sanchez, the High Treasurer of Aragon, who was another of the explorer's most fervent patrons, was of full Jewish blood, being a son of a *converso* couple..."

[26]Two hundred years later a fully equipped sailing vessel might have cost $30,000.

Columbus including Mastre Bernal, a physician; Marco, a surgeon; Roderigo Sanchez, an inspector; Luis de Torres, an interpreter; and sailors Alfonso de la Calle[27] and Roderigo de Triana, who is claimed to be "the first white man ever to see the new world."[28] Torres settled in Cuba and has been credited with introducing tobacco to Europe from his vast tobacco plantations.[29]

Cecil Roth's *History of the Marranos:*

> The connection between the Jews and the discovery of America was not, however, merely a question of fortuitous coincidence. The epoch-making expedition of 1492 was as a matter of fact very largely a Jewish, or rather a Marrano, enterprise.[30]

Columbus, the Jew?

A few scholars, including Roth, present strong evidence that Columbus was himself a Jew. He hid his Jewishness, they say, because "no Spanish Jew could ever have expected aid from the king and queen of Spain, so the explorer claimed to be an Italian Catholic."[31] Tina Levitan, author of *Jews in American Life,* found the first reference to Columbus' Jewishness in print in a diplomatic document dated fifty-eight years after the discoverer's

---

[27]Roth, *Marranos,* pp. 272-73: "Mestre Bernal, who had been reconciled in 1490 for Judaizing"; "Rodrigo Sanches, a relative of the High Treasurer, joined the party as Superintendent at the personal request of the Queen"; Luis de Torres, the interpreter, was, according to Golden and Rywell, the first European to set foot in the new land; Alonso de la Calle, whose very name denoted that he was born in the Jewish quarter."

[28]According to Golden and Rywell, p. 9: "It was two o'clock in the morning when he shouted 'Land, Land.' The sails were shortened and at daybreak Friday, October 12, 1492, a new world was before them." Columbus claimed that it was he who first sighted land in order to claim the royal gratuity of ten thousand maravedis and a silk waistecoat promised to the one who made the first sighting. See Kayserling, *Christopher Columbus,* pp. 91, 110.

[29]Tina Levitan, *Jews in American Life* (New York: Hebrew Publishing, 1969), p. 4; Golden and Rywell, p. 9, claim that Torres "acquired great tracts of land from the Indians." A family member, Antonio de Torres, later commanded twelve of Columbus' fleet (Golden and Rywell, p. 7). Israel Abrahams, *Jewish Life in the Middle Ages* (New York: Atheneum, 1969), p. 138: "Tobacco, so far as its use in Europe is concerned, was also discovered by a Jew, Luis de Torres, a companion of Columbus. The Church, as is well known, raised many objections to the use of tobacco, and King James I's pedantic treatise only voiced general prejudice. Jewish Rabbis, on the other hand, hailed the use of tobacco as an aid to sobriety." Abrahams, p. 139: "It is worth noting that Jews early took to the trade in tobacco, a trade which they almost monopolize in England today." Torres is also claimed to have named the turkey calling it "tukki," the Hebrew word for peacock. See Jack Wolfe, *A Century with Iowa Jewry, 1833 - 1940* (Des Moines: Iowa Printing, 1941), p. 10.

[30]Roth, *Marranos,* p. 271.

[31]Levitan, *Jews in American Life,* p. 4. See also Cecil Roth, *Personalities and Events in Jewish History* (Philadelphia: Jewish Publication Society of America, 1953), pp. 192-211.

death. The French ambassador to Spain, she reveals, refers to "Columbus the Jew."[32] Furthermore she states:

> From him we learn that Cristobal Colon (who never called himself Christopher Columbus and never spoke or wrote Italian) was the son of Susanna Fontanarossa [also spelled Fonterosa] and Domingo Colon of Pontevedra, Spain, where those bearing such surnames were Jews, some of whom had been brought before the Spanish Inquisition....Letters written by him to strangers have the customary X at the top to indicate the faith of the writer, but of the thirteen letters written to his son only one bears an X, and that letter was meant to be shown to the King of Spain. The others have in the place of the X a sign that looks like the Hebrew characters B and H, initials used by religious Jews meaning in Hebrew, "With the Help of God."[33]

Harry L. Golden and Martin Rywell, authors of *Jews in American History: Their Contribution to the United States of America,* are quite insistent about the Jewishness of Columbus. They cite where Ferdinand, Columbus' son, writes that his father's "progenitors were of the blood royal of Jerusalem..."[34] In Columbus' words, "for when all is done, David, that most prudent king was first a shepherd and after wards chosen King of Jerusalem, and I am a servant of that same Lord who raised him to such a dignity."[35] One Jewish author insists that "all existing portraits of the discoverer gave him a Jewish cast of countenance." Another claimed that a "certain soft-heartedness in Columbus is a Jewish trait."[36] His lineage also pointed to Jewish roots—his mother's maiden name was Suzanna Fonterosa, "daughter of Jacob, granddaughter of Abraham and a Jewess. His father, Domingo Colon, was a map-seller. Did not Columbus write the King of Spain that his ancestors were interested in maps?"[37]

---

[32]Levitan, p. 5.

[33]Levitan, p. 5.

[34]Golden and Rywell, p. 7; Friedrich Heer, *God's First Love: Christians and Jews over Two Thousand Years* (New York: Weybright and Talley, 1967), pp. 104-6: Heer discusses Columbus' interest in the messianic implications of his western explorations and his repeated references to prophecy as well as other indications of his Jewish descent.

[35]Golden and Rywell, p. 7.

[36]Lee M. Friedman, *Jewish Pioneers and Patriots* (Philadelphia: Jewish Publication Society of America, 1942), pp. 62-3.

[37]Golden and Rywell, p. 7, cite the works of Celso G. de la Riega (Geographical Society of Madrid, 1898) and Henry Vignaud (American Historical Review, n.d.).

Columbus, the Slave-Dealing Jew?

Christopher Columbus was an experienced sailor long before his infamous voyage west. Sir Arthur Helps writes that "In the course of [his] letters, [Columbus] speaks after the fashion of a practised slave dealer." In fact, in 1498, his five-ship expedition brought 600 Indians to Spain as slaves. Two hundred were given to the masters of the ships and four hundred sold in Spain.[38] Columbus employed slave labor in gold mining even before sailing for the New World. He helped to start the Portuguese West African slave-labor settlement of San Jorge El Mina (St. George of the Mines) in present-day Ghana, formerly known as the Gold Coast.[39]

When the Spaniards found gold in the New World, reports Eric Rosenthal in his book *Gold! Gold! Gold!: The Johannesburg Gold Rush,* they started

> on a gold hunt of such intensity that the natives came to believe the white men suffered from some disease curable only by the limitless application of this metal....[When] Columbus discovered that, apart from some poor alluvial deposits, the gold simply did not exist, he forced the harmless Indian aborigines into slavery....The entire importation of gold from the New World for the first 20 years after 1492 represented in cash only $300,000 a year, and the total then recovered, worth about $5 million, cost at least 1 $^1/_2$ million Indian lives.[40]

Columbus was anything but a blessing to the New World population. The Europeans, led by Columbus, brought unprecedented brutality to the West, leaving the remains of whole

---

[38]Golden and Rywell, p. 18 note; Sir Arthur Helps, *The Spanish Conquest in America,* vol. 1 (New York, 1900), pp. 113-14.

[39]Eric Rosenthal, *Gold! Gold! Gold!: The Johannesburg Gold Rush* (Johannesburg: MacMillan, 1970), p. 71 note.

[40]Humboldt is paraphrased in Rosenthal, p. 71. According to a translation of the Spanish-Jewish historian Joseph ben Joshua Hakkohen found in Richard J. H. Gottheil's, "Columbus in Jewish Literature,"*PAJHS*, vol. 2 (1894), p. 136, upon Columbus' arrival in the "New World":

> Columbus rejoiced when he saw that the natives had much gold, and that they were disposed to be friendly....He placed [among the Indians] thirty-eight men in order that they might learn the language of the people and the hidden places of the country, until the time when he should return to them....Columbus took with him ten Indians...

Columbus' chief aim was to find gold, writes M. Kayserling, *Christopher Columbus*, p. 86:

> [I]n a letter to the queen he frankly declared that this gold might even be the means of purifying the souls of men and of securing their entrance into Paradise. Thus he stipulated that he was to have a tenth of all pearls, precious stones, gold, silver, spices, and other wares, — in short, a tenth of everything found, bought, bartered, or otherwise obtained in the newly discovered lands...

communities of Red people in their wake.[41] On Hispaniola Columbus found gold and a docile Arawak population. He lavished praise on the natives and gained their trust and affection and then proceeded to enslave them. According to Columbus: "They are without arms, all naked, and without skill at arms and great cowards, a thousand running away from three, and thus they are good to be ordered about, to be made to work, plant, and do whatever is wanted, to build towns and be taught to go clothed and accept our customs."[42] Cities began to spring up all over the island of Hispaniola. The traffic in slaves—African and Indian—grew rapidly, and some Jews were engaged in this trade as agents for the royal families of Spain and Portugal.[43]

Whether or not Columbus was a Jew, as so many Jewish historians now claim, has not been definitively proven; however, it is clear that Columbus' brutality against and enslavement of the indigenous population was financed by Jewish investors. The history books appear to have confused the word *Jews* for the word *jewels*. Queen Isabella's *jewels* had no part in the finance of Columbus' expedition, but her *Jews* did.[44]

---

[41]See Mark A. Burkholder and Lyman L. Johnson's, *Colonial Latin America* (New York: Oxford University Press, 1990), pp. 28-33, in which they chronicle the legacy of Christopher Columbus and the brutal conditions imposed by the Spaniards on the indigenous citizens of the "New World."

[42]Carl Ortwin Sauer, *The Early Spanish Main* (Berkeley: University of California Press, 1966), p. 32; Burkholder and Johnson, p. 26.

[43]Burkholder and Johnson, p. 28; Liebman, *The Jews in New Spain*, p. 47.

[44]G. Cohen, pp. 33, 37. See also Kayserling, *Christopher Columbus*, p. 110.

The Jews and Slavery in Colonial South America and the Caribbean

> *"With the spread of sugar, cotton, cocoa, and other plantations the slave ships began to plow those waters, nor can it be said that Jewish traders were absent from the hideous traffic."*[45]

The Jewish Caribbean presence began in earnest with Columbus' initial foray into the region. With these early Jewish colonists the economic motivation for the exploitation of millions of Black Africans was introduced to the Western Hemisphere. The strategy seemed simple enough: wealth would be amassed through a plantation economy driven by sugar cane. The two companion enterprises of trading sugar and slaves were common occupations of Jews in the Middle Ages.[46] The early European explorers had ascertained that the climate, both temperately and financially, made the Caribbean a logical enterprise zone, and in this transfer of the sugar industry into the eastern Caribbean, the history of the industry became entwined with the western migration of the Jews. They were primarily the financiers and merchants and in a few cases they were also the plantation masters.[47] Jews from Portugal, Holland, England and all over Europe advantaged themselves through the domination of the commerce of these island regions, particularly in sugar.[48]

---

[45]Rufus Learsi, *The Jews in America: A History* (New York: KTAV Publishing House, 1972), p. 25.

[46]*EHJ*, p. 189, cites the Cairo *Genizah* records. The Jews maintained a formidable influence over sugar production even until the twentieth century. For example, in the Soviet Union, see *EHJ*, p. 190: By 1872, Jews such as M. Halperin and M. Sachs helped put one-quarter of the total sugar production in Russia in Jewish hands. In 1914, 86 refineries in Russia (32% of the total) were owned by Jews; 42.7% of the administrators of the joint-stock sugar companies were Jewish, and two-thirds of the sugar trade was in Jewish hands.

As for slavery, the Jews of the Middle Ages "regarded the Slavic east as the land of slaves par excellence." They are recorded as dealers of castrated slaves (eunuchs) as early as 870 AD in China. They appear involved in the trade in documents dated 906, 1004, 1009 and 1085. See *EHJ*, p. 271 and also *EJ*, vol. 14, pp. 1661-62.

[47]J. H. Galloway, *The Sugar Cane Industry* (Cambridge University Press, 1989), p. 79. Daniel M. Swetschinski, "Conflict and Opportunity in 'Europe's Other Sea': The Adventure of Caribbean Jewish Settlement," *AJHQ*, vol. 72 (1982-83), p. 222: "The number of sugar plantations in Portuguese America rose from 70 in 1570, to 130 in 1585, to 230 in 1610, and to 346 in 1629."

[48]Learsi (p. 25) said that Jews played a "leading part." See also Marc Lee Raphael, *Jews and Judaism in the United States: A Documentary History* (New York: Behrman House, 1983), p. 14.

Jewish slave traders procured Black Africans by the tens of thousands and funnelled them to the plantations of South America and throughout the Caribbean.[49] There remains no documented trace of protest over this behavior—it was a purely commercial venture with which Judaism did not interfere. Whether the local influence was Portuguese, Dutch or English, the Black man and woman fared the same. In Curaçao in the seventeenth century, as well as in the British colonies of Barbados and Jamaica in the eighteenth century, Jewish merchants played a major role in the slave trade. In fact, in all the American colonies, whether French (Martinique), British, or Dutch, Jewish merchants frequently dominated.[50]

This study is only slightly concerned with the particular European influences governing the region at various times—that subject has been addressed elsewhere. All western settlements simply required Black labor for their very survival. This passage in Samuel Oppenheim's study of Jews in Guiana applies throughout the region:

> The demand for slaves for the colony seems to have been quite brisk. They were regarded as necessary for its support, its sole salvation...as valuable as burnished silver, and were not allowed to be made the subject of sale to other localities.[51]

With the help of the Jewish slave traders, Blacks poured in and in some locales eventually outnumbered whites by as much as 5 to 1 in the cities and 30 to 1 in the rural plantation areas.[52] The expertise that Jews previously developed in the sugar islands of Madeira and Sao Thome, made them indispensable to the New World scheme. Daniel M. Swetschinski estimates that the Jewish share in overall trade was disproportionately large: "[They] constituted about 65-75% of the total Portuguese mercantile community while hardly totalling more than 10% of the population."[53] This dominance of trade by the Jewish community

---

[49]Galloway, p. 81: "As sugar grew in significance, so did African slavery: from about 6,000 slaves in 1643 to 20,000 in 1655 and 38,782 in 1680." See Learsi, p. 22. He characterizes the settlements as being based on a "slave economy on which all the plantations of the New World rested."

[50]Raphael, p. 14.

[51]Samuel Oppenheim, "An Early Jewish Colony in Western Guiana: Supplemental Data," *PAJHS*, vol. 17 (1909), pp. 57-58; Stephen Alexander Fortune, *Merchants and Jews: The Struggle for the British West Indian Caribbean, 1650-1750* (Gainesville: University Presses of Florida, 1984), p. 66. L.L.E. Rens, "Analysis of Annals relating to early Jewish settlement in Surinam," in Robert Cohen, *The Jewish Nation in Surinam: Historical Essays* (Amsterdam: S. Emmering, 1982), p. 33, calls the slaves "indispensable."

[52]For examples see Herbert S. Klein, *African Slavery in Latin America and the Caribbean* (New York: Oxford University Press, 1986), pp. 133, 134.

[53]Swetschinski, p. 217.

made them the most prominently poised of any group to exploit the slave markets.[54]

Brazil

Brazil was the anchor Jewish community from which other Western communities took root. Portuguese Jews arrived in Brazil in 1503 led by explorers Fernando de Norohha and Gaspar da Gama, who had obtained from the king of Portugal a virtual monopoly on settlement in the region. They brought sugar cane, technical skills and slaves and soon transformed Brazil into the "most important area of sugar production in the world." So important, that the scholars concede that Portugal could not have survived as an independent nation without the Brazilian sugar trade.[55] Sugar was first produced in Asia but as late as the beginning of the fifteenth century, sugar was so expensive in Europe that it was sold only in pharmacies for medicinal purposes. Portuguese Jews developed their mastery in the trade by establishing plantations on the island of Sao Thome off the west coast of Africa, "employing at times as many as 3,000 Negro slaves."[56]

The first colonists came annually on "two ships with criminals, Jews and prostitutes, for the purpose of catching parrots." Those condemned as sinners sought refuge in Brazil's open range,[57] and the Jews saw the commercial potential and established as many as 200 settlements along the Brazilian coast in the 16th century.[58] They "quickly became the dominant class," writes Lee M. Friedman; "[a] not inconsiderable number of the wealthiest Brazilian traders were [Jews]."[59]

---

[54]*MCAJI*, pp. 96-97.

[55]Herbert I. Bloom, review of *The Dutch in Brazil, 1624-1654*, by C.R. Boxer, *PAJHS*, vol. 47 (1957-58), p. 115.

[56]Arnold Wiznitzer, "The Jews in the Sugar Industry of Colonial Brazil," *Jewish Social Studies*, vol. 18 (July 1956), pp. 189-90.

[57]Herbert I. Bloom, "A Study of Brazilian Jewish History," *PAJHS*, vol. 33 (1934), pp. 62-63; Lee M. Friedman, "Some References to Jews in the Sugar Trade," *PAJHS*, vol. 42 (1953), p. 306; Peter Wiernik, *The History of Jews in America: From the Period of the Discovery of the New World to the Present Time* (New York: Hermon Press, published, 1912; revised, 1931; reprinted, Westport, Connecticut: Greenwood Press, 1972), pp. 29-30.

[58]Maslin, p. 159; *EHJ*, p. 189.

[59]Friedman, "Sugar," p. 306. Friedman cites Werner Sombart, *The Jews and Modern Capitalism*, translated by M. Epstein (1913; reprint, Glencoe, Illinois: Free Press, 1951), p. 32. See also Anita Novinsky, "Jewish Roots of Brazil," in Judith Laikin Elkin and Gilbert W. Merkx, *The Jewish Presence in Latin America* (Boston: Allen & Unwin, Inc., 1987), pp. 35-36; Burkholder and Johnson, p. 198. David

The Jewish sugar planters prospered living on large plantations and making extensive use of local Indian labor and imported Black slaves.[60] By 1600, the plantations, the bulk of the slave trade, the more than one hundred sugar mills with at least 10,000 Black Africans, and most of the exports of processed sugar "were in the hands of the Jewish settlers."[61] Stephen Fortune: "As early

---

Grant Smith, "Old Christian Merchants and the Foundation of the Brazil Company, 1649," *Hispanic American History Review*, vol. 54 (May 1974), pp. 233-34: "To contemporaries the problem appeared so compelling that in 1629 D. Felipe IV called a council of ecclesiastics and jurists to consider measures for dealing with the New Christians, whose monopoly of trade allegedly caused prices to soar 'thus sucking all the money from the populace, so that there was nowhere to be found a rich man who was not of the [Hebrew] nation.'"

[60]Arkin, *AJEH*, p. 199. Professor Gilberto Freyre describes the Brazilian plantation owners of this period in his book *The Masters and the Slaves — A Study in the Development of Brazilian Civilisation* as follows:

> Power came to be concentrated in the hands of the country squires. They were the lords of the earth and the lords of the men and women also. Their houses were the expression of the enormous feudal might – ugly, strong, thick walls, deep foundations. For safety's sake, as a precaution against pirates and against the natives and the Africans, the proprietors built these fortresses and buried gold and their jewels beneath the floors. Slothful, but filled to overflowing with sexual concerns, the life of the sugar planters tended to become a life that was lived in a hammock. A stationary hammock with the master taking his ease, sleeping, dozing. Or a hammock on the move with the master on a journey or a promenade beneath the heavy draperies or curtains. He did not move from the hammock to give orders to his Negroes, to have letters written by his plantation clerk or chaplain, or to play a game of backgammon with some relative or friend. It was in a hammock that, after breakfast or dinner, they let their food settle as they lay picking their teeth, smoking a cigar, belching loudly, emitting wind and allowing themselves to be fanned or searched for lice by the piccaninnies as they scratched their feet or genitals – some of them out of vicious habits, others because of venereal or skin disease.

For a summary of the conditions of slavery in this period, particularly the treatment of African and Indian women, see Sean O'Callaghan's, *Damaged Baggage: The White Slave Trade and Narcotics Traffic in the Americas* (London: Robert Hale, 1969), pp. 15-32. Galloway, p. 72: "As on Hispaniola, the average plantation in Brazil had about 100 slaves....Even as late as 1583, two-thirds of the slaves on the engenhos of Pernambuco were Indian."

There are also other corroborating statements of Jewish wealth, including those in George Alexander Kohut's article "Jewish Martyrs of the Inquisition in South America," *PAJHS*, vol. 4 (1896), pp. 104-5: "The Marranos appear to have been quite prosperous for a while..." And on pages 127-28 Mr. Kohut quotes from R. G. Watson's *Spanish and Portuguese South America During the Colonial Period*, vol. 2 (London, 1884), p. 119: "If the New Christians were in Brazil a despised race, they could at any rate count on opportunities of gaining wealth and retaining it when gained."

[61]Arkin, *AJEH*, p. 200; Arnold Wiznitzer confirms in *Jews in Colonial Brazil* (Morningside Heights, New York: Columbia University Press, 1960), pp. 50-51, that

> In return for a payment of 200,000 cruzados the New Christian merchants, by a royal decree of July 31, 1601, had been granted the right to trade with the colonies, but in 1610 this concession had been revoked. The Portuguese New Christian merchants suffered tremendous losses as a result of this act of revocation, since almost all of the country's export trade had been in their hands.

Friedman, "Sugar," p. 307, says that in Brazil, "Many [Jews] became successful planters and mill owners, and not a few became sugar brokers and slave dealers or combined both operations, bartering slaves against sugar." Mr. Friedman referenced N. Deerr, *The History of Sugar*, 2 vols. (London: Chapman & Hall, Ltd.,

as the sixteenth century, Jews were interested in the large profits to be derived from the slave trade as a consequence of the sugar industry, and they appear to have had no compunction regarding their activity in human merchandising."[62] In *Voyage of Francis Pyrard,* the author returns to Portugal from Bahia in 1611 and describes a fellow passenger:

> The Jew had more than 100,000 crowns worth of merchandise, most of it his own; the rest put in his care by the principal merchant and others. There was also another Jew on board as rich as he, and four or five other Jewish merchants. The profits they make after being nine or ten years in those lands are marvelous, for they all come back rich; many of these new Christians, Jew by race, but baptized being worth 60, 80, or even 100 thousand crowns...[63]

Though the Portuguese had staked a claim to the region, they could not find enough colonists for its development, despite the fabulous profits of those who risked settlement. There was, say the historians, a "desperate need for European manpower in the face of Indians who died rather than submit to regimented labor and blacks who died of too much regimented labor."[64] The Portuguese difficulties presented an opportunity to the Dutch, who heard of the immense wealth of the New World and sought to gain access. Dutch merchants had been carrying on a profitable commerce with the Portuguese Jewish colonists, and this relationship was a major factor in the establishment of the Dutch West India Company, the all-powerful but private European land-development corporation formed to conquer the rich northeast coast of Brazil.

The Dutch West India Company

It is necessary to look more closely at the entity responsible for seizing and administering colonies in Brazil and throughout the Caribbean. The Dutch West India Company was founded in 1621 for the sole purpose of making money. There was little concern as to how this was to be achieved. Its primary method was to

---

1949), vol. 1, p. 107; Galloway, p. 79, describes the Jewish involvement: "In both Pernambuco and Amsterdam, the Sephardic Jews became involved in the sugar trade as financiers and merchants; in Pernambuco a few became [plantation masters]." Dimont, p. 30, says that sugar production was "an industry controlled by the Marranos."

[62]Fortune, p. 71.

[63]Max J. Kohler, "Phases of Jewish Life in New York Before 1800," *PAJHS*, vol. 2 (1894), p. 95; Anita Novinsky, "Jewish Roots of Brazil," in Elkin and Merkx, p. 36.

[64]Judith Laikin Elkin, *Jews of the Latin American Republics* (Chapel Hill: University of North Carolina Press, 1980), pp. 14-15.

establish colonies and trading posts in the New World and exploit the natural resources to then trade with Europe and the other colonies[65]—an endeavor requiring many thousands of Black slaves. According to Company founder William Usselincx: "Some people were so vile and slavish by nature that they were of no use either to themselves or to others and had to be kept in servitude with all hardness."[66]

The Dutch West India Company raised capital by selling shares and by pirating Spanish and Portuguese silver ships and plundering their cargoes.[67] Wiznitzer's *Jews in Colonial Brazil* is more explicit about the Company's origins and methods:

> Year after year, Dutch merchants equipped privateers and captured Portuguese ships with cargoes destined for the mother country. In 1616, twenty-eight, and in 1623, seventy such ships were captured. This is the context in which the East India and West India Companies were founded in Amsterdam, in 1602 and 1621 respectively. Their economic objective was the acquisition of goods in India, West Africa, and America through purchase, barter, or piracy and without Portuguese interference. Another aim was political: to divide the Spanish fleet and, in general, to weaken Spain to the greatest possible extent.[68]

Jews invested heavily and became willing partners in the Company, seeking "dividends from silver, gold, furs, and [the] slave trade."[69] At the time, Holland was the only country where

---

[65]Arnold Wiznitzer, *Jews in Colonial Brazil* (Morningside Heights, New York: Columbia University Press, 1960), p. 48: The Dutch West India Company was authorized to appoint its own governors and officials in conquered areas. The company was administered by a board of nineteen directors, called the Heeren XIX.

[66]Ernst van den Boogaart and Pieter C. Emmer, "The Dutch Participation in the Atlantic Slave Trade, 1596-1650," in *The Uncommon Market*, eds. Henry A. Gemery and Jan S. Hogendorn (New York: Academic Press, 1975), p. 357.

[67]*EAJA*, pp. 124-25.

[68]Wiznitzer, *Jews in Colonial Brazil*, p. 48.

[69]Golden and Rywell, pp. 11, 13; *EAJA*, pp. 125-26 and notes 27 and 28. Bloom states that there is no accounting of the exact investment of the Jews in the Company but cites the works of others who concur that while their numbers were not more than 10%, their investment was much greater. Eighteen Jews of Amsterdam, by 1623, had reportedly invested 36,100 guilders of the 7,108,106 guilders raised (one half of 1%), in the West India Company though actual figures have not been determined. Later, the influence of these investors in the establishment of a Jewish community in colonial New York, over the objection of the Company's own governor, suggests that the reported investment of the Jews is understated. See this document, section entitled "New York." See also Arkin, *AJEH*, p. 201, and Jonathan I. Israel, *The Dutch Republic and the Hispanic World 1606-1661* (Oxford: Clarendon Press, 1982), p. 127. It is reputed that Dutch Jews may have owned as much as "five-eighths" of the Dutch *East* India Company, whose profits from precious metals, spices, coral and drugs were magnificent. See John M. Shaftesley, *Remember the Days: Essays on Anglo-Jewish History presented to Cecil Roth by members of the Council of The Jewish Historical Society of England* (Jewish Historical Society of England, 1966), pp. 127, 135, 139.

Jews were permitted some semblance of religious and economic liberty. The Dutch rulers, in promoting economic development, encouraged the immigration of Jews for their business expertise and international connections and Holland soon became a center of Jewish wealth and power. The Dutch had invented the doctrine of mercantilism, the notion that the state existed not to save souls but to increase wealth, and for this the Jews were reputed to be expert.[70] Marcus Arkin writes: "Since the main industries in which [Jews] participated (silken textiles, sugar refining, diamond cutting, and tobacco blending) were dependent on colonial sources of supply, it is not surprising to find the Jews of Amsterdam concerned with Dutch commerce to the Far East and the New World....In the eighteenth century approximately one-quarter of the [Dutch East India] company's shareholders were Jews, and its ultimate decline brought ruin to many a wealthy [Jewish] family."[71]

Another venture confirms Jewish interest in such enterprise. In describing the formation of the armored shipping Brazil Company, David Grant Smith, pp. 237-38, suggests that "New Christians" were considered to be "the only possible source for funds of such magnitude."

[70]Arthur Hertzberg, *The Jews in America: Four Centuries of an Uneasy Encounter: A History* (New York: Simon and Schuster, 1989), p. 22: "...and the purpose of this firm was not to foster Christianity among the Indians; it existed to make money for its stockholders..." Also *ibid*, p. 25.

[71]Arkin, *AJEH*, pp. 96 and 97; Roth, *Marranos*, p. 286. The East India Company brought the opium that later infected the Orient. Jewish families like the Sassoons profited handsomely, and more than a few American shipping firms made their wealth in this drug trade. According to Stanley Jackson's *The Sassoons* (New York: E. P. Dutton & Co., 1968), p. 22: "With rapid national addiction, the drug developed into one of the East India Company's most profitable commodities. It became a very convenient medium of exchange when the Company began buying more tea and silk from the Cantonese who insisted on being paid in silver. Since exports of cotton could not balance the trade, opium was the only answer."

When the Chinese rulers, fearing the total destruction of their people, tried to stop it, the British stepped in (Jackson, p. 23):

> The East India Company's food ship *Lord Amherst* had docked at Shanghai in 1832 with members of a trade mission eager to buy tea and silk in exchange for their own piece – goods and opium....They seized and burned twenty thousand chests worth upwards of £2 million. (Some outraged shippers valued their losses as high as £5 million.) It was the long-expected, and not unwelcome, signal for British warships to come to the aid of all honest merchants in the sacred name of free trade. They demolished the weak Chinese forces in an operation which would pay the plumpest of dividends for a full century....At the end of the so-called "war" in August 1842, a defeated Emperor signed the Treaty of Nanking. Five ports, Canton (previously the only one in which the British were allowed), Amoy, Foochow, Ningpo and Shanghai, were set aside for the conquerors....The opium trade remained illegal, but a kindlier and half-blind eye was now turned on smugglers who promptly set up their main base on the island of Hong Kong, ceded to Britain. China had flowered overnight like a monstrous poppy.

The name of the ship, *Lord Amherst*, is a significant coincidence in that it was Sir Jeffrey Amherst—with the help of Jewish traders—who used blankets deliberately infected with smallpox to destroy the North American Indian population in a

A Private Venture

It must be clarified that the bulk of the exploration of the West was promoted by private firms and financed for the most part with private capital. The benefits of their discoveries accrued to the investors in the firm, not necessarily to the government or the people of the nation of origin. The monarch would invest the nation's military as his or her *personal* investment in the enterprise.[72] The expeditions of Columbus, for instance, were private ventures of Jewish financiers, who received notice of his "discoveries" even before Ferdinand and Isabella.[73]

With the protection of the Dutch military, the principal maritime power at that time, the Dutch West India Company colonized and settled the Western Hemisphere solely to establish a steady flow of natural wealth back to its European investors, not to any national authority. This is a critical distinction and the source of much of the animosity against the Jews. The Gentiles were, for the most part, nationalists, owing their allegiance to the nation in whose territory they resided. They respected the edicts of their government particularly with regard to international relations. The Jews, on the other hand, considered themselves as Jews first, *particularly* in international commerce. They remained internationalists without the patriotic fervor of their Gentile countrymen. When their host country was at war with a trading partner of the Jews, and on whom an embargo had been placed, the Jews would continue trade by various methods including changing the name of the ship and/or its owner to one suiting the law in the port where they desired entry.[74] They did not see this smuggling as illegal or even harmful—just business.[75] These were, after all, private transactions among private businesses and individuals—not with any government agency or national authority. But as these arrangements flourished, the national interests were circumvented and the local governments taxed and

---

similar use of chemical warfare. See this document, section entitled "Jews and the Red Man."

[72]For example, S. D. Goitein, *Jewish Letters of Medieval Traders*, p. 10.

[73]Golden and Rywell, pp. 5-9; Kohler, "Columbus," *PAJHS*, vol. 10 (1902), p. 162: "Winsor, in his 'Christopher Columbus'...judges the advance of funds to have been by Santangel from his private revenues and in the interest of Castile only. And this seems to be proved by the invariable exclusion of Ferdinand's subjects from participation in the advantages of trade in the new lands...'"

[74]*EAJA*, p. 147.

[75]George Horowitz, in *The Spirit of Jewish Law* (New York: Central Book, 1963), pp. 79-80, claims that Jews always made a distinction with regard to laws they were bound to respect: "For a Jew, compliance with 'Gentile' law in [some] matters was not required....For Jews, the law of the nation, the general system of law prevailing among the people in whose midst they dwelt was not binding..."

restricted the Jews as the leading traders.[76] These restrictions led to the historical application of the term "persecution," but evidence shows that the practice of subordinating the national interest in pursuit of personal profit—and not religion, per se—raised the ire of the Gentile.[77]

---

[76]An example: Isaac S. Emmanuel's, *The Jews of Coro, Venezuela* (Cincinnati: American Jewish Archives, 1973), p. 8, recounts an ordinance passed on December 14, 1835, which taxed foreign merchants – apparently targeted at Jews.

[77]The arguments against the Jews in the Western settlements were primarily economic, with religious bias playing a minor role. The Jewish historians seem to support this contention in a number of recorded incidents: Bloom, in *EAJA*, pp. 146-47, cites a classic example of the conflict in Curaçao in 1653 when the governor complained that "the Jews were carrying on smuggling with Venezuela and the Greater Antilles, and that they charged too much for goods they traded in, remonstrating that they demanded three times the price asked for the same article in Holland. The Jews, on the other hand, complained that their trade was hindered and that they were not granted enough privileges." See also Frank W. Pitman, *The British West Indies* (London, 1917), p. 136. Also Bloom, *EAJA*, p. 136 and note 61, states that the Jews in Brazil "were accused [in a petition] of sharp practice, trickery and frequent bankruptcy. Curiously enough, the names of some of the signatories might be considered Jewish." *EAJA*, p. 146, states plainly that "Jews were very active in this horse smuggling," in clear violation of their Curaçaon charter. The government of Barbados makes explicit reference to Jews in illegal economic activities in their Council Minutes of 1705 (see this volume "Barbados" section). Another statement indicative of the permeation of scurrilous business practices can be found in *Emmanuel HJNA*, p. 74. Of the Jewish businessman, the authors seem to imply that due to the closeness of the small Jewish community and the recourse afforded by the Jewish tribunal and for no other reason, "he was *forced* to trade fairly and honestly" (italics ours). In the larger society, apparently, buyer beware. Marcus Arkin, in his book *Aspects of Jewish Economic History*, p. 200, states that Jews opened restricted sugar markets by the "judicious bribery" of local officials. Fortune, p. 98: "By 1750, Jews were brokers, stockjobbers, and careful speculators in schemes like the South Sea Company. Indeed, they were accused of flagrant stock manipulations, and during the 1750s a Jewish agent negotiated with some wealthy London and Dutch Jews to cause a fall in English stocks that would bring them fabulous profits." Wiernik, p. 55: "The merchants of England were opposed to the admission of Jews, because of their ability to control trade wherever they entered and because they would divert it from England to foreign countries."

In colonial America, Jews violated the non-importation agreements by selling banned British goods (see this document, "Jews and the American Revolution" section), creating tension among the colonists and wealth among the Jews. The American Civil War brought similar accusations, which inspired General U. S. Grant's expulsion Order No. 11 of 1862, described by Bertram Wallace Korn in *American Jewry and the Civil War* (Philadelphia: Jewish Publication Society of America, 1951), pp. 122-23, and later in this study.

All of these references bear no indication of a theological dispute. In fact, Judaism seems to be defined in terms of the economic practices of Jews, who acted in business and religion as a group, maintaining a separate community, and who were therefore addressed in that manner. Wiernik writes (p. 44) of the seventeenth-century Portuguese Jews of Surinam: "There was no desire or striving for assimilation on either side in those times." Richard Gottheil, "Contributions to the History of the Jews in Surinam," *PAJHS*, vol. 9 (1901), p. 130, claims that Surinam Jews "naturally clustered together..." And later in the colony of Georgia, where all but Blacks "are tolerated and are permitted to enjoy all manner of liberty," the Jews chose to remain among their own and even made distinctions between Jews from Spain and Germany, with the Germans "demand[ing] the preference for

The power of the Company's rulers rivaled that of the kings and queens of Europe, evidenced by this exchange described by Arnold Wiznitzer:

> In a letter of July 20, 1645, Gaspar Dias Fereira had proposed to the Portuguese king that he buy Brazil from the Dutch for the sum of 3 million crazados, payable in six monthly installments. Sousa Coutinho, the Portuguese ambassador at The Hague, considered this proposal very practical. The Jesuit priest Antonio Vieira a man who exercised considerable influence in Lisbon and Brazil at the time, also advocated this solution. The negotiations, however, yielded no results, since the West India Company declined the offer.[78]

The power to sell, and perhaps to buy, nations was in the hands of the Company's rulers, not the monarch's, and even with such power writes Arthur Hertzberg, "The Jewish leaders in Amsterdam...knew that they had the power to cajole or even to intimidate the West India Company..."[79]

The Company performed governmental functions including the licensing of expeditions, issuing permits for slaves and collecting taxes from settlers engaged in commerce.[80] In 1674, the debt-ridden Company dissolved, no longer able to administer its territories. Soon thereafter it was reorganized, though undercapitalized, to attempt to maintain its former power. Slave dealing was its major income source and, again, Jews invested heavily.[81]

---

themselves." See Leon Hühner, "The Jews of Georgia in Colonial Times," *PAJHS*, vol. 10 (1902), pp. 76-77. The assimilation of the Jewish community into the American society is a unique phenomenon in Jewish history. Jews acted as a single entity when petitioning for rights or privileges, when pursuing business opportunities, when developing their communities, when defending their interests and when worshipping. The references to Jews as a class, therefore, are not as indicative of religious prejudice as they are in recognition of and respect for the preferred social status of the Jews.

[78]Wiznitzer, *Jews in Colonial Brazil*, pp. 106-7.

[79]A. Hertzberg, p. 25; Bloom, "Book Reviews: *The Dutch in Brazil*, p. 114: "It is obvious that Jewish and Marranos' influence must have been very great."

[80]Bloom, "Brazilian," p. 63. Bloom states: "Tax-farming, a traditional Jewish occupation was not lacking in Brazil. In 1638 Moses Navarro bought the right to farm the tax on sugar from the region Pernambuco for 54,000 guilders. Benjamin de Pino purchased the right to farm the tax on the mills from the region S. Antao Popica and Serinhaim for 43,000 guilders. The total amount of taxes accruing to the West India Company from this source was 280,900 guilders." A further study of the Jewish economic affairs in Brazil can be found in Bloom's, *EAJA*, pp. 128-47.

[81]*EAJA*, pp. 169-70. The reasons for the failure of the Company were manifold. Greed at several levels is probably the most accurate description. Infringement on the slave monopoly by private shippers, many of whom were also Jewish; depletion of the soil from overplanting, piracy, and slave revolts are some of the causes cited by historians.

Dutch Conquest in Brazil

The Dutch West India Company set its sights on the rich northeast coast of Brazil. They failed in a 1624 attempt to take Bahia but succeeded in 1630 when they took the stronger port center of Recife, better known as Pernambuco. Jews participated in planning the raids, went out with the expeditions as soldiers, and then settled in the conquered areas.[82] Soon thereafter, they set their sights on the slave trade:

> Portuguese merchants, many of them [Jews], had controlled most of the slave trade between Africa and America until the Portuguese rebellion of 1640....In 1635, however, the Dutch West India Company had captured the African center of Elmina Castle, and, in 1641, the great centers of Luanda and Sao Tome. Thus, as the Portuguese were forced out of the slave trade in 1640, their place was taken by the Dutch West India Company and a few competitors, amongst whom only the English proved to be formidable. The Company first turned Brazil and, after 1654, Curaçao into large slave depots and concentrated most of its remaining financial and military strength to supplying the Caribbean and the Spanish colonies with slaves.[83]

The Dutch had a settlement policy more lenient than the Portuguese and Jews flocked in from all over Europe. As fortunes grew, the Jewish scholars report, the Jews "appear to have been among the major retailers of slaves in Dutch Brazil" between 1630 and 1654.[84] In fact, slaves and sugar were the two main revenue sources for these Brazilian Jews.[85] Ownership of land and slaves

---

[82]Elkin, p. 16.

[83]Swetschinski, p. 236; Wiznitzer, *Jews in Colonial Brazil*, pp. 67-68; Smith, pp. 246-47; Israel, *The Dutch Republic*, p. 276.

[84]*EHJ*, p. 273. The trade practices of the slave merchants are described in Sean O'Callaghan's, *Damaged Baggage*, p. 16 (O'Callaghan makes no mention of the religious affiliation of the slave dealers to whom he refers below):

> Every big house had its slave pen where men and women were herded together like cattle....Because of the vast profits from sugar a superior type of slave could be brought. The sugar planter could afford the most beautiful women and highly intelligent men....When the Portuguese bought slaves they paid particular attention to the Negroes' sexual organs, in order to avoid acquiring individuals in whom they were underdeveloped, for it was feared that they would prove to be bad procreators.

On page 22 he adds: "It is an undisputed fact that the vast majority of plantation owners treated their slaves abominably."

[85]*EHJ*, p. 273. See also Friedman, "Sugar," pp. 305-9; Bloom, "Brazilian," and Gilberto Freyre, *Masters and Slaves: A Study in the Development of Brazilian Civilization* (New York: Alfred A. Knopf, 1946). Also confirming this account is Arkin, *AJEH*, p. 203. These works outline the primary role that the cultivation of sugar, and therefore Black African slavery, played in the development of the Western continents.

conferred status, and apparently anyone who could acquire the means to live like a lord was allowed to become one.[86] Dr. Bloom confirms that Jews "were among the leading slave-holders and slave traders in the colony."[87] The Jews involved in agriculture can be divided into three social categories:

> [W]ealthy plantation owners who purchased as many as ninety slaves to work in their mills; small-scale farmers who grew sugar on rented land and owned from ten to twenty slaves; and poor farmers who grew corn, manioc, and fruit on their own or with the help of their wives and children. In certain cases, members of this last group came to own one to four slaves.[88]

So extensive was this trade that in a three-and-a-half-year span, the Dutch West India Company collected 27 "lists" of slave buyers who purchased Africans from them. Slaves could be paid for in sugar and where payment was postponed, the Jews charged from 3 to 4% monthly interest.[89] Subsequently, Jewish immigrants moved out of the sugar-growing business to the more lucrative and liquid plantation supply trades. Dr. Wiznitzer claims that Jews "dominated the slave trade," then the most profitable enterprise in that part of the world.[90]

> The West India Company, which monopolized imports of slaves from Africa, sold slaves at public auctions against cash payment. It happened that cash was mostly in the hands of Jews. The buyers who appeared at the auctions were almost always Jews, and because of this lack of competitors they could buy slaves at low prices. On the other hand, there also was no competition in the selling of the slaves to the plantation owners and other buyers, and most of them purchased on credit payable at the next harvest in sugar. Profits up to 300 percent of the purchase value were often realized with high interest rates....If it happened that the date of such an auction fell on a Jewish holiday the auction had to be postponed. This occurred on Friday, October 21, 1644.[91]

---

[86]Elkin, p. 14.

[87]*EAJA*, p. 133.

[88]Elkin and Merkx, p. 36; Wiznitzer, *Jews in Colonial Brazil*, p. 70: "Unquestionably, they played a more important part as financiers of the sugar industry, as brokers and exporters of sugar, as suppliers of Negro slaves on credit, accepting payment of capital and interest in sugar."

[89]Bloom, "Brazilian,"p. 63; Fortune, p. 71.

[90]Bloom, "Book Reviews: *The Dutch in Brazil*, p. 113, note 114.

[91]Wiznitzer, *Jews in Colonial Brazil*, pp. 72-73; Raphael, p. 14.

On June 13, 1643, Adriaen Lems wrote to his Company employers that the non-Jewish planters could not prosper because "negroes" were too dear and interest was too high. The price was prohibitive for non-Jews, who were forced to rent Black slaves from the Jews at exorbitant rates.[92] Judith Laikin Elkin describes the arrangement:

> Those who succeeded in establishing themselves under Dutch jurisdiction prospered as traders, middlemen, interpreters, and brokers of slaves. The Dutch West India Company monopolized the import of slaves, but private entrepreneurs ran the slave auctions. Among these were numerous [Jews], who also provided the credit that [plantation masters] needed until the sugar crop was brought in. Considering that the mill owners found it cheaper to replace a slave every seven years than to feed him adequately, business was brisk.[93]

Many individual Jews are recorded as participants in the trade. David Israel and Abraham Querido of Amsterdam bought a number of slaves from the Dutch West India Company in 1658. In 1662, Abraham Cohen Brazil bought 52 slaves from the Company, while Jeudah Henriquez of Amsterdam bought twelve.[94] In 1673, N. & N. Deliaan offered the Dutch West India Company 500 African slaves and two years later Jan de Lion (a.k.a. Joao de Yllan), as the agent of others, proposed selling the Company 1,500 - 2,000 Black African slaves from Rio Calabary.[95] Don Manuel Belmonte of Amsterdam was "a Spanish-Jewish nobleman of culture and refinement, high in royal and religious circles, [who] had no qualms about carrying on the slave trade. He and a gentile associate conducted it on an extensive scale."[96]

Jewish Expulsion

The massive numbers of imported and brutally treated Black slaves caused slave rebellions, weakening the Dutch. The Portuguese regrouped and mounted a military campaign to retrieve Brazil as well as the slave centers of Africa. The ensuing battles, between 1645 and 1654, besieged the population with shortages of provisions, which soon began to take a heavy toll. Many of the Jews, who sided with the Dutch, were killed in the

---

[92]Bloom, "Brazilian,"pp. 63-64.

[93]Elkin, p. 17.

[94]*Emmanuel HJNA*, p. 75 note 52. See also Liebman, *New World Jewry*, p. 170; Johan Hartog, *Curaçao From Colonial Dependence to Autonomy* (Aruba, Netherland Antilles, 1968), p. 178; and Swetschinski, p. 222.

[95]*Emmanuel HJNA*, p. 75; *ibid*, vol. 2, p. 747.

[96]*Emmanuel HJNA*, pp. 75-76 and note 55.

battle, many died of starvation, the remainder were exposed to death from various causes. "Those who were accustomed to delicacies were glad to be able to satisfy their hunger with dry bread," wrote Peter Wiernik, "soon they could not obtain even this. They were in want of everything, and were preserved alive as if by a miracle."[97]

> Many people died of inanition; swelling of the limbs was a symptom of approaching death. Cats and dogs came to be regarded as delicacies. Negro slaves dug out the cadavers of horses and greedily devoured them. The sight of the starving Negroes in the city was truly distressing.[98]

In the first Hebrew poem written in the Western Hemisphere, Isaac Aboab related the events and his experiences between the outbreak of the rebellion in 1645 and the arrival of two relief ships. His bitter contempt for a Black freedom-fighting ex-slave is evident in the following paraphrase:

> In the year of 5404 [1645], Portugal's king in his wrath schemed to destroy what was left of Israel. From the gutter he raised an evil man, whose mother was of Negro descent, a man who did not know his father's name [Joao Fernandes Vieira, the leader of the rebellion]. This evil man gathered much gold and silver and led the revolt. He tried to overcome the ruling Dutch by ruse, but his schemes were discovered. Then he fled to the woods until the hoped-for troops of the Portuguese king came to his rescue. He then caused great trouble for the Jews. The revolt led to the siege of the cities from the land and from the sea. I prayed and wept and implored the shepherd of Israel to send help. I asked the people to fast to atone for their sins and to conciliate God.[99]

By 1654, the Jews sought refuge in Amsterdam, the Caribbean Islands, and further north in New Amsterdam, later to be called New York.[100] They continued in slave dealing, either as buyers or sellers wherever they found refuge. Jews who returned to Amsterdam were no less dependent on the Black slave. Nearly a century later in 1743, according to tax records, of 422 Jews, 2 had seven slaves, 5 had six slaves, 14 had four slaves, 21 had three slaves, 54 had two slaves, 282 had one slave, and 39 reported none.[101]

---

[97]Wiernik, p. 39.

[98]Wiznitzer, *Jews in Colonial Brazil,* p. 101.

[99]Wiznitzer, *Jews in Colonial Brazil,* p. 103. The poem is entitled *Zekher asiti leniflaot El* (I have set a memorial to God's miracles).

[100]Bloom, "Brazilian," pp. 62-64; Golden and Rywell, pp. 10-15; Lucien Wolf, "American Elements in the Re-Settlement," *Transactions of The Jewish Historical Society of England,* vol. 3 (1896-1898; reprint, 1971), p. 80.

[101]*EAJA,* p. 214, note 36.

Jewish Slave Legacy

The legacy of this Jewish dominance over colonial Brazil is manifested centuries later in the language and folklore of its citizenry. "There are even Bush Negroes," says Jacob Beller, "with Jewish names who use Hebrew words in their language — no doubt descendants of the slaves who worked on the Jewish-owned sugar plantations."[102] Beller observed the lingering remnant of Jewish oppression:

> The time-honored anti-Semitic stereotypes were used, accusing Jews of being Communists, capitalists, profiteers, bloodsuckers, etc. I was told that even the creoles, the great-grandchildren of the slaves, now accuse the Jews of having enslaved and robbed their ancestors who were the true owners of the land.[103]

The residual effect of the Jewish presence in Brazil has been codified in the language. The *Diccionario de la Academia Espanola,* for example, includes the following:

> **Judio** (fig.). Avaro, usurero [miser, usurer].
> **Judiada** (fig. y fam.). Accion inhumana. Lucro excesivo y escandaloso. [Inhuman action. Excessive and scandalous profit].
> **Hebreo** (fig. y fam.). Mercado [merchant]. Usurero [usurer].
> **Sinagoga** (fig.). Conciliabulo, en su a acepcion, vale decir, una junta para tratar de cosa que es o se presume ilicita. [Conspiracy. In its 2nd meaning, a meeting called to deal with something that is, or is presumed to be, illicit].
> **Cohen** [Name borne by priests of Israel]. Adivino, hechicero, alcahuete. [Soothsayer, sorcerer, bawd].[104]

---

[102]Jacob Beller, *Jews in Latin America* (New York: Jonathan David Publishers, 1969), p. 110.
[103]Beller, p. 112.
[104]Elkin, p. 22.

The Spanish Inquisition

Much of the history of the Jews in the New World was affected by the forced conversion drives initiated by the Catholic church. The infamous Spanish Inquisition brought a reign of terror throughout Europe as the Church attempted to forcibly impose its doctrine upon the world. The Inquisitors fueled the expulsion of the Jews from Portugal and Spain and reached even across the Atlantic to the New World settlements. The gruesome tortures employed by the Inquisitors to secure allegiance had more than a religious connotation. The Jews were a target of the wave, but not just for practicing Judaism—but because they were suspected of teaching the "false doctrine" to the Black slaves. Frederick P. Bowser's *African Slave in Colonial Peru: 1524-1650,* though not known to be a Jewish source, is nonetheless instructive:

> Portuguese slave traders were not merely smugglers who robbed Spain of silver; they were also Jewish heretics who practiced their faith in secret behind a public facade of Catholic orthodoxy and who inundated the American colonies with blacks indoctrinated in their own false beliefs. These beliefs, embellished with African superstitions, were in turn spreading among the Indians. The Seville merchants questioned whether African labor was worth all the smuggling and undermining of the Church's work among the Indians, but they stopped short of appealing for the abolition of the slave trade.[105]

More than once, Jews were accused not just of being Jews, but for slave dealing and sometimes for that alone. The Inquisitors charged their subjects for either crime, and frequently Jews were found guilty on both counts.[106] If the practice of Judaism was the crime, then the question remains, why the concern over the slaves? Slave dealing and slavery and their *connection* with Judaism and Jews were offensive to the Spanish reformers. To the Inquisitors, conversion to Judaism by the Black slaves was more than a religious ritual—it was a business arrangement in which the Blacks were the productive partner. As in the case of Diogo Dias Querido, an Amsterdam Jew engaged in "large-scale

---

[105]Frederick P. Bowser, *African Slave in Colonial Peru: 1524-1650* (Stanford, California: Stanford University Press, 1974), p. 34; Wiernik, p. 34, reports that the "public facade" mentioned in this quote included Marranos or secret Jews taking some extraordinary actions: "...it was reported that the physicians of Bahia, who were mainly new-Christians, prescribed pork to their patients in order to lessen the suspicion that they were still adhering to Judaism." See also Bertram Wallace Korn, *The Early Jews of New Orleans* (Waltham, Massachusetts: American Jewish Historical Society, 1969), pp. 3-4.

[106]Bowser, p. 58.

operations on the west coast of Africa," where he employed ten large vessels and many smaller ships: The Inquisitors alleged that Querido employed in his household several Black slaves who were natives of that coast. In his home they received instruction in the Portuguese and Dutch languages "so that they could serve as interpreters in Africa," presumably to be a more effective trader. Moreover, it was alleged, these slaves were given instruction in Mosaic Law and converted to Judaism.[107]

Jews were also known to have instructed the Indians of New Spain in "Mosaic Law," sealing their relationship with drops of blood from pricked fingers.[108] The Indian's knowledge of the land and its resources, trails and tribes was expansive, and their allegiance was highly valued. Europe's experience with "Mosaic Law" was that it very closely resembled business law, and that money, not worship, was the main objective.

Advancing a "kind master" delusion about the nature of slavery, Lady Magnus nonetheless points to the underlying concern of the Inquisition:

> So fond grew the grateful slaves of their Jewish masters, that they very often desired to become Jews themselves, and were thus the indirect cause of an immense deal of harsh and suspicious legislation. The Church conscientiously abhorred Jews. It could not be expected to look on calmly at the possible manufacture of more of them. So council after council of the Church busied itself in devising plans to prevent, or in imposing penalties to punish, any conversions to Judaism.[109]

The Black population in many of these regions was greater than that of whites, sometimes manifold greater, and as such these Blacks were expected to fight as well as work. The question for the Inquisitors was not only "Which God will they fight for?" but, maybe more important, "Which God will they dig gold and silver for?" Jacob Beller, author of *Jews in Latin America,* wrote that the mission of the Spanish Crown "was to extract as much gold as possible from the colonies, to spread Catholicism and to pursue those who were practicing Judaism in secret..."[110]

---

[107]Wiznitzer, *Jews in Colonial Brazil,* p. 46.
[108]Liebman, *The Jews in New Spain,* p. 48.
[109]Magnus, p. 107.
[110]Beller, p. 82.

Where there were slaves, there were immense profits and Jews were frequently found at the source.[111] The Spanish Inquisition cannot be seen as a purely religious or a purely economic phenomenon. The interests were varied and variable depending on the condition encountered and the temperament of its local authorities. Clearly though, Black slaves and native inhabitants played a significant role as the subject of many charges leveled at Jews in this period.

Surinam

The Jews arrived in Surinam with their many slaves between 1639 and 1654. Joseph Nunez de Fonseca, also known as David Nassi, led the last influx, established a synagogue and built a whole colony based on slave labor.[112] He crafted a little "Jewish homeland" on a large island in the Surinam River that became known as the "Savannah of the Jews."[113] Soon they owned vast sugar, coffee, cotton, and lumber plantations and used many thousands of African slaves,[114] for the Indians were not able to adapt to compulsory labor and "died away rapidly."[115]

By May of 1667, an inventory of an area of the country known as Thorarica showed the Jewish holdings to be considerable:

> [Thorarica] consisted of nine plantations for raising sugar cane with 233 slaves, 55 sugar kettles, 106 head of cattle, and 28 men

---

[111]Bowser, p. 57; Magnus, p. 107.

[112]Edwin Wolf and Maxwell Whiteman, *The History of the Jews of Philadelphia* (Philadelphia: Jewish Publication Society of America, 1957), pp. 190-91. Samuel Oppenheim, "An Early Jewish Colony in Western Guiana, 1658-1666: And Its Relation to the Jews of Surinam, Cayenne and Tobago," *PAJHS*, vol. 16 (1907), p. 98: There seems to be some discrepancy over the actual settlement dates. In *EAJA*, p. 154, Bloom cites evidence in the archives of the Dutch-Portuguese Jewish Congregation that Jews were residents in 1639. See also Felsenthal and Gottheil's chronology on p. 48, note 158. Suffice it to say that by the mid-seventeenth century a settlement of Jews was established in Surinam.

According to Seymour B. Liebman, *New World Jewry, 1493 - 1825: Requiem for the Forgotten* (New York: KTAV, 1982), p. 186: "The name has been spelled Sarinan, Sarinhao, Serenamm, Surinamme, and Serrinao. It has been mistaken for Essequibo, Demarary, and Berbice, which are part of what became known as British Guiana. These territories, together with French Guiana, were also known as the "Wilde Kust."...The word "Surinam" stems from the name of the original Indian inhabitants, the Surinese, who called their area Surina."

[113]Learsi, pp. 21-22.

[114]Arkin, *AJEH*, p. 97.

[115]John Gabriel Stedman, *Narrative of an Expedition Against the Revolted Negroes of Surinam* (London, 1796; reprint, Amherst: University of Massachusetts Press, 1971), p. vii.

> plus an additional six plantations with 181 slaves, 39 sugar kettles, and 66 animals. All these plantations were owned by eighteen Portuguese Jews.[116]

Africans were brought in in large concentrations and warehoused by Jews as the slave trade became a "major feature of Jewish economic life."[117] The "fear of the slave masses" was a phrase that frequently appeared in the official documents.[118] At no time did the number of whites exceed 7% of the number of slaves. By the end of the eighteenth century, in the plantation region outside the city, there was one white for every 65 blacks, despite the repeated instructions from the authorities that there should be at least one overseer for every 25 slaves.[119] The Jews at times made up half of the white population.[120]

Many special privileges were granted to the Jewish colonists, especially when the English were in control.[121] When the Dutch took over in 1667 and promised the Jews free exercise of their religion, Jews "went so far as to demand that their slaves be permitted to work on Sunday," the Christian Sabbath, when all

---

[116]Liebman, *New World Jewry*, p. 188.

[117]Raphael, p. 24.

[118]Just the threat of such uprisings, real or imagined, caused stock market fluctuations in Amsterdam in the 1770s, tightening credit for the Surinam planters and forcing some of them out of business. See *MCAJ1*, p. 161; Stedman, p. ix.

[119]Laura Foner and Eugene D. Genovese, eds., *Slavery in the New World, A Reader in Comparative History* (Englewood Cliffs, New Jersey: Prentice Hall, 1969), p. 182. Joseph Lebowich, "Jews in Surinam," *PAJHS*, vol. 12 (1904), p. 169: In 1792, Paramaribo contained 1,000 Jews, 1,000 whites and 8,000 slaves; the plantations contained 1,200 Jews and whites and 35,000 slaves; total population for Surinam, 3,200 whites (probably half Jewish) and 43,000 slaves.

[120]Foner and Genovese, p. 180; Arkin, *AJEH*, p. 97.

[121]Albert M. Hyamson, *A History of the Jew in England* (London: Methuen & Company, Ltd., 1908), pp. 201-2:

> As early as 1665 they were allowed a court of justice of first instance for civil cases, and they were exempted from prosecution by their creditors on the high festivals. It was specifically stated in a Government proclamation that immediately on reaching the colony "every person belonging to the Hebrew nation...shall possess and enjoy every liberty and privilege possessed by, and granted to, the citizens and inhabitants of the colony, and shall be considered as English-born." It was decreed that they should not be compelled to serve in any public office; their persons and their property were placed under the special protection of the Government; they were permitted to practice their religion without hindrance, and land was assigned to them for the erection of synagogues and schools, and for use as a cemetery. All these advantages were granted, "whereas we have found that the Hebrew nation [have] proved themselves useful and beneficial to the colony."

Oppenheim, "Guiana," pp. 108-9. According to Dr. B. Felsenthal and Prof. Richard Gottheil, "Chronological Sketch of the History of the Jews in Surinam," *PAJHS*, vol. 4 (1896), p. 8, "The Jews occupy an honorable position and hold the principal property in the colony." See also Wiernik, p. 44, and Lucien Wolf, "American Elements in the Re-Settlement," p. 95.

work was curtailed.[122] Such a demand was a clear indication of the relative confidence and power exercised by the Jews.

The Jewish community continued to prosper and by 1694 the Jewish families totalled nearly 100, in all about 570 persons; they possessed more than 40 estates and 9000 slaves.[123] Africans were given away as gifts by Jews, as in 1719 when "Governor Coutier receive[d] a present of two cows and 50 casks of sugar. Commn Raineval receive[d] 10 casks of sugar and 24 slaves. Commander de Vries 24 slaves..."[124]

By 1730, Surinam reached its greatest affluence with its 400 plantations—with 80,000 African slaves footing the bill.[125] By 1791, the Portuguese Jews numbered 834 and the German Jews 477, with 100 "Jewish mulattoes"—the unwanted result of the rape of African women by Jewish slave masters—constituting in

---

[122]*EAJA*, pp. 155-56; Wiernik, p. 45; Cyrus Adler, "A Traveler in Surinam," *PAJHS*, vol. 3 (1895), p. 153, quoting from Stedman, p. 378: "These people possess particular rights and privileges in this colony, with which they were endowed by King Charles the Second, when the settlement of Surinam was English; and such are these privileges I never knew Jews to possess in any other part of the world whatever."

[123]Wiernik, p. 47; *EJ*, vol. 15, p. 530.

[124]The wealth of the Jews is demonstrated in *EAJA*, p. 155, in which Bloom says that ten Jews departed for Jamaica in 1675 with 322 slaves. See also *MCAJ1*, p. 159. Another indicator is in 1695, when the governor of Surinam solicited donations for the construction of a hospital at Paramaribo. The Jews who subscribed are listed by J. S. Roos in an article entitled "Additional Notes on the History of the Jews in Surinam," *PAJHS*, vol. 13 (1905), pp. 130-32. These donations appear to have been made in quantities of sugar ranging from 25 to 1400 pounds. The below listed Jewish donors, therefore, may be considered plantation owners or brokers, who were the prime exploiters of Black African labor. The names marked with an asterisk are mentioned on other lists and in documents relating to slave-holding Jews.

Daniel Messiah
Joseph Coronel
Jacob Rodriguez de Prado, Jr.
Abraham Nunez Henriquez
Abraham Pereyra
Abraham de Pina
Abraham Crespo
*Abraham Arias
Abraham Israel Pizarro
Abraham Pinto de Affonseca
Samuel Cohen Nassy
Abraham Nunez de Castro
*Abraham Isidro
*Abraham Henriquez de Barrios
Alexander Car Moseh
Aharon Pereira
*David Mendes Meza
David Lopez Henriquez
*David de Meza
David Carrillo
David de Moseh C. Nassy
David de Moseh Montesinos
David Juden
Daniel Nunez Henriquez
Debora de Souza Montesinos
*Ester de Avilar
Gabriel de Matos
Jacob Rodriguez de Prado
*Jacob de Caseres Bravo
Jacob de Meza
Jacob Rodriguez Monsanto
Jacob Coronel Chacaon
Jacob Coronel Brandon
*Jacob y Jedidda Costa
Jacob Cohen Nassy
Jacob Abenacar
Jeosuah Serfati Pina
Joseph de Britto
Joseph Peregrino
Ishack de Brito
Ishack de David Pereyra
Ishack de Pina
Ishack Israel de Payva
Ishack Lopez Mirandela
[I]shack Israel Ardinez
*Ishack Israel Moreno
Ishack Israel Lorencillo
Moseh C. Nassy
Moseh Henriquez
Moseh da Costa
Moseh Mendez
Jacob Nunez Henriquez
Moseh Rodriguez de Prado
*Moseh Bueno de Mesquita
Michael Lopez Arias
Ribca de Aharon da Costa
Sara de Joseph C. Nassi
Sara de David de Fonseca
Sara de Abraham da Costa
Sara da Silva
Sabatay de Zamora
Selomoh Gabay Sid
Selomoh Rodriguez
*Samuel de la Parra
Samuel y Jeosuah Drago
widow of Isaac Israel Pereira

[125]*EAJA*, p. 157.

all more than one-third of the white population of the colony.[126] When authorities considered legislation requiring that slaves be idle on the Christian Sabbath, the Jews protested calling such an ordinance a "crippling disability."[127] The Black African was so critical to the development of the Jewish community that "[t]he economic decline of the community was largely connected with the abolition of the slave trade in 1819 and the emancipation of the slaves in 1863."[128]

Jewish Plantations

In May of 1668 an inventory of fifteen plantations owned by 18 Portuguese Jews counted 414 Black Africans being held as slaves.[129] In Richard Gottheil's article "Contributions to the History of the Jews in Surinam," he lists those plantations "which evidently belonged to Jews...showing how the Jews, even here, naturally clustered together."[130] Obviously, many thousands of Black African slaves were required to make these plantations productive.

Plantations on Surinam River w/ Acres

Plantation	Acres	Plantation	Acres
Widow of Jo. Co. Nassi (Porto Bello)	800	Heirs of Mess. Penco (Wayapinnica)	550
Sa. Meza	1000	Widow of Ab. M. Maeza (Bersaba)	250
Ishak de David Meza (Venetia)	1000	Heirs of B H Granada (Pomibo)	
Solomon Meza (d'Otan)	1000	Heirs of Jos. Arias (Guillgall?)	500
I. Gr. de Fonseca (Carmel)		Bene H Granada (Nahamoe)	450
Abraham Cohen Nassi (Kayam)		Jos. Coh. Nassi (la Confianza)	430
David Cohen Nassi (bon Esperansca)		B. H Granada (Zaut Punt)	1558
Abraham de Brito (Guerahr)		Moses Naar (Sarga)	
Moses Nunez Henriquez (Hebron)		Is. de David d'Meza (Boavista)	
David de la Pera (Abocha Ranza)		Heirs of Granada (By Zaut Punt)	1000
David idem (Warjamoe)		M de Britto (Vrapanica ?)	100
Ab. Mementon (Byanerahr)	600	Widow of Coc. Nassi (de Sonusco)	750
Ab. H de Barios (Moria)		Is. de Britto (de Goede Fortuyn)	1081
Ab. de Pinto (Cadix)	400	Ab. Dovalle (?)	250
Ab. Bueno: bibax		Is. Henriq (Jusego)	140
Wid. of Sam. de la Para (Anca doel)		Ab. Pinto	224
Heirs of Sam. Co. Nassi (Inveija)		Is. Carilho (Roode Bank)	1700
Ab. Nun. Henriq.		Ab. & Is. Pinto (Stretta Nova)	1800
Jac. Gabai Craso (Jeprens)		Ard' Ab. da Costa (Aboa Pas)	1042
Neph. Messias (Porfio)		Heirs/Baeza/da Costa (Cabo Verde)	
Is. Careleo (Lucha d'Jacob)	2250	Jos. Gabay Faro (Gooscen)	1452

---

[126]Hilfman, p. 12. See also Klein, p. 133.

[127]*MCAJ1*, p. 154.

[128]*EJ*, vol. 15, p. 531. See also Klein, p 134: "By 1817 Surinam had lost some 25,000 slaves and was down to 50,000 such workers, along with 3,000 free colored and just 2,000 whites."

[129]*EAJA*, p. 155. Also, Friedman, "Sugar," p. 308. Mr. Friedman referenced Deerr, vol. 1, p. 210; Werner Sombart, *The Jews and Modern Capitalism*, translated by M. Epstein (1913; reprint, Glencoe, Illinois: The Free Press, 1951), p. 36; *EJ*, vol. 15, p. 530.

[130]Gottheil, "Contributions to the History of the Jews in Surinam," pp. 130-33.

Widow of Sam. de la Para (Anca)	1050	Iaq de Prado (la Recuperada)	288
Jac. Gab. de Crasto		Pardo Gen Carthago (Rake Rak)	400
Heirs of Moses Cotinhio (Retro)		Mos. Isidro (de Goe de Buurt)	
Heirs of Meza (Quamabo)		Widow of Ab. de Pina (Beherseba)	
Sam. d'Avilar (la Diligenza)	1775	Sam. Uz. d'Avilar (de 3 gelroeders)	1000
Joode Savane		1. Wid. of Jac. d'Avilar	1200
Jac. H de Barios	800	2. Esth. Lorenco	200
Iz. Uz. de Avilas	800	3. Beni H Moron (Klyn Curacau)	
Jac. H de Barios (Uncultivated)		4. Iac. de Pina (Haran)	130
Widow of Gab. Baeza (Mahanaem)		5. Iac. Coh. Nassi (Petak Enaim)	130
David d'Iz. Messias (Floreda)		6. Dav. Uz. d'Avilar (Parmllk?)	130
Ab. Fonseca Meza (Abroea)		7. Heirs of Sol. Ies. Levi	300
Mord. M. Quiro (Klyn Amst.)	110	Heirs of Ab Arias (Gelderland)	
Mos. C. Baeza (Sucoht)	200		

Plantations on the Caswinika Creek

E.R.R. de Prado (Waico rebo) 2300 acres
Prado (Prado?) 300 acres
G. Jacobs (?)

Plantations on the Para Creek

Samuel Nassy

Plantations on the Right Bank of the Surinam River

S. Nassy
S. Nassy
Simson
M. Nassy
Montesinus
Isaque Pereira
Nunes
Rafael Aboafe.
Iosoe en Jacob Nassy
Mose I. de Pona
Parera(?)
Mesa
Josef Nassy
Solis.

Plantations on the Left Bank of the Surinam River

De Fonseca Ioods Dorp en Sinagoge
David (?) Nassy
De Pina Elias Ely
Aronde Silva
Serfatyn Abram de Pina
Nunes da Costa Jacques da Costa
Parada (?) Barug de Costa

Plantation on the Cottica River

Saare Brit (i.e. Sha'are Berit)

According to Jewish author Herbert I. Bloom, "[the] slave trade was one of the most important Jewish activities here as elsewhere in the colonies." The following is a list of Jewish buyers of Black slaves from the Dutch West India Company in Surinam, February 21, 22, 23, 1707.[131]

Jew	Male	Female	Children	Guilders
Abraham Arias	6	3		2,250
Jacob Cardoso	2	1		750
Salomon la Para	4	2		1,500
Jacob Henriques de Barrios	2	1		750
Isaak da Costa	4	2		1,500
Joseph Costelho	2	1		750
Jacob Barugh Carvalho	2	1		750
David Gradis d'Affonseca	2	2		840
Moses Henriques Cothino	1	1		500
Elias Chayne	3	1		965
David Mendes Mesa	1	1		505
David Simon Levi	1	1		425
Juda Abrahamse	3	1		800
Wed. van Moses boeno bias	1	1		455
Isaack Carrera Brandon	2	2		975
David d'Isaak Messiah/d'Afonseca & Co.	1	1	2	1,155
Jacob bunes	1	1		610
Jacob de Casseres Bravo	1	1		600
Jacob da Costa	4	2	2	2,020
de Weed. Esther d'Avilaar	1	1		455
Moses Nunes	1	1		505
Moses bueno de Musquito	4	3		1,430
Abraham da Costa	1	1		420
Samuel d'Avilaar	2	2		1,250
Isaack Labadie	5	1		1,685
Jacob d'Avilaar	4	2		755
David Marcado	3	1		835
Abraham Isidro	2			500
Isaak da Costa	1	1		425
Jacob Benjamin Abenakar	2			665
David de Mesa			1	210
Henricus de Barrios			1	170
Isaak de Jacob de Mesa			2	540
Rica da Costa			2	520
Abraham de Lima			2	510
Erasmus Marcus*			4	935
Abraham Arias			2	250
Abraham, Rachel Cohen	6		2	2000
Totals**	74	41	21	32,160

***Sic*. Figures as listed in original. Actual totals are 75 Male, 39 Female, and 20 Children.

[131]*EAJA*, pp. 159-60. Other sales took place in March 1707, wherein ten Jews bought slaves amounting to 10,400 guilders, which was more than one-fourth of the total amount of money expended at the sale (38,605 guilders).

The Jews were naturally heavy buyers in the African slave markets, and in 1755 even the synagogue invested in a house and 14 slaves, purchased from another Jew, A. Perera. Other registered investments of the synagogue include a plantation called "Nahamu" (Comfort ye) with its 112 slaves. Isahak de Joseph Cohen Nassy, of a most prominent Jewish family, purchased "Tulpenburg" (Tulip Castle) with its 72 Africans, many of whom died in 1772, forcing him into financial crisis.[132]

Thousands of enslaved Africans labored for the Jewish plantation masters in the cruelest, most inhuman conditions.[133] The list below is composed of names that appeared on maps of settlements in Surinam circa 1750-1780.[134]

Aboafe (=Aboab), Rafael
Arias, Abraham
Arias, Joseph
Aron
Avilar, Izak de
Avilar, Jacob Uziel d'
Avilar, Samuel de
Avilar, Samuel Uziel de
Avilas (Avilar?) David Uziel d.
Baeza
Baeza, Gabbai
Baeza, Moses C.
Barios, Abraham Henriquez de
Barios, Jacob Henriquez de
Brito (or Britto), Abraham de
Brito, Isak de
Brito, Moses de
Bueno, Abraham
Careleo, Is[aac]
Carilho,(=Careleo?), Is[aac]
Costa
Costa, Abraham da
Costa, Barig(=Baruch) de
Costa, Jaques da
Costa, Nunes de
Cotinhio, Moses
Crasto, Jacob Gabai
David,(?)
Dovalle (?), Abraham
Ely, Elias
Faro, Joseph Gabay
Fonseca, de
Fonseca, I. Gr. de
Granada, Henriquez
Henriques, Abr. Nunez
Henriques, Is[aac]
Henriques, Moses Nunez
Isidro, Moses
Levi, Solomon Ies
Lorenco, Esther
Mementon, Abraham
Messias, David de Izhac
Messias, Naphtali
Mesa (=Meza)
Meza
Meza, Abraham Fonseca
Meza, Abraham M.
Meza, Isaac de David
Meza, Salomon
Meza, Samuel
Montesinus
Moron, H(enriquez?)
Naar, Moses
Nassi (Nassy)
Nassi, Abraham Cohen
Nassi, Coc (?)
Nassi, David Cohen
Nassi, Isaac Cohen
Nassi, Jacob
Nassi, Joseph Cohen
Nassi, Joseph
Nassi, Samuel
Nunes
Para, Samuel de la
Parada(?)
Parera (=Pereira?)
Penco, Messias
Pera (=Para?) David de la
Pereira, Isaque
Pina, de
Pina, Abraham de
Pina, Jacob de
Pinto, Abraham de
Pinto, Is[aac,]
Pona, Mose, I. de
Prado, Gent. Carthago
Quiro, Mordecai M.
Serfatyn
Silva, de
Simson
Solis

[132]*EAJA*, pp. 162-63; *MCAJ1*, 159; R. Bijlsma, "David de Is. C. Nassy, Author of the *Essai Historique sur Surinam*," in Robert Cohen, *The Jewish Nation in Surinam*, p. 66.

[133]Foner and Genovese, p. 182: "[T]hose living in the worst conditions in Surinam were those working on the sugar plantations (and these were in the majority)..."

[134]Gottheil, "Contributions to the History of the Jews in Surinam," pp. 133-34.

The Jews Murder the Blacks of Surinam[135]

> *"From time to time the Negro slaves revolted and escaped to the jungles, whence they descended on their masters. For nearly a century the 'Savannah' suffered from these depredations, and to fight them off the Jewish planters had only themselves to depend on."*[136]

Between 1690 and 1772, the Black man of Surinam rebelled against the Jewish slavemakers.[137] The "Maroons," or runaway former slaves, formed several communities in the inaccessible parts of the woods, "and were the most implacable and cruel enemies of the colonists."[138] Some 6,000 ex-slaves had escaped into the interior of the colony by the early 18th century and proved too stubborn for the Dutch to overcome. Three major groups of Maroons became established in the interior regions and became known as the Djukas, Saramaacanes, and Matuaris.[139] Jacob R. Marcus reported the conditions of the time:

> The whites felt they were being persecuted by their own slaves! The result was a vicious circle of white insecurity, inducing Negrophobic repression and inhuman cruelty, to which the blacks reacted by murdering their white oppressors and escaping into the jungle. It was common for fugitive slaves to join the Bush Negroes who had been taking refuge in the wilderness ever since the days of the English occupation during the 1650's. From their jungle villages and fortresses the embittered blacks sallied forth to wage a relentless war against their former masters. Plantation life thus had its full complement of perils, and the Jewish planters led by their own militia captains not only

---

[135]Simon Wolf, *The American Jew as Patriot, Soldier and Citizen* (Philadelphia: Levytype Company, 1895), pp. 462-73; Korn, *Jews of New Orleans*, pp. 1-4; *EJ*, vol. 15, pp. 529-31; *EHJ*, pp. 273-74; *MCAJ1*, p. 157.

[136]Learsi, p. 22.

[137]*EAJA*, p. 163. Bloom says that "especially those in Jewish hands" rebelled, though he does not explain why. See the section of this study entitled "Treatment and Torture of the Black Slave."

[138]A society of Black people who escaped their kidnappers in Panama was visited and described by Sir Francis Drake and quoted in Sean O'Callaghan's, *Damaged Baggage*, pp. 30-31: "In this Towne we saw they lived verie civilly and cleanly for as soone as we came thither, they washed themselves in the river and changed their apparel which was verie fine and fitly made (as also the women do weare) somewhat after the Spanish fashion, though nothing so costly....Escaped maroons who were recaptured were treated with special severity." Similarly, Captain Stedman (p. 368) reports, "The cleanliness of the negro nation is peculiarly remarkable, as they bathe above three times a day."

[139]Klein, pp. 133-34.

> defended themselves against Negro raids but also made frequent retaliatory incursions into the jungle. Captain David C. Nassy engaged in more than thirty expeditions as a frontier ranger against the well-organized and desperate Negroes. The Indians, whose language Nassy spoke, were employed as scouts.[140]

During the course of a Maroon incursion in 1690, a wealthy Jewish plantation owner named M. Machado was put to death by the freedom fighters, and as the threat of full-scale insurrection grew the Jews organized a militia to attack the Black settlements and recapture the "marauding band of negroes." The Jews participated in the suppression of the revolts, and from 1690 to 1722 they took the lead. As a matter of fact, writes Cecil Roth, the revolts "were largely directed against them, as being the greatest slave-holders of the region."[141] Some of the Jewish leaders were

David Nassy
Captain Forgeoud
Captain Jacob D'Avilar
Manuel Pereira
Isaac Arias
Abraham De Brito
Captain Isaac Carvalho
Moses Naar
Gabriel de La Fatte
Isaac Nassy
J. G. Wichers
Sir Chas. Green
Abraham De Veer

In 1730, a desperate effort was made to punish the Black guerrillas by a detail of the Jewish militia including fourteen volunteers and thirty-six of their slaves. They devastated the African settlements but their actions "did not, by any means, intimidate the lawless hordes who were intent upon rebellion and plunder. On the contrary it only roused their anger all the more."

David Nassy, nephew of the biggest slave dealer in Surinam, joined with Captain Boeyé of the 500-man Jewish Citizens' militia and offered freedom to their slaves if they participated in an attack on the Blacks. Their sole function: to murder all Blacks that they could not re-enslave. The Africans, led by Brother Corydon, had engineered a series of attacks on the Jewish plantations, which angered the Jews.

The greatest of the leaders of the Black rebels was named Baron. He had formerly been the slave of a Swede, who had promised to free him. The master then broke his word and sold him to a Jew. "Baron obstinately refused to work, in consequence of which he was publicly flogged under the gallows. This usage the negro so violently resented, that from that moment he vowed revenge against all Europeans without exception..."[142]

---

[140] *MCAJ1*, p. 160.

[141] Roth, *Marranos*, p. 292.

[142] Stedman, p. 50.

In one raid, Nassy "was arrayed against the Creoles, who by reason of their more acute intelligence and culture (having been long associated with Europeans) were yet the most dangerous of all their foes....[Nassy] set their huts ablaze; tore their fruits out of the ground; killed many on the spot and dragged about forty slaves along with them as captives."[143] Captain Moses Naar, in his seventeenth attack against the freedom-seeking Africans, "burned down a whole negro village [and] made a number of captives." Naar and Gabriel de La Fatte were presented with silver cups "in recognition of their active zeal in suppressing a revolt of the negroes in their colony."[144] But silver cups did not suffice and so they severed the hands of the Blacks, which were then used by Jews as trophies.[145]

Treatment and Torture of the Black Slave

> *"One is permitted to make a slave serve with rigor. Yet, though that be the legal rule, it is the way of wisdom and the practice of saintliness that a man should be considerate, and following the path of righteousness, should not make yoke of slavery more heavy nor cause his slave anguish....One should not abuse a slave by word or deed. He is subjected to service but not to humiliation. One should not give free course to much anger and shouting and one should talk to him only with gentleness."*[146]

The harsh and cruel conditions faced by the Black slave and the unspeakable tortures employed by the Europeans for the most minor offenses drove the African to hopeless rebellion.[147] The English explorer Captain John Gabriel Stedman assisted the colonists in their wars with the Maroons and wrote a narrative of his expeditions.[148] He described the Black slaves in Surinam as being kept nearly naked, with a diet of little more than a few yams

---

[143]Wolf, p. 466.

[144]Wolf, pp. 468-69.

[145]Wolf, p. 465; Stedman, p. 87.

[146]George Horowitz, quoting the Jewish philosopher Maimonides in *The Spirit of Jewish Law* (New York: Central Book Company, 1963), pp. 137-38. See also Abrahams, pp. 97, 101, and Philip Birnbaum, *A Book of Jewish Concepts* (New York: Hebrew Publishing Company, 1975), pp. 452-53.

[147]Stedman, p. vii.

[148]Stedman's narrative gives explicit detail of the relationship between the European colonists and their Black slaves.

and bananas. The slave women "must yield to the loathsome embrace of an adulterous and licentious manager, or see her husband cut to pieces for endeavouring to prevent it." Many destroyed themselves by suicide, ran away, or if they stayed, they would grow "sad and spiritless, and languish under diseases...which render the patient a shocking spectacle." Many contracted tape worms "sometimes two yards in length," and leprosy, which covers the whole body with scales and ulcers; "the breath stinks, the hair falls off, the fingers and toes become putrid, and drop away joint after joint. [T]he unhappy sufferer may linger sometimes for many years...separated from all society, and condemned to a perpetual exile in some remote corner of the plantations."

The tortures were horrifying and included flogging, mutilation, hanging, and quartering, drowning, starving to death, breaking out of the teeth, stinging to death by mosquitoes and other insects, as well as burning alive at the stake.[149] These sadistic tortures were performed seemingly for the sheer pleasure of the Caucasian master: "slitting up their noses, and cutting off their ears, from private pique, these are accounted mere sport." When one master died, "the principal part of his slaves were beheaded and buried along with him."[150] There was one report of a Jewish woman who murdered a Black woman "by running a red-hot poker through her."[151]

The Black slaves often chose suicide and at times would throw back their heads and swallow their tongue, choking them to instant death in the presence of their masters. The practice had become so prevalent that the Caucasian sought to prevent it by "holding a firebrand to the victim's mouth." This method being prevented,

> some have a practice of eating common *earth*, by which the stomach is prevented from performing its ordinary functions, and thus dispatch themselves without any immediate pain, but linger perhaps for a twelve-month in the most debilitated and shocking condition. Against these ground-eaters the severest punishments are decreed by the laws, but without much effect, as they are seldom detected in this act of desperation.[152]

Finally, Stedman concluded that "by such inhuman usage this unhappy race of men are sometimes driven to such a height of desperation, that to finish their days, and be relieved from worse

---

[149]Stedman, p. vii.

[150]Stedman, p. 369.

[151]*MCAJ1*, pp. 160-61.

[152]Stedman, p. 368.

than Egyptian bondage, some even have leaped into the caldrons of boiling sugar, thus at once depriving the tyrant of his crop and of his servant."[153]

Jews participated in these activities and sometimes led them. Stedman describes a remarkable scene he witnessed of a Black man being "broken alive upon the rack, without the benefit of the coup de grace or mercy-stroke"—a slow execution presided over by a Jew named De Vries. The Black man was laid upon a wooden cross with arms and legs expanded and was fastened by ropes. The executioner, himself a slave, chopped off his left hand,

> next took up a heavy iron bar, with which, by repeated blows, he broke his bones to shivers, til the marrow, blood, and splinters flew about the field; but the prisoner never uttered a groan nor a sigh. The ropes being next unlashed, I imagined him dead, and felt happy; till the magistrates stirring to depart, he writhed himself from the cross, when he fell on the grass, and damned them all, as a set of barbarous rascals; at the same time removing his right hand by the help of his teeth, he rested his head on part of the timber, and asked the by-standers for a pipe of tobacco, which was infamously answered by kicking and spitting on him; till I, with some American seamen, thought proper to prevent it. He then begged that his head might be chopped off; but to no purpose. At last, seeing no end to his misery, he declared, "that though he had deserved death, he had not expected to die so many deaths: however, (said he) you christians have missed your aim at last, and I now care not, were I to remain thus one month longer." After which he sung two extempore songs (with a clear voice) the subjects of which were, to bid adieu to his living friends, and to acquaint his deceased relations that in a very little time he should be with them, to enjoy their company for ever in a better place. This done, he calmly entered into conversation with some gentlemen concerning his trial; relating every particular with uncommon tranquillity – "But," said he abruptly, "by the sun it must be eight o'clock; and by any longer discourse I should be sorry to be the cause of your losing your breakfast." Then, casting his eyes on a Jew, whose name was *De Vries*, "A-propos, sir," said he, "won't you please to pay me the ten shillings you owe me?" – "For what to do?" – "To buy meat and drink, to be sure – don't you perceive I am to be kept alive?" Which speech, on seeing the Jew stare like a fool, this mangled wretch accompanied with a loud and hearty laugh. Next, observing the soldier that stood sentinel over him biting occasionally on a piece of dry bread, he asked him "how it came to pass, that he, a *white man*, should have no meat to eat along with it?" – "Because I am not so rich," answered the soldier. – "Then I will make you a present, sir," said the negro; "first, pick my hand that was chopped off clean to the bones, next begin to devour my body, till you are glutted; when you will have both bread and meat, as best becomes you"; which piece of humour was followed by a second laugh; and thus he continued, until I left him, which was about three hours after the dreadful execution.

---

[153]Stedman, pp. 370-72.

> Wonderful it is indeed, that human nature should be able to endure so much torture, which assuredly could only be supported by a mixture of rage, contempt, pride, and the glory of braving his tormentors, from whom he was so soon to escape.[154]

"At Demerary, so late as October, 1789, thirty-two wretches were executed in three days, sixteen of whom suffered in the manner just described, with no less fortitude, and without uttering one single complaint."[155]

Amid the brutality, the Jews prayed[156]:

Old Hebrew Prayer in Time of Revolt of the Negroes

> God, blessed and mighty through Eternity, Oh Lord of Hosts, we come as supplicants before Thee to pray for the peace of the country as Thou hast commanded by Thy prophet.
>
> Seek the peace of the city whither I have banished you and pray on its behalf unto the Lord, for in its peace shall you have peace. (Jer. xxix, 7.)
>
> Oh, Lord our King! Exalted, mighty and tremendous Creator of all, who givest answer in times of trouble, have compassion upon us; have mercy, save and deliver those who are setting out to fight our enemies the negroes, cruel and rebellious.
>
> Oh, Lord of Hosts, lead them in peace and guide them towards life according to their desires. Redeem them from the hand of the wicked and the oppressor; from sickness and ambush, from spoilers and plunderers on the road, from evil and dangerous beasts, from the snakes and serpents in the woods and on the plains from all injury and loss both by day and by night. As it is written: "Thou shalt not fear the terror of the night nor the arrow that flieth by day, nor the pestilence that stalketh in the darkness nor the disease that wasteth at noonday. (Ps. xci, 5, 6.)

---

[154]Stedman, p. 38; R.A.J. Van Lier, "The Jewish Community in Surinam: A Historical Survey," in Robert Cohen, *The Jewish Nation*, p. 23.

[155]Stedman, p. 383.

[156]"Miscellaneous Items Relating to Jews of North America," *PAJHS*, vol. 27 (1920), pp. 223-24.

> [Here follows a number of additional appropriate quotations from scripture.]
>
> Teach and guide them with good counsel and the spirit of Thy knowledge, be to them strength and refuge to subdue, to conquer and destroy beneath their feet all cruel and rebellious Africans, our enemies who are planning evil against us. ...Listen to our prayer for Thou art He who heareth the prayers of all. Amen.

The Black former slaves vigorously rebelled for over seventy years, never relented, and in 1749, 1760, and 1762 concluded peace treaties, forcing the Surinam government and the Jews to respect their communities.[157] By the 1840s, when their numbers had increased over 8,000, government policy shifted from isolation to incorporation as the labor situation turned increasingly critical.[158] The Maroon communities never lost their status as self-governing, self-sufficient entities and stand today as the greatest of the Black fighting forces in New World history.[159]

---

[157]*EAJA*, p. 157; Stedman, p. viii; Wiernik, pp. 46-48, also gives a brief account of these events.

[158]Klein, pp. 133-34. Additional references to these events are provided in Felsenthal and Gottheil's, "Chronological Sketch of the History of the Jews in Surinam," pp. 3-5. Their chronology is as follows:

> 1691 Samuel Nassy – with the title Capitein – is mentioned as the richest planter in Surinam.
> 1717 Continued trouble of the Jews with the bush-negroes.
> 1718 The bush-negroes destroy the plantation of David Nassy. They are chastised by the Jews under the leadership of Capitein Jacob D'Avilar. David Nassy serves under D'Avilar with distinction. His praises are sung by the Judaeo-Spanish poetess, Benvenida Belmonte.
> 1726 The Jews have still further trouble with the bush-negroes.
> 1738 Manuel Pereira in Surinam murdered by the bush-negroes of his estate. Isaac Arias (a former officer of the Jewish company), David Nassy and Abram de Brito avenge his death.
> 1743 David Nassy in Paramaribo, 71 years of age, is successful in more than 30 engagements with the bush-negroes. But he is eventually killed, and Isaac Carvalho takes his place as Capitein.
> 1749 Uprising of Auka-negroes, which the Jewish Capitein Naar successfully combats. For this he is liberally rewarded by the Raad.
> 1750 Isaac Nassy, a very young man, wishes to make an end of the bush-negroes. He arms his friends and his slaves and starts out. But he had not reckoned upon meeting so large a number of them. He is killed, together with 200 of his men.
> 1772 In spite of the peace concluded on May 23, 1761, with the bush-negroes, the aid of the mother country had to be called in. 500 men were sent to put them down. In 1774 forts were erected and a military line drawn from the Savannah of the Jews along the river to the sea.

[159]For a reference to Jews of Jamaica selling arms to Maroons, see Mavis C. Campbell, *The Maroons of Jamaica, 1655-1796: A History of Resistance, Collabration, and Betrayal* (Massachusetts: Bergin & Garvey Publishers, 1988), pp. 68-73.

Essequebo, Guiana (also called **Nova Zeelandia**)

The Dutch West India Company controlled territory in South America known as Guiana. Though fertile, it was left idle in favor of the development of Brazil. When the Portuguese reclaimed Brazil in 1654, the Company drew up a prospectus inviting Jews, "under tempting conditions," to settle the wild coast of Western Guiana including provisions for slave labor.[160]

A Rulle in What Manner and Condition That the Negroes Shall Be Delivered in the Wilde Cust [sic]

1. That there shall bee delivered in the said Cust soe many negroes as each shall have occasion for, The which shall be Paide heere shewing the Receipt, in ready money at one hundred and fifty guilders for each man or woman.
2. Children from eight to twelve years that shall counte, two for one piece, under the eight yeares three for one the breeding goeth with the mother.
3. Hee that shall advance the Paiment before the Receipt comes shall enjoy the discounnte of Tenn £Cent.
4. To all them that shall Paye and buy for Ready mony if thei will thei shall have sutch number of negroes. Trusted to pay within five years and after them shall Pay for each man, woman or child as above the sume of two hundred and fifty and he that shall advanse the Paiment shall have discount of Tean Per Cent a yeare and them that shall buy for ready money shall be ingaged for the Paiment of the others.[161]

Rule 14 stated that if the settler owned a sugar plantation with 50 Africans he may not be taxed for 12 years; if he owned a plantation with oxen and 30 Negroes, he may not be taxed for 9

[160]Samuel Oppenheim, "The First Settlement of the Jews in Newport," *PAJHS*, vol. 34 (1937), p. 5. Oppenheim, "Guiana," p. 105: "...every inducement was offered to intending settlers; that pamphlets were published, some of them being translated into German, giving exaggerated accounts of the wonderful fortunes to be made by the growing of sugar in Nova Zeelandia, and promising slaves on credit..." Oppenheim, "Guiana," p. 109: "Other clauses provided for the free and untaxed mining for gold and silver and the precious stones; for hunting and fishing in certain woods, mountains, and waters; for the transportation of slaves from the coast of Guiny; for allotments of land to the colonists, with all rights of ownership; for admission to rights of citizenship, and particularly for the election of representatives to advise in meetings concerning the welfare and commerce of the colony, and for various privileges and exemptions independently of those specially applicable to Jews."

[161]Oppenheim, "Guiana," p. 178.

years; lesser businesses taxed accordingly. After the non-taxable period, the owners were to be taxed 10 percent of their profits.[162]

Some of these documents, discovered among the *Egerton Manuscripts* in the British Museum, are evidence of an English grant of privileges to the Jews.[163] They were apparently drafted by Jews in Holland in 1657, and approved by the colonization committee on November 12 of that same year, though some amendments were added later.[164]

The price and availability of Black Africans to the Jewish settlers appeared as a critical issue throughout the documentation. The agreement appears to have been revised through negotiations with "a committee of the Jewish nation." The addendum is entitled "Request for the Enlargement of the Printed and Published Conditions Relating to the Colonization of the Continental Wild Coast," and alters the initial contract in a number of ways, but primarily assures the colonists that the authorities

> [intend] to keep the wild coast well provided with merchandise and negroes so as to promote their local sale and use. [W]hen the country is developed and provided with everything they will then make regulations to let merchandise and negroes go out from there upon a certain toll.[165]

A ship sailing from the Netherlands on the second of February 1658, called the *Joannes*, carried the first Jewish colonists to Guiana.[166] A cargo of slaves was introduced, and among the first settlers were a number of Jewish "refugees" from Brazil, headed by David Nassy. They were expert in sugar manufacture and cultivation, and it was they who introduced the industry to the area.[167] Samuel Oppenheim writes of their development plans:

---

[162]Robert Cohen, "The Egerton Manuscript," *AJHQ*, vol. 62 (March 1973), pp. 341-43; Oppenheim, "Guiana: Supplemental Data," p. 65.

[163]Oppenheim, "Guiana," p. 118; Oppenheim, "Guiana: Supplemental Data," p. 54.

[164]Oppenheim, "Guiana: Supplemental Data," p. 54. The identity of the grant of privileges was claimed to be an English grant of 1654 for a Jewish colony in Surinam, but may also refer to a Dutch grant to David Nassy, dated January 25, 1658, for a Jewish colony in the Essequibo, which settled in what is now British Guiana.

[165]Oppenheim, "Guiana: Supplemental Data," pp. 60-61.

[166]Oppenheim, "Guiana," p. 104.

[167]Friedman, "Sugar," p. 308, cites Deerr, vol. 1, p. 208; Oppenheim, "Guiana," p. 105.

> It was decided to send out two ships, fully equipped, one to bring colonists to Essequibo, and the other to purchase slaves in Africa to be brought to the new colony, and it was also resolved not to restrict the colonists to trading with the Indians for logwood, but also to grow sugar, for which negroes would be necessary.[168]

David Nassy made an agreement on January 25, 1658, to deliver "several hundred slaves" to Guiana.[169] Philipe de Fuentes, described as a "Jew planter," wrote a letter on November 29, 1660, that describes a new settlement in what is now known as Venezuela:

> I consider this land better than Brazil, but in order to become acquainted with its virtue one has need of a quantity of negroes and particularly a Governor with twenty-five soldiers in order to keep the land quiet, etc....

In a letter dated April 25, 1661, Fuentes stated further:

> Negroes are required here....Do not regard this otherwise than it is written or as anything but the honest truth, without exaggeration or hypocrisy and upon which you may rely.[170]

As he did previously in Brazil, Paulo Jacomo Pinto (probably an alias for Abraham or David Pinto) acted in Holland as the representative of the Jews in making the necessary arrangements to enable them to emigrate and also to provide them with slaves when required. The Pinto family were millionaire financiers of Holland and were active about this time in the Jewish community of Rotterdam and Amsterdam.[171]

Samuel Oppenheim, writing for the American Jewish Historical Society, has published portions of documents relating to Jews and their being supplied with slaves. They are here displayed, as in Mr. Oppenheim's piece, as raw data that sheds some light on the nature of the colonies and of the Jews themselves. Primarily, they consist of correspondences of negotiations between Jews and Dutch and/or English authorities:

- "Monday, November 26, 1657. Came to a closer understanding with representatives of the Hebrew nation, and contracted with them regarding the delivery of slaves on the Wild Coast, according to the agreement relating thereto entered separately in the agreement book, yet to be inserted in these minutes under date of January 24, 1658."

---

[168]Oppenheim, "Guiana," pp. 102-3.
[169]Oppenheim, "Guiana," p. 103.
[170]Oppenheim, "Guiana," p. 131.
[171]Oppenheim, "Guiana," p. 103.

- "We have, however, the exact terms of the contract with the Jews regarding the price and delivery of slaves. These are set out in the Extracts from the Dutch archives in the Appendix, under date of January 24, 1658..."[172]
- "Friday, January 25, 1658. Engaged to-day in passing ordinances regarding slaves. This relates to the Jews under the contract made with them as well as to other Netherlanders. Among others, closed the contract made between the committee and David Nassy, and one on his order upon the surety of Dr. Paulo Jacomo Pinto, as may be seen in the dispatch book of ordinances relating to slaves."[173]
- "March 22, 1658. Read a request from the Hebrew nation at Leghorn, asking to be permitted to go from there to Essequibo. Whereupon, after deliberation, it was resolved to speak with Paulo Jacomo Pinto and to sound him as to what sum he should like to be paid by each person for transportation. Whereupon he has undertaken to write regarding this, and on receipt of answer to notify this meeting. The above named Pinto asks for 140 slaves to be paid for in ready money and a like number of 140 on time."[174]
- "Tuesday, February 24, 1659. Paulo Jacomo Pinto appears and requests to arrange with the commissioners regarding the transportation of the people from Leghorn, who are to provide their own food, for 120 persons; secondly, he asks for 200 slaves for ready money and 200 on receipt. Whereupon, after consultation, it was resolved to answer that the commissioners propose to deliver to him 200 slaves to be paid for in ready money and 200 slaves on time, and, if he wishes, 100 on receipt shall be at his option."[175]
- "The Extracts also show that in February and March, 1659, the committee in charge of the colonization were asked to accommodate the Jews with slaves, indicating that they and not Nassy supplied them."[176]
- "Tuesday, March 5, 1659. There appeared Dr. Paulo Jacomo Pinto with five of his nation from Amsterdam and requested to be accommodated with slaves, and that an executive be sent, and thirdly, that a ship may be made ready to transport folk, also with regard to those from Leghorn."[177]

---

[172]Oppenheim, "Guiana," p. 117.
[173]Oppenheim, "Guiana," p. 164.
[174]Oppenheim, "Guiana: Supplemental Data," p. 66.
[175]Oppenheim, "Guiana," pp. 67-8.
[176]Oppenheim, "Guiana," p. 115.
[177]Oppenheim, "Guiana," p. 166.

- "March 31, 1659. The minutes were submitted, and the Committee was also authorized to provide Pinto with passports for those from Leghorn, and also regarding slaves."[178]
- "Thursday, January 15, 1660. Messrs. Morthamer and van der Heyden were designated to confer with a certain Jew regarding a private trade in slaves, on the same terms as those made in Amsterdam."[179]
- "Thursday, May 21, 1660. It is considered by those present whether the Jew named Latorre, who has come from the colony, leaving his wife and children there, shall, together with others of his nation, consisting of 40 souls, including women and children, be permitted to depart from there and return to the Director the slaves received by them, and that they be not required to take more and further that of what they remain indebted one-half be remitted to them and the other half be paid here, for which said Pinto agrees to become surety....Likewise considered what shall be done in case the Jews arriving at Tobago from Leghorn remain there and refuse the...slaves contracted to be received from us in our colony, to be used there for agricultural purposes. It was resolved if those people do not readily receive the slaves contracted for, that, through Director Goliath, a bill be presented and in case of non-acceptance the same be protested for non-payment instead of making delivery."[180]
- "Monday, March 3, 1663. There appeared Abraham Levy showing that he received orders and advice from a Jewish broker in Amsterdam...offering to contract for the furnishing of 500 slaves every six months in the river Essequibo for 100 pieces of eight each, or as many more as may be engaged, payment to be made here and for such number and such period as may be agreed with the others in an offer to be made later on, provided that there are proper vessels ready for convenient transportation of the said slaves to Cartagena or Cape Debero [de Verd], it being understood that for each head there shall be paid on the clearance four to five pieces of eight or as much more as shall be stipulated."[181]
- "It was decided and resolved not to oppose the slave trade, but yet not to engage the city in it, and on that account to ask the committee to think of another expedient."[182]
- "The aforenamed colonists shall be allowed all the privileges of trading for slaves as may hereafter be decided by the Council of Nineteen. This accommodation to be the same as that allowed to the colony of Essequibo, under the Chamber of Zeeland."[183]
- "There appeared Paulo Jacomo Pinto with Jacomo Nunes Pereira, with commissioners for Nova Zeelandia, in order to contract for the receiving of 12 slaves at Pomeroon, and also at the same time to receive 12 more slaves against an old receipt."[184]
- "There also appeared Paulo Jacomo Pinto requesting delivery of

---

178Oppenheim, "Guiana," p. 166.
179Oppenheim, "Guiana," p. 172.
180Oppenheim, "Guiana," p. 166.
181Oppenheim, "Guiana," p. 170.
182Oppenheim, "Guiana," p. 174.
183Oppenheim, "Guiana," p. 121.
184Oppenheim, "Guiana," p. 70.

205 slaves heretofore contracted for on behalf of the people from Leghorn or those empowered by them; if not all at once, then at least a part, and so successively until the full delivery."[185]

- "There appeared Mr. Paulo Jacomo Pinto showing how that between him and the company a contract was heretofore made regarding the sale of a number of slaves for certain colonists from Leghorn, for which a considerable sum of money was heretofore paid to the commissioners for Nova Zeelandia, which colonists, through an accident, were deviated to the island of Tobago and reduced to the utmost poverty, and since it was not possible to transport these people to Pomeroon because there was great mortality and weakness in Nova Zeelandia he requests that the money paid by them [for the slaves] may be returned."[186]
- "Also a certain draft agreement with David Nassy in regard to the procuring by Albertus Chinne at his own risk of 200 slaves from Nova Zeelandia and to transport them where he wills, except to Tobago or the nearest colonies, paying *f*200 for the adults, conditioned that they may be allowed by the commissioners to go free, as is more fully therein set out, which being seriously deliberated upon it was understood that the slaves there must be considered as the sole salvation of the colony, and in all cases of trouble, &c., regarded as burnished silver; and because of this the said request was refused. Of this Mr. Pinto shall be notified."[187]

The exact circumstances which frame the correspondence above have not been fully analyzed from the Black African perspective. The historians refer to the "negroes" as inanimate tools in the development of the Jewish colonial presence and so the true nature of the Black experience as chattel of these Jews has not been adequately researched.

---

[185]Oppenheim, "Guiana: Supplemental Data," pp. 69-70.
[186]Oppenheim, "Guiana: Supplemental Data," p. 69.
[187]Oppenheim, "Guiana: Supplemental Data," pp. 68-69.

Slave Contracts

> *"They came with ships carrying African blacks to be sold as slaves. The traffic in slaves was a royal monopoly, and the Jews were often appointed as agents for the Crown in their sale. When the king granted Pedro Gomez Reinal the exclusive right to import slaves into the colonies, the contract contained a clause permitting Gomez to have on his ship two Portuguese who would be in charge of the sale of the Negroes and do anything else necessary 'among the people of the sea.'"*[188]

The Jewish movement into the Caribbean and South American regions was so dependent on free African labor that nearly every surviving document relating to these settlements discusses the supply of slave labor. The inducements to potential settlers always included the promise of an ample supply of "negroes"—and in many or most cases it was the primary determinant. Each migration and settlement has its own social and political characteristics with regard to the condition and circumstances of its Jewish community. Among the Jews, however, the common characteristic of their New World settlements was the demand for African slaves.

The European monarchies designated firms to supply slaves to their colonies. These contracts, known as *asientos*,[189] were awarded for a specific time and covered a specific geographical area. The firm forming the *asiento* could sub-contract some of its functions to others, and here the Jews were well represented.

In 1698, the Spanish Government granted the *asiento* to the Portuguese Royal Guinea Company. It commissioned Andrew Lopes as its agent and he assumed the name of Andreas Alvares Noguera for this purpose. Lopes had been active in the slave trade between Africa and Mexico, and he introduced other Jews into the business. Two Jewish ship owners of London, Isaac Rodrigues and Isaac da Costa Alvarenga, sent their ship to Africa for Black slaves, who were carried to Vera Cruz. The voyage of this ship seems to have been typical for two reasons, writes author Gedalia Yogev:

---

[188]Liebman, *New World Jewry*, p. 170.

[189]The term has been spelled variously: asientos, asentistas, assientos, etc.

> Firstly there was the private business which the captain transacted in violation of his contract and to the detriment of the Company. Lopes maintained that the captain, in violation of the contract's provisions, took many slaves on his own account, thus causing serious overcrowding on board ship which resulted in a high death rate among the slaves. He also accused him of selling the best slaves for his own account at various ports, before reaching Vera Cruz. Lopes said he had known that such practices were common, and therefore included in the contract explicit provisions forbidding them. Secondly there was the predominance of Jews in the undertaking. It was just this sort of illegal private trade, as well as the important role which Jews played in the Company's affairs, that prevented the renewal of the Assiento contract by the Spaniards, when it expired in 1701.[190]

Transporting the slaves across the Atlantic and then ferrying them about the region was the kind of trade in which the Jews had ancient experience. They recognized the obvious need for Black labor and opened yet another fruitful enterprise.[191]

Barbados

> *"The wealth of Barbados, the extravagance of its businessmen, and the reputed prosperity of the Jews contrasted with the inexcusable and disgraceful plight of the slaves: A ship, a chain, a distant land. A whip, a pain, a white man's hand. A sack, a field of cotton balls, The only thing grandpa recalls."*[192]

The island of Barbados was first "discovered" by the English in 1605 and was inhabited by Jews twenty years later, with steady immigration thereafter as a result of regional political events.[193] They are generally believed to have been among the earliest colonists and among the pioneers of sugar-planting.[194] Where there was sugar cultivation, there were slaves and it was the Jews who dominated the market.[195] Barbados was also the site of

---

[190]Gedalia Yogev, *Diamonds and Coral Anglo Dutch Jews and 18th Century Trade* (Leicester: University Press, 1978), p. 36.

[191]See the section entitled "Slave Ships and Jews."

[192]Fortune, p. 109.

[193]Wilfred S. Samuel, *A Review of The Jewish Colonists in Barbados in the Year 1680* (London: Purnell & Sons, Ltd.,1936), p. 12.

[194]Hyamson, p. 198; Roth, *Marranos*, p. 289, believes the date to be approximately 1655; Wiernik, p. 55: "The oldest settlement under the English flag in the West Indies was probably on the island of Barbados, where, it is believed, Jews came first in 1628."

[195]James S. Handler and Frederick W. Lange, *Plantation Slavery in Barbados* (Cambridge, Massachusetts: Harvard University Press, 1978), p. 16: "With the aid

unusually heavy illicit trade and smuggling. Stephen Fortune's study found that "Between 1660 and 1668, when the illegal trade of the island was least restricted and quite remunerative, Jewish traders became more prominent in Barbados."[196] The Gentiles were offended:

> By 1665, Barbadian businessmen, more awed by than envious of local Jewish prosperity connected with the Dutch, exclaimed in derision: "The Governor has countenanced Jews who have become very numerous, and engrossed the greatest part of the trade of the island, to the great discouragement of the English merchants, their dealings being principally with those of their own tribe in Holland; and being a people minding to trade and to be useful to each other, they will not be helpful in case of insurrection or invasion."[197]

By 1670, Barbados had already reached its boom phase in sugar production and economic growth. When the lucrative Spanish trade and other clandestine activities shifted from Barbados to Jamaica, so did Jews.[198] But Barbados remained a point of embarkation for much of this trade. Vast numbers of slaves were held on Barbados to feed the Caribbean markets. The mere numbers of these "ferocious" Africans being kept and transported by Jewish merchants, well out of proportion to the island's immediate needs, caused anxiety among the Gentiles. The Jews had left the security of the island to the Gentiles, whose primary security concerns were the Black slaves stockpiled by Jews.

The island's citizenry moved in 1679 to limit the Jews in their African slave commerce. Jews made up 22% of the nearly 20,000 white inhabitants[199] and the slave population neared 40,000,[200] so the Barbadian Assembly passed an "Act restraining the Jews from keeping or trading with negroes."[201] Again in 1688, they passed another such restrictive act prohibiting Jews and others from

---

of Dutch and Sephardic Jewish capital and credit, Barbados became the first British possession in the Caribbean to cultivate sugar on a large scale, and during the 1640s its economy began to be based on plantation production and slave labor."

[196]Fortune, p. 103.

[197]Fortune, p. 109.

[198]Fortune, p. 105.

[199]*MCAJ 1,* p. 101; Fortune, p. 59.

[200]Fortune, p. 58; Wiernik, p. 56, estimated the Jewish population of the island in 1681 to be 260. The Barbados slave population in 1629 was estimated to be 29; In 1643, 6,000; 1655, 20,000; 1673, 33,000; 1690, 40,000; 1712, 41,970; 1734, 46,360; 1748, 47,025.

See also Richard S. Dunn, "Barbados Census of 1680: Profile of the Richest Colony in English America," *William and Mary Quarterly*, vol. 26, no. 1 (January 1969), p. 22.

[201]Hyamson, p. 199; Vincent T. Harlow, *A History of Barbados, 1625-1685* (New York, 1926; reprint, Negro Universities Press, 1969), p. 265.

keeping more than one slave each. "I gather," wrote historian Davis, "that the Jews made a good deal of their money by purchasing and hiring out negroes; and this order by council was intended, evidently, to place them under disability in that direction."[202]

An Act for the Governing of Negroes

> Be it therefore enacted...that no person of the *Hebrew* nation residing in any Sea-port Town of [*sic*] Island, shall keep or employ any Negro or other Slave, be he Man or Boy, for any use or service whatsoever, more than one Negro or other Slave, Man or Boy, to be allowed to each of the persons of the said Nation, excepting such as are denizened by His Majesty's Letter Patent, and not otherwise, who are to keep no more than for their own use, as shall be approved of by the Lieutenant Governor, Council and Assembly: And if any Negro, Man or Boy, more than is before allowed by this Act, shall be found three months after the publication hereof, in the custody, possession or use of any of the persons aforesaid, then every such person or persons shall forfeit such Negro or other Slave; one moiety of the value thereof, to whomsoever shall inform, and the other moiety to this Majesty to the use in this act appointed. Passed August 8, 1688.[203]

Herbert Friedenwald characterized the Barbadian Jews and the laws restricting their slave holding: "No one familiar with the history of the West Indian colonies, particularly of Jamaica, can have failed to notice the constant fear in which the inhabitants lived of a slave uprising. In many cases the treatment of the slaves was particularly cruel, and they frequently revolted and committed horrible atrocities. Stringent laws governing the many slaves of Jews were therefore enacted."[204] The ordinary Barbadian planter usually treated his slaves with great harshness, wrote Wilfred Samuel, "whilst the horrors of the journey from the African Coast on the slave ships simply cannot be described."[205]

More legislation was introduced to regulate Jewish commercial slaving activities, and in July of 1705 the governmental council enacted the following:

---

[202]N. Darnell Davis, "Notes on the History of Jews in Barbados," *PAJHS*, vol. 18 (1914), pp. 143-44.

[203]Herbert Friedenwald, "Material for the History of the Jews in the British West Indies," *PAJHS*, vol. 5 (1897), pp. 60, 97.

[204]Friedenwald, p. 60; Fortune, p. 60, says that the sugar plantation owners "used a blatantly inhumane slave system to improve their standing in the eyes of their fellow men."

[205]Samuel, pp. 46-47.

> Whereas it appears to this Board that the Jews in this Island are very prejudicial to Trade, by not buying the Produce of this Island; but, on the contrary, Ship off all the ready money they can get, It is ordered that the Solicitor General and Queen's Counsel procure a list of what Negroes belong to the several Jews in this Island, and that they prepare a Proclamation to Revive and put in Execution a Law relating to Jews keeping negroes.[206]

Barbados Jews were considered by the Gentiles to be transients with exploitative intentions because their landed-proprietor class principally owned freehold and leasehold house property in Bridgetown and were not planters, an occupation that would indicate a long-term communal interest. In fact, back in 1681, they had decreed that "the presence of Jews is inconsistent with the safety of Barbados."[207] But the local concerns were overruled by the tax-conscious monarchy in Europe, and, continues Friedenwald, "The increasing importance of the Jewish community in the island led to the absolute repeal of this obnoxious clause in September, 1706."[208]

Another of the complaints of the Gentile centered around the smuggling trade, which was seen as being dominated by Jews. Though Jews were not the only group that participated in smuggling, they were the only group with the marketing capabilities that could maximize profits in this illicit trade. The acts of the locals may have centered around limiting the Jews' access to slave labor, which was required to move the volume of goods throughout the islands and other ports; limiting the slaves would subsequently cripple their trade.[209]

---

[206]Davis, pp. 142-43, Appendix B ("Minutes of Council," July 9, 1705, p. 83). The reader should notice that the wording of these Acts refers exclusively to commercial matters and not to any religious difference.

[207]Samuel, p. 9.

[208]Friedenwald, p. 60. Note what Friedenwald believes to be "obnoxious." The repeal order is in Friedenwald, p. 98. The Jews apparently would not consider physical work and the restrictions imposed on Jewish slave owners were considered oppressive. See Wilfred S. Samuel, p. 9:

> [T]he Jews were not allowed to employ Christian servants, and this – combined with the limitation as to the number of negroes to be owned – proved obviously a real hardship in a Colony where plentiful white labour was actually available, thanks to the transportation thither of numerous felons, rebels and paupers. Thus the Barbados Jews of the employer class when in need of indentured white servants had to make use exclusively of poor Jews.

[209]Liebman, *New World Jewry*, p. 177; Vincent T. Harlow, described the process in some detail in his book *A History of Barbados*, pp. 263-64, and quotes specific examples of the illicit commercial practices of Jews. Israel, *The Dutch Republic*, pp. 141, 425, says some smuggling routes were considered "specialties" of Jews.

In another example, a royal customs agent came across a large vessel from Barbados on its way to Amsterdam, and

> being suspicious he made a thorough examination, and found that on the general cargo the aliens' duty (amounting to over £84) had been evaded, and that quantities of white

By 1741, the Gentile population of the island had had enough of the Jews' method of commerce and proposed and passed a special tax and enumerated several reasons calling for such action. The act was read to the legislature on May 7, 1741, a portion of which follows:

> ...That the Jews in this island are a very wealthy body, their gains considerable, and acquired with great ease and indolence, and with little risk, and their fortunes so disposed, that the usual methods of laying taxes will not affect them; they are generally concerned in, nay have almost entirely engrossed, the whole retail trade of this island, furnish people with materials of luxury, tempt them to live and dress above their circumstances, carry on a traffic with our slaves greatly prejudicial to the planter and fair trader, encouraging the negroes to steal commodities from their masters, which they sell to or barter with the Jews, at inconsiderable and under values; and, when by such means they have amassed great wealth, they lay out their money at interest, by which the public stock is no way increased; and it must ever be against the interest and policy of every country, to encourage the heaping up of such riches among them: That it is in this light the Jews are taxed separately, and not on account of religion or country, nor does the present tax exceed what they have paid forty years ago, when their riches were not so great as they are at present, and their numbers have been daily increasing under a taxation of this sort ever since...[210]

The bill goes on to state that the Jews had avoided paying taxes on their slaves and other imported items, though they had benefitted greatly from the services of the government, primarily military defense. Jews were apparently exempt from civil and military duties on account of their religion and yet reaped the benefits of governmental services.[211] It was the economic disparity created in part by the special civil status of the Jews that appeared to motivate the actions of the Barbadian government.

---

sugar, tobacco, ginger, fustick, lignum vitae, and three large copper guns had been concealed from the officials – thus escaping a further sum of over £67. It is significant of the influence possessed by this Jewish fraternity that Mr. Hayne was offered large bribes to desist from his prosecution, and that when he refused, his career as a customs officer was gradually ruined by their unscrupulous hostility.

[210]George Fortunatus Judah, "The Jews' Tribute in Jamaica," *PAJHS*, vol. 18 (1909), pp. 170-71.

[211]Judah, pp. 171-74. For an example, see Hartog, *Curaçao*, p. 134.

Barbadian Jews and Personal Slaves

The Jewish community in Barbados was a "compact and self-contained unit"[212] that centered around their commerce. Here, there were no ghettos — each family of Jews was well maintained by a cadre of enslaved Africans.[213] One Barbadian family of three was waited upon by ten servants, some of whom were available for hire.[214] One Bridgetown businessman is on record as the owner of twenty-six slaves. Even the rabbi of the island, Haham Lopez, had the "enjoyment of his own two negro attendants."[215]

Besides "the horrors of negro risings," there were other perils of Barbadian life — there were destructive hurricanes, diseases like elephantiasis, to them known as "Barbados Leg," and yellow fever, which "claimed its victims by the score." These maladies had, according to the governor, "swept away many of our people and our slaves."[216] In the seventeenth century Barbados and Jamaica were described by a Jewish writer as "sinks of iniquity....The traders and planters guzzled and drank and were steeped in immorality and profanity."[217]

A review of Jewish wills found that none of these Barbadian slave owners were planters, but nearly all were slave holders[218]:

> Wealth is relative, of course, but practically every Barbadian Jewish will documents ownership of slaves, jewelry, plate, or real estate, and often all four. Hester Valverde, who left legacies to friends and relatives and owned ten slaves, went out of her way to mention in her will that her estate was small.[219]

---

[212]Samuel, pp. 8-9.

[213]Liebman, *New World Jewry,* p. 175: "The mean number of white persons per Jewish family was 3.4, and the mean number of persons of these Jews was 6.4, with slaves running 3.0 per family."

[214]*MCAJ1,* p. 120. Davis, p. 141: Jews confined their business to Swan Street, more commonly known as "Jew Street," where they carried on a vigorous trade in slaves.

[215]Samuel, p. 7.

[216]Samuel, p. 10.

[217]Samuel, pp. 46-47.

[218]*MCAJ1,* p. 119.

[219]*MCAJ1,* p. 120; Wilfred S. Samuel published the wills, the details of which are listed in the last chapter of this study entitled "Jews of the Black Holocaust." See also Howard Morley Sachar, *The Course of Modern Jewish History* (New York: Dell Publishing, 1958), p. 161.

Below are published lists of Jewish inhabitants of the island who held Africans as slaves during the colonial era. (See Dr. Cyrus Adler, "Jews in the American Plantations Between 1600-1700," *PAJHS*, vol. 1 (1893), pp. 105-7.)

"A List of the Inhabitants in and about the Towne of St. Michaells with their children hired Servants, Prentices, bought Servants and Negroes"

Jews	Slaves	Jews	Slaves
Isack Abof	1	Isack Meza	4
Gabriell Antunes	4	David Namias	5
Abraham Burges Aron	2	Aron Navaro	11
Moses Arrobas	2	Judith Navaro	1
Abraham Barruch	3	Samuel Navarro	1
Aron Barruch	5	Isaac Noy	2
Rabecah Barruch	1	Jacob Franco Nunes	1
Daniell Boyna	14	Abraham Obediente	2
Daniell Boyna	11	Jacob Pacheco	4
Rachell Burges	2	Rebecah Pacheco	4
Soloman Cordoza	2	Isaac Perera	3
Abraham Costanio	6	Isaac Perera	4
Samuell Dechavis	4	Jacob Preett	1
Mrs. Leah Decompas	1	Abraham Qay	2
David R. Demereado	11	Judith Risson	2
Moses Desavido	3	Anthony Rodrigus	10
Paul Deurede	3	Mordecai Sarah	1
Lewis Dias	8	Joseph Senior	4
Isaac Gomez	2	Jaell Serano	5
Moses Hamias	1	Hester Bar Simon	1
David Israell	3	Abraham Sousa	2
Abraham Lopes	1	David Swaris	2
Eliah Lopez	2	Judieah Torez	2
Rachel Lopez	1	Jacob Fonceco Vale	4
Moses Mercado	2	Abr: Valurede	4
		List Total	**177**

In reviewing the records of Jewish owners of Black slaves, one must be aware of the warning of Wilfred S. Samuel, who studied the Barbadian archives for the Jewish Historical Society of England:

> [I]nquiries as to the size of their households, as to their land, and as to the number of their negroes, would raise a hundred apprehensions as to increased taxation – not only among the Jews, who were already heavily burdened, but among all the planters and merchants of the Island, and it may well be that here and there an attempt would be made by an anxious taxpayer to underrate the importance of his possessions. Certain of Haham Lopez' congregants would have been prone to such an offence, for some of them, not being planters, owned more than the stipulated number of slaves and hired them out to the

planters as and when required — a convenient arrangement, doubtless, but in breach of the law.[220]

Other surveys yielded information on the slave holdings of the island's Jewish population:

PARISH OF ST. PETER. BARBADOS.
A list of the Servants Negroes & Land in the parish of St. Peter Allsaints taken the 15th of December 1679.[221]

	Servant	Negroes
Jacob Defonsequa	-	6
Deborah Burgis	-	1
Sollomon Chafe	1	5
Jerrimiah Burgis	-	3
Abraham De Silver	-	5
Joseph Mendas	-	10
David Chelloe	-	2
Mosias Delyon	-	3
Sollomon Mendas	-	3
David Velloa	-	2
Abraham Barrow	-	2
Simon Mendas	-	1
Jacob Massias	-	2
Simon 'ffretto	2	4
Paule De Verede	1	4
Total		53

Records at the American Jewish Historical Society list the Jewish plantation owners of Barbados in approximately 1692.[222] Of course, plantations required slave labor:

Mrs. Gratia de Meriado
Joseph Mendez
Abraham Baruk
Heneriquez
Luiz Diaz
Roel Gideon
Abraham Gomez
Abraham Buino Demesquieta
Fernandez Nunez
Luiz Camartho

The decline of the Jewish community of Barbados came as a result of the great hurricane in 1831, which devastated the island, and also destroyed the synagogue. Though a new edifice was erected and dedicated in 1833, the emancipation of the slaves in 1834 was the final blow.[223] The members continued to leave the

[220]Samuel, p. 7.

[221]Samuel, p. 51.

[222]Frank Cundall, N. Darnell Davis, and Albert M. Friedenberg, "Documents Relating to the History of the Jews in Jamaica and Barbados in the Time of William III," *PAJHS*, vol. 23 (1915), pp. 28-29.

[223]E. M. Shilstone, "The Jewish Synagogue Bridgetown Barbados," *The Journal of the Barbados Museum and History Society*, vol. 32, no. 1 (November 1966), p. 6.

island for the United States, with, according to Peter Wiernik, "most of them going to Philadelphia."[224]

Curaçao

As early as 1634, Curaçao, a South Caribbean island about thirty-eight miles from the coast of Venezuela, was explored and conquered by a Dutch West India Company expedition that included a Jewish interpreter, Samuel Coheno. Coheno became the first governor of the island that was considered "the mother of American Jewish communities."[225] In 1651, Joao de Yllan and 12 Jewish families were given free passage to Curaçao by the Dutch government, in order to cultivate the land. They possessed letters to the governor, Matthias Beck, directing him to furnish them with sufficient land and oxen, and to loan them slaves. Large tracts of land were assigned to them two miles north of Willemstad.[226] Among the early Jewish families who settled in Curaçao were such prominent names as Aboab, De Messa, Perera, De Leon, La Parra, Cordoze, Marchena, Chaviz, Oleveira, Henriquez Cutinho, Cardoza, Fonseca, Fernandez, De Castro and Jesurun, and they were "consistently honored as ranking citizens, and guaranteed the same freedom of worship enjoyed by their counterparts in Amsterdam."[227]

The island itself had no real plantations producing for the world market. The initial efforts of the Company to cultivate cotton, sugar, and tobacco were confronted with the problem of the dry climate, so another familiar enterprise was pursued:

> Curaçao very soon developed into a mercantile colony, with heavy trade in slaves, in contraband, and in arms for the surrounding Caribbean region. What were (and are) called "plantations" were, in Curaçao, no more than large expanses of arid terrain, where a little sorghum was grown for the livestock and a piece of irrigated land on which some vegetables and fruit were grown for local and city consumption.[228]

---

[224]Wiernik, p. 57.

[225]Maslin, p. 160; Liebman, *New World Jewry*, p. 179.

[226]*EAJA*, p. 145. The name of Joao de Yllan has been spelled variously in the historical literature as Juan Dilliano, Jan de Illan, Jan de Lion, Juan Delino and Jean Dillan. See Cornelis CH. Goslinga, *A Short History of the Netherlands Antilles and Surinam* (The Hague, 1979), pp. 54-55.

[227]Beller, p. 83; G. Herbert Cone, "The Jews in Curaçao," *PAJHS*, vol. 10 (1902), p. 142; Goslinga, p. 57.

[228]Foner and Genovese, p. 181.

The Dutch West India Company desired that Curaçao would be the largest slave center of the Caribbean, and by 1648 they had reached their goal.[229] The Company held a monopoly on the slave trade, which netted a 240 per cent profit on each slave,[230] but Jewish shippers involved in *asientos* ignored that arrangement. Portuguese Jewish merchant-bankers financed this *asiento* business, as well as other inter-island colonial trade.[231] This competition caused the Dutch West India Company to attempt to prohibit trade in Curaçao, and in 1653 the Jews were forbidden, temporarily, to buy any more Black slaves.[232] This, despite the heavy Jewish influence in the Company, indicating the severity of the offense.[233]

Governor Peter Stuyvesant, the appointed Company authority of that region, was well aware of the Jewish trade practices and that the Jews had been guaranteed religious freedom provided that they fulfill certain obligations—an agreement on which the Jews reneged.[234] He was also aware that the Jews had breached their original contract with the Dutch West India Company when the Jews engaged in illegitimate commerce in lumber and horses. A letter from the Company director in Holland to Governor Stuyvesant dated March 21, 1651, tipped him off: "[Joao de Yllan] intends to bring a considerable number of people there to settle and cultivate, as he pretends, the land, but we begin to suspect, that he and his associates have quite another object in view, namely, to trade from there to the West Indies and the Main."[235] Another letter dated June 6, 1653, came from the disgruntled Dutch authorities:

---

[229]*Emmanuel HJNA*, p. 75; Hartog, *Curaçao*, pp. 101-2.

[230]*EAJA*, p. 128.

[231]Swetschinski, p. 226.

[232]*EAJA*, pp. 146-47; Swetschinski, p. 233. In his book *History of the Jews in America*, Peter Wiernik provides an instructive example (p. 52) of the callous disregard for the humanity of Black people by a Jewish historian: "...despite the favorable conditions under which they settled there," he writes, "they were even prohibited in 1653 from purchasing additional negro slaves which they needed for their farms." This sentiment, which considers restrictions on their use of African slave labor as oppression, exists throughout the Jewish historical record.

[233]According to Goslinga, p. 57, the Jews wielded enough power to challenge and overturn such edicts. When Vice-Governor Beck wanted to use the Jews' slaves, along with those of other slave owners, to work on the new fort on Saturdays:

> The Jewish community, addressing to the Amsterdam Chamber, violently objected to what was to them a serious religious offense. The Chamber forthwith responded by ordering the governor to refrain from harassing their Jewish subjects, and expressed their surprise at Beck's order because "the Jews, in times of danger and distress have yet to shirk their responsibility."

[234]*EAJA*, p. 145.

[235]Cone, p. 147.

> We concluded from the informations which we receive now and then from Curaçao, that this colony [of Jews] is rather detrimental than profitable to the company, as a colonist, Joao de Yllan, and his adherents, have no aim to cultivate the soil and promote the increase of its products as the intention was of the company, but their only employ is limited to cutting away the stock visch hout and exporting the horses from the island of Aruba and Bonaires to the Caribbean and other neighboring isles, so that [before] long nothing shall be left from either article on this island....We are informed that this Nation is so unwearied in this traffick that they not only neglect to cultivate tobacco, Indigo, cotton and other produce of the soil, but do not even provide themselves with the first necessaries of life, so that there is much reason to apprehend that they in time shall become a burthen on the magazines of the company.[236]

This illegal trade had also served to deplete the island of all but "a lot of broken down" horses unfit for the strain of cultivation.[237]

The Jews had become notorious for their perceived ability to control trade and for flouting established rules of trade. And when they attempted to buy still more slaves, the Company refused.[238]

Though de Yllan was denied, another Jew, Joseph Nunes de Fonseca, alias David Nassi, was reluctantly granted settlement rights. The directors in Holland were cautious: "Time must show whether we shall succeed well with this nation; they are a crafty and generally treacherous people in whom therefore not too much confidence must be placed."[239] The settlement agreement was clear:

> It is further permitted to Fonseca and partners, in the form of a lease, to select and take possession of all such lands as he, with his colonists, shall be able to cultivate, to obtain every sort of produce, to increase the number of cattle in that country...with the express condition that they shall be obliged to make a beginning with their cultivation within a year, and that they shall

---

[236]Cone, pp. 150-51. Subsequent letters were also critical, not of Judaism, but of the trading practices of the Jewish community; 7th of July 1654 – from the directors of the Dutch West India Company:

> And first we have with regret and great displeasure the misconduct and extortions made there by the Jewish nation and the colonist John de Yllan, in the sale of their wares and old shreds at such an exorbitant price; wherefore we command you to prevent this in future by all possible means.

[237]Cone, p. 150. Letter to Stuyvesant from DWIC directors dated December 13, 1652.

[238]Max J. Kohler, "Jews and the American Anti-Slavery Movement," *PAJHS*, vol. 5 (1897), pp. 141-42; also reported by Elizabeth Donnan, *Documents Illustrative of the Slave Trade in America*, 4 vols. (Washington, D.C.: Carnegie Institution of Washington, 1930), vol. 3, p. 415 note.

[239]Cone, p. 147.

> bring within four years the stipulated number of settlers in that country under the penalty of the forfeiture of said lands.[240]

Even after the initial conflict the Jews were given extraordinary privileges. There were vessels trading between Stuyvesant's home base in New Amsterdam (now New York) and Curaçao as early as 1657—trade conducted principally by Jews.[241] Curaçaoan Jews not only were owners of some two hundred vessels, but they were captains, sailors, and even privateers (legal pirates) preying actively on Spanish commerce.[242]

An observer of the time wrote, "The large number of Israelites that came from Brazil and the immense quantity of wealth they brought with them, caused the old prejudices against the Jewish nation to disappear. They were allowed to take up their abode in any part of the country they wished; and later, they not only possessed the best houses in the city, but also lands, and almost the entire commerce of the Island was in their hands."[243] Historian Yosef Hayim Yerushaimi:

> At a time when most of the Jews in continental Europe were ghettoized, or repressed in myriad other ways, these Jews engaged in an almost untrammeled range of economic activity, bore arms in the militias, owned land and ran plantations, and were represented in local councils.[244]

By 1659, they received a certain number of slaves to work on their plantations which increased by breeding and by the purchase from the Company of *macarons*—weak or sickly slaves. The inhabitants could not buy sound slaves for their private use until 1674.

On every estate there were slave prisons, frame shacks divided into boxes in which offenders were chained up by the hands or the feet.[245] The punishments inflicted upon the slaves were atrocious, and they "often lived in misery." Whippings were issued for minor offences, and in times of drought and inflation slaves had actually starved to death. Manumission on the ground of old age was another inhuman practice favoured by some.[246]

---

[240]Cone, p. 148.

[241]Cone, p. 147; Learsi, p. 23: "The trade between Curaçao and New Amsterdam was largely in Jewish hands..."

[242]Yerushaimi, p. 191; *Emmanuel HJNA*, p. 681; Hartog, *Curaçao*, pp. 115-16.

[243]Cone, p. 145.

[244]Yerushaimi, p. 190.

[245]Hartog, *Curacao*, p. 176.

[246]Hartog, *Curacao*, p. 174-75.

Also in 1674 the Company permitted the Jews to buy slaves for the export trade,[247] and the Jews did not hesitate to become fully involved. Judith Elkin has claimed that

> Sephardim based on Curaçao worked as sailors, navigators, merchants, slavers, and pirates. In 1715 they probably accounted for 36 percent of the white population of Curaçao, and they dominated the island's shipping.[248]

Jewish slave entrepreneurs functioned as the local agents responsible for transportation of the slaves from Curaçao to the Spanish American ports—a natural endeavor for the Jews, who owned 80 percent of the Curaçao plantations.[249] David Senior and Jacob Senior (a.k.a. Philipe Henriquez) came to Curaçao from Amsterdam in 1685 to deal in Black human beings. Born to the most prominent and respected Jewish family, Jacob has been described as "the only Jew to whom the Holland Board of Admiralty ever granted a concession to fetch slaves from Africa and transport them in his vessel, *De Vrijheid*, to Curaçao."[250] On June 30, 1701, Senior chartered *Het Wappen van Holland* from Curaçao Governor Nicolaas van Beck to get slaves from Africa. Beck's report to the Company says that out of the 664 slaves placed on board at Africa, 205 died en route to Curaçao.[251]

Jacob Senior also served as director of the Curaçao *asiento* for the Royal African Company, one of the largest slave-trading firms of the day. Jointly with his brother David and associate Johan Goedvriend he would reship these slaves to other parts, chiefly to Cartagena.[252] Senior was seized and imprisoned by the Spanish Inquisition but was released and prohibited from the trade. He nevertheless continued his heavy slave traffic along the Spanish Main, according to a record of 1711.[253]

---

[247]*Emmanuel HJNA*, p. 75.

[248]Elkin, p. 18. Another well-documented description of the Jewish settlement in Curaçao can be found in *MCAJ1*, pp. 180-87, *passim*.

[249]Raphael, p. 24.

[250]*Emmanuel HJNA*, p. 76 and note 63.

[251]*Emmanuel HJNA*, p. 77.

[252]*Emmanuel HJNA*, p. 77.

[253]*Emmanuel HJNA*, p. 77.

Emanuel Alvares Correa (1650-1717) was active in the local slave trade for many years, and served as an intermediary between the Dutch and Portuguese for the transfer of a shipment of slaves from Africa to Mexico via Curaçao.[254] Another Jew notable in the practice was Manuel de Pina (a.k.a. Jahacob Naar). They, however, were not alone. The Emmanuels state that

> Almost every Jew bought from one to nine slaves for his personal use or for eventual resale. Prominent among such purchasers were the cantors David Pardo in 1701 and David Lopez Fonseca in 1705, and the physician Isaacq da Costa in 1705.[255]

In the last decade of the 17th century a considerable number of Jews began leaving the island, many en route to Newport, Rhode Island. Author Peter Wiernik maintains that this emigration left Curaçaoan Jewry unaffected: "The prosperity of those who remained in Curaçao went on increasing in the eighteenth century....They were prosperous merchants and traders, and held positions of prominence in the commercial and political affairs of the island. By the end of the century they owned a considerable part of the property in the district of Willemsted; and as many as fifty-three vessels are said to have left in one day for Holland, laden with goods which for the most part belonged to Jewish merchants."[256]

Many of these ships carried Black Africans. Jewish participation in the slave trade with the Company was extensive in the twenty-five years between 1686 and 1710, as the following figures indicate. The Jews are the recorded owners of approximately 867 African citizens during this time period[257]:

---

[254]*EHJ*, p. 273; Swetschinski, p. 237; Hartog, *Curaçao*, p. 133.

[255]*Emmanuel HJNA*, p. 78.

[256]Wiernik, p. 53.

[257]*Emmanuel HJNA*, p. 78. It should again be noted that as in Barbados Jews had every reason to underreport their taxable holdings—they were, after all, prominent as tax-collectors (tax-farmers). This, coupled with a lively smuggling trade with Africans as the prime profit-making commodity, would cause one to question the validity of the slave holdings reported by the Jews. These figures, therefore, represent the lowest possible number of Africans held as slaves by the "chosen people." See Samuel, p. 7.

Jewish Purchaser	Slaves	Value in Pesos	Year
Philipe Henriquez, David Senior	30	2,483	1700
Idem & Idem & Juan Goedvriend	249	22,816-5-2	1701
Manuel Alvares Correa	482	46,754	1701
Abraham Lucena & Gabriel Levy	10	1,000	1701
Moses [Levy] Maduro	11	1,100	1701
Philipe Henriquez, David Senior	102?	10,200	1702
Mordechay [Namias] de Crasto	56	14,800	1705
Idem & Moseh Lopez Henriquez	29	2,900	1705
Moses [Levy] Maduro	10	1,000	1705
Jacob Benjamin Jesurun Henriquez	?	1,850	1705
Ferro & Neyra	46?	4,572	1710

The Most Complete List of Jewish Curaçaoan Slaveholders with the number of their slaves

(July 1, 1764 - July 1, 1765)

Several lists of Curaçaoan Jews and their slave holdings have been uncovered by researchers of the island's history. The most comprehensive study is by Isaac S. and Susan A. Emmanuel, entitled *History of the Jews of the Netherland Antilles,* in which they detail the economic development of the Jews in the region. Below listed are those Jews who participated in the slavery of Black Africans and the number of their African slaves. See Appendix 22, pp. 1036-45.

Slaveholder	Slaves
Abraham & Isaac de Marchena	80
Abraham de Jacob Juda Leon	6
Aron Motta	4
Abraham Dias Cotino	1
Abraham Curiel	3
Aron Henriquez Moron	8
Abraham de Jacob Lopez Dias	2
Abraham Rodrigues Mendes	1
Abraham de Pina Junior	4
Aron de Molina	1
Abraham de Mordechay Senior	2
Abraham de Mordechay de Crasto	2
Abraham de Benjamin L. Henriquez	1
Abraham de David Jesurun	4
Aron Mendes	3
Abraham de Isaac Senior	6
Abraham Lopes Penha	1
Abraham Henriquez Cotino	4
Abraham de Salomon Levy Maduro	2
Abraham Rodriguez Pimentel	1
Abraham de Isaac Levy Maduro	4
Abraham L. Dias	2
Abraham Calvo	4
Abraham Henriquez Melhado	3
Benjamin Raphael Henriquez1	5
Benjamin Vaz Faro	5
Benjamin de M. Jesurun	2
Cohen Henriquez Junior	2
David de Gabriel da Costa Gomez	3
David Lopez Laguna & Samuel de Joseph da Costa Gomez	8
David Haim Castillo	1
David de Molina	2
David Ricardo	3
Daniel Lopez Castro	2
David Morales	4
David da Costa Andrade	6
David Jesurun	6
David Bueno Vivas	6
Daniel Aboab Cardozo	1
David de Isaac Senior	2
David Taboada	1
David de Jacob Lopes de Fonseca	1
David Abenatar	2
David Gomes Casseres	4
David Suares Junior	2
Daniel Mendes de Castro	5
David Ulloa	3
Elias Lopes	1
Elias Haim Parera	2
Elias Rodrigues Miranda	3
Francisco Lopes Henriquez	40
Gabriel Pinedo	3
Jacob de David Jesurun	25

Isaac Mendes	40
Josias de Casseres	1
Isaac Haim Rodriques da Costa	25
Jacob Monsanto	3
Jacob Haim Rodrigues Parera	2
Isaac Pardo	12
Isaac Suares	4
[Dr.] Joseph Caprillis	10
Jacob de David Suares	1
Jacob Jesurun Henriquez	6
Jacob de Joseph Jesurun Henriquez	2
Jacob Levy Maduro	6
Jacob Fidanque	6
Jacob Gabay Henriquez	2
Jeosuah Henriquez Junior	6
Isaac de Elias Juda Leon	2
Isaac de Jacob Juda Leon	2
[Dr.] Isaac Cardozo	1
Jacob de Elias Jesurun Henriquez	2
Jacob Lopes de Fonseca	3
Josias Dovale	6
Isaac Parera	8
Jacob de Mordechay Andrade	3
Jacob de Abraham Andrade	4
Isaac Motta	10
Jacob Aboad Cardoza	4
Jacob Garcia de Pas	2
Isaac Touro	1
Jacob de Josuah Naar	3
Joseph Curiel	4
Isaac Curiel	2
Josias Idanha de Casseres	4
Isaac de Mordechay de Crasto	2
Isaac Hisquiau Andrade	1
Isaac de Jacob Hz. Fereyra	6
Jacob Hisquiau Suares	10
Isaac Rodrigues Miranda	3
Jacob Lopez Dias	1
Isaac Haim Namias de Crasto	2
Jacob Cohen Henriquez	2
Isaac Jesurun	1
Joseph Obediente	4
Isaac de Abraham Senior	3
Jeosua Naar	12
Jacob de David Senior	2
Jacob Pinedo	2
Isaac Mendez	2
Judah Cohen Henriquez	2
Isaac de Salomon Levy Maduro	3
Jeosuah Henriquez	40
Manuel de Raphael Alvares Correa	32
Moses de David Lopes Henriquez	12
Mordechay Henriquez	4
Mordechay de Moses Penso	1
Manuel de Moses Alvares Correa	12
Mordechay de Jacob Henriquez	1
Mordechay Motta	2
Mordechay de Crasto	8
Moses de Isaac Levy Maduro	2
Manuel Pinedo	2
Moses Lopez Penha	1
Moses Naar Henriquez	3
Moses de Benjamin Jesurun	2
Moses Henriquez	6
Mordechay de Salomon L. Maduro	4
Raphael Alvares Correa	3
Raphael Molina Monsanto	2
Rachel Bueno Vivas	3
Samuel de Gabriel da Costa Gomez	4
Samuel de David Hoheb	5
Samuel & Manuel Juda Leon	8
Saul & Josias Idanha de Casseres	2
Salomon de Jacob Curiel	2
Salomon de Salomon Levy Maduro	4
Salomon Lopes Henriquez	5
Selomon Keyser	1
Samuel Habib	1
Salomon de Mordechay Senior	2
Saul Pardo	7
Samuel de Isaac Levy Maduro	4
Sara da Costa Gomez	6
Widow Moses de Abm. de Chaves	4
Widow Moses Penson	10
Widow Salomon de Is. Levy Maduro	4
Widow Benjamin de Casseres	8
Widow Abraham de Chaves	3
Widow Isaac Penso	7
Widow Benjamin da Costa Andrade	1
Widow David Cohen Henriquez	2
Widow David Lousada	2
Widow Isaak Levy	3
Widow Moses Naar	2
Wid. Benjamin de E. Jn. Henriquez	1
Widow Abraham Flores	3
Widow Moses Cohen Henriquez	1
Widow Benjamin Athias de Neyra	4
Widow Joseph Israel Touro	2
Widow Jacob Pinedo	2
Widow Moses de (Crasto) [Castro]	3
Widow Elias Judah Leon	1
Widow Jacob Curiel	6

In 1720, the six top-ranking Jewish slavemasters had a combined minimum total of 165 slaves.[258] These Jews were:

Widow Mordechay Henriquez	60
Gabriel Levy	39
Widow Mordechay de Crasto	26
Widow Balthazar de Leon	17
Daniel Aboab Cardozo	16
Jeosuah Henriquez	16

[258]*Emmanuel HJNA,* p. 228.

In 1744, the Jews reportedly owned 310 African hostages. In 1748, they furnished the Curaçao government with 126 African slaves to fortify the island.[259]

Jeosuah Henriquez	16
Francisco Lopez Henriquez	16
Jacob Hisquiau de Leon	12
Moses Penso*	12
David Senior	10
Joseph da Costa Gomez	10

*Penso bought two plantations with 300 Africans from Gentile Willem Meyer.[260]

In 1749, just five big Jewish slaveowners had a combined minimum total of 91 slaves.[261]

Samuel & Benjamin de Casseres	35
Jeosuah Henriquez	16
Francisco Lopez Henriquez	18
Jacob Hisquiau de Leon	12
Joseph da Costa Gomez	10

A "very strict slave census taken in 1765 showed that the Jews owned 860 slaves."[262] The Jesurun family owned a record number of 366 Black people. The closest Gentile was Eva van Wijk with 240 slaves. A century later, in 1863, when the Blacks were emancipated, the Jews owned 1,851. The government paid all the slaveholders an indemnity of 200 florins per slave. At that time 45% of all private wealth in Curaçao was in Jewish hands.[263] The Jew, in 1894, was three and one-half times richer than the Protestant and six to eight times richer than the Catholic.[264]

---

[259]*Emmanuel HJNA*, p. 229.
[260]*Emmanuel HJNA*, p. 228 note.
[261]*Emmanuel HJNA*, p. 228.
[262]*Emmanuel HJNA*, p. 228.
[263]*Emmanuel HJNA*, p. 364.
[264]*Emmanuel HJNA*, p. 364 note 52. This volume clearly states that the Jew was "sixty-eight" times richer than the Catholic, but this may be a misprint. If the statement refers to white Catholics, it may likely be corrected as "six to eight." If to Black Catholics, then it is probably accurate.

Coro

Curaçaoan Jews branched out into Coro, Venezuela, which had become a haven for their runaway slaves. Between 1729 and 1796, 112 African slaves of Jews, identified by their brand marks, reportedly found refuge in Coro.[265] Soon, the Jews initiated business activities that aroused the concern of the local business establishment.[266] They had extended loans to the public administration and to the army but, in 1854, decided to cease that policy. The tightened money supply sparked anti-Jewish riots, leading to yet another expulsion.[267] The charges, recounted by Isidoro Aizenberg, were familiar: "The 'misery and Helplessness' that the people of Coro are enduring are caused by the Jews as a result of their 'distorted avarice,' usurious practices and price-fixing through deception and monopolistic controls.'...[O]ne evil consequence of the poverty caused by the Jews was 'to see the many daughters of Coro, previously models of virtue, being prostituted by the Jews.'"[268]

Though anti-Semitism is charged by the departing Jews, no Jewish historian explains the anti-Black behavior of the Coro Jews. According to Aizenberg: "Two hundred and fifty souls left Coro for Curaçao: 168 Jews and 88 slaves, among them."[269]

Jamaica

Jews had resided in Jamaica since about 1625 and, as in Barbados and elsewhere, they were among the pioneers of sugar-planting in the island. Jamaica welcomed Jewish settlement and their commercial expertise.[270] Historian Albert Hyamson:

---

[265]Liebman, *New World Jewry*, p. 184.

[266]Isidoro Aizenberg, "The 1855 Expulsion of the Curaçoan Jews from Coro, Venezuela," *AJHQ*, vol. 72 (1982-83), *passim;* Isaac S. Emmanuel, *The Jews of Coro, Venezuela* (Cincinnati: American Jewish Archives, 1973), *passim.*

[267]Aizenberg, p. 496.

[268]Aizenberg, p. 497. By this time some Jews were involved extensively in international prostitution. See Sean O'Callaghan, *Damaged Baggage: The White Slave Trade and Narcotics Traffic in America* (London: Robert Hale, 1969); Edward J. Bristow, *Prostitution and Prejudice: The Jewish Fight Against White Slavery, 1870-1939* (New York: Schocken Books, 1983); William W. Sanger, *History of Prostitution* (New York: Eugenics Publishing, 1937); Francesco Cordasco, *The White Slave Trade and the Immigrants* (Detroit: Blaine Ethridge Books, 1981).

[269]Aizenberg, p. 500.

[270]Hyamson, p. 200. Jamaica was discovered for Europeans by Columbus in 1494 during his second voyage to the New World.

> Their numbers increased and they continued to flourish. Some of them were engaged in retail trade, but the majority were wholesale merchants, and the greater portion of the trade with the Spanish Main was in their hands....Their economic position was by then so strong that they practically monopolized the trade in sugar, rum and molasses.[271]

Direct from their Brazilian expulsion in 1654, the Jews set up the same kinds of slave sale credit arrangements they practiced in Brazil.[272] "It was not any more uncommon," writes Max Kohler, "for the many Jewish residents...to be enumerated as possessors of a number of slaves, than was the case with non-Jews."[273] David Henriques, Hyman Levy, and especially Alexander Lindo were the major slave importers.[274] As a measure of their wealth and comfort, Isaac Contino, a Jamaican merchant, had ten personal slaves; Isaac Henriques Alvin, a wealthy Port Royal fisherman, had eighteen; and Daniel Sueyroe, a goldsmith, had twelve.[275]

The records of 1692 list the plantation and property holdings of some of the island's Jews.[276] Below they are listed as presented in the American Jewish Historical Society record:

> Mr. Karbona [h]as a plantation in Leganee(?) wh[ich] he has bought and paid for.
> Mr. Solomon Gabay has a Plantation for many yeares in magitt Savana.
> Mr. Joseph Ridana [h]as a Plantation in ye same place.

---

[271]Hyamson, pp. 202-3, states that "...the greater portion of the industry and the commerce was in the hands of that [Jewish] section." See also Hyamson, pp. 200, 204. It was widely known that Jews prospered inordinately. Picciotto's *Sketches of Anglo-Jewish History* (p. 94), as cited in Adler's "A Traveler in Surinam," *PAJHS*, vol. 3 (1895), pp. 78-79: "By mid-century the Jamaican trade was principally in Jewish hands, with about 200 Jewish families residing in the island." In "Notes: Jewish Merchants and Colonial Slave Trade: Documents from the Public Record Office Memorial of the Jews about their Taxes Presented to Sir William Beeston, Governor-in-Charge of the Island of Jamaica," *PAJHS*, vol. 34 (1937), p. 285, the author, Charles Gross, presents a letter, dated Jamaica, September 6, 1736, in which an incredulous John Meriwether writes: "at our last quarter Sessions I was surpris'd to see a Jew, one of the top Supra Cargoes in the Illicit Trade for Negroes and dry goods making Application to be reliev'd in his taxes by reason of his poverty, and he had an allowance."

[272]*MCAJ1*, p. 114. Other evidence of abrasive business practices includes that from Frank W. Pitman, *The British West Indies* (London: 1917), p. 136: Planters could obtain loans at five percent interest from the English. Those who could not, however, "were forced to pay the higher rates demanded by Jews and other merchants or factors resident in the islands. In many cases bonuses had to be given, so that, actually, rates as high as twenty per cent were commonly paid."

[273]Max J. Kohler, "Jews and the American Anti-Slavery Movement II," *PAJHS*, vol. 9 (1901), p. 45.

[274]*EHJ*, p. 273.

[275]*MCAJ1*, p. 119.

[276]Cundall, Davis, and Friedenberg, pp. 28-29.

Mr. Solomon Acton [h]as a plantation in ye North Side in port Mary.
Mr. Abraham Gabay has a plantation in white hood.
Mr. Benjiamen Corvalo [h]as a plantation in ye same place.
Mr. Moses Jessurun Cardezo [h]as 15 houses.
Mr. Joseph da Costa Alvaringa [h]as 10 houses.
Mr. David Alvarez
Mr. Jacob Mendez Gutierez
Mr. Jacob Detorez
Mrs. Sarrah Gabay

The trading practices of the Jewish inhabitants became an irritant to the Jamaican government. In the island's archives there is a letter, dated January 28, 1691 or 1692, from the president and the Council of Jamaica to the Lords of Trade and Plantations, in which he says:

> The Jews eat us and our children out of all trade, the reasons for naturalising them not having been observed; for there has been no regard had to their settling and planting as the law intended and directed. We did not want them at Port Royal, a place populous and strong without them; and though told that the whole country lay open to them they have made Port Royal their Goshen, and will do nothing but trade. When the Assembly tries to tax them more heavily than Christians, who are subject to Public duties from which they are exempt, they contrive to evade it by special favours. This is a great and growing evil and had we not warning from other Colonies we should see our streets filled and the ships hither crowded with them. This means taking our children's bread and giving it to Jews. We believe that it could be avoided by giving a little more confidence to the Council.[277]

---

[277]"Calendar of State Papers, Colonial Series, America and West Indies, 1689-1692" (published 1901), p. 593, and cited in Cundall, Davis, and Friedenberg, pp. 26-27. The island's government offered still more evidence of the civil advantages of the Jewish community. Jewish historians have charged that anti-Semitism created a separate status and taxation for the Jews as a class. A review of the written deliberations of the Jamaican government, however, shows a more reasoned approach than the charges allow (the Jews' status as slave dealers notwithstanding). Below is a portion of the Council records of 1741 that address taxation of the Jews (See George Fortunatus Judah, "The Jews' Tribute in Jamaica," *PAJHS*, vol. 18 [1909], pp. 172-73):

> That, admitting the Jews did pay taxes equally with other traders and inhabitants, in case this separate tax had not been laid, yet their exemptions from offices civil and military, from juries, and other burthensome and expensive services, which others are obliged to perform, amply make up for this taxation; all posts civil and military in the gift of this Government, are toilsome and expensive, and attended with no profit, except the posts of Chief Justice and Captain of the Port; the other offices in this island, that are honorable and advantageous, are held by Patent immediately from his Majesty; the civil posts, Jews have been always, or till very lately, exempt from, on account of their religion, which did not allow them to qualify themselves for such posts, and as to military posts in our Militia, they were very unfit for, never desirous of, nor would they accept of them:
>
> That the Jews have always been excused from serving as Jurors, and, by that indulgence alone, saved much more than the amount of this tax; supposing that each person who pays a share of this tax, was to attend the Courts, once in a year, as other inhabitants do, in which case it costs them from ten to twenty pounds, one with another,

The records show other references to Jews and Blacks. In 1700, Jews complained about excessive taxation of their negroes and cattle, etc.[278] Haham Jeossuha His advertised in the *Royal Gazette* of Kingston, Jamaica, on December 15, 1792, for the return of a runaway slave.[279] In 1731, Captain Nassy was accused of misconduct on an expedition against the so-called Bush-Negroes, but was acquitted,[280] and in some Jewish wills, slaves were left to the synagogue.[281] A Jewish shopkeeper in Kingston "boxed the ear" of a Gentile-owned African slave, causing Jamaica's House of Assembly to take action.[282]

There was an active trade with the Jews of North America. The Rhode Island slave trade employed 100-150 vessels annually, each

---

besides the loss of time or disadvantages of being absent from their private affairs; besides, the Jews would be liable to other inconveniences in this service, in which the public must be involved; on their Sabbaths and holy days, which happen frequently in the times the Courts are held, the Courts must be adjourned; their own causes, which make a great part of the business, would be postponed, and public justice delayed; on the other hand were they compelled to serve on those days, such an oppression upon their consciences, and violation of their religion, would be hardships still greater upon them, and, however valuable an institution a trial by juries is, yet an exemption from attendance as jurors has been, in particular cases, looked upon as a favour and privilege; by the Law of England, apothecaries are excused from that duty, and by the Act of Toleration, dissenting Teachers were excused from juries; and the Legislature, at the time that Act was passed, was not in a temper to impose any severities upon them; nor have the Jews, in the catalogue of their pretended grievances, ever suggested that any partial distinctions had ever been made in determining upon their properties: That the Jews in this island have their Synagogues, and public profession of their Religion, without any restraint whatsoever; they have equally the benefit of our laws, advantages of our trade, and the same security for their properties, with all his Majesty's subjects, and have all the indulgencies they require on account of their religion, though they have not complied with the terms of the grants of denization, act of naturalization, referred to in their petition to his Majesty, their estates consisting chiefly in shop goods and other moveable effects; and, consequently, they cannot be looked upon as any lasting security or advantage to us; and, if some of them have purchased houses in the Towns, no great benefit accrues to the public, by such purchases; and it is notorious they were made, for the greatest part, with a view of defeating their creditors, houses having never, or until very lately, been extended or sold in this island for debt...

In 1693, Governor William Beaston answered charges of unfairness to the Jews by citing the Windsor Proclamation signed on December 14, 1661, by Charles II and brought to Jamaica in August 1662, which was aimed at encouraging settlement. The Jews were more interested in being merchants, he said, and were not devoting themselves to planting as called for by the Proclamation. See Samuel J. Hurwitz and Edith Hurwitz, "The New World Sets an Example for the Old: The Jews of Jamaica and Political Rights, 1661-1831," *AJHQ,* vol. 55 (1965-66), pp. 39-40. Compare with R. A. Fisher, "A Note on Jamaica," in *Journal of Negro History,* vol. 28 (April 1943), pp. 200-203.

[278]Dr. Charles Gross, "Documents from the Public Record Office (London)," *PAJHS,* vol. 2 (1894), p. 166.

[279]Bertram W. Korn, "The Haham DeCordova of Jamaica," *AJA,* vol. 18 (1966), p. 148.

[280]Max J. Kohler, "Jewish Factors in Settlement of the West," *PAJHS,* vol. 16 (1907), pp. 11-12.

[281]*MCAJ1,* p. 130.

[282]*MCAJ1,* p. 110.

carrying to Jamaica 80-100 Black men, women, and children.[283] By the 1700s, however, Jamaica experienced an economic decline primarily because of the "growing commercial importance of Curaçao, which became, with St. Eustatius, a center of clandestine activities and a hub of Jewish commercial enterprise, legal and illegal."[284]

Here listed is the estimated slave population of Jamaica during the years when Jews were acknowledged to be significant in the trade. The extraordinary increase far exceeded the island's internal needs and is indicative of a brisk wholesale slave export business in which Jews were highly active.

Jamaican Slave Population[285]

Year	Slaves
1661	514
1670	2,500
1673	9,504
1677	20,000
1703	45,000
1722	80,000
1739	99,239

Jews had been excluded from voting and from positions in the civil service until 1831, even though "the doors of economic opportunity were wide open."[286] Until this time they'd been "content" to "avoid open conflict by studiously avoiding politics." They were "happy with their religious privileges, and the fact that they suffered from no governmental economic discrimination..."[287]

---

[283]*MEAJ1*, p. 141.

[284]Fortune, pp. 126-27.

[285]Fortune, p. 58.

[286]Hurwitz and Hurwitz, p. 40. The authors offer some curious reasoning (p. 37) as they argue for the suffering Jews: "Where no man was equal, the Jews were the most unequal of all. If slaves might seem even less equal, this rested on the premise that, unlike the Jews, who were considered to be human, the slaves were not so regarded at all. They were instruments, property, tools, albeit in human form. The Jews never fell into the non-human category even when they were adjudged to be agents of the devil."

[287]Hurwitz and Hurwitz, p. 43. They further quote other contemporary observers of the condition of the Jewish community (p. 45): "Many of the travellers who visited Jamaica reported that the Jews were very important to the Island's economy. For example, in The *Port Folio* (Philadelphia, [Magazine]), for May, 1812 (p. 12), there appears in 'Letters from Jamaica' the observation that 'Kingston contains a great number of Jews who have spread all over the Island.' Describing two synagogues, the writer characterized them as showing 'very little taste or beauty.' The Jews were 'excluded from every office and the enjoyment of every privilege,' but, 'as usual, they acquire great wealth.'"

When, however, the ex-slave was afforded the same rights and privileges as the Jews, they became fearful and moved to nullify the political restrictions. "For the first time, possession of a white skin, if by a Jew, carried with it no more privileges than that of a colored citizen of Jamaica."[288] By 1835, Alexander Bravo became the first Jewish member of the Jamaican Assembly, and fourteen years later eight of the forty-seven members were Jews.

Listed below are Jews who attained notoriety as appointed members of the Jamaican military, which served to maintain the slavocracy.[289]

Myer Benjamin
Alexander Bravo
Aaron Gomez DaCosta
Isaac Gomez DaCosta
Samuel Delisser
Jacob DePass
Moses Q. Henriques
Abraham Isaacs
Barnet Isaacs
George Isaacs
Daniel Jacobs
Alexander Joseph Lindo
David Lopez
Philip Lucas
Moses Gomez Silva

Martinique

The first large plantation and sugar refinery in Martinique was established in 1655 by Benjamin D'Acosta (also Dacosta), who had come from Brazil with 900 coreligionists and 1100 slaves.[290] These Jews, says Professor Marcus, "fled to Martinique where they furthered the sugar industry and the Negro slave economy which it created."[291]

---

[288]Hurwitz and Hurwitz, p. 46.

[289]Wolf, pp. 483-84.

[290]Friedman, "Sugar," p. 307. Mr. Friedman cited Werner Sombart, *The Jews and Modern Capitalism*, p. 36. See also Roth, *Marranos*, p. 290.

[291]*MEAJ1*, pp. 21-22; Friedman, p. 307, cites Deerr, vol. 1, pp. 230-31.

The family of David, Benjamin, and Moses Gradis owned extensive territory in St. Domingo and Martinique.[292] The DePas family garnered special consideration from the French tax collector in his report back to the mother country. He counted at least ten estates between them with hundreds of slaves and servants.[293] By 1680, "every [Jewish] householder had at least one slave; seven had ten or more. Of these seven, one had twenty-one slaves, while another had thirty slaves."[294]

Nevis

The Nevis community was a wealthy one comprised largely of Portuguese Jews.[295] They settled in about 1670, having been refugees from high taxation on Barbados.[296] The 1707 census shows that the Jews were all slaveowners, including Abraham Bueno DeMezqueto (Mesquita) and Solomon Israel. Israel's was the largest Jewish household of family and slaves in the census. Ralph Abenduna was a resident of Boston in 1695 and also appears as a slaveholder in Nevis in 1707.[297] The census also indicates that planter Isaac Lobatto headed a household of two white females and twelve Blacks. Isaac and Esther Pinheiro's census record reads: "2 Wh. M.; 4 Wh. F.; 9 Bl." Esther had purchased a slave woman in New York on February 13, 1707.[298]

The following is a "List of the Inhabitants of Nevis, with the number of their Slaves," dated March 13, 1707, which appears in the third volume of *Caribbeana*.[299] This census gives the following data about Jewish residents of the island:

---

[292]Korn, *Jews of New Orleans*, p. 2.

[293]Lee M. Friedman, *Jewish Pioneers and Patriots*, p. 92.

[294]*MCAJ1*, p. 88.

[295]*MCAJ1*, p. 99.

[296]Malcolm Stern, "A Successful Caribbean Restoration: The Nevis Story," *AJHQ*, vol. 61 (1971), p. 21.

[297]Stern, "Notes on the Jews of Nevis," pp. 155-57. See also Stern, "Nevis Story," p. 22.

[298]Stern, "Notes on the Jews of Nevis," pp. 157-58.

[299]Stern, "Some Notes on the Jews of Nevis," pp. 153-54.

Jews	White Males	White Females	Blacks
Isaac Lobatt		2	12
Isaac Pinheiro	2	4	9
Abraham Bueno De		1	8
Ralph Abenduna			1
Solomon Israel	4	1	13

The decline of Nevis' white and Jewish population occurred when in 1838 the emancipation of the slaves "saw the departure of most of the remainder [of them]."[300]

Saint Dominique

To the African, life and conditions on Saint Dominique were particularly painful. As a consequence, Jewish plantation owners found that their "greatest difficulties...were offered by runaway Negro slaves."[301] Jacob Beller, in his study of Latin American Jews, described the breaking point:

> [The African's] drive for freedom was finally attained on the island of Saint Domingue in a great uprising in 1801. The slaves seized weapons, and gained control of the interior mountain passes. Greatly outnumbering their masters, they overran sugar and coffee plantations and massacred all whites they captured. Awaiting execution at dawn was the captive French-Jewish plantation owner, Aaron Soria.[302]

The Saint Dominique revolt caused many Europeans to seek permanent refuge in other regions, including North America. Word of the ferocity of the uprising reached all over the world, and slaveholders everywhere took brutal measures to guard against a similar fate. Jews like the Moline family were run out of Saint Dominique in 1793. They brought with them some African captives branded with the Moline name to work for them in Pennsylvania.[303] The Gradis family owned extensive territory on

[300]Stern, "The Nevis Story," p. 23.

[301]*MCAJ1*, p. 159.

[302]I. Harold Sharfman, *Jews on the Frontier* (Chicago: Henry Regnery Company, 1977), p. 139. Another Jewish account is in "Items Related to the Jews in South America and the West Indies," *PAJHS*, vol. 27 (1920), pp. 476-77: "They were attacked by negroe-forces and defended themselves the best way they could....The negroes massacred the whites whenever an opportunity afforded; every white citizen therefore was compelled to take up arms in defence of the city. The blacks, who greatly outnumbered the white male population, had full possession of the mountains and all their passes, they were well armed and drilled and made frequent attacks by night on the city."

[303]Wolf and Whiteman, p. 191; Rosenbloom, p. 116.

the island as well as a major shipping enterprise. Abraham Gradis later planned to develop the state of Louisiana with a massive infusion of 10,000 slaves, though it was never implemented. There is evidence, to be expanded upon ahead, that Jews were actually breeding female slaves for sexual purposes on the island.

Though Blacks were held as slaves under the most brutal of conditions by Jewish Europeans, Jacob Marcus, the esteemed Jewish historian, saw the *Jews* as victims. After a slave echoed a Jewish slur he had obviously heard from his Gentile master, Marcus complained that "anti-Jewish prejudice was not absent on Saint Dominique even among the Negroes."[304]

Saint Eustatius

In 1722, Saint Eustatius Island in the Caribbean Netherlands had 1,204 inhabitants, of which 4 families (22 people) were Jewish with 3, 7, 4 and 2 slaves respectively.[305] According to Marcus, it soon became the center of the smuggling traffic, particularly in munitions during the American Revolution, and the largest North American Jewish settlement. "Jews flocked to the 'golden rock' and some North American Jewish merchants even established branch offices there."[306]

Saint Thomas

"Already in the year 1492 Portuguese Jews settled in Saint Thomas, where they were the first plantation owners on a large scale....[T]hey set up many sugar factories and gave employment to nearly three thousand Negroes."[307] By the year 1550, this industry had reached the height of its development on the island. There were sixty plantations with sugar mills and refineries, producing a substantial supply for export.

---

[304]*MCAJ1*, p. 93.

[305]John Hartog, "The Honen Daliem Congregation of St. Eustatius," *AJA*, vol. 19 (April 1967), p. 61.

[306]*MCAJ1*, p. 142; N. Taylor Phillips, "Items Relating to the History of the Jews of New York," *PAJHS*, vol. 11 (1903), p. 149.

[307]Friedman, "Sugar," p. 306. "Employment" here does not mean that they were paid. These "three thousand Negroes" were Black citizens of Africa seized and "employed" against their will—with no compensation provided.

Smuggling

> *"[A]mple evidence [exists] that in matters of contraband and the like, Jewish merchants were at one with their Gentile counterparts; they smuggled when they could."* [308]

Throughout the New World, merchant shippers had established inter-island relationships based on the plantation economy. Slaves and equipment, seed and harvest, chains and ammunition had to be ferried about to meet the demands of the market. But commercial relations were subject to the demands of governments that were frequently at odds. Taxes applied to different products in different ports at different times were exacted from the merchants by the kingdom or company that ruled the port. The embargoes of warring nations restricted trade, interrupting many a profitable commercial relationship, turning many into outlaws and contraband smugglers for the sake of personal profit.

Jews were involved extensively in such illicit trading and employed a number of skillful methods to avoid taxes and to circumvent governmental regulation. The most profitable of the contraband items were the Black African slaves—the very fuel of the economy. The smuggling of Black people into various Western markets was so extensive that nearly every "legitimate" bill of lading of the African trade listed in port or merchant records may have underreported slave quantities by manifold. An observer of this traffic in the Caribbean in the early 17th century noted that

> every slave trader who obtained licenses for 100 Africans casually loaded five times that number and ran into no difficulties with the authorities in Cartagena; he merely distributed between twelve and twenty slaves among the parties concerned, and was then given free rein to sell the rest of his cargo. The slave trader Manuel Bautista Perez...matter-of-factly listed in his account book for 1618 that he had bribed the governor, treasury officials, and various minor functionaries of Cartagena with slaves and cash totaling 6,170 pesos to get them to let him land twice as many slaves as his registry called for. Even the convoy system was riddled with fraud — to the point where the newly appointed corregidor of Ica, Gregorio Rico, felt obliged to write the Crown from Puerto Belo about the

[308] *MCAJ2*, p. 790.

> scandalous numbers of illegally imported slaves who had made the voyage with him.[309]

Human beings had a distinct advantage as contraband. They could walk, load and store themselves and did not require a crew of laborers to move them about, not to mention the immense per-slave profit. They could also carry the other marketable items in the clandestine trade such as molasses, tobacco, ammunition and tea, and as unpaid laborers, all benefits and profits accrued to the smuggler.[310]

At the foundation of this traffic were Portuguese Jews who fled Brazil in the wake of the Inquisition and built up the illegal commerce of Buenos Aires, Argentina, "importing West African slaves and exporting the silver of Potosi, [Bolivia]."[311] Jews in Jamaica and South America, in cooperation with Jesuit priests and Spanish authorities, created an extensive emporium for smuggling centered in Jamaica.[312] It had been declared in a sworn statement made for the Spanish government in 1728 that there was not a mariner of a slave-shuttling packet-boat who did not carry two or three thousand pesos worth of human property "from some Jamaican Jew on every one of the four or five trips made annually by such boats."[313]

As the royal duties and restrictions on goods carried legally to America became more and more expensive, "Portuguese merchants, eager for profit, began supplementing their legitimate cargoes with quantities of illegal slaves and merchandise."[314] Rhode Islanders were notorious for their participation in this

---

[309]Bowser, p. 56; Hartog, *Curaçao,* p. 139. Three varieties of this trade are described by Swetschinski, pp. 234-35:

> ...contraband under cover of the slave trade, contraband in the guise of *arribadas* and contraband pure and simple. Simple contraband consisted in a ship landing at an out-of-the-way port and the merchant selling his wares at an inland market....Contraband in the guise of *arribadas* called for a Dutch or English ship to enter a Spanish port claiming to have been blown off course, to have been damaged or simply to have run out of victuals. Once inside the Spanish harbor it was fairly easy to sell some or all of the ship's cargo surreptitiously. Here is where the real advantage of the Portuguese Jews came through. For they possessed in many of the harbors along the coast between Panama and Guyana Portuguese New Christian associates, if not more or less immediate kinsmen, who weathered the inquisitional storms of the mid-century.

[310]Frances Armytage, *Free Port System in British West Indies* (New York: Longmans Green and Co., 1953), p. 47.

[311]Elkin, p. 13.

[312]Fortune, p. 123.

[313]Vera Lee Brown, "Contraband Trade: A Factor in the Decline of Spain's Empire in America," *The Hispanic American Historical Review*, vol. 8, no. 2 (May 1928), p. 180.

[314]Bowser, p. 34.

traffic. Jewish businessmen like Naphtali Hart & Company sought their share,[315] and Aaron Lopez engaged in the practice rather extensively.[316]

But this was the eighteenth century, reasons Stanley Chyet of the Jewish Institute of Religion, "when a merchant had little choice but to regard deceiving the authorities as a commercial necessity; no merchant saw a dishonor in violations of the trading laws."[317] Jacob Rader Marcus agrees:

> Every effort was made to evade payment of the requisite duties, and the core of the navigation laws, the requirement that most imports and exports from and to Europe clear through English ports, was often flouted. Smuggling in tea, dry goods, and gunpowder, not only from the Dutch West Indies, but also from Holland herself, was something less than uncommon....There seems for the most part to have been no strong moral scruples about smuggling. Substantial merchants like the Browns, the Hancocks, and Lopez all smuggled, whenever the opportunity to do so safely presented itself.[318]

Where slave cargoes were taxed is also where bribes were paid and books were falsified—while the Black carnage mounted. Undocumented and unaccounted for are the untold numbers of Africans who were thrown to the sea to avoid port authorities. Central and South American Jews carried on the trade with Holland and "knew the location of all the ports of the Gulf of Mexico where illegal shipments could be made and the onerous Spanish taxes avoided."[319] A British official remarked, "The Jews with us know very well how to land goods at our wharfs in the

---

[315]*MCAJ2,* p. 791; Andrea Finkelstein Losben, "Newport's Jews and the American Revolution," *Rhode Island Jewish Historical Notes*, vol. 7, no. 2 (November 1976), p. 262. William G. McLoughlin, *Rhode Island: A History* (New York: W.W. Norton & Company, 1978), pp. 66-67, described the trade:

> The prime means of circumvention was smuggling. Smuggling meant chiefly bringing sugar or molasses from French or Spanish colonies into Rhode Island without paying the duties required by the Molasses Act of 1733 and its more restrictive revisions in 1764 and 1766. Designed to regulate trade rather than produce revenue, the Molasses Act was an attempt to force the colonists to trade only with the British West Indies. But the British planters did not produce enough sugar and molasses to satisfy the commercial needs of the New England colonists, especially for making rum. The Molasses Act seemed unfair. It gave the West Indian planters a monopoly, while depriving New Englanders of a principle source of raw material needed to support their export trade. The result was to encourage smuggling despite the risks. Risks in fact increased profits.

[316]*MCAJ2,* p. 793. Stanley F. Chyet, "Aaron Lopez: A Study in Buenafama," *Karp, JEA1,* p. 197, writes, "...we discover...on frequent occasion – that Lopez had no aversion to illegalities like smuggling and bribery....Lopez did, to be sure, engage extensively in smuggling."

[317]Chyet, p. 198.

[318]*MCAJ2,* p. 789.

[319]Liebman, *The Jews in New Spain,* p. 216.

night time, without any notice being taken of them."[320] J. Savary des Bruslons in his *Dictionaire universal de commerce* (1748) testifies that "[t]he Jews of Amsterdam are so expert that, after disguising the merchandise by mingling it with other goods, or packing it in another way or re-marking it, they are not afraid to go to certain Portuguese ports and resell the goods there. Very often they even dispose of it to the same merchants from whom the booty was taken."[321] The use of false names was very common among English Jews of Portuguese extraction, a practice which conceals the true extent of the Jewish smuggling trade.[322]

The authorities of the various colonies had little hope of regulating the flow of the smuggling trade despite edicts from Europe. The opportunities to profit were too apparent to the skilled trader. When the Jews were expelled from Martinique by the French, they simply moved to the English Barbados, which became the new seat of their smuggling operations.[323] The English Jamaican Jews engaged in the illicit trade with the Spanish in what is now Central America.[324] Even while the English and French were bitter enemies, it was reported that several Jewish stores in Kingston were full of French coffee.[325] In at least one documented case, the volume and revenues of the illicit trade were so extensive that when Isaac de Fonseca of Barbados threatened to abandon Curaçao and turn his smuggling trade towards Jamaica, Curaçaoan authorities refrained from interfering.[326] In 1723, Governor Worsley of Barbados claimed that the network of illicit trade in Barbados was so extensive that he was "incapable of preventing it."[327] According to Isidoro Aizenberg, the smugglers and pirates became the undisputed authorities where trade was concerned. The governor in Venezuela, for instance, had to accept the fact that unless he allowed local products to be smuggled in Dutch ships, they would

---

[320]Arthur S. Aiton, "The Asiento Treaty As Reflected in the Papers of Lord Shelburne," *The Hispanic American Historical Review*, vol. 8 (May 1928), p. 174.

[321]Arkin, *AJEH*, p. 94.

[322]Harold Pollins, *Economic History of the Jews in England* (East Brunswick, NJ: Associated University Presses, 1982), p. 51.

[323]Liebman, *New World Jewry*, p. 177.

[324]Liebman, *New World Jewry*, pp. 62-63.

[325]Armytage, p. 46.

[326]Wiernik, p. 52.

[327]Fortune, p. 102. Fortune, p. 103: Customs Commissioner Cox claimed that "[t]he French traders land in the night and nail up the gunns of the batterys on the Leeward coast, for want of matrosses being at their posts, they steal and carry away our negroes, and put prohibited goods on shoar, all my care to the contrary being ineffectual to prevent it."

never reach Europe. A large proportion of these ships were owned by Jews who became active participants in the trade between Venezuela and the Old World.[328]

Jean Laffite, Jewish Pirate

The smuggling business boomed after the United States prohibition on imported Africans in 1808 unleashed feverish activity in the Mexican gulf area as the price for a Black male soared from $300 to $1,000 in New Orleans. Plantation owners from all along the Mississippi River and its tributaries arrived to purchase more and more slaves in the clandestine trade. Jewish pirate Jean Laffite smuggled goods and slaves into Louisiana, about 50 miles west of New Orleans. From that station, river craft transported the slaves and merchandise north to St. Louis and to nearby New Orleans.[329]

Laffite, whose enterprise spanned the Caribbean, marshalled the forces of the area's maritime thugs in a massive operation against free trade. Rabbi Sharfman described the organizational process:

> ...Jean Laffite noted that instead of taking advantage of the principle of supply and demand, the buccaneer captains...in rivalry, stole each other's blacks, and offered prime males for sale at a mere dollar a pound. Accusations and arguments between them would soon result in open warfare that threatened the very existence of Barataria. It was then that the fighting captains agreed to unite under Jean Laffite. Standing on a hillside before a motley assemblage of almost 500 sabre-rattling sea robbers and cut-throats, knife-and-gun-brandishing felons and desperados, the Jewish Creole dandy stood firm, yet relaxed, speaking in his gentlemanly fashion.[330]

Laffite dispatched 60 ships throughout the Caribbean to hunt Spanish slave ships and then held weekly slave auctions at his retreat at Barataria on the Louisiana coast.[331] The trade was under the total control of Laffite, and as Sharfman put it, "No Baratarian dared disobey." Amsterdam Jewish merchants were involved in arming these ships of terror as well as disposing of the booty captured by these pirates.[332]

---

[328]Liebman, *New World Jewry*, p. 184. For discussion of Dutch involvement see Fortune, p. 104. See also Swetschinski, p. 222.

[329]Sharfman, p. 234.

[330]Sharfman, p. 144.

[331]Sharfman, p. 151.

[332]Arkin, *AJEH*, p. 94. *EAJA*, p. 98: "Barbary Jews chose Leghorn as the market for slaves and booty. It was often cheaper to buy piratical goods from there than to

Jewish merchants of New Orleans became closely associated with Jean Laffite. The auction house of Jacobs & Asbridge operated by Maurice Barnett preferred the quality of Laffite's African product. They "were sturdy and healthy, for only the hardiest blacks survived confinement in the deep dark stuffy hulls of the slave ships, not to mention the contagious diseases and brutal treatment that marked their months-long journey."[333] Antonio Mendez, Civil Commandant of a district outside of New Orleans, aided the slave-smuggling efforts,[334] and another Jew, New Orleans businessman David G. Seixas, a slaveowner himself, "acquired a schooner and possibly arranged for their [the enslaved Africans'] shipment and transport."[335]

As many as 400 Blacks were sold in a single day and smuggled into New Orleans by Laffite and his agents. His operation was so extensive that he was said to monopolize Louisiana's import trade and the commerce of the entire Mississippi Valley. By 1812, it was claimed that Jewish pirate Jean Laffite had become the "greatest trader in all the West."[336]

---

procure them directly from Barbary. Dutch Jews took advantage of this trade. Beside their well-known transactions in slaves, they bought cotton, drugs, gall nuts, fabrics, Tripolitan silks, [pearls}, etc. in Leghorn."

[333]Sharfman, p. 151. Also in Sharfman, pp. 152-53: "And Virginia's native slaves did not compare to imported African 'Black Ivory' offered at Laffite's 'Temple.' Slaves from Africa's Gold Coast, pitch black and ferocious, brought the lowest prices. Preferred were those from French Dahomey, tobacco-colored and gentle. Males in their twenties brought higher prices than females of that age, and children lesser prices."

[334]Sharfman, p. 151.

[335]Sharfman, p. 145.

[336]Sharfman, p. 154.

Summary

Jewish influence within the great western migration has been considerably understated—and yet for the African it was of critical significance. Under the historical cloak of a national identity, rather than a religious one, Jewish entrepreneurs ventured west and formed the commercial base that made possible the settlement of the New World. Seymour Liebman, for example, stated the unwritten—that "almost all historians attest that in the seventeenth century in the New World, 'Portuguese' was synonymous with 'Jew'..."[337]

The commercial tradition of the European Jewish communities and their advantages in international trade are indisputable. Sugar had transformed the islands into "agricultural bonanzas and entrepots of commerce, creating the need for shipping, credit and capital, merchants, wholesalers of dry goods and other manufactures, insurance of freight, and all the other visible and invisible items of trade that broadened the economic base of the plantations."[338] In 1712, Joseph Addison wrote:

> They [Jews] are so disseminated through all the trading parts of the world, that they are becoming the instrument by which the most distinct nations converse with one another and by which mankind are knit together in general correspondence. They are like the pegs and nails in a great building which, though they are but little valued in themselves, absolutely necessary to keep the whole frame together.[339]

Slavery was essential to the New World mission of wealth building and therefore became the most lucrative enterprise of the times—nothing moved without Black labor. The 1661 letter from the newly explored colony in Venezuela is our best insight:

> Negroes are required here....Do not regard this otherwise than it is written or as anything but the honest truth, without exaggeration or hypocrisy and upon which you may rely.[340]

Jews, as an elementary fact, participated in the process by which millions of African citizens were enslaved and murdered. Jewish wealth and freedom established, they set their sights to the north.

---

[337]Liebman, *New World Jewry*, p. 169.

[338]Fortune, pp. 64-65; Shaftesley, p. 138.

[339]Liebman, *New World Jewry* p. 189.

[340]Oppenheim, "Guiana," p. 131.

Jews and Slavery in Colonial North America

The Jews arrived in North America primarily as refugees from Brazil and from the islands of the Caribbean and met a population quite different from their own. The American colonies represented a land of farmers and seaport merchants, and as late as the mid-eighteenth century, nine-tenths of the inhabitants made their living from the soil.[341] As many as one-third to one-half of the entire Revolution-era population came from the class of indentured servants, a class whose members were primarily the purged criminals of European jails.[342] The Jews, on the other hand, were of the mercantile class, with an entrepreneurial tradition and a worldwide network of commercial relationships. The majority of these Jews were by no means poor and destitute "huddled masses," but instead were highly skilled and savvy businessmen whose wealth on arrival far surpassed that of many other immigrants. "As almost all the early Jewish settlers in America belonged to the wealthy classes," writes historian Peter Wiernik, "it was natural for them to accept the institution of slavery as they found it, and to derive as much benefit from it as other affluent men."

The earliest Jewish settlements were established in Newport, Rhode Island, and New York, where there were numerous Jewish slave holders long before and right through the American Revolution.[343] Jews adapted to the business climate of colonial North America and operated with the same skill they had demonstrated in the island regions to the south—and accepted Black slavery without question. In the North before 1800 and in the South all through the colonial period, slaves were stocked as commodities by Jewish merchants.[344] Countless thousands of

---

[341]Stanley Feldstein, *The Land That I Show You* (New York: Anchor Press/Doubleday, 1978), p. 12.

[342]*MCAJ2*, p. 799.

[343]Wiernik, p. 206; David Brener, *The Jews of Lancaster, Pennsylvania: A Story With Two Beginnings* (Lancaster: Congregation Shaarai Shomayim, 1979), p. 2.

[344]*MUSJ1*, p. 585. The Jewish historian Leon Hühner, "The Jews of Virginia from the Earliest Times to the Close of the Eighteenth Century," *PAJHS*, vol. 20 (1911), p. 86, comments on the business acumen of the colonial Jews:

Africans were brought here in colonial times as slaves by Jewish merchant-shippers, and in the South Jews began to enter the planter class in substantial numbers.[345]

The New York- and Newport-area Jews had established a highly efficient trans-Atlantic shipping operation. Jews who settled in North Africa with access into the African mainland arranged with African tribal traitors for the transport of Blacks to the Atlantic coast for sale to the New World merchant-shippers. Liquor, feverishly distilled in the American northeast, was used in Africa in much the same way as it was in the destruction of American Indian civilization. The New England colonies became so dependent on the alcohol-for-slaves trade that its absence, they claimed, would have idled two-thirds of all of their ships and caused massive unemployment, crippling their economy.[346] The colonies' very lifeblood was slavery and the slave trade. Jewish historian Henry L. Feingold, in a fit of understatement, put it this way: "The traffic in human beings by the Portuguese, Dutch, French and English was an essential ingredient of the early capital formation necessary for the development of the capitalist system, and Jews who were frequently found at the heart of commerce could not have failed to contribute to the [slave] trade directly or indirectly."[347]

It should be made very plain at this point that even until the Civil War era, Jews as a community never interfered with the practice of slavery or registered any reservation about its dehumanizing effects. When some colonies had proposed high tariffs on the importation of slaves, intending to discourage the slave trade, Jewish merchants Joseph Marks, Samson Levy, and David Franks protested, for they "were among those who wished to see the traffic continue."[348] Slavery was a business concern

---

It must be confessed that the Jew has a peculiar aptitude for mercantile enterprise. Whether carrying on commerce on a large scale as at Newport or New York in colonial days, or as the small tradesman in less important communities, he generally appears in our early records primarily as the merchant...

[345]Lenni Brenner, *Jews in America Today* (Secaucus, New Jersey: Lyle Stuart, 1986), pp. 221-22. Priscilla Fishman, ed., *Jews of the United States* (New York: Quadrangle, 1973), p. 8: From the early colonial times, "Jewish entrepreneurs were engaged in the slave trade on the North American mainland, participating in the infamous triangular trade..."

[346]"Thomas Fitch Papers," *Collections* (Hartford: Connecticut Historical Society), vol. 18 (1920), pp. 262-73.

[347]Feingold, *Zion*, pp. 42-43; Marc Lee Raphael, *Jews and Judaism in the United States: a Documentary History* (New York: Behrman House, 1983), p. 14.

[348]Abram Vossen Goodman, *American Overture: Jewish Rights in Colonial Times* (Philadelphia: Jewish Publication Society of America, 1947), p. 127.

mitigated only by the bottom line. Regionally, one can discern no difference in the Jews' attitude or philosophy with regard to *non-Jewish* human bondage. Says Bertram W. Korn, "It would seem to be realistic to conclude that any Jew who could afford to own slaves and had need for their services would do so."[349] The eminent Dr. Marcus confirms this in his recent book, *United States Jewry, 1776-1985:*

> All through the eighteenth century, into the early nineteenth, Jews in the North were to own black servants; in the South, the few plantations owned by Jews were tilled with slave labor. In 1820, over 75 percent of all Jewish families in Charleston, Richmond, and Savannah owned slaves, employed as domestic servants; almost 40 percent of all Jewish householders in the United States owned one slave or more. There were no protests against slavery as such by Jews in the South, where they were always outnumbered at least 100 to 1....But very few Jews anywhere in the United States protested against chattel slavery on moral grounds.[350]

Joseph Weinberg was just as direct in his paper to conservative American rabbis:

> [L]ike other white men in the caribbean and North America, some Jews were slave traders and slave holders. There were occasional attempts to restrict Jewish activity by limiting the number of slaves they could own and prohibiting the purchase of baptized slaves by Jews, but these provisions were not enforced. Like other merchants of their day, the Jews found the slave trade to be a profitable business. Some purchased Negroes to hire them out, while others worked them on their plantations. In their treatment and dealings with slaves Jews behaved no better and no worse than other white men; at times they beat recalcitrant slaves and had their share of black runaways.[351]

Several Jewish communities throughout North America took root and continued the same lucrative commercial operations that had brought them so much success in other areas of the globe. The slave market continued to offer the best return and the mercantile experience of the Jews found them tooled and ready to take full advantage.

---

[349]Bertram W. Korn, "Jews and Negro Slavery in the Old South, 1789-1865," in *Karp, JEA3*, p. 184.

[350]*MUSJ1*, p. 586; Robert G. Weisbord and Arthur Stein, *Bittersweet Encounters* (Westport, Connecticut: Negro Universities Press, 1970), p. 20.

[351]Weinberg, p. 34.

New York

> *"In May 1654 sixteen ships carrying the Jews of Brazil set out for Holland. Fifteen reached their destination, but the sixteenth, carrying twenty-three Sephardi Jews, was blown off course. It was captured by Spanish pirates and its cargo confiscated; the vessel was sunk, and the passengers held to be sold as slaves. But the pirate ship was sighted by a French bark, the St. Charles, and the prisoners were rescued. The penniless Jews were taken to New Amsterdam, the nearest port."*[352]

This, the humble beginnings of the greatest of the world's Jewish communities, as described by Max I. Dimont. Today, more Jews live in New York City than in any other single place on the globe—including Israel. There they wield immense influence and there they first entered North America. When the first Jews arrived in New Amsterdam (later called New York) in 1654, it was to the chagrin of Peter Stuyvesant, the appointed director of the Dutch West India Company's western affairs. Speaking of a shipment of African slaves he had just received from Curaçao,

---

[352]Dimont, p. 37. Though there is, as yet, no definitive proof, the pirates who accosted that refugee ship may have also captured the Black slaves of these Jews. When the Portuguese recaptured Recife from the Dutch in 1654, instead of reprisals, they pardoned all defenders of the Dutch colony which included the Jews and gave them three months to sell their homes and to prepare to leave for Holland. It would be, at the very least, unusual, for this class of wealthy merchants (reportedly 150 families) to be without slaves. They demonstrated no aversion to the practice and used the African in every facet of their lives; from the plantation to the kitchen, and from the synagogue to the docks, Blacks were well-represented as slaves of Jews. One would be hard pressed to believe that these Jews would have boarded sixteen ships to establish new homes and left their most valuable commodity on shore. That act alone would have been unprecedented since their westward migration from European soil and would warrant careful historical scrutiny in and of itself. For just two of many examples, see Max J. Kohler, "New York," *PAJHS*, vol. 2 (1894), p. 96, who quotes Thomas Southey's, *Chronological History of the West Indies* (London, 1827), vol. 1, p. 335: "They proceeded to Guadeloupe and were civilly received by M. Houel, the governor; upwards of 900 persons of all ages landed — soldiers, merchants, women, children and slaves, bringing with them immense riches." And second, Aizenberg, p. 500, describes the expelled Jews of Coro in 1855 as consisting of "168 Jews and 88 slaves, among them." Also *EAJA*, p. 155; Arnold Wiznitzer, "The Number of Jews in Dutch Brazil (1630-1654)," *Jewish Social Studies*, vol. 16 (1954), pp. 112-13; Arnold Wiznitzer, "The Exodus from Brazil and Arrival in New Amsterdam of the Jewish Pilgrim Fathers, 1654," *PAJHS*, vol. 44 (December 1954), pp. 81-83.

Stuyvesant said he preferred them to the "unbelieving Jews."[353] He petitioned the Company's directors in Holland to exclude further Jewish colonists, but they replied that such action "would be unreasonable and improper, especially in view of the big losses which this nation suffered from the conquest of Brazil and in view of the great fortune which they have invested in the company."[354]

Stuyvesant's unwelcome of those twenty-three Jewish refugees from Brazil has been perceived as the Jews' first encounter with American anti-Semitism, but as Arthur Hertzberg writes: "though [Stuyvesant] did use such terms as 'Christ killers' or 'Christ rejecters,' as he fought against letting them stay in town, his quarrel with them was primarily economic." Generous land grants and privileges were awarded to those who agreed to farm the Caribbean island frontiers to provide much needed staple crops for the western settlements. The Jews, through Jo'ao de Yllan, were offered a Curaçaoan settlement under these conditions but preferred instead to raise and smuggle horses and deal slaves. Stuyvesant, who was the former governor of Curaçao and whose jurisdiction included the Caribbean islands, was left to continue the expensive importation of European crops.[355]

---

[353]Robert St. John, *Jews, Justice and Judaism* (New York: Doubleday and Company, 1969), p. 7. An extensive account of the circumstances surrounding the arrival of the Jews in New Amsterdam (New York) has been offered by Samuel Oppenheim, "Early History of the Jews in New York, 1654-1664: Some New Matter on the Subject," *PAJHS*, vol. 18 (1909), pp. 37-53.

[354]Arkin, *AJEH*, p. 97; St. John, p. 14; Howard Morley Sachar, *The Course of Modern Jewish History* (New York: Dell Publishing, 1958), p. 161. It is reported that the original Jewish investment in the Dutch West India Company of 1623 amounted to only one half of 1% of the total investment – hardly enough to be considered a "great fortune." By 1654, this investment must have been increased substantially or the initial investment was underreported.

[355]A. Hertzberg, pp. 20-21, 23; Goslinga, p. 55; Goodman, p. 75; Hartog, *Curaçao*, p. 131. See also Friedenwald, p. 50: In September of 1670, Governor Thomas Modyford of Jamaica made a list of Jamaican landholders with the "surprising" absence of Jewish names. According to historian Friedenwald: "This gives some standing to the charges that they [Jews] would not become planters, but remained traders and merchants, made against them a few years later." Also, Friedenwald, p. 59: A list of eminent planters in Barbados made in May of 1673 "contains the name of no Jew." Though Jamaica and Barbados were English possessions at the time and not subject to Stuyvesant or the Dutch West India Company, it nonetheless represents a Jewish behavior pattern that supports Stuyvesant's claims. Stuyvesant also felt that Jews received unfair advantages in other Company settlements. Author Peter Wiernik in *History of the Jews in America*, pp. 52-53: "Peter Stuyvesant (1592-1672), the Governor of New Netherlands, complained to the directors of the West India Company in the following year, that the Jews in Curaçao were allowed to hold negro slaves and were granted other privileges not enjoyed by the colonies of New Netherlands; and he demanded for his own people, if not more, at least the same privileges as were enjoyed by 'the usurious and covetous Jews.'"

After this initial conflict, reports Leo Hershkowitz in his study of Jewish community development in New York, "[t]here was a high degree of toleration with few examples of overt anti-Semitism."[356] For the most part the Jews formed a separate class by their own predilection. There were no ghettos, nor were they confined to any portion of the city, but they tended to congregate in the Dock Ward fronting the East River.[357] Their houses were exactly the same as all the other houses in town,[358] and in 1777 the German mercenary John Dohla commented that "the Jews of New York were not like those of Europe — they were clean shaven, dressed like everyone else, ate pork and intermarried without scruple."[359]

In colonial New York, Jews constituted a major segment of the mercantile population, and were an important part of colonial trade, "a fact often overlooked by historians," complains Hershkowitz.[360] They were engaged in money-lending, brokering, and banking from the earliest colonial age.[361] Slave dealing, then the most profitable of ventures, was financed through the New York banking firms; and though few records exist, the critical capital provided by these firms—capital that launched the African expeditions—cannot be understated.[362] The trade of the Jewish merchants was primarily in agricultural products exchanged for rum, slaves, and manufactured goods.[363] One recorded cargo included "coconuts, coral, tobacco, turpentine, sturgeon, wine, rum, two Negro boys, and one mulatto slave."[364]

The Jews traded with their co-religionists in Curaçao, Surinam, Saint Thomas, Barbados, Madeira, and Jamaica—referred to as the principal trading ports for New York outside of England. It

---

[356]Leo Hershkowitz, "Some Aspects of the New York Jewish Merchant and Community, 1654-1820," *PAJHS*, vol. 66 (1976), p. 12; Fishman, p. 5.

[357]Kohler, "New York," p. 91; Hershkowitz, "New York," p. 11. Lee M. Friedman, *Pilgrims in a New Land* (Philadelphia: Jewish Publication Society of America, 1948), p. 9: "The history of Israel in the United States is no ghetto history, walled off from the history of the land."

[358]A. Hertzberg, p. 24.

[359]Hershkowitz, "New York," p. 28.

[360]Hershkowitz, "New York," p. 25.

[361]Kohler, "New York," p. 85, notes that "It is of considerable interest in this connection to note that Jews were among the founders of the New York Stock Exchange in 1792."

[362]Philip S. Foner, *Business and Slavery* (Chapel Hill, North Carolina: University of North Carolina Press), pp. 164-68.

[363]Hershkowitz, "New York," pp. 11, 19, 26.

[364]Hershkowitz, "New York," p. 26.

should be mentioned that these ports were the very same places where Jewish settlements had been formed at an earlier day, and hence Jewish traders in New York "had a marked advantage over others in this West Indian trade."[365] Historian Peter Wiernik flatly stated that this trade "was principally in the hands of Jews,"[366] and Stanley Feldstein describes the benefit:

> America's Jewish merchants, using their religio-commercial connections, enjoyed a competitive advantage over many non-Jews engaged in that same lucrative intercolonial trade. Since the West Indian trade was a necessity to America's economy and since this trade was, in varying degrees, controlled by Jewish mercantile houses, American Jewry was influential in the commercial destiny of Britain's overseas empire.[367]

---

[365]Kohler, "New York," p . 79. A. Hertzberg, p. 25: "They kept in touch with other Jews all over the world, even with secret communities in England and France, so that [wrote the French envoy in Holland] 'the Jews in Amsterdam are the best informed about foreign commerce and news of all people in the world.'" Kohler, "Settlement of the West," p. 24: "The inter-colonial trade which promptly sprang up in colonial times between Jewish settlers in different and often distant colonies afforded further opportunities..." Fishman, pp. 7-8: "For a variety of reasons, Jewish settlers were heavily involved in overseas trade....Jewish merchants had built-in advantages and special skills. They had a knowledge of the international market and a network of kinsmen-business associates in the Caribbean, Italy, Spain, the Near East, and India. Knowledge of languages – Hebrew, Yiddish, German, Spanish, Portuguese, Dutch – was an additional asset. In commercial correspondence of the period, letters were written in three and sometimes four languages." See also S. D. Goitein, *Jewish Letters of Medieval Traders*, p. 6.

See also Herbert I. Bloom's "A Study of Brazilian Jewish History," *PAJHS*, vol. 33 (1934), p. 67: "Jews are known to have made use of their international connections to operate efficiently as purveyors of supplies....[S]ome Jewish traders in Brazil utilized their connections with their coreligionists in Amsterdam to furnish New Holland with provisions and stores." See also the reference in Marcus Arkin, *Aspects of Jewish Economic History* (Philadelphia: Jewish Publication Society of America, 1975), p. 97, and Swetschinski, p. 235.

[366]Wiernik, p. 52.

[367]Feldstein, p. 13. Sachar, p. 163: "As in Europe, the Jews in colonial America were almost exclusively a trading people, active in intercolonial, Indian, and foreign trade. Their experience, literacy, and contacts overseas enabled them to play a disproportionately large role in coastal shipping and ocean commerce." Raphael Mahler, *A History of Modern Jewry: 1780-1815* (New York: Schocken Books, 1971), p. 2:

> The Jewish share in commerce with the West Indies – a vital sector in the economy of the American colonies – was particularly prominent. The Jews of Newport took an outstanding position in this trade. Their contacts with the local Jewish Kehillot, in some instances members of their own families, was a great advantage to Jewish merchants in West Indian ports of call such as Barbados, Jamaica, Surinam, and Curaçao. Jewish businessmen in most of the important seaport towns played a conspicuous role in this commerce, finance and industry of the prospering colonies.

In 1717 and 1721, the *Crown* and the *New York Postillion,* owned by Nathan Simson and his New York and London associates, sailed into the northern harbor with a total load of 217 Africans. The shipments came directly from the African coast and were "two of the largest slave cargoes to be brought into New York in the first half of the eighteenth century."[368] In August of 1720, "Simon the Jew" (probably Simon Bonane or Bonave) was slave dealing.[369] New York Jewish merchants were in several instances charged with and found guilty of "selling demented and unsound slaves they had warranted as sound."[370]

Jews also held Black slaves for their personal comfort and status. During the first half of the 1700s, Black slaves constituted 20% of New York's population, with some Indians also held in slavery[371] and with every New York family of any wealth or comfort owning slaves.[372] By the 1720s Jews formed their religious community with some paying their dues by sending "a Negro slave to clean the synagogue."[373]

The Gomez family of New York "were for many years the recognized heads" of the Jewish community,[374] and in 1741 slaves belonging to them, and to Abraham Myers Cohen, were accused of being involved in a threatened riot and insurrection.[375] Sampson Simson, "one of the most prominent members of the New York Chamber of Commerce" and one of the drafters of its constitution, "was the largest trader among the New York Jews during the years 1757-1773." He was the owner of "a number of vessels engaged in trade with the East and West Indies," the

---

[368]*MEAJ1,* pp. 64-5.

[369]Kohler, "New York," p. 84.

[370]*MCAJ2,* p. 795.

[371]Hershkowitz, "New York," p. 12. On page 11 Hershkowitz adds: "Trade was primarily in agricultural products exchanged for rum, slaves, and manufactured goods."

[372]Kohler, "New York," p. 84. Lee M. Friedman, *Early American Jews* (Cambridge, Massachusetts: Harvard University Press, 1934), p. 62: "[M]any of the early Jewish settlers were slave-owners..."

[373]*MCAJ2,* p. 916. Saul Jacob Rubin, *Third to None: The Saga of Savannah Jewry 1733-1983* (Savannah, 1983), pp. 117-18, provides evidence of the use of Black labor by Jews to perform duties in the synagogue: "The case of the *Shammash* Henry was identified as a slave who was compensated five dollars "for his attention in cleaning and lighting the lamps, etc. of the synagogue." According to Rubin, Henry was needed because the kindling of lights on *Shabbat* is forbidden to Orthodox Jews, so that "a non-Jew is required to handle the 'work-related' chores of the synagogue."

[374]Miriam K. Freund, *Jewish Merchants in Colonial America* (New York: Behrman's Jewish Book House, 1939), p. 34.

[375]Kohler, "New York," p. 84.

Hardy, Sampson, Snow Union, Polly among them.[376] Jacob Franks "occasionally" imported household slaves.[377]

The wealthiest Jewish families had domestic servants as a rule. Moses Beach's list of affluent New Yorkers includes the following Jewish names with their estimated wealth[378]:

Samuel Abrams [Abrahams]	$150,000
A.L. Gomez	$200,000
David Hart	$250,000
Uriah Hendricks	$300,000
Widow Hendricks [Mrs. Harmon]	$300,000
Hyman Solomon [Haym M. Salomon]	$100,000

The following Jews were known dealers, owners, shippers, or supporters of the slave trade and of the enslavement of Black African citizens in early New York history.[379]

Issack Asher
Jacob Barsimson
Joseph Bueno
Solomon Myers Cohen
Jacob Fonseca
Aberham Franckfort
Jacob Franks
Daniel Gomez
David Gomez
Isaac Gomez
Lewis Gomez
Mordecai Gomez
Rebekah Gomez
Ephraim Hart
Judah Hays
Harmon Hendricks
Uriah Hendricks
Uriah Hyam
Abraham Isaacs
Joshua Isaacs
Samuel Jacobs
Benjamin S. Judah
Cary Judah
Elizabeth Judah
Arthur Levy
Eleazar Levy
Hayman Levy
Isaac H. Levy
Jacob Levy
Joseph Israel Levy
Joshua Levy
Moses Levy
Uriah Phillips Levy
Isaac R. Marques
Moses Michaels
(E)Manuel Myers
Seixas Nathan
Simon Nathan
Rodrigo Pacheco
David Pardo
Isaac Pinheiro
Rachel Pinto
Morris Jacob Raphall
Abraham Sarzedas
Moses Seixas
Solomon Simpson
Nathan Simson
Simja De Torres
Benjamin Wolf
Alexander Zuntz

---

[376]Freund, p. 36; Kohler, "New York," p. 83.

[377]*MEAJ1*, pp. 64-65.

[378]Ira Rosenwaike, *On the Edge of Greatness: A Portrait of American Jewry in the Early National Period* (Cincinnati: American Jewish Archives, 1985), p. 72.

[379]A more detailed documentation of their involvement is provided in the chapter entitled "Jews of the Black Holocaust." Also, Hershkowitz, "New York," pp. 29, 32, APPENDIX II.

Jewish Heads of Households in New York City, Census of 1830[380]		
Head of Household	Number of Black Slaves	
	M	F
Emanuel Abrahams	1	
L. B. Borwick		1
Rebecca Canter		1
Joseph Dreyfous		1
Nathan Emanuel		1
Bernard Hart		1
Joel Hart		1
Joseph L. Hays		1
Harman Hendricks	1	
Henry Hendricks	1	
David Henriques		1
Sampson M. Isaacks		1
Isaac Isaacs		1
Joseph Jacobs		1
Naphtali Judah		1
Aaron Levy		1
Jacob Levy Jr.		2
Moreland Michell		1
Moses L. Moses		2
Joshua Naar		1
Seixas Nathan	3	
Abigail Phillips		1
Moses S. Phillips		1
M. B. Seixas		3
Benedict Solomon		1
Sophia Tobias		1

[380]Rosenwaike, *Edge of Greatness*, pp. 119-23, Table A-6.

Newport, Rhode Island

> *"The Almighty Dispenser of all Events [now beholds] a Government which gives to bigotry no sanction, to persecution no assistance but generously affording to all liberty of conscience and immunities of citizenship deeming everyone of whatever nation or tongue or language, equal parts of the great Government machine."*[381]
>
> Moses Seixas

Mr. Seixas, of course, saw no irony in the fact that Newport, Rhode Island, had become one of the most active slave-trading ports of North America—with the significant assistance of his Jewish community. Indeed, as Jewish historians Edwin Wolf and Maxwell Whiteman have reported, the Newport Jews "traded extensively in Negroes,"[382] and for the thirty years during which Newport was a major commercial center, Jewish traders saw their most prosperous and successful times.[383] Rhode Island became the second largest slave dealing center behind only South Carolina.[384] Its three primary sources of wealth were the sugar trade, the slave trade, and the fisheries—especially whaling—and most Rhode Island merchants engaged in all three.[385] By 1760, 15 percent of Newport's population were Black slaves supplying labor to the lucrative port industries and to the lavish estates of the Caucasian merchants.[386]

---

[381]See Morris U. Schappes, *Documentary History of the Jews in the United States* (New York: Citadel Press, 1950), p. 79: Moses Seixas, the Jewish representative of Newport's Masons and warden of the synagogue, is quoted from a letter from the Newport Congregation to the President of the United States, George Washington, August 17, 1790. After the Revolutionary War, the Jews were accorded equal rights and freed of all legal restrictions, and then continued to finance the enslavement, shipment and murder of Black Africans. See also William G. McLoughlin, *Rhode Island: A History* (New York: W.W. Norton & Company, 1978), p. 105.

[382]Wolf and Whiteman, pp. 190-91.

[383]Max J. Kohler, "The Jews in Newport," *PAJHS*, vol. 6 (1897), p. 62.

[384]"Some Old Papers Relating to the Newport Slave Trade," *Newport Historical Society Bulletin*, no. 62 (July 1927), p. 12: "As many as 184 vessels were engaged in this trade at one time from the State of Rhode Island....Let us realize that this meant that every day witnessed the arrival or departure of a slave ship."

[385]McLoughlin, p. 63.

[386]McLoughlin, pp. 64-65, and 106: "Census statistics in 1755 indicate 4,697 slaves (or 11.5 percent of the population). Of these, 1,234 were in Newport, constituting 15 percent of that city. By 1774, census reports show only 3,761 slaves in the state, constituting 6.3 percent of the population." Peter T. Coleman, *The Transformation of Rhode Island, 1790-1860* (Providence: Brown University Press,

Newport was also the rum-producing center of the colonial world and the primary destination of the bulk of the sugar and molasses coming out of the West Indies. The infamous Triangular slave traders carried the rum into Africa in exchange for kidnapped Black Africans, many of them murdered in the process. From here many were taken to the West Indian plantations to produce the sugar for the insatiable profiteers of colonial America.

The Jewish presence in Newport dates back to 1658, with another wave arriving in 1694 on a ship with "a number of Jewish families of wealth and respectability on board" who settled there possibly from the Jewish stronghold of Curaçao.[387] But a new order was established in the 1750s when "hundreds of wealthy Israelites, a most distinguished class of merchants, removed here from Spain, Portugal [and] Jamaica...and entered largely into business." Among those were the families Lopez, Rivera, Polock, Hart, and Hays.[388] Dr. Henry Feingold described the Jewish pilgrims:

> The first group of fifteen Jewish families who arrived in Newport from Holland in the spring of 1658 were simple folk – soap boilers, brass workers, and small merchants....They owned seventeen candle-making factories related to a wholly Jewish-owned spermacetti trust, twenty-two distilleries, four sugar refineries for the making of rum to be used domestically and for the African trade, five rope-walk factories, a Castile soap-manufacturing combine, several furniture factories, a potash trust, and several smaller merchandizing establishments. The Jews of Newport also maintained a sizable representation in the shipping and whaling industries.[389]

1969), p. 14: "By mid-century, Rhode Island numbered over 40,400 inhabitants, but many of them lived in towns newly acquired from Massachusetts, and in Newport, particularly, about a sixth of the residents (over 1,100 people) were Negroes."

[387]Kohler, "Newport," p. 66. According to Leon Hühner in his article, "The Jews of Virginia," p. 89: "It is interesting to note that after the earthquake at Lisbon in 1755, a company of secret Jews embarked thence for America. The captain of the vessel intended to land them on the Virginia coast, but adverse and violent winds led him to seek refuge in Narragansett Bay, and these Jews subsequently became some of the most enterprising merchants of Newport." One should also note that Jewish families of "wealth and respectability" *invariably* owned slaves and likely migrated to Newport with many. The points of origin of these Jewish families were notoriously central to the Jewish slave-dealing empires of the Caribbean, where wealth was measured in numbers of Black slaves.

[388]Kohler, "Newport," p. 69. Andrea Finkelstein Losben, "Newport's Jews and the American Revolution," *Rhode Island Jewish Historical Notes*, vol. 7, no. 2 (Nov. 1976), p. 260: "Jews came to Rhode Island because of Roger Williams' liberal policies toward religion and because Newport's harbor offered excellent commercial opportunities."

[389]Feingold, *Zion*, p. 41. "Some Old Papers Relating to the Newport Slave Trade," *Newport Historical Society Bulletin*, no. 62 (July 1927), p. 12: The author here

The people whom Henry Feingold describes as "simple folk" in fact were the high-powered commercial engine of the Northeast. The Newport Jewish merchants played a "leading and very important part" in this commerce utilizing their well-established ties in the West Indies and all the other Colonies, as well as in England. From every port in the Caribbean, Jewish merchants sent so many ships to Gentile as well as Jewish merchant-traders that their rivals "often complained bitterly that they were monopolizing the West India trade."[390] Spermacetti candle making, the "electric utility" of the colonial age, was controlled by Jews and was, in fact, the first American business monopoly. As in all colonial commerce it required Black slaves. Distilling required Black cultivators and later, Black processors.[391] The manufacture of soap, a craft monopolized by Jews since the fourteenth century,[392] required Black manufacturers—most of whom were unpaid slaves of Jews. Even "Negro mechanics of some skill" helped build the Newport synagogue.[393]

Newport's Slave-Trading Jews

Many Jews, if not directly implicated in the slave trade, showed passive acquiescence by engaging in trades directly tied to slavery, such as distilling, financing and insuring, shipbuilding and outfitting (installers of bondage hardware). The Rhode Island slave trade employed 100-150 vessels annually, estimated Dr.

---

claims that "there were no less than 22 Stills waiting to turn the sugar into rum..." This, coupled with Feingold's statement, seems to suggest that *all* the stills in Newport were owned by the Jews. Dr. Eric E. Hirshler, ed., *Jews From Germany in the United States* (New York: Farrar, Straus & Cudahy, 1955), pp. 21-22: "Indeed, the Jews were leading in the establishment of the spermacetti oil and candle syndicate." See also Fishman, p. 8, who claims that Jews controlled other products: "Jewish traders were among the first to introduce cocoa and chocolate to England, and at times they had a virtual monopoly in the ginger trade." According to Harold Pollins, p. 53, the diamond-coral trade was nearly Jewish-dominated. Though Jews have claimed that discrimination barred them from participation in some trades, Pollins asserts that "the main reason for specialisation was probably the Jews' conservative adherence to known goods and known routes."

[390]S. Broches, "Jewish Merchants in Colonial Rhode Island," *Jews in New England* (New York: Bloch Publishing, 1942), p. 10.

[391]William G. McLoughlin, *Rhode Island: A History* (New York: W.W. Norton & Company, 1978), p. 64.

[392]Feingold, *Zion*, p. 41.

[393]*MCAJ3,* p. 1498; Weisbord and Stein, pp. 23-24.

Marcus, each carrying to Jamaica 80-100 Black men, women, and children.[394] Feingold described how the Jews were connected:

> From Africa they imported slaves and from the West Indies they received molasses from which they distilled rum. A key aspect of the triangular trade involved the notorious middle passage, the transportation of slaves from the west coast of Africa to the West Indies and eventually directly to the Colonies. Newport was the major Colonial port for this traffic in people, so that it comes as no surprise that Colonial Rhode Island boasted a higher proportion of slaves than any other colony.[395]

Nearly all Jews in Newport "had Negro domestic slaves....Bartlett, *R.I. Census, 1774,* shows only two Newport Jewish families without slaves."[396] Some of those Jews with direct ties to slavery as slave owners and/or traders were Saul Brown (a.k.a. Pardo), Isaac Elizer, Naphtali Hart, Jacob Isaacs, Aaron Lopez, Abraham Sarzedas, Sarah Lopez, Abraham Rivera, Moses Seixas, Jacob Rodriguez Rivera, Joseph Isacks, Simon Bonan, Amon Bonan, Delancena Jew, Moses Levey, Widdow D. Roblus, Isaac D. Markeys, [Luis] Gomas.[397]

The Newport Jewish community declined rapidly as a result of the Revolutionary War, as it was targeted by the British as a center of commerce.[398] Newporters, however, plunged back into slaving after the Revolution in a desperate attempt to rebuild the town's shattered economy.[399] Newport's economy and untold lost Black lives notwithstanding, the Jews prospered immensely and secured a significant part of their economic foundation from this port city.

Pennsylvania

---

[394] *MEAJ1,* p. 141. These figures are exceedingly low but are included as a substantiation of participation of Jews in the slave trade by an impeccable Jewish source.

[395] Feingold, *Zion,* p. 42; Raphael, p. 14. Rudolf Glanz, "Notes on Early Jewish Peddling in America," *Jewish Social Studies,* vol. 7 (1945), p. 121: "Doubtless they were active in Indian trade, supplying the Army, and in real estate deals, but the center of their activities was triangular trade between the American colonies and the motherland *via* the West Indies."

[396] *MCAJ3,* p. 1528. According to Ira Rosenwaike, "An Estimate and Analysis of the Jewish Population of the United States in 1790," *Karp, JEA1,* p. 393. Dimont, p. 44: "At the time of the Revolution, the Jewish community in Newport comprised but fifty to seventy-five Jewish families, but their wealth and prestige outstripped that of the Jewish community in New York."

[397] *MCAJ3,* p. 1528. See also this document, chapter entitled "Jews of the Black Holocaust."

[398] Wiernik, p. 99.

[399] Peter T. Coleman, p. 54.

The Jews formed communities in Pennsylvania with diverse economic bases. To the west were Jewish Indian traders and military arms suppliers, while the eastern Jewish community based in Philadelphia comprised mainly merchant shippers.

Philadelphia in 1663 was a small settlement of tiny cabins called Wicaco. Individual Jews appear in Philadelphia records as early as 1703, but it would not be until 1738 that Jewish leadership formed to start a bona fide Jewish community.[400] Joseph Simon, Jacob Franks, Nathan Levy, Solomon Etting, and the Gratz family, among others, were the most prosperous colonial families — and all practiced slavery. Levy Andrew Levy, an agent for Joseph Simon's operation, "with his bride Susannah and their Negro female slave, proceeded westward on horseback trailed by a file of horses laded with Simon goods....Her slave, one of the first blacks in Pittsburgh...drew water, milked the cow, and cared for the horses."[401] Two Jewish writers on the region's history, Edwin Wolf and Maxwell Whiteman, cite a local example of a Jewish clergyman as an owner of slaves:

> The Reverend Jacob Cohen's short, teen-age, bound girl wore a spotted jean jacket, a striped linsey petticoat, a spotted coarse shawl and a black wire-framed bonnet, when she ran away, and he was forced to offer a dollar's reward for anyone who would bring her home or take her to the gaol [jail]. The Jews who could afford them had both servants and slaves. The Quakers were the only people who as a religious denomination opposed the institution of slavery.[402]

Jews became increasingly prominent and influential in colonial Pennsylvania. The firm of Levy, Franks & Simon (founded 1751) became the most powerful western merchant conglomeration of its time. It was their 250-ton, 10-gun ship *Myrtilla* that brought the 2,000 pound Liberty Bell to the Philadelphia State House.[403] Jacob Franks is said to have gotten his share of business in armaments and slaves during Queen Anne's War (1702-1713), which gave Britain a monopoly in the slave trade.[404]Philadelphia merchant Isaac Moses appears to have been associated with Joseph Reed, Robert Morris, and other businessmen in launching the first bank in the United States which supplied provisions to the Continental

---

[400]Brener, p. 2.
[401]Sharfman, p. 21.
[402]Wolf and Whiteman, p. 190.
[403]Sharfman, p. 13.
[404]*JRM/Memoirs 2*, p. 293.

Army of the United States.[405] Again, the wealthiest among them held slaves, who tended their businesses, ships, and homes. A published list of the wealthy residents of Philadelphia included estimates of the estates of the following Jews in 1820[406]:

Jacob I. Florance	$500,000
William Florance	150,000
Hyman Gratz	75,000
Jacob Gratz	50,000
A. Hart	150,000
Dr. Joseph Leon	50,000
Joseph Levy	75,000
L. J. Levy	50,000
E. L. Moss	50,000
John Moss	300,000
Isaiah (Estate)	60,000
G. D. Rosengarten	150,000

The Census of 1830 provides "official" data on the slave holdings of Philadelphia Jews.

Jewish Heads of Households in Philadelphia, Census of 1830[407]

Head of Household	Number of Black Slaves	
	M	F
Sarah Andrews		1
Lewis Bomeisler	1	
Michael H. Cardga		1
Henry Elias	1	
David Etting	1	
Reuben Etting	1	
M. Gratz	1	
Sarah Hart		1
Samuel Hays	2	
Lewis Lipman	1	
Joseph Marks		1
Elias Mayer		2

405Kohler, "New York," p. 87.
406Rosenwaike, *Edge of Greatness*, pp. 72-73.
407Rosenwaike, *Edge of Greatness*, p. 124, Table A-7.

(Jews in Philadelphia and their slaves, Census of 1830, continued)

S. Moses	1	1
Eliazor L. Moss		1
Samuel Moss	1	
Isaiah Nathans		1
Jacobs Nathans		1
Nathan Nathans		2
David B. Nonas		1
Joseph Parara	1	
Mr. Peixotto		1
Zalegman Phillips		2
Isaac Phillips	1	

The Jews of western Pennsylvania were at the edge of the frontier and helped to link the pioneers with the imported and manufactured goods found in the port cities. They established lucrative arrangements with the native population that anchored their capital growth.

Jews and the Red Man

Jews were among those Europeans who saw the value of the fur pelts supplied by the native American (Indian) and became known as *Indian traders.* Max J. Kohler writes that the Jews "entered the new world through the Atlantic colonies controlled by the English charters, and finally worked their way west, trading with the Indians."[408] At first this trade was forbidden to Jews in some Dutch-controlled regions but they appealed to the West India Company at Amsterdam, and in 1656 the restrictions were lifted.[409]

Second only to the slave trade, Indian trading was the most profitable of commercial ventures.[410] Cheap European trinkets and baubles were traded for the fur pelts of the Indian trappers.[411]

---

[408]Kohler, "Settlement of the West," p. 33. Frances Dublin, "Jewish Colonial Enterprise in the Light of the Amherst Papers (1758-1763)," *PAJHS*, vol. 35 (1939), p. 3: Among the Indian traders "number many Jews." Dublin, p. 14: "Jews, considering their total number, formed a fairly large proportion of those engaged in the fur trade."

[409]Harry L. Golden and Martin Rywell, *Jews in American History: Their Contribution to the United States of America* (Charlotte: Henry Lewis Martin, 1950), p. 15.

[410]Dublin, p. 14: "The fur trade was one of the cornerstones of the colonial structure."

[411]Joseph L. Blau and Salo W. Baron, eds., *The Jews of the United States, 1790-1840*, 3 vols. (New York: Columbia University Press, 1963), vol. 1: 112-13. Jacob Marks,

Jacob Marcus recounts the involvement of some of the Jews in this commerce:

> Da Costa of Charleston advertised Indian goods in 1757; Isaac De Lyon and James Lucena of Savannah shipped out deerskins in the 1760's to pay for their English imports; and back in the woods the Nunez brothers traded with the Indians among whom they lived and fathered a brood of half-breeds.[412]

But this commerce was more than a matter of bartering with "local savages." They had in mind vast projects in the fields of western trade and land development,[413] and for this they would necessarily have to gain the trust of the various Indian organizations whose welcoming spirit opened the west to the Jews. The traders found themselves in a unique position to encourage and assist the Europeans in the extermination of the Indians. As traders in the wilderness they knew the trails and the tribal locations as well as the customs, wants, and needs of the Indians. As the European encroachment created lethal conflict, these Jewish traders often supplied the European with weapons, staples, and critical military intelligence. Once the Red man was removed there was no one more advantageously positioned to seize the valuable land than the Indian trader.

Rabbi I. Harold Sharfman points out that the Indians came to hate the white settlers with a passion, "for they hacked down trees, leveled roads where the deer trails ran, killed off their buffalo and deer, and drove away wild game."[414] But still they

---

for example, furnished what were called "mock garnets" to the Office of Indian Trade for trade with the Indians.

[412]*MCAJ2*, p. 732. See the example in Leon Huhner, "Daniel Gomez, A Pioneer Merchant of Early New York," *Karp, JEA1*, p. 183. Gomez owned a tract of land that "had been selected, no doubt, because the purchaser realized its immense advantage for purposes of barter and traffic with the natives. But 'Gomez the Jew' was not content to utilize this advantage on a small scale. Accordingly, between about 1717 and 1720, he built a massive stone house in this hollow, close to the main Indian trail leading across the mountains to the *Dans Kammer*. The site too, had been carefully selected, for near the house was a spring, which from time immemorial, was a favorite stopping place for the Indians."

[413]Goodman, p. 129. Brener, p. 16: "...[T]he first major venture into the area [was] for the purpose of earning the confidence of the Indians for future land concessions from them."

[414]Sharfman, p. 6. George P. Graff, "Michigan's Jewish Settlers, Frontiersmen in Every Sense of the Word," *Michigan Jewish History*, vol. 10 (January 1970), p. 10, quotes Rabbi Richard C. Hertz in the "Introduction" to *The Beth El Story*: "...the Indians regarded all white men, regardless of their national loyalties or creedal beliefs, as predatory interlopers preying upon their precious hunting grounds." According to an account published by Reverend Henry Cohen, "A Brave Frontiersman," *PAJHS*, vol. 8 (1900), p. 63, the Indians tried to reason with the settlers:

were intrigued by the strange wares of the peddlers and the new sensation that came with the spirit in a bottle. Joseph Simon was one of those Jewish peddlers that, according to Rabbi Sharfman,

> barter[ed] with the tribes exchanging colorful trinkets and a variety of eye-catching beads and the like for valuable furs....Little did [the Indians] realize...that they were bartering away their civilization. The iron kettles, shooting irons, and sundries they acquired for furs meant that they had to kill for many pelts that exceeded their needs for clothing, food, and shelter. Dependency on the white man's whiskey led to quarrelsomeness and murder of fellow braves. They fell prey to the diseases of the pale faces for which they had no immunity — smallpox, measles and sexual diseases.[415]

Simon was one of those who supplied those items that would eventually degenerate the Indian nation. He came to Lancaster, Pennsylvania, about 1735 and soon became one of the most prominent Indian traders and merchants and one of the largest land-holders in America. His land claims extended over Pennsylvania, Ohio, Illinois and to the Mississippi River.[416] In the Indian territory he had business interests with fellow Jews Barnard and Michael Gratz, David Franks, Solomon Etting, Challender and Levy Andrew Levy.[417] Simon, John Miller and brewer Mordecai Moses Mordecai decided to process hard liquor to introduce into the Indian trade. When it appeared that war was imminent between the French, Indians and the British, Simon

---

> This chief spoke at some length and to the point. It was the old story of honest, oppressed Indians, and treacherous, tyrannical white men. Much truth was told with native eloquence, and the Great Father was asked to stop the building of the iron road, which would soon drive away the buffalo and leave his children without food.

But the white man saw it another way (Rev. H. Cohen, p. 61):

> The Indians...became aggressive, exacting, and insulting. They preyed upon the settlers, stopped and robbed the overland stages, seized stock, took possession of station-houses, and, when hungry passengers were seated at their meals, turned them out, and themselves consumed all the scanty supply of provisions, and sometimes added murder to their other offenses. Seeing the weakness of our military posts, they insulted and taunted the garrisons, and occasionally robbed them.

[415]Sharfman, pp. 2, 8-9; Brener, pp. 2, 8.

[416]This, despite a ban on settlement west of the Alleghenies by Parliament. See Henry Necarsulmer, "The Early Jewish Settlement at Lancaster, Pennsylvania," *PAJHS*, vol. 9 (1901), p. 31, citing Ellis and Evans' *History of Lancaster County* (p. 18).

[417]Markens, "Hebrews in America," *PAJHS*, vol. 9 (1901), p. 33. Eric E. Hirshler, ed., *Jews From Germany in the United States* (New York: Farrar, Straus & Cudahy, 1955), p. 25: "Simon was one of the foremost Indian traders of his time." Hirshler, p. 26: "Between Indian attacks and French ambitions Simon helped to shape American and English policy at the source; as one of the largest landholders he was vitally interested in the promotion of settlements." See also "Notes: Joseph Simon, of Lancaster, Pennsylvania," *PAJHS*, vol. 1 (1893), p. 121.

began to make guns.[418] By the 1770s it was said that the Simon conglomerate had a "virtual monopoly" on the western trade.[419]

Other Jews made their fortunes exploiting the hapless Indian population. Hayman Levy Company was a leading Indian trader and Benjamin Lyon was its agent.[420] Later, Levy, Lyons & Company became "the largest fur trader of the colonies and one of the most opulent merchants in the city."[421] Hayman Levy shipped many goods to the western frontier, including a 1763 shipment that included "Iron, steel, paints, drygoods, scalping knives, Negro slaves..."[422] Levy's business ethics were challenged in this 1774 letter to Levy from the copybook of colonial merchant Ephraim S. Williams:

> ...I am far from being satisfied with your persisting in charging me the $2^1/_2$ percent more in my supplies than what you began with and what I expected would be the rule you should stick to. Had I judged you capable of taking such an advantage without my approbation I would never have dealt with you, nor am I yet so involved with you, but I can easily be off...[423]

Chapman Abraham was among the early merchants of Detroit and in 1765 he was selling rum in partnership with a man by the name of Lyons (possibly Benjamin Lyon).[424] Before them was Isaac Miranda, a Jew who, "posing as a 'fashionable Christian,' gained the political appointment of judge, swearing his oath upon

---

[418]Sharfman, pp. 19, 20. Brener, p. 12: "The partnership of Simon with Mordecai Moses Mordecai and John Miller produced 'Distill'd Liquors,' 'Annesses, Caraway seeds, Callamus, Cinnamon, orange, Snake root and spirits' combined to produce what we hope was an acceptable beverage." See also *ibid*, p. 16, for evidence of the connection that liquor had with land negotiations with the Indians.

[419]Brener, p. 15. Jacob R. Marcus, *The Jew and the American Revolution* (Cincinnati: American Jewish Archives, 1974), p. 14: One of Simon's companies, Simon & Campbell, is said to have "provided the Indian commissioners with goods for pacifying the natives."

[420]Sharfman, p. 16. Hayman is sometimes spelled Heyman.

[421]Freund, p. 39.

[422]Jacob R. Marcus, *Studies in American Jewish History* (Cincinnati: Hebrew Union College Press, 1969), p. 233. The widely held belief that Indians scalped the white settlers is challenged by this very order. This shipment is clearly intended for white frontiersmen who will likely use these knives on the scalps of Indians to collect a bounty. In 1706, in the colony of Massachusetts, for instance, a white man could reap a £50 reward for the scalp of an Indian. See *The Boston News-Letter*, August 19, 1706. See the case of Jewish bounty hunter Sigmund Shlesinger herein, p. 114.

[423]"Olden Times in Detroit," *Michigan Pioneer and Historical Society Collections and Researches*, vol. 28 (Lansing, 1900), p. 562.

[424]Irving I. Katz, "Chapman Abraham: An Early Jewish Settler in Detroit," *PAJHS*, vol. 40 (1950-51), p. 84.

a New Testament, but His Honor was soon dismissed for defrauding the Indians."[425]

Sending their packhorse trains across the mountains, the Jewish merchants fully hoped to dominate the western trade, to control mercantile sales, to build new towns and colonies, and to populate the vast territory between the Alleghenies and the Mississippi.[426] This required the expulsion of the owners and reallocation of the valuable land and resources—a fitting assignment for the Royal forces of Britain and France.

Jews as Military Contractors

The pioneer Jews were squarely aligned with the Europeans, primarily the British, and were suppliers of their military. It was they who ox-trained to the distant fortresses with all of the necessities for the troops to maintain their positions, some with exclusive contracts with London. Army supply, says Marcus,

> was, in consequence, a big business, and it was a business which the Jews knew well....Some of them were massive suppliers, involved in operations requiring sums of money in the millions; others were petty sutlers or army peddlers....Supply as big business came into its own during the vast military operations required by the French and Indian War. The large French and English armies had to be provisioned, and both armies looked to Jewish suppliers for food.[427]

Jacob Franks and son David of Philadelphia had contracts for provisioning British troops totaling over £750,000.[428] George III of England signed authorization to pay Moses Franks for supplies to his North American troops,[429] and Joseph Simon supplied the British in Pontiac's War of 1761–64.[430] Later, the firm of Simon, Levy & Franks "managed to secure the highly profitable Fort Chartres provisions contract to supply the English troops stationed there."[431] In the French and Indian War, Marcus reports

---

[425]Sharfman, pp. 2-3; Brener, p. 2.

[426]*MCAJ2*, p. 816. Brener, p. 15: "The interest of the Jew in that area was intense."

[427]*MCAJ2*, pp. 707, 714. See also Kohler, "Settlement of the West," p. 24: There was "very active participation of well-known Jewish families during the 18th century, in trade with the Indians, in extensive purchase and speculation in western lands, and in enterprises for provisioning armies engaged in interior warfare."

[428]Freund, p. 40.

[429]"Selected Acquisitions," *AJA*, vol. 32 (1980), p. 100.

[430]"Acquisitions," *AJA*, vol. 4 (1952), p. 42; Sharfman, p. 20.

[431]Sharfman, p. 46. See also Leon Hühner, "The Jews of Virginia from the Earliest Times to the Close of the Eighteenth Century," *PAJHS*, vol. 20 (1911), p. 91.

that the New Yorkers did a thriving business as sutlers and shopkeepers, satisfying the wants of soldiers and militiamen.[432]

The Anglo-Dutch merchant Uriah Hendricks reportedly did considerable trade with the British army; the Jewish firm of Lyon & Company supplied the infamous British General Jeffrey Amherst; and, according to documents,[433] Hyam Myers and Gershon Levy were also suppliers of Amherst's troops.[434] In fact, the conquest of Canada, a major military operation, involved numbers of Jewish tradesmen, including Aaron Hart, a Bavarian Jew who became a notable Canadian businessman in the post-revolutionary period.[435]

Other Jews in the trade were gun dealer Samuel Judah, Naphtali Hart Myers, Sampson Simson, Hayman Levy, Joseph Bueno, Simpson Levy and Nathan Levy. Again, Dr. Marcus could not have been clearer about the motive of the Jewish war supply operations:

> It was also during the French and Indian War that Jewish merchants from Philadelphia and Lancaster helped supply the army and the militia in their efforts to crush the Indians on the transallegheny western frontier.[436]

German Jews fought in the Royal American Regiment in the war against the Indian, both as officers and privates.[437] In 1774, during Cresap's War, which saw the Indians rise to save their hunting grounds from the oncoming settlers, another of Joseph Simon's firms, Simon & Campbell, "sold supplies to the Virginia troops in Pittsburgh and also helped outfit and finance the soldiers and workmen repairing and building Fort Pitt and Fort Fincastle (present-day Wheeling)."[438] They appear, seemingly, in every conflict as suppliers of either *or both* sides. Marcus confirms that the tomahawk — the weapon popularly believed to have

---

[432]*MCAJ2*, pp. 708-10. It is here stated that "Pacheco, then in London, was exporting large quantities of guns to the colonies, and one of the Gomezes was selling muskets, swords, and bayonets to George Clinton, the governor of New York. The records of the French and Indian War, which lasted from 1754 to 1763, reveal that there were Jewish sutlers and supplymen active in the vast territory between the Altamaha River in southeastern Georgia and the St. Lawrence River in Canada."

[433]*MCAJ2*, p. 710; "Selected Acquisitions,"*AJA*, vol. 32 (1980), p. 100.

[434]"Acquisitions," *AJA*, vol. 16 (1964), p. 94.

[435]*MCAJ2*, p. 708.

[436]*MCAJ2*, p. 710.

[437]Hirshler, p. 24.

[438]*MCAJ2*, p. 711.

been manufactured by the "marauding Indians"[439] — may have been sold or given to them by Jews:

> Mathias Bush, another member of the Lancaster-Philadelphia Jewish merchantry, supplied Pennsylvania with relatively large amounts of arms and munitions. (The same accounts credit Benjamin Franklin with 100 tomahawks, which he no doubt supplied for the use of loyal Indian allies.)[440]

Jews and Smallpox

Sir Jeffery Amherst, the genocidal commander-in-chief of His Majesty's Forces in North America, came in 1758 to fight the French, after gaining a solid reputation as a British officer in Germany in the War of the Austrian Secession. One of his responsibilities in his new position was to annihilate the Indian population, and it was he who conceived the strategy to spread smallpox among them by way of infected gift blankets. His greatest adversary was Chief Pontiac, who had organized a coalition of Indian tribes to defend their homeland and had been successful in frustrating the European encroachments. Amherst felt that the Native American "was the vilest race of beings that ever infested the earth, and whose riddance from it must be esteemed a meritorious act, for the good of mankind" and who should, upon capture,

> immediately be put to death, their extirpation being the only security for our future safety, and their late treacherous proceedings deserves no better treatment from our hands.[441]

Amherst's pathological hatred for the Indian knew no limits — co-existence was not an option. In a postscript of a 1763 letter to Col. Henry Bouquet, Amherst wrote:

> Could it not be contrived to send the smallpox among these disaffected tribes of Indians? We must on this occasion use every stratagem in our power to reduce them.

---

[439]Feingold, *Zion*, p. 45. See also Kenneth Libo and Irving Howe, *We Lived There Too* (New York: St. Martin's/Marek, 1984), p. 56.

[440]*MCAJ2*, p. 711; Brener, p. 16.

[441]"Acquisitions," *AJA*, vol. 4 (1952), p. 42; "Acquisitions," *AJA*, vol. 16 (1964), p. 94; "Acquisitions," *AJA*, vol. 17 (1965), pp. 85, 91; Sharfman, p. 38. Other sources that can provide background on Pontiac and events surrounding the conflict are Howard H. Peckham, *Pontiac and the Indian Uprising* (New York: Russell & Russell, 1947); Alvin M. Josephy, Jr., *The Patriot Chiefs: A Chronicle of American Indian Resistance* (New York: Viking Press, 1958); Francis Parkman, *The Conspiracy of Pontiac* (New York, 1962).

Rabbi Sharfman explains the events that followed and the involvement of the Jewish Indian traders:

> Captain Ecuyer then called upon Levy Andrew [Levy] at his trading post. He told how he tricked the chief into accepting the deadly gifts and placed an order to replace the blankets and handkerchiefs. This grim invoice accompanied the new goods, receipt of which was duly acknowledged by Ecuyer:
>
> Debtor: The Crown to Levy, Trent & Co., for sundries had by order of Captain Simeon Ecuyer, Commandant...to sundries, got to replace in kind those which were taken from the people in the hospital to convey the smallpox to the Indians, viz.,

2 blankets @	2.00.
1 silk handkerchief @	.10.
1 linen do.	3.6
Total:	2.13.6

> Fort Pitt, August 15, 1763
> I do hereby certify that the above articles...were had for the uses above-mentioned.
>
> S. Ecuyer, Captain, Commandant
>
> Seventy Shawnee, Mingo, and Delaware, fell before the unseen enemy, smallpox. Many more undoubtably died, for the Indians had no resistance to the white man's diseases.[442]

The inevitable defeat of the Indians left vast tracts of land available for white development, and the Indian traders were the primary beneficiary. "There was only one hope on which the future of western commerce could be secured," writes Rabbi Sharfman:

> Indian land to which the Jewish and Quaker firms had rightful claims. Both sought compensation for their losses at Bloody Run near Fort Detroit, suffered during the Pontiac Uprising in 1763.

---

[442]Sharfman, p. 38. Dr. Marcus, in *MCAJ2*, p. 717, says that these Jews were associated with David Franks and his family of Philadelphia, who he says seem to have been "the leading Jewish supplyman in North America for more than twenty years from about 1755 until about 1778," and whose firm (p. 715) was "to become England's chief, though not sole agents for army supply during the French and Indian War." And on p. 716: "It was [Franks'] syndicate, the largest among the army purveyors, that secured the contracts for victualling his majesty's forces in North America, including the thirteen colonies along the coast below the Bay of Fundy, the Canadian provinces, the transallegheny frontier, the Illinois country, and the Old Southwest along the lower Mississippi. The syndicate reached out into the West Indies as well and shipped provisions to the armed forces in the Bahamas and on Bermuda, Martinique, Guadeloupe, and Jamaica."

Also Sharfman, p. 290: Colonel Bouquet replied that he would try to distribute germ-laden blankets among the Indians, "as it is a pity to expose good men against them, I wish we could make use of the Spanish method, to hunt them with English dogs...who would, I think effectually extirpate or remove that vermin."

> Though fierce competition divided the two major western firms in the Ohio, they united to seek joint compensation.
> Simon, Levy & Franks, in concert with Baynton, Wharton & Morgan, claimed their despoiled goods totaled an astronomical 86,000 pounds. Referring to themselves as 'suffering traders,' the merchant-princes of the western trade consolidated to form a land company by which they attempted to gain compensation in Indian land. They called their proposed colony 'The Indiana Company,' seeking Indian territory south of the Ohio, in western Virginia, the region then known as Indiana.[443]

On November 5, 1768, 3,000 men from the Iroquois Six Nations "bartered" for trinkets and goods an immense expanse of territory stretching from western New York to eastern Kentucky. Of this, the Jewish and Quaker Indiana Company would receive 2,500,000 acres — a land eventually divided into the states of Ohio, Kentucky, and West Virginia.[444]

As each tribe succumbed to either disease, slaughter, or retreat, "rightful claims" were made. On July 5, 1773, the different tribes of the Indian nations in Illinois conveyed to twenty-two residents of Lancaster and the surrounding country a tract of land that now encompasses the southern half of Illinois. Eight Jews were interested in its purchase: Moses Franks, Jacob Franks, David Franks, Bernard Gratz, Michael Gratz, Moses Franks, Jr., Joseph Simon, and smallpox co-conspirator Levy Andrew Levy.[445]

It was only a matter of time before the pogrom reduced the once mighty Indian nation to but a few holocaust survivors. Those who had won the trust of the Indians were the greatest beneficiaries of their extinction.[446] Augusta Levy, wife of Winnebago Indian trader John Meyer Levy, witnessed the Indian's expulsion from the Minnesota area in 1848 with these words:

> ...in the spring there was a great excitement over the removal of the Indians. [John] was very glad they were going...he had had enough of the Indians.

There are other references to Jews and Indians in the Jewish historical record. In the Battle of Beecher Island, the "Little Jew," Sigmund Shlesinger (1848-1928), entered into his diary on Monday September 21, 1868, that he had "Scalpt 3 Indians which

---

[443]Sharfman, p. 45.

[444]Sharfman, p. 45.

[445]Henry Necarsulmer, "The Early Jewish Settlement at Lancaster, Pennsylvania," *PAJHS*, vol. 9 (1901), pp. 33-34. See also Kohler, "Settlement of the West," p. 24, and Fishman, p. 9.

[446]Brener, pp. 15-16.

were found about 15 feet from my hole consealt in grass. For purpose of collecting bounty."[447] Records show that as late as the 1880s Solomon Bibo of New Mexico was charged with defrauding the Indians of grazing land.[448]

The disregard for the humanity of the Red man and woman is demonstrated in the scholarship of the foremost Jewish historian, Jacob Rader Marcus, who describes the mockery of an Indian by Hyam Myer's "Wild West" show, and further calls it "the spirit of enterprise":

> Like many of his fellow merchants in the Canadian fur trade, Myers had suffered reverses during the French and Indian War and presumably in the Indian uprising that followed it. To recoup his fortunes, he had his friend Sampson Simson intercede with Sir William Johnson for formal permission to exhibit some Mohawks in Europe. Myers sailed with the Indians before the proper certificate was forthcoming from the Indian Commissioner, and had already begun to parade them in Holland and in the taverns of London when the Lords of Trade urged Lieutenant-Governor Cadwallader Colden in New York to have Johnson put an end to the undertaking. From all indications Myers made no money on his grand European tour, for he ended up owing the Indians money – or refusing to pay them. Then, as now, there was "no business like show business!"[449]

---

[447]Burt A. Siegel, "The Little Jew Was There: Biographical Sketch of Sigmund Shlesinger," *AJA*, vol. 20 (1968), p. 25; Jacob R. Marcus, *Studies in American Jewish History* (Cincinnati: Hebrew Union College Press, 1969), p. 235. See the full account by Rev. H. Cohen, p. 59.

[448]"Trail Blazers of the Trans-Mississippi West," *AJA*, vol. 8 (June 1952), p. 83. Also see the *Records of the Bureau of Indian Affairs: 1884-1885*, "Bibo Lease of Acoma Lands."

[449]*MCAJ2*, p. 814.

Jews and the American Revolution

As the American Revolution approached, Jews, who by this time numbered nearly 1,500, became the subject of concern among the colonists when it was widely believed that they were acting in accord with the royal wishes of London rather than with their colonial brethren. As a result of the French and Indian War, England possessed one of the largest empires in the world with a debt of £140,000,000, approximately one half of which was incurred in defending the American colonies. The King of England, therefore, felt it was well within his rights to tax and regulate the commerce of the colonists to offset this huge liability. Of course, his subjects in the colonies disagreed and implemented a number of measures to protest and avoid these edicts.[450]

The Stamp Act was enacted and then repealed by Parliament and the tax on tea cost more to collect than it took in, so it was also abandoned. But the tax on sugar and molasses, the critical and profitable link in the slave trade, had the potential to cripple the colonial commerce.[451] Britain sent to the New England coast twenty-seven warships with soldiers and revenue agents to enforce the tax. Outraged, the colonial merchants joined in non-importation agreements refusing to purchase British goods, calling such taxation without representation "tyranny"—all except the Newport merchants, "chiefly Jews," who carried on their trade as usual. Merchants in other colonies felt that these Rhode Islanders were taking advantage of their loss by maintaining their trade relations with the enemy.[452]

"Resentment in other colonies turned into rage," wrote historian David Lovejoy, when it was reported in several places that the non-importation agreement had broken down completely in Newport. Rumors spread that three vessels from London had

---

[450]Losben, p. 259. Historian Max I. Dimont, *The Jews In America,* p. 59, takes the British point of view:

> Viewing the Revolution with hindsight, one finds little to quarrel about with the English....Actually, the Colonies had borne no more than a third of the cost of the French and Indian Wars, and England two thirds. In 1775, the per capita tax on the British was fifty times that paid by the Americans. The Sugar and Stamp Acts imposed on the Americans were mild compared to those levied on the British. The cry "No taxation without representation" disguised the issues. The colonists were objecting to a potential tyranny rather than an actual one. They were looking for a reason to rebel, rather than being pushed into rebellion. In fact, after the war, the Americans had to tax themselves more severely than the British had.

[451]J. A. Rogers, *Africa's Gift to America* (St. Petersburgh, 1961), p. 42; "Thomas Fitch Papers," vol. 18, pp. 262-73.

[452]Losben, p. 262.

unloaded in Newport, and not only had they sold their goods but it was claimed that the Newporters were actually advertising them for sale.[453] An increasing number of people in other colonies became incensed at Rhode Island and launched a general boycott of the colony's trade.[454] Only after eight colonies had placed a temporary embargo on their trade did the Newport merchants honor the non-importation pact.[455] In Lovejoy's book *Rhode Island Politics, 1760-1776*, he examines the issue:

> The blame for breaking the nonimportation agreement was primarily laid at the feet of the Jews. The irate merchants of Boston claimed that the Newport culprits were "chiefly Jews," while Ezra Stiles reported that "five or six Jews & three or 4 Tories" had drawn "down Vengeance upon" a whole country....Ezra Stiles singled out Aaron Lopez as the chief violator. Because he refused to come into the agreement the customs officials showed him great lenity and favor. The captains of his twenty-five vessels were exempted from swearing their cargoes at the Customs House while oaths were strictly exacted from all those who had agreed not to import English goods. Once by mistake a man-of-war in the harbor seized one of Lopez' vessels with a cargo of wine which was being taken off at night by five small boats....Stiles was no bigot; he had great admiration for the Jews of Newport, often attended their services in Touro Synagogue, and read Hebrew with the rabbis. When he blamed them for violating the nonimportation agreement, he probably knew what he was talking about.[456]

But this was not the only place where Jews openly defied the Revolution. While the Bostonians were throwing tea from British vessels into the Boston harbor, the Gratzes of Philadelphia smuggled it into America. Though impossible to sell this tea in the "super-patriotic" cities of the east coast, another Jew, Joseph Simon, did offer it for sale in his store near Pittsburgh. When discovered, the patriots resolved to put a stop to it and on the night of August 24, 1775, they confiscated the unsold contraband and burned it.[457]

---

[453]David S. Lovejoy, *Rhode Island Politics, 1760-1776* (Providence: Brown University Press, 1958), p. 144.

[454]Lovejoy, p. 144.

[455]Losben, p. 264.

[456]Lovejoy, p. 146; Virginia Bever Platt, "And Don't Forget the Guinea Voyage: The Slave Trade of Aaron Lopez of Newport," *William and Mary Quarterly*, vol. 32, no. 4 (1975), p. 607. Stanley F. Chyet, "Aaron Lopez: A Study in Buenafama," *Karp, JEA1*, p. 204: "[Lopez] supported the agitation only with great reluctance. When the Revolution finally erupted into its military phase in 1775, he did cast his lot with the Whigs, but no revolutionary ardor informed his decision."

[457]Brener, p. 15.

A Newport Jew named Pollock, having imported tea contrary to the command of the Rhode Islanders, was driven from the Caribbean island of St. Eustatius with loss of all his property.[458] In 1776, the Continental Congress was having doubts as to the neutrality of Jewish trader David Franks and his ability to conduct business without passing information to the enemy.[459] The Congress may have been reacting to the known history of Jews in the Caribbean conflicts of the previous century. Stephen Fortune has written that merchants in Barbados in 1667 strongly suspected that Jews were passing military secrets to enemy troops.

> The merchants were indeed aware that Jews had offered intelligence and army supplies to Cromwell in the conquest of Jamaica, and in the grandiose plans for the conquests of Chile and Peru. They may also have recalled how quickly and easily Jamaican Sephardic Jews changed their allegiance from Spain to England after the conquest of Jamaica in 1655. Observing the long history of Jews as victuallers and intelligencers, the colonists questioned their loyalty. Jews were perceived as opportunists and masters of duplicity with loyalties colored by hopes of profit.[460]

There is "much evidence" to show that many Jews decided to remain loyal to the Crown in the American Revolution. Many of these Loyalist Jews were from Newport, Rhode Island. Some were openly in favor of Britain and some tried to remain neutral, "but decided that their conscience and economic interests led them to loyalty to Great Britain."[461] The British, after all, were the muscle behind the economic advances of the Jews. Many who were Indian traders found their fortunes claiming the spoils of British extermination policies. Jews, with their inter-regional shipping network and high volume commercial enterprise, stood the most to lose from colonial independence.[462] The protection of their ships by the British navy and the stability of the British monetary system were reason enough to resist the cry of their fellow colonists for freedom.[463] Not only were the Jews

---

[458]J. F. Jameson, "St. Eustatius in the American Revolution," *American Historical Review* (October 1902 - July 1903), vol. 3, p. 705.

[459]Brener, p. 18.

[460]Fortune, p. 67.

[461]Losben, p. 266; Jonathan D. Sarna, Benny Kraut, and Samuel K. Joseph, *Jews and the Founding of the Republic* (New York: Markus Wiener Publishing), p. 31; Jacob R. Marcus, *The Jew and the American Revolution* (Cincinnati: American Jewish Archives, 1974), pp. 2-3.

[462]Marcus, *The Jew and the American Revolution*, p. 3.

[463]Bernard Bailyn, *New England Merchants in the Seventeenth Century* (Cambridge, Massachusetts, 1955), pp. 86-87.

economically aligned with the British, but they provided the weapons for the ensuing battle.

British Military Supply and the Jews

Even as their community vacillated, the Jews saw the opportunities in the lucrative military supply trade. Many, if not most, Jewish merchants of that day were purveyors on a large or small scale. As in the French and Indian War, Jewish military suppliers provisioned the British forces and one, Jacob Franks, was appointed an official purveyor to the British army.[464] When the Revolution broke out in 1775, Samuel Jacobs undertook to provision British regulars and German mercenaries in Canada. Jacobs was, and remained, a staunch Loyalist and had no sympathy for the Americans.[465]

Chapman Abraham was an accredited British loyalist and in a letter written in 1778, emphasized his loyal conduct toward the British and his animosity toward the rebels. He mentions that he supplied several regiments during the War, was one of those who repelled the rebels at Long Point, and served as a volunteer with the troops when the Americans were defeated at Three Rivers.[466]

Other Jews in the military supply trade were Ezekiel and Levy Solomons, Benjamin Lyon, and Gershon Levy. Some other notable Jews included in a list of British Loyalists were[467]:

---

[464] *MCAJ2*, pp. 712-15; Marcus, *The Jew and the American Revolution*, p. 3; Sarna, Kraut, Joseph, p. 7. Jews were heavily involved in army supply trade and some have argued that their role may have been pivotal in some conflicts. An account of an extraordinary private effort by a French Jew is in *MCAJ2*, p. 714:

> Abraham Gradis devoted himself wholeheartedly to the promotion of French imperialism in the Americas, Gradis constantly urged the French crown to greater efforts for its North American colonial empire and supplied Montcalm with provisions, munitions, and transport for the French general's push into northern New York. When the French tide began to ebb during the crucial year of 1758, Gradis assembled a fleet of ships, some of which he owned, others of which he chartered, and sent them to Montcalm's aid....In his heroic effort to help save France's North American domain, Gradis dispatched many ships to Canada, but even those which did succeed in piercing the blockade fell into enemy hands on their way back to Europe.

[465] *MCAJ2*, p. 709.

[466] Irving I. Katz, "Chapman Abraham: An Early Jewish Settler in Detroit," *PAJHS*, vol. 40 (1950-51), p. 85.

[467] Losben, pp. 266, 267, 273; Schappes, pp. 51-52; Morris Jastrow, Jr., "Notes on the Jews of Philadelphia, From Published Annals," *PAJHS*, vol. 1 (1893), p. 61.

Solomon Aaron
Abm. J. Abrahamse
David Franks
Jacob Franks
Abraham Gomez
Moses Gomez, Jr.
Isaac Hart*
Barrak Hays
Moses Michael Hays
Uriah Hendricks
Levy Israel
Aaron Keyser
Joseph Solomon Kohn
David Levison
Henry Marx
Jacob Mayer
Rachel Myers*
Samuel Myers
David Nathan
Myer Polock
Sam. Samuel
Isaac Solomon
Isaac Touro*

*Touro and Rachel Myers had to flee Newport when the British left, as did Isaac Hart, who lost his life and fortune for his allegiance to the Crown.[468]

Summary

The Jewish influence over the burgeoning colonial commerce had been well established in key seaboard locations by the American Revolution. The trade channels of the Caribbean had now expanded to include the North American settlements and Jews were clearly the pioneers. The overland routes to the western fur-trading posts were well worn by Jewish peddlers, and supply routes to the Royal armies almost exclusively carried the goods of Jewish merchants. They exploited these opportunities and gained advantages by rooting themselves firmly in the urban centers of the New World.

With the Jews and their skillful commercial practices came their Black slaves. The condition of the Black African remained unchanged with this northward migration. He adapted to the commercial flexibility of the various Jewish enterprises, providing the essential ingredients—skill and brawn—which made the Latin/Jewish experience so profitable. For the first time, Jews settled into an environment amenable to their economic and social interests, with the freedom to pursue opportunities and, as far as the Africans were concerned, with little moral restraint.

As in the settlements to the north, the American South provided opportunities for Jewish entrepreneurial activity. Agricultural commerce was familiar to the New World Jewish experience, and this experience—and the sweat and blood of the Black slave—facilitated the transition.

---

[468]Losben, p. 273.

Jews in the South

> *"For the most part they had acquired wealth and owned numerous slaves whom they exploited for the development of their resources. Their prosperity and long tenancy had won them prestige equal to that of the non-Jewish natives, and they were not only completely at home amid their surroundings, but, naturally, supported and sanctioned the institutions that had been so propitious to them, providing them with wealth, position and comfort. Like other wealthy Southern land and slave owners they were convinced that their financial stability depended upon maintaining the services of the negro slaves. It is, therefore, hardly surprising that they became staunch upholders of the slavery system, in their unwillingness to relinquish these personal benefits."*[469]

George Cohen's statement, published in 1924, is a most direct indictment of the Jewish community in the crime of slavery. "They were slave traders in major cities like New Orleans, Mobile, and Richmond," writes Leonard Dinnerstein,[470] and as slavery became the chief distinguishing characteristic of the South:

---

[469]G. Cohen, pp. 84-85. See also Eugene I. Bender, "Reflections on Negro-Jewish Relationships: The Historical Dimension," *Phylon*, vol. 30 (1969), p. 60; Lewis M. Killian, *White Southerners* (Amherst: UMass Press, 1985), p. 73; Harry Simonhoff, *Jewish Participants in the Civil War* (New York: Arco Publishing, 1963), pp. 310-11; Korn, "Jews and Negro Slavery," p. 218.

[470]Leonard Dinnerstein, *Uneasy At Home* (New York: Columbia University Press, 1987), p. 86.

> the test of the true Southerner was his acceptance of the institution. Southern Jews appear to have had little ambivalence on this score. Rabbi David Einhorn of Baltimore is the only prominent southern Jew who is known to have spoken out against slavery. Others either kept silent or gave wholehearted support to the Southern ideology.[471]

Jews were indistinguishable from other white Americans in their attitudes and treatment of Blacks.[472] When "King Cotton" dominated the South, Jews began to enter the planter class in substantial numbers.[473] Slave-dealing was an extremely profitable business particularly in the lower South, which required a constant resupply for its newly developed plantations. The upper South produced more slaves through natural increase and breeding than its over-worked soil required, creating interregional commercial opportunities.[474] Plantation supply became the bread-and-butter Jewish enterprise, with their goods of all descriptions keeping the Southern slave economy in motion.

At no time did Southern Jews feel tainted by the slave trade,[475] and they were found at every level of the slavocracy. Ansley, Benjamin, George and Solomon Davis of Richmond and Petersburg, Virginia, for example, went on the road and sold whole gangs of Blacks beginning in 1838. Benjamin Mordecai of Charleston, West Virginia, had large slave pens alongside his warehouses, and at one sale in 1859 he purchased $12,000 worth of Africans.[476] Jacob Levin of Columbia, South Carolina, and Israel I. Jones of Mobile, Alabama, were leaders of their Jewish communities and among the biggest dealers of Black people of the mid-nineteenth century. One of the leading auctioneer houses of New Orleans was operated by Levy Jacobs, who paraded Blacks on the auction block, selling slaves bred right in America.[477]

---

[471]Dinnerstein, *Uneasy at Home*, pp. 86-87. See also Wiernik, pp. 206-7.

[472]Julius Lester, lecture at Boston University, January 28, 1990; Weisbord and Stein, p. 20.

[473]Brenner, pp. 221-22.

[474]Korn, "Jews and Negro Slavery," p. 199.

[475]*EHJ*, p. 274.

[476]*EHJ*, p. 274; Korn, "Jews and Negro Slavery," pp. 181-82; Myron Bermon, *Richmond's Jewry 1769-1976: Shabbat in Shockoe* (Charlottesville, Virginia: Jewish Community Federation of Richmond; University Press of Virginia, 1979), p. 166; Feldstein, p. 81.

[477]Sharfman, p. 152.

Feingold, in his *Zion in America,* said: "We can fairly assume that Jews did not differ substantially from their fellow Southerners in their animus toward 'people of color.' [Mississippi] Jews approved of, or at least did not think of opposing, the slave system."[478] The most prominent of Southern Jews rose in defense of the slavocracy. "As might be expected," writes Jacob Marcus, "Southern Jews defended the slave system; individuals among them were among the institution's most vigorous apologists."[479] David Yulee (born Levy), the first Jew elected to the U.S. Senate, retired to join the Confederacy. Another Jew, Judge Samuel Heydenfeldt, regularly demonstrated that his sympathies were with the Confederacy.[480]

Slave owning was a status symbol among Jews, who held slaves in higher proportions than other Southern families—in fact by almost 2 to 1 higher.[481] Three quarters of the Jewish households in Charleston, West Virginia, and Savannah, Georgia, and one third in Baltimore, Maryland, held one or more Africans—the average in Savannah was five—and according to the census of 1820, the average Jewish household nationwide had three slaves.[482]

Distribution of Slaves Among Slaveholders, Southern Households & Jewish Southern Households, 1830 Census[483]

Number of Slaves	% of Total Southern Households	% of Jewish Households
1	18.8	16
2-4	30.2	38
5-9	24.3	26
10-19	17.1	13
20-49	7.7	6
50+	1.8	1
Total	100.0	100

---

[478]Feingold, *Zion,* p. 62.

[479]*JRM/Memoirs 1,* p. 20.

[480]G. Cohen, p. 87.

[481]Rosenwaike, *Edge of Greatness,* p. 66.

[482]Ira Rosenwaike, "The Jewish Population of the United States as Estimated from the Census of 1820," Karp, *JEA2,* p. 17.

[483]Rosenwaike, *Edge of Greatness,* p. 68, Table 21.

Slaves in Southern Jewish Households, 1830 Census.[484]

Place	House holds	None	1	2-4	5-9	10-19	20-49	50+
Baltimore	30	26	4	0	0	0	0	0
Charleston	104	10	14	32	30	9	1	0
Columbia (S.C.)	11	0	0	3	4	3	1	0
Georgetown Co. (S.C.)	14	4	1	1	3	3	0	2
New Orleans	35	10	3	11	7	3	1	0
Richmond	28	4	4	15	3	2	0	0
Savannah	20	2	1	6	4	5	2	0
Georgia (residual)[a]	9	1	3	1	1	3	0	0
Kentucky	7	3	0	3	1	0	0	0
Missouri	5	2	0	3	0	0	0	0
No. Carolina	5	2	0	2	0	1	0	0
So. Carolina (residual)	18	3	2	1	4	1	7	0
Virginia (residual)	24	4	3	11	5	0	1	0
Other[b]	12	3	3	3	1	1	1	0
Total	322	62	38	92	63	31	14	2

There appeared to be no reason, other than lack of purchase price, for a Jew to be without a Black slave.[485] Even those Jews who review American Jewry of that period prove the wealth of an individual by the number of slaves they held. Some use a high slave count as proof of Jewish industry, diligence, and business prowess.

A study of the different centers of Southern Jewry reveals a common dependence on the Black African and a definite self-interest in maintaining the slave system. As William Toll has written, "Long tradition and business instincts told him, when in Rome to act as a Roman....While hardly a flattering picture, Jewish historians of southern communities do not contradict it."[486]

---

[484]Rosenwaike, *Edge of Greatness*, p. 67, Table A-20.

[a]. Excludes 1 household, number of slaves illegible.

[b]. Alabama, Arkansas, Florida, District of Columbia, Mississippi, balance of Louisiana and Maryland.

[485]"Some Old Papers Relating to the Newport Slave Trade," *Newport Historical Society Bulletin*, no. 62 (July 1927), p. 11: "And it is certain that Protestants, Quakers, and Jews were all holders of slaves. It was a question not of creed or race, but of the possession of sufficient money."

[486]William Toll, "Pluralism and Moral Force in the Black-Jewish Dialogue," *AJHQ*, vol. 77 (September 1987), p. 91; Dieter Cunz, *The Maryland Germans: A History* (Princeton, New Jersey: Princeton University Press, 1948), p. 285.

Virginia

Virginia was originally established by staunchly Anglican Britons who were uninterested in assimilating with any other religionists. For this reason, and for the lack of populous centers for commerce, Jews were not attracted to Virginia in the same way as they were to other states and never reached the economic pinnacle that the Jews of Newport and New York achieved.[487]

But the Jews did not exempt themselves from Virginia's slave trade. This slave-breeding state saw the immigration and establishment of many Jews in the plantation economy: Elias Legardo came on the ship *Abigail* in 1621; Joseph Mosse and Rebecca Isaacke came in 1624 on the *Elizabeth*; John Levy had 200 acres at James City County in 1648; Manuel Rodrigues owned a plantation in Lancaster County in 1652; David Da Costa exported tobacco from his plantation in 1658; Michael Israel was a border ranger and militiaman in 1758 and purchased 80 acres in Albemarle County in 1757, and in 1779 he had 300 acres on Mechum's River; John Abraham also owned a plantation in Virginia.[488]

The founders of Richmond's Jewish community were men such as Israel and Jacob I. Cohen, Samuel Myers, Jacob Modecai, Solomon Jacobs, Joseph Marx, Zalma Rehine, and Baruch and Manuel Judah — all slave holders.[489] In post-Revolutionary days, Richmond was a town of 2000 people, half of whom were slaves.[490] By 1788, 17% of the white population were Jews and all but one of the Jewish householders held "a domestic servant (a slave); one of them had three."[491] Author Myron Berman confirmed that "Most of the Jews of Richmond in the early 19th century possessed slaves..."[492]

A famed nineteenth-century historian travelled through the South and gave an account of the growing Jewish post-Civil War presence among the Blacks: "There is a considerable population of

---

[487]*MUSJ2,* p. 30: "Jews nearly always prefer the cities."

[488]Hühner, "The Jews of Virginia," p. 88; Golden and Rywell, p. 23.

[489]Berman, p. 159.

[490]*MEAJ2,* p. 188.

[491]*MUSJ1,* p. 211; *MUSJ2,* p. 28.

[492]Berman, p. 166. Feingold, *Zion,* p. 60: "[T]he possession of one or two house servants was fairly widespread. As many as a quarter of the South's Jews may have fallen into this category....It is a clue to the relative prosperity of [Mississippi] Jewry because slave ownership was also an indication of wealth and social status." This accounting, however, is of domestic servants only and makes no accounting of the Blacks held as stock in trade.

foreign origin [in Virginia]," wrote Frederick Law Olmsted in *The Cotton Kingdom,*

> generally of the least valuable class; very dirty German Jews, especially, abound, and their characteristic shops (with their characteristic smells, quite as bad as in Cologne) are thickly set in the narrowest and meanest streets, which seem to be otherwise inhabited mainly by negroes.[493]

Virginia's Jewry remained and prospered with little resistance from the white Gentile. They were well respected and became pillars of their local communities.

Jewish Heads of Households in Virginia Census of 1830[494]

Head of Household / *County*	Number of Blacks			
	Slave		Free[a]	
	M	F	M	F
Lynchburg				
George Davis		4		
Norfolk				
P. J. Cohen	1	5		
J. J. Levy	2	1		
Frederick Myers	3	4		
Petersburg				
Ansley Davis	1	4		
Benjn Davis			1	
David Davis	1	1		
Henry Davis	2			
Mark Davis	1			
Saml Mordecai	1			
Saml H. Myers	1	2		
Henry Solomon		1		
Albemarle				
David Isaacs	1	2	2	

[493]Frederick Law Olmsted, *The Cotton Kingdom* (New York: Alfred A. Knopf, 1953), p. 38. Olmsted has been labeled an "antisemite" by some Jews.

[494]Rosenwaike, *Edge of Greatness*, pp. 132-33, Table A-11 (Excludes Richmond).

a.) "Free," as meant here, either means indentured servant, rented from another owner, or manumitted and in the service of the Jewish household. There were no truly free Africans in America. Blacks of whatever class by law could not be free. In fact, the "free" Blacks (applied regionally) were prohibited from the use of firearms; restricted from the purchase or use of liquor without a recommendation from a reputable white man; required to report to a white guardian periodically; required to observe curfews; denied the right of assembly except for church; restricted in movement; restricted from immigration; denied educational opportunities; among other restrictions. Violation of these laws could mean severe fines, corporal punishment, or resale into slavery.

(Jews in Virginia Census of 1830, continued)

Isaac Raphael	2	4		
Franklin				
Emanuel Judah		2		
Henrico				
Jacob Mordecai	13	10		
Louise				
Myer Angel		2		
Powhatan				
Simon Z. Block	3	6		
Aaron N. Cardozo		2		
David N. Cardozo	1	3		
Isaac N. Cardozo	2	2		
Moses N. Cardozo	4		1	
Saml A. Cardozo			1	2

Jewish Heads of Households in Richmond Census of 1830[495]

Head of Household	Number of Blacks			
	Slave		Free	
	M	F	M	F
Simon Abrahams	3	5		
Adolph Ancker	1	2		
Mitchell Ancker	1	2		
Myer Ansel	1	2		
Jacob Block		2		
Abraham Cohen		1		
Samuel Daniels		3		
Hetty Jacobs	1	1		
Baruch Jadah		2		
Abraham Levy		2		
Alexander Levy	3	7		
Jacob Levy		1		
Isaac Lyon		2		
Jacob Lyon		1		1
Joseph Marx	6	6	1	
A. Myers		1		
Judah Myers	1	2		
Moses M. Myers	4	3		
Myer Myers	2	1		1
Samuel Myers	3	2	1	
Solomon Pallen		2		
W. B. Pyle		2		
Zalmi Rehine		2		
S. Solomon		3		

[495]Rosenwaike, *Edge of Greatness*, p. 128, Table A-8.

Carolinas

In 1826, the value of the slaves in the South was about three hundred million dollars; of this about a fifth belonged to residents of South Carolina. The demand for slaves had grown to such an extent that a slave was worth seven to ten times as much in 1860 as at the end of the Revolutionary War.[496]

In Charleston, South Carolina, resided "the most cultured and wealthiest Jewish community in America."[497] The Jewish community expanded from the start with the help of a brisk business in Black slaves. Charleston was once one of the great centers of Jewish commerce that declined only after the slave emancipation.[498] Joseph Salvador purchased 100,000 acres in the Carolinas in 1755, and in 1773 his son Francis purchased 6,000 acres to grow indigo, working "at least thirty slaves." Solomon Isaacs imported some slaves into Charlestown in 1755.[499] "All told," says Marcus, "1,108 cargoes of Negro slaves were entered at the port of Charleston, 1735-1775. Solomon Isaacs brought in four small cargoes in 1755; Da Costa & Farr, two cargoes, 1760-1763. During 1752-1772, five other cargoes were brought in by Jews."[500] The firm of Mordecai & Levy operated in the Carolinas and placed this advertisement in the *Gazette of the State of South-Carolina* on August 12, 1778:

> RUN AWAY the 4th of August, inst. a negro wench named Clarinda, of a yellow complexion, had on when she went away a cross-bar check coat, a coarse white linen shift, and a blue handkercher on her head, and formerly belonged to Mrs. Gordon. Whoever will deliver the said wench to the warden of the work-house in Charlestown, or to the subscribers in King-street, shall receive a reward of fifty pounds currency and all reasonable charges and whoever harbours or entertains her, may depend upon being prosecuted to the utmost rigour of the law.
>
> Mordecai & Levy[501]

---

[496]Charles Reznikoff and Uriah Z. Engelman, *The Jews of Charleston* (Philadelphia: Jewish Publication Society of America, 1950), p. 276 note 22.

[497]*Historia Judaica*, vol. 13 (October 1951), p. 160.

[498]*JRM/Essays*, p. 275.

[499]*MEAJ2*, p. 322.

[500]*MCAJ3*, p. 1504.

[501]Lathan A. Windley, compiler, *Runaway Slave Advertisements: A Documentary History from the 1730s to 1790*, vol. 3 (Westport, Connecticut: Greenwood Press, 1983), p. 356.

The "cultured and wealthy" Jews of Charleston included the families Cardoza, Carvalho, Da Costa, Tobias, Harby, Mordecai, Noah, Benjamin, Baruch, and Lewisohn.[502]

Jewish Heads of Households in S. Carolina, Census of 1830
(Excluding Charleston and Columbia)[503]

Head of Household/	Number of Black Slaves	
County	M	F
Barnwell		
Barnett A. Cohen	11	13
Beaufort		
A. H. Abrahams	6	4
Rebecca Benjamin		2
Myer Jacobs	16	13
Henry C. Solomons	9	16
Saul & Hart Solomons	15	8
Chesterfield		
Joshua Lazerus	20	1
Colleton		
Isaac Moise	3	3
Isaac C. Moses	10	12
Georgetown		
S. M. Boss	1	
Jacob Cohen	134	160
Solomon Cohen	11	6
Charlotte Joseph	4	2
A. Lopez	5	5
Abraham Myers	4	3
Mordecai Myers	24	40
Benjamin Solomon	4	10
Israel Solomon	1	5
Sampson Solomon		3
Kershaw		
Abraham DeLeon	4	5
Hannah DeLeon		1
Chapman Levy	23	13
Hayman Levy	2	3
Sumter		
Franklin J. Moses	4	3
Mark Solomon		1

[502] *Historia Judaica,* vol. 13 (October 1951), p. 162.
[503] Rosenwaike, *Edge of Greatness,* pp. 130-31, Table A-10.

Jewish Heads of Households in Charleston, Census of 1830[504]				
	Number of Blacks			
Head of Household	Slave		Free	
	M	F	M	F
Moses Aarons	2	1	1	
Elias Abrahams	7	5		
Moses Abrahams	1	4		
Abraham Alexander	3	6		1
Isaac Barrett	5	3		
Jacob Bensaden			1	
Emanuel Canter	1	1		
Rebecca Canter		1		
David N. Cardoza	1	4		
D. D. Cohen	3	3		
Hartwig Cohen	2			
Hyam Cohen	4	4		
Mordecai Cohen	10	13		
Mrs. M. Cohen	1	7		
Nathan A. Cohen		2		
Philip Cohen	7	3		
Solomon J. Cohen	2	5		
Jane E. DaCosta	1	7		
Henry Davis	1	1		
Jacob DeLaMotta	2	3		
Isaac DeVaga	1	2		
Moses J. Ellis		3		
Isaac Emanuel		2		
Abraham Goldsmith		1		
Francis Goldsmith	1			
Morris Goldsmith	6	6		
Henry J. Harby	5	6		
Rebecca Harby	1	6		
Jacob Harris	1	9		
Rebecca N. Harris	2	6		1
Bella Hart		5		
Nathan Hart	2	5		
Samuel Hart		1		
Jacob Henry	5	4		
Jacob Hertz	2	2		
C. M. Hyams	5	2		
Moses D. Hyams	1	2		
Samuel Hyams	8	5	4	1
Solomon Hyams		2		
Abraham Hyman	3			
Hyam Jacobs	1			

[504]Rosenwaike, *Edge of Greatness*, pp. 113-15, Table A-2.

(Jews in Charleston, Census of 1830, continued)

Joseph Joseph	1	5		
Jacob C. Labat		1		
C. Lazarus		1		
Marks Lazarus	2	8		
Elias Levy	1	2		
Jacob C. Levy	2	3		
Lyon Levy	4	7		
Moses C. Levy	3	3		
Priscilla Lopez	1	5		1
George Lyons		1		
Simon Mairs	1	4		
Mark Marks	2	2		
Aaron Moise	1	1		
Abraham Moise	1	3		
Isaac Mordecai		1		
Joseph Mordecai	2	2		
Moses C. Mordecai	1	1		
R. Mordecay	2	2		
Isaac C. Moses	6	3		
Isaih Moses		3		
Israel Moses		2		
Levy Moses		2		
Simon Moses		1		
Solomon Moses	4	5		1
Joseph Moss	2	5		
Caroline Motta	2	5		1
Jacob Arias Motta	1	1		
Henry Nathan	2	4		
Nathan Nathans		6		
William Nauman	3	9		
Aaron Phillips		1	2	5
Benjamin Phillips	1	5		
S. C. Piexotta	1			
Moses Rodregues		1		
Sarah Salomon	3	3		
Abigail Sampson		4		
Jane Sampson	2	2		
Abraham M. Seixas		2		
Joseph Solomon	2			
Solomon Solomon	2	2		
Alexander Solomons	2	2		
Judith Suarez		2		

Jewish Heads of Households in Columbia (S.C.) and Vicinity, Census of 1830[505]				
Head of Household	Number of Blacks			
	Slave		Free	
	M	F	M	F
Judith Barrett	8	4	1	
I. S. Cohen	2	2		
M. H. DeLeon	3	5		
Samuel Levy	3	3	1	1
Abm Lipman	1	1		
Isaac Lyons	7	6		
A. Marks	2	3		
Dr. E. Marks	11	11		
H. Marks	5	5		
Polock & Solomons	1	3		
C. Solomon	1	5		

Georgia

In 1733, a group of Jewish immigrants arrived in Georgia from London as the land grants were being awarded.[506] It was the first colony that absolutely prohibited slavery from the very start and it was this feature that most severely affected the settlement. In all other colonies slavery was an established institution, and in neighboring South Carolina most of the manual labor was performed by Black slaves.[507]

Jews from other regions of Europe came to Georgia, possibly induced by wine and silk manufacturing in the colony, and found more discrimination among themselves than with the Gentile neighbors. Leon Hühner says that in 1737 deep South red-neck Georgia there was "no discrimination against Jews in the matters of trade."[508] In fact, he reports that in that state "both sets of [Jewish] settlers kept very much apart. The prejudice existing in that day between the Portuguese and German Jews was too great to allow close relations."[509] The second wave of Jews to Georgia, writes Max I. Dimont, "was a sad lot of down-and-out Ashkenazi Jews who had emigrated from Germany to England....The British

---

[505]Rosenwaike, *Edge of Greatness*, p. 117, Table A-4.

[506]Roth, *Marranos*, p. 294; Leon Hühner, "Jews of Georgia in Colonial Times," *PAJHS*, vol. 10 (1902), p. 66.

[507]Hühner, "Jews of Georgia," pp. 83-84.

[508]Hühner, "Jews of Georgia," pp. 80, 81.

[509]Hühner, "Jews of Georgia," pp. 70-71.

Jews were embarrassed by their distant cousins from Germany and looked for ways to be rid of them."[510] Soon, as was the case in the Caribbean, the inhabitants felt that they could not function without Black slaves,[511] and they petitioned the English trustees for "the right to use Negro labor." The Jews, by now more than a third of the total population, applied to the Gentile colonists for the "liberty to sign" the petition, but the Gentiles "did not think it proper" for Jews to participate with them "in any of our measures." The trustees refused the petition, triggering a general exodus from the colony, by both Christians and Jews.[512] By 1740, only three Jewish families were left in Georgia due to the slave prohibition.[513] They left, according to Marcus, "for the same reasons the others did: Negro slavery was prohibited, the liquor traffic was forbidden."[514] The Earl of Egmont reported in his diary of 1741 that every one of the Jews were gone from Savannah, Georgia, and that a Jewish wine maker named Abraham De Lyon said he left for "the want of Negroes...whereas his white servants cost him more than he was able to afford."[515]

One Jew named Saltzburger stood up to those that demanded that Africans be enslaved in the colony, but he, according to author Leon Hühner, "did not object to the principles of negro slavery, but opposed rather because they did not care to live in the same place with negroes."[516]

Finally, in October of 1741, the *Trustees' Journal* reported that "there are various reports that negroes had at last been allowed in the Colony, upon which the Jews and...others were preparing to return to the Colony."[517] It wasn't until 1749, however, with the "model colony...falling apart," that the trustees permitted slavery

---

[510]Dimont, p. 46. For more evidence of this internal "vehemence and animosity," see *MCAJ1*, pp. 164-68 and Goodman, pp. 173, 190-91.

[511]One Jew intending to prepare his 45-acre lot complained of his "present inability to be at such an expense as to employ servants for hire." See Charles C. Jones, "The Settlement of the Jews in Georgia," *PAJHS*, vol. 1 (1893), p. 12.

[512]Hühner, "The Jews of Georgia," pp. 84-85; *MEAJ2*, p. 287. Marcus seemed to feel that it was a sign of anti-Semitism that the Jews were refused the right to sign the request. See also Leonard Dinnerstein, "Neglected Aspects of Southern Jewish History," *AJHQ*, vol. 61 (1971-72), pp. 53-54.

[513]St. John, p. 60; Hühner, "The Jews of Georgia," p. 82: "The reasons which ultimately induced most of the Jews to leave the colony had nothing whatever to do with religious prejudice."

[514]*JRM/Memoirs 2*, p. 288.

[515]Edward D. Coleman, "Jewish Merchants in the Colonial Slave Trade,"*PAJHS*, vol. 34 (1938), p. 285.

[516]Hühner, "The Jews of Georgia," p. 85.

[517]Hühner, "The Jews of Georgia," p. 87; *MEAJ2*, p. 306.

as well as the use of hard liquor[518] and economic life began to flourish.[519] By 1771, half of Georgia's 30,000 population were Black slaves.[520] As the Black population grew, Jews were at the forefront in their slave training.

A Jew Teaches Slave Religion

Once slavery was introduced into the colony, it became essential to condition the Africans to the requirements of being slaves. The case of Joseph Ottolenghe, a Jewish resident of Georgia, provides explicit evidence of the use of Christianity to pacify and subdue the Black African. Upon hearing "that a number of Negroes to the amount of 300 and upwards were fix'd in that colony," Joseph Ottolenghe applied to the Georgia trustees and to two English religious organizations who hired him in February of 1750, to train the slaves. They saw the opportunity, as Jacob Marcus wrote, to "thriftily use one stone — one missionary — to kill three birds....Ottolenghe was not only to work at the [silk factory], but he was also to train Negroes in the industry and at the same time to covert them to Christianity."[521]

He assumed the position in July of 1751, and five months later wrote to one of his sponsors, The Society for Promoting Christian Knowledge of London, whose devotion was "the furtherance of the Christian religion among Indians and Negroes":

> I would instruct their Negros three days in the week...[and] that I might make it easie to the masters of these unhappy creatures, I have appointed the time of their coming to me to be at night when their daily labour is done.
>
> And in order to get their love, I use them with all the kindness and endearing words that [I] am capable of, which makes them willing to come to me and ready to follow my advice. And as rewards are springs that sets less selfish minds than these unhappy creatures possess, on motion, I have therefore promised to reward the industrious and the diligent, and I hope thro' Xt's grace that 'twill have its due effect...[522]

---

[518]*MCAJ1*, p. 366.

[519]*JRM/Memoirs 2*, p. 297.

[520]*JRM/Memoirs 2*, p. 324.

[521]*MCAJ1*, pp. 472-74; mentioned by Hühner, "The Jews of Georgia," pp. 89, 91. A full account of Ottolenghe's life in Georgia can be found in *MEAJ1*, pp. 307-14. See also Albert J. Raboteau, *Slave Religion: The "Invisible Institution" in the Antebellum South* (New York: Oxford University Press, 1978), pp. 118-19.

[522]Note the use of the abbreviation "Xt" as an apparent replacement for *Christ* and/or *Christianity*. The symbol *x* (coincidentally?) is the universal mathematical symbol for the unknown.

He went on to say how he would travel to the plantations to "spur them on" and to give them "a little more sense of religion than they have at present." In November of 1753, he lamented that

> ...It is true that [the] number [of slaves I teach] is not so great as I could wish, by reason of their penurious masters who think that they should be great loosser (sic) should they permit their slaves to learn what they must do to be saved, not considering that he would be a greater gainer if his servant should become a true follower of the blessed Jesus, for in such a case he would have, instead of an immoral dishonest domestic, a faithful servant.[523]

One year later he added,

> ...Again slavery is certainly a great depressor of the mind which retards thus their learning a new religion, proposed to them in a new unknown language, besides the old superstition of a false [African] religion to be combated with. And nothing harder to be remov'd (you know) than prejudices of education, riveted by time and entrench'd in deep ignorance, which must be overcom'd by slow advances, with all the patience and engaging means that can be studied to make them fall in love with the best of all religions, and so to captivate their minds as to give all their very little leisure to the study of it.

In 1755, the colonial legislature had decreed that Blacks were not to be taught to write, so Ottolenghe probably only taught the reading and reciting of Bible passages. In another letter of October of 1759, he details the hardships he has encountered exhorting Black people to "forsake paganism and embrace X'ty." Later that year he ceased employment over a salary dispute.

Ottolenghe had other interests in Georgia. As a land owner he started with 50 acres and gradually built up a series of farms and plantations totalling over 2,000 acres. By 1754, he reportedly owned two slaves and later twelve. In 1757, as a Justice of the Peace, he tried a Black man for theft and ordered his execution.[524]

While Georgia's Jews took care, as German Jew Eben Ezer saw it, "to keep down negro slaves and the Roman Catholics,"[525] there was "no discrimination against Jews in matters of trade" and "no obstacle to Jews holding office in the colony."[526] Blacks had no such freedoms in Georgia's early years due in part to the efforts of the Jewish community. Despite this distressing report of the

---

[523]*MEAJ2*, p. 310. Punctuation added to text for grammatical clarity.

[524]*MEAJ2*, pp. 313-14.

[525]Hühner, "The Jews of Georgia," p. 76.

[526]Hühner, "The Jews of Georgia," pp. 81, 92.

condition of Georgia's slave population, much of it from his own pen, Jewish historian Leon Hühner concludes: "In the record of the Jews of the Colony of Georgia there is no stain."[527]

Jewish Heads of Households in Savannah and Vicinity, Census of 1830[528]

Head of Household	Number of Blacks			
	Slave		Free	
	M	F	M	F
A. D. Abrahms	6	3		
Isaac Cohen	1	3		
E. DeLaMotta	3	4		
A. DeLyon	1	2		
Isaac DeLyon	2	4		
L.S. DeLyon	10	13		
Saml Goldsmith	4	5		
Levi Hart		1		
Jacob P. Henry	1	1		
David Leion	10	13	4	2
Abby Minis	7	3		
Isaac Minis	8	8		
M. Myers	10	9		
Isaac Russell	1	1		
A. Sheftall	4	8		
M. Sheftall Sr.		2		
Moses Sheftall	4	6		
Solomon Sheftall	3	1		

[527]Hühner, "The Jews of Georgia," p. 95.
[528]Rosenwaike, *Edge of Greatness*, p. 129, Table A-9.

Other Southern Jewish communities where data exists include Louisiana, where New Orleans supported an active community of traders, including slave traders.

Jewish Heads of Households in New Orleans, Census of 1830[529]

Head of Household	Number of Blacks			
	Slave		Free	
	M	F	M	F
S. Audler	1	3		
M. Barnett Senr	5	3		
Aaron Daniels	3	5		
Danl Goodman	2	1		
Edw. Gottschalk	3	4		
Abraham Green		2		
Geo. W. Harby		1	1	
Moses Harris	2	1		
Nathan Hart		1		
Samuel Hart	2	3		
Samuel Herman	8	10		
Manis Jacob	2	3		
L. Jacobs	15	18		
Samuel Jacobs	2	4		
Andre Kerkhan				1
Samuel Kohn	5	6		
Widow Kokernote	1	2		
Joseph Lasalle	1	2		4
B. Levy	4	4		
L. S. (?) Levy		2		1
Alexander Philip	4	6		
Isaac Philip		3		
Asher Philips	1	2		
A. Plotz		1		
Lewis Salomon	1	1		
Abraham Solomon	3	5		
Danl Warburg	1	1		

[529]Rosenwaike, *Edge of Greatness*, p. 118, Table A-5.

Jews in the West

Evidence of Jews and Blacks in the American western frontier is sketchy, though it is known that Jews were miners and traders in the far west with extraordinary success. The utilization of slave labor by Jews in these endeavors has not been well documented, though their economic achievements are impressive.[530] In Don W. Wilson's paper entitled "Pioneer Jews in California and Arizona, 1849-1875," published in the *Journal of the West*, he outlines the Jewish influence on trade in the region. As they had done in the East, the Jews in California concentrated in the clothing and dry goods trades.[531] By the middle 1860s, the labor-intensive tobacco trade in the San Francisco area, wholesale and retail, was almost entirely in the hands of Jewish merchants. According to Wilson, it was not an exaggeration in 1865 when a newspaper editor wrote:

> Merchandise, from the time it is freighted on the clipper ships until it is consumed, passes principally through the hands of Jewish merchants. As importers, jobbers, and retailers, they seem to monopolize the trade. Their commercial position is high indeed, and without them now, trade would almost become stagnated in the State. The express companies in the interior depend mainly upon them for support, and the freight and package lists continually abound with their names.[532]

Dr. Samuel Lilienthal of Philadelphia asked a group of San Francisco businessmen to write down the names of San Franciscans who they believed had assets of one million dollars or more. Of the fifty-seven names compiled in less than ten minutes, there were seventeen Jews among them. A taxpayer list of 1865 included the tax assessments of Jewish firms in the following manner: one firm with an assessment of over $300,000; one over $150,000; one over $100,000; four over $75,000; five over $50,000; seventeen over $20,000; and twenty over $10,000.[533]

---

[530]For further information on this subject see Jack Benjamin Goldmann, *A History of Pioneer Jews in California, 1849 - 1870* (thesis, University of California, 1939); Rudolf Glanz, *The Jews of California from the Discovery of Gold until 1880* (New York: Southern California Jewish Historical Society, 1960); Allen du Pont Breck, *The Centennial History of the Jews of Colorado, 1859 - 1959* (Denver: Hirschfeld Press, 1960); Ida Libert Uchill, *Pioneers, Peddlers and Tsadikim* (Denver: Sage Books, 1957). These books, however, are not explicit about the role of Blacks in the westward migration of the Jews.

[531]Don W. Wilson, "Pioneer Jews in California and Arizona, 1849-1875," *Journal of the West*, vol. 6 (April 1967), p. 228.

[532]Wilson, p. 230.

[533]Wilson, p. 231. *Ibid*, pp. 232-33:

> Dr. Lilienthal reported on his return to the East that Messrs. Scholle, Sacks, Strauss, Lippman, and Longersheim owned 60,000 acres of land in Los Angeles County which had been purchased for $125,000.00 from Former Governor Pico. In 1860 I. J. Benjamin visited

A leading newspaper in 1882 reported that the firm of B. Dreyfus and Company owned the largest vineyards in the world. Benjamin Dreyfus had a total of 14,500 acres of vineyards and was the leading figure in the industry for many years. In a correlated industry, the Castle Brothers, Guggenheim Brothers, and Rosenberg Brothers were among the top fruit producers in California.[534] An editorial that appeared in the *Jewish Chronicle* is "probably accurate": "Take Hebrew energy and capital from California and the state would be bankrupt."[535]

Los Angeles and wrote that "the Jews here also possess great flocks of sheep and herds of cattle." One form of farming, the wine industry, proved particularly profitable for several Jews including the well-known Lachman families. Practically all whiskey and brandy on the West Coast was distilled or distributed by Jews. Other Jews whose economic fortunes are notable include Herman Ehrenberg, Charles Poston who began filing claims which amounted to eighty mines and 20,000 acres of land within five years. Mr. M. Goldwater who is recorded to have procured a contract for 500,000 pounds of corn, to be delivered at Camp Verde. Solomon Barth who won several thousand dollars and several thousand head of sheep in a card game....He was assured a place in Arizona history by virtue of a treaty with the Navaho Indians entitling him to be the sole owner of the Grand Canyon.

[534]Wilson, p. 231. These plantation industries must certainly have required many hands of cheap or slave labor—as they do today.
[535]Wilson, p. 231.

Jews, Slavery and the Civil War

> *"What sociological phenomena would lead the Southern Jew to fight so fervently for the principle of slavery? Why was he willing to sacrifice his life so readily for a cause that he knew was contrary to religious principle? In their former European lands of oppression Jews actually sought to avoid conscription by any means; yet here in the South they fought willingly and with zest."*[536]

The Civil War and the slavery issue caused no great moral convulsion among the Jews of America.[537] By this time the total population of the United States was estimated to be 31,443,321 and Jews numbered about 150,000.[538] So many of their fortunes were founded and maintained on the backs of the African that only a tiny fraction of Jews, North or South, spoke for his freedom. Author Roberta Strauss Feuerlicht saw a contradiction:

---

[536]Rabbi Leo E. Turitz and Evelyn Turitz, *Jews in Early Mississippi* (Jackson: University Press of Mississippi, 1983), p. xvii; Learsi, p. 95, concurs. He states that the Jews of the South "embraced its cause promptly and enthusiastically."

[537]Learsi says that money and not morality was the motivating concern (p. 91): "It cannot, however, be said that this lofty tradition had an important part in determining the side which the Jews in America took in the conflict....And as for the recent Ashkenazic immigrants who established themselves in the South, they were nearly all traders or peddlers...and no trader can prosper who openly opposes the politics of his customers."

[538]G. Cohen, pp. 92-93; Sylvan Morris Dubow, "Identifying the Jewish Serviceman in the Civil War: A Re-appraisal of Simon Wolf's *The American Jew as Patriot, Soldier and Citizen*," *AJHQ*, vol. 59 (1969-70), p. 359 note. Jayme A. Sokolow, "Revolution and Reform: The Antebellum Jewish Abolitionists," *Melus* (1981-82), p. 28: After the 1840s, there was a mass migration of German and Eastern European Jews (Austria, Hungary, Poland, Bohemia) which raised America's Jewish population from 50,000 in 1850 to 150,000 by the Civil War. During this decade the number of Jewish congregations increased from 37 to 77, the seating capacity almost doubled from 19,588 to 34,412, and there was a threefold increase in the value of religious property.

> For all the self-righteousness of the North, slavery had been implanted and nourished by Northern merchants, Christian and Jewish. During the eighteenth century, Jews actively traded in slaves; some Jews ran slave markets.[539]

Professor Salo Baron perceived no moral dilemma on the part of nineteenth-century Jews: "Jewish merchants, auctioneers, and commission agents in Southern states continued to buy and sell slaves until the end of the Civil War....[A]t no time did Southern Jews feel tainted by the slave trade."[540]

Many historians have concluded that slavery was not the pivotal issue in the American Civil War—saving the Union was more important. The Jews in the North, as with others of the merchant class, were quite content with the huge quantities of cotton money being funnelled through New York banks fueling the industrial expansion, and as such they were unmotivated by moral concerns. Their brethren to the south would consider no other option than chattel slavery for Blacks, having based their livelihood fully on African labor. The secondary and tertiary industries that profited from free labor production had a heavy Jewish representation. The textile and clothing trades relied totally on cotton.[541] The ship building of the colonial period, and later the railroad and steamship building, was fueled by the finance houses of Philadelphia, Boston and New York with plantation revenues, and the colonial shippers moved slaves and their produce around the world.

The South, seeing the opulence and splendor that their slave produce had brought to the North, agitated to keep the profits below the Mason-Dixon line—an unbearable concept for the Northerners, who wanted to *Save the Union* and thus the flow of slave-based capital.[542] Many in the South began to speak rather

---

[539]Feuerlicht, p. 73.

[540]*EHJ*, p. 274; also Fishman, p. 8.

[541]Raphael, pp. 15-16, 17. See Samuel Maas' commentary of the time in *MUSJ1*, p. 588.

[542]Philip S. Foner, *Business and Slavery* (Chapel Hill, North Carolina: University of North Carolina Press, 1941), *passim*. Theories and opinions abound speculating on the causes of the Civil War. The economic aspect must be considered as the primary motivation. There is no evidence that more than a handful of whites—North or South—wanted the African free out of any moral concern. Even the great symbol of the Abolitionist cause, Abraham Lincoln, wanted to emancipate *and deport* the African, and then only if by doing so the Union would be saved. The economy, prior to and since the Civil War, was the root of all significant events in American history and provides the strongest and most reasonable argument for the "irrepressible conflict"—the American Civil War. See Thomas P. Kettell, *Southern Wealth and Northern Profits* (New York, 1860), pp. 126-27; Charles A. and Mary R.

boldly about sending their product directly to foreign markets from the Southern ports and then banking the proceeds in the South. The produce, like the capital, was shipped to the New York brokers and exported from Northern ports. The *Charleston Mercury* opined: "Why does the South allow itself to be tattered and torn by the dissensions and death struggle of the New York money changers? Why not trade directly with our customers? What need is there of this go-between to convey to the markets of the world our rich products, for which the consumers stand ready, gold in hand, to pay the full value?"[543]

England, King Cotton's biggest customer, was particularly interested in this no-middleman idea as a cost-cutting measure.[544] The Northern money houses quaked at the concept and actually saw the doom of their economy and standard of living. The Southerners resented having to go to these bankers every year for planting and harvesting loans as well as hearing the growing irritant of abolitionism. Thus—a war.

It was this economic argument that carried the most weight within the American Jewish community. Still, some, especially Blacks, expected the moral lead in the abolition of slavery to be assumed by the "people of the Bible." But many commentators during and since were puzzled by such fervent defense of a system out of which Jews presumably made their Biblical trek. The American and Foreign Anti-Slavery Society in their report of 1853 expressed their frustration:

> The Jews of the United States have never taken any steps whatever with regard to the slavery question. As citizens, they deem it their policy to have every one choose which ever side he may deem best to promote his own interests and the welfare of his country. They have no organization of an ecclesiastical body

---

Beard, *The Rise of American Civilization*, vol. 2 (New York, 1927), pp. 3-10; Algie M. Simons, *Class Struggles in America* (Chicago, 1906), pp. 32-36; Louis M. Hacker, "Revolutionary America," *Harper's Magazine*, March 1935, pp. 438-40, 441; Editorial, *Vicksburg Daily Whig* (January 18, 1860); Hinton R. Helper, *Impending Crisis of the South* (New York, 1857), pp. 21-23; Joel A. Rogers, *Africa's Gift to America* (St. Petersburgh, 1961), pp. 141-42. Some of these sources have been presented in Kenneth M. Stampp's *The Causes of the Civil War* (New Jersey: Prentice Hall, 1965).

[543]Foner, p. 147.

[544]According to Learsi (p. 92), the "steam-powered spinning jenny and the power loom had been installed in factories in England. The demand for cotton took a tremendous leap, and the planters were enabled to meet it by the cotton gin, the machine for separating the seed from the fiber which Eli Whitney invented in 1793. Those landmarks in the Industrial Revolution transformed the attitude of the planters towards slavery. The wealth which King Cotton showered down upon the South could not be renounced, and there was an enormous increase in the demand for slaves."

> to represent their general views; no General Assembly, or its equivalent. The American Jews have two newspapers, but they do not interfere in any discussion which is not material to their religion. It cannot be said that the Jews have formed any denominational opinion on the subject of American slavery....The objects of so much mean prejudice and unrighteous oppression as the Jews have been for ages, surely they, it would seem, more than any other denomination, ought to be the enemies of caste, and friends of universal freedom.[545]

This report "was substantially correct,"[546] wrote Rabbi Bertram Korn, the foremost authority on nineteenth-century American Jewry, in his study of the period. Individual Jews who had participated in the development of the institution of slavery, as well as in the discussion of its merits, from the very beginning were not so willing to forego its advantages for the sake of an uncivilized servant class of property.[547]

It was a system with which Jews were completely familiar and its abolition was, to them, both unreasonable and resistible. In this section, we will focus on various segments of the Jewish community to examine their behavior when the Union and the Confederacy clashed over the profits produced by the Black slaves. Ms. Feurlicht, in her book *Fate of the Jews,* frankly concluded: "Not only were a disproportionate number of Jews slave owners, slave traders, and slave auctioneers, but when the line was drawn between the races, they were on the white side."[548]

---

[545]Louis Ruchames, "Abolitionists and the Jews," *PAJHS*, vol. 42 (1952), pp. 153-54; the complete text is in Schappes, pp. 332-33. The original source is *The Thirteenth Annual Report of the American and Foreign Anti-Slavery Society*, pp. 114-15. See also Sokolow, p. 27.

[546]Korn, *Civil War*, p. 15. Feldstein, *The Land That I Show You*, p. 96, agrees: "For the most part, the statement was correct."

[547]Korn, *Civil War*, p. 15.

[548]Feuerlicht, p. 187.

Jewish Clergy and Black Slavery

> *"The pursuit of wealth in slaves and usury not only violated Jewish ethics but destroyed the rough democracy imposed upon a people in exile. Initially, the Jews looked to their rabbis and scholars for guidance. Eventually, the aristocracy of learning gave way to the aristocracy of wealth. Leadership of the community passed from the wise man to the rich man, a curse of organizational Jewry even today."*[549]

The slavery debate raged across the country, but no Jewish leaders of the Old South "ever expressed any reservations about the justice of slavery or the rightness of the Southern position."[550] Jewish clergy did not even discuss *Black* slavery until 1860, and then primarily in support of it.[551] Arthur Hertzberg sums up their position:

> As was to be expected, the Jewish clergy in the South, without exception, endorsed the Confederacy. These preachers, most of whom were quite recent immigrants from Germany, summoned up great passion in their defense of states' rights. They repeated the conventional platitudes of that day, that the black race was incapable of taking care of itself, that slavery was a way of discharging the responsibility of whites toward their childlike inferiors...[552]

Rev. J. M. Michelbacher was completely convinced of the justice of Negro slavery, and Rabbi George Jacobs of Richmond, Virginia,

---

[549]Feuerlicht, p. 39.

[550]Abraham J. Karp, *Haven and Home: A History of Jews in America* (New York: Schocken Books, 1985), p. 80; Karp, *JEA3*, p. 209.

[551]*EJ*, vol. 12, p. 932. Frequently discussed, however, was *Jewish* slavery, which was the centerpiece of their moral crusade. According to Robert V. Friedenberg, *"Hear O Israel," The History of American Jewish Preaching, 1654-1970* (Tuscaloosa and London: University of Alabama Press, 1989), p. 41: "By the 1850s, there were at least sixty Jewish religious leaders in the country, of whom at least eighteen have left us printed sermons." Friedenberg, p. 46: "It is highly significant that the first important statement on slavery to be made from any Jewish pulpit in the United States was not made until January 1861, after South Carolina had already left the Union over the question of slavery and while six other states were in the process of deciding to do the same." See also Korn, *Civil War*, pp. 29-30.

[552]A. Hertzberg, pp. 123-24.

owned and rented slaves.[553] Rabbi Raphall called those who opposed slavery "blasphemous."[554] Rev. A. Grunzberg of Rochester wrote a letter complaining of the "high standing politicians who are very zealous for the half-civilized Negro, [but] so illiberal against our nation."[555] Rabbis Simon Tuska of Memphis and James K. Gutheim of New Orleans both defended the enslavement of Blacks to their congregations.[556] Gutheim, the most distinguished of the South's Jewish clergymen, chose to move his family to the home of his in-laws in Mobile rather than take an oath of allegiance to the United States and the "Dictator of Washington," Abraham Lincoln.[557] Similarly, Rev. Henry S. Jacobs, who had served *Beth Shalome* of Richmond for three years (1854-1857) before moving on to Charleston, denounced Rev. Samuel Isaacs of New York for writing an appeal for loyalty to the Union.[558]

All twenty-one Southern Jewish congregations were staunchly Confederate; of those in the North, there is no record of any

---

[553]Korn, *Civil War,* p. 29; and on pp. 88-90, Michelbacher also composed a prayer for his cause, which read in part:

> Be unto the Army of this Confederacy, as thou were of old, unto us, thy chosen people – Inspire them with patriotism! Give them when marching to meet, or, overtake the enemy, the wings of the eagle – in the camp be Thou their watch and ward – and in the battle strike for them O Almighty God of Israel, as thou didst strike for thy people on the plains of Canaan – guide them O Lord of Battles, into the paths of victory, guard them from the shaft and missile of the enemy..."

See also Lewis M. Killian, *White Southerners* (Amherst: University of Massachusetts Press, 1985), p. 73; Korn, *Civil War,* p. 29. Feldstein, pp. 100-101: Rabbi Michelbacher justified the enslavement and the prison-like atmosphere of the slave states in this prayer, reasoning that it was the only means to prevent a repetition of the Saint Dominique massacre of the 1790s:

> The man servants and maid servants Thou has given unto us, that we may be merciful to them in righteousness and bear rule over them, the enemy are attempting to seduce, that they, too, may turn against us, whom Thou has appointed over them as instructors in Thy wise dispensation....Behold, O God, [the abolitionists] invite our man-servants to insurrection, and they place weapons of death and the fire of desolation in their hands that we may become an easy prey unto them; they beguile them from the path of duty that they may waylay their masters, to assassinate and to slay the men, women and children of the people that trust only in Thee. In this wicked thought, let them be frustrated, and cause them to fall into the pit of destruction, which in the abomination of their evil intents they digged out for us, our brothers and sisters, our wives and our children.

[554]Feldstein, p. 97.

[555]Letter to G. F. Train, in *Civil War,* by Bertram Korn, p. 252, note 66.

[556]Korn, *Civil War,* pp. 29-30; Karp, *Haven and Home,* p. 80.

[557]Nathan M. Kaganoff and Melvin I. Urofsky, *Turn to the South: Essays on Southern Jewry* (Charlottesville: American Jewish Historical Society, University Press of Virginia, 1979), p. 29; Bertram W. Korn, "The Jews of the Confederacy," *AJA,* vol. 13 (1961), p. 38.

[558]Kaganoff and Urofsky, p. 29.

official rebuke of the slave system. Kaganoff and Urofsky's *Turn to the South*:

> The Northern rabbinate remained divided on the issue. Isaac Leeser — living in Philadelphia but with strong ties to Richmond — tried hard to remain aloof and neutral and was condemned by both sides.[559]

Rabbi Bernard Illowy, distinguished leader of Baltimore's Orthodox Hebrew Congregation, defended the status quo. Though he did not preach secession, he did declare his open sympathy for the secessionists and their Negro property rights:

> Who can blame our brethren of the South for seceding from a society whose government cannot or will not protect the property, rights and privileges of a great portion of the Union against the encroachments of a majority misguided by some influential, ambitious aspirants and selfish politicians who, under the color of religion and the disguise of philanthropy, have thrown the country into a general state of confusion, and millions into want and poverty?[560]

Illowy, as with the other slave-making religionists, turned to the Bible for justification: "Why did not Moses...prohibit the buying or selling of slaves?" "Where was ever a greater philanthropist than Abraham, and why did he not set free his slaves?"[561] When federal troops occupied New Orleans and military authorities ordered all citizens to take the oath of allegiance to the United States or go behind the Confederate lines, the rabbi and most of his congregation refused to take the oath and were deported.[562]

The rabbis were already enforcing a system of apartheid within their places of worship that was entirely compatible with their

---

[559]Kaganoff and Urofsky, p. 29; Feldstein, p. 96.

[560]Isaac M. Fein, "Baltimore Jews During the Civil War," Karp, *JEA3*, p. 326.

[561]Fein, "Baltimore Jews," p. 327. Even Isaac Mayer Wise, himself a vociferous negrophobe, contradicted this view of Moses. See Bertram W. Korn, *Eventful Years & Experiences* (Cincinnati: American Jewish Archives, 1954), p. 130: "It is evident," claimed Wise, "that Moses was opposed to slavery from the facts:

1. He prohibited to enslave a Hebrew, male or female, adult or child.
2. He legislated to a people just emerging from bondage and slavery.
3. He legislated for an agricultural community with whom labor was honorable.
4. He legislated not only to humanize the condition of the alien laborers, but to render the acquisition and the retention of bondmen contrary to their will a matter of impossibility.

> ...We are not prepared, nobody is, to maintain it is absolutely unjust to purchase savages, or rather their labor, place them under the protection of law, and secure them the benefit of civilized society and their sustenance for their labor. Man in a savage state is not free; the alien servant under the Mosaic law was a free man, excepting only the fruits of his labor.

[562]Killian, p. 74.

public positions on the issue. The rules of Southern Jewish synagogues, says Joseph P. Weinberg, writing to American rabbis, "reflect a clear and conscious desire to exclude Blacks from Jewish fellowship."[563] Dr. Jacob Rader Marcus writes that Richmond's *Beth Shalome* or House of Peace, the most *democratic* of all the nation's synagogues, was dedicated to "peace and friendship," and yet membership was restricted to "any free man." This stipulation, he says, "would seem to be directed against Negro slaves who might be attracted to the synagogue of their masters." Likewise, in the 1820 constitution of *Beth Elohim* of Charleston, "people of colour" were excluded from membership.[564]

These positions taken by the rabbinate "reflected rather than contravened the views of their congregants," according to Henry L. Feingold of the Jewish Theological Seminary of America, who added that in general,

> Jews shared the unfavorable view of the Negro, which was at the base of the slave system....During the antebellum period, Southern Jewish congregations in Richmond, New Orleans and Charlestown specifically indicated in their constitutions that membership was restricted to white Israelites.[565]

One of the most respected rabbis in America, Max Lilienthal of Cincinnati, "agreed with most of his colleagues that the abolitionists were incendiary radicals who were bringing the nation to the brink of disaster." Lilienthal delivered an after-the-fact sermon on April 14, 1865, in which he publicly apologized for not having been anti-slavery until Lincoln issued the Emancipation Proclamation. When a lay member of the "chosen" community wrongly believed Lilienthal to be an abolitionist, he sent to Lilienthal a picture of the rabbi with a note scrawled across the front:

> Sir:
> Since you have discarded the Lord and taken up the Sword in defense of a Negro government, your picture that has occupied a place in our southern home, we return herewith, that you may present it to your Black Friends, as it will not be permitted in our dwelling. Your veneration for the Star Spangled Banner is, I presume, in your pocket, like all other demagogues who left their country for their country's good. I shall be engaged actively in

---

[563]Weinberg, p. 35. According to Bertram W. Korn, "Jewish Chaplains During the Civil War," *AJA*, vol. 1 (June 1948), p. 7: Some rabbis were directly employed by the Confederate Army because "the Confederate Congress was *more liberal and tolerant* than its Washington counterparts" with regard to the appointment of Jewish chaplains in the army (italics ours).

[564]*JRM/Memoirs* 2, p. 224.

[565]Weinberg, p. 35.

> the field and should be happy to rid Israel of the disgrace of your life. Be assured that we have memories; our friends we shall not forget. Should you ever desire to cultivate any acquaintance with me, I affix my name and residence, and you may find someone in your place who can inform you who I am.
>
> Jacob A. Cohen
> New Orleans, La., C.S.A.[566]

This is indicative of the immense pressure that the Jewish religious leaders were facing from the at-large Jewish population, who, by all accounts, were four square in favor of maintaining Black slavery in America.

Jews and Abolitionism

Even the Jewish scholars can find but a few sentences of Jewish protest over the plight of the Black slave. It is now clear, writes Dr. Marcus, "that most antebellum Jews, those in the North as well as in the South, cared little about the moral issues of human bondage."[567] Jews not only accepted this doctrine, Dr. Korn admits, but "some of them helped to formulate and circulate it..."[568] Those few Jews who stood against the institution of slavery were scorned and rebuked—most harshly by their own brethren in the synagogue. Even the anti-slavery Jews opposed the spread of slavery not out of sympathy for the condition of Blacks, but because it was a threat to their jobs. For "Every sensible farmer knew that his laboriously conquered farm land would lose enormously in value if a plantation worked by Negroes could be established on the land adjoining it."[569]

At its height, the abolitionist movement "was more smoke than real strength." When it ventured into the political arena as the Liberal Party, it received only 65,000 votes out of a total of 2,500,000 ballots cast.[570] "We should not be surprised to discover that there was not a single abolitionist among the Jews of the

---

[566]Korn, *Civil War*, p. 28.

[567]Jacob Rader Marcus, *Studies in American Jewish History* (Cincinnati: Hebrew Union College Press, 1969), p. 38.

[568]Korn, "Jews and Negro Slavery," p. 216.

[569]Feingold, *Zion*, p. 89; Cunz, p. 286.

[570]Hirshler, p. 56. Fein, "Baltimore Jews," p. 338: In Maryland, for example, in the 1860 Presidential elections, Lincoln, who was perceived as anti-slavery, received only 2,294 votes out of a total of 92,502.

South," wrote Dr. Korn.[571] Another author wrote that in general, "Jews were everything in the Old South except abolitionists."[572] They "profited economically and psychologically from slavery," says Sokolow, and even in northern and midwestern abolitionist territory, "Jews also maintained a discreet silence on the subject."[573]

Prior to 1848 and the immigration of German Jewish political liberals, there were Jews interested in the manumission societies, but their numbers were "pitifully small." The protection of Blacks was among the primary aims of these associations,[574] and some, like the Society for Promoting the Manumission of Slaves, acted in defense of Blacks against Jewish masters. The minutes of meetings describe actions taken against "Solomon a Jew," Moses Gomez, a Mrs. Judah, the wife of either of Aaron or Carey Judah, Jacob Levy, Simon Moses, and Levi Hyman.[575]

Jews sat out this battle over slavery in favor of the status quo resolution. In a weak nod to the edicts of their own religion, some like Louis Stix:

> expressed sympathy for the plight of blacks but did nothing to promote their liberation. Though he classified himself as an "outspoken" opponent of all involuntary servitude, he still advocated gradual emancipation and a government indemnity for "[his] southern neighbors for their pecuniary losses in parting with their slaves."[576]

Except for the Orthodox rabbi Sabato Morais of Philadelphia, there were no Orthodox Jews in the antislavery movement.[577] Ernestine Rose, however, the Polish-born daughter of a rabbi, offered something other than silence:

> [E]ven if slaveholders treated their slaves with the utmost kindness and charity; if I were told they kept them sitting on a sofa all day, and fed them with the best of the land, it is none the less slavery; for what does slavery mean? To work hard, to fare

---

[571]Korn, "Jews and Negro Slavery," p. 215. Certainly, no Jews who came to live in the antebellum South were deeply affected by abolitionism, and their ethical anxiety over the peculiar institution was "sometimes demonstrated," wrote Stephen J. Whitfield, "but not abundantly." See Whitfield, *Voices of Jacob, Hands of Esau: Jews in American Life and Thought* (New York: Archon Books, 1984), p. 226.

[572]Oscar R. Williams, Jr., "Historical Impressions of Black-Jewish Relations Prior to World War II," *Negro History Bulletin*, vol. 40 (1977), p. 728.

[573]Sokolow, p. 27. In Barbados, for instance, the Jews regarded manumission as "a curious eccentricity." See Samuel, pp. 46-47.

[574]*MUSJ1*, p. 586.

[575]Schappes, p. 597.

[576]Feldstein, p. 98.

[577]Sokolow, p. 32.

> ill, to suffer hardships, that is not slavery; for many of us white men and women have to work hard, have to fare ill, have to suffer hardship, and yet we are not slaves. Slavery is, not to belong to yourself – to be robbed of yourself.[578]

Regrettably, Jewish voices of abolition were few and unheeded.

God Supports Slavery?

No event caused the forces of bondage to rejoice more than when Rabbi Morris Jacob Raphall of Congregation *B'nai Jeshurun* in New York issued a sermon that was to become known as the "Bible Defense of Slavery."[579] On January 4, 1861, he preached the most publicized sermon ever delivered by an American Jew up to that time.[580] Said he:

> [I]t remains a fact which cannot be gainsaid that in his own native home, and generally throughout the world, the unfortunate negro is indeed the meanest of slaves. Much had been said respecting the inferiority of his intellectual powers, and that no man of his race has ever inscribed his name on the Parthenon of human excellence, either mental or moral.[581]

"What he did," Dr. Korn wrote, "was to place Judaism squarely in opposition to the philosophy of abolitionism...and insisted that...biblical tradition and law guaranteed the right to own slaves."[582] This critical confirmation of "God's will" from a prominent and respected Jewish authority, indeed the highest paid American clergyman, gave the slavemaster all he needed to fight the righteous battle against the abolitionists. Raphall went a step further and actually condemned abolitionism and its practitioners:

> How dare you, in the face of the sanction and protection afforded to slave property in the Ten Commandments — how dare you denounce slaveholding as a sin? When you remember that Abraham, Isaac, Jacob, Job — the men with whom the Almighty conversed, with whose names He emphatically connects His own most holy name, and to whom He vouchsafed to give the

[578]Feldstein, p. 99.

[579]For full text see Schappes, pp. 405-18. Another account by Harry Simonhoff in *Jewish Participants in the Civil War* (New York: Arco Publishing Co., Inc., 1963), pp. 10-13.

[580]Robert V. Friedenberg, p. 40.

[581]Schappes, p. 412.

[582]Korn, *Civil War*, p. 17.

> character of "perfect, upright, fearing God and eschewing evil" — that all these men were slaveholders, does it not strike you that you are guilty of something very little short of blasphemy?[583]

He accused the abolitionists of being "impulsive declaimers, gifted with great zeal, but little knowledge; more eloquent than learned; better able to excite our passions than to satisfy our reason." To Rabbi Raphall, slave property was placed under the same protection as any other species of lawful property. Slave ownership was not only lawful but a religious obligation.[584]

A Southern rabbi praised Raphall for "the most forceful arguments in justification of the slavery of the African race."[585] The Southern press played Raphall's proclamation prominently and often, for one of the "chosen" had cleared the moral obstacle from perpetual slavocracy. The *Richmond Daily Dispatch* called Raphall's proslavery doctrine "the most powerful argument delivered." The *Charleston Mercury* hailed his message as "defend[ing] us in one of the most powerful arguments put forth north or south."[586] After all, writes Robert Friedenberg, "[h]is explanation is clear, plausible, and entirely consistent with the thrust of Hebrew commentary...[and] compares favorably with the proslavery sermons delivered from Christian pulpits."[587] His speech was so well received that two weeks later he repeated it and raised funds for its issue as a pamphlet.[588]

Raphall was made an honorary member of the American Society for Promoting National Unity, a group of pro-slavery Northerners and Southerners whose membership included his co-religionists Rabbis George Jacobs, James Gutheim, and J. Blumenthal.[589]

---

[583]Feuerlicht, pp. 74-75.

[584]Feldstein, p. 97; Sokolow, p. 34.

[585]Feuerlicht, p. 75.

[586]*Richmond Daily Dispatch* of January 7, 1861; *Charleston Mercury* of May 12, 1861; Korn, *Civil War*, p. 18; Sokolow, p. 34.

[587]Robert V. Friedenberg, pp. 51, 52.

[588]Feuerlicht, p. 75.

[589]Korn, *Civil War*, p. 249, note 19.

Rabbi David Einhorn, The Voice of Judaism

As the rabbinate lined up with the commandment of their pro-slavery national leader, Rabbi David Einhorn was the lonely Jewish voice of abolition. Described by Henry L. Feingold as "the only noteworthy Jewish Rabbi opposed to slavery," Einhorn was indeed a lone voice, for which he paid a heavy price.[590]

As editor of the German-language newspaper *Sinai*, he consistently reminded his Baltimore readers of the evils of slavery. Einhorn's eloquent rebuke of the evil institution found no sanction, however, among the Jewish community. Even as the community of abolitionists welcomed him into their ranks, the Jews of his own congregation rejected his uncompromising stand on the issue.

Einhorn's views were unrelenting. Commenting on why the Southern church defends slavery, he said that it is because the church "unfortunately is not a free agent [and] is not independent of the state, it follows the politics of the ruling party....[T]he church leaders read the Bible according to its letter, not according to its spirit."[591]

Of the religious hypocrisy within his own faith:

> A Jew, a sapling of that stem, which praises the Lord daily for the deliverance out of Egyptian yoke of slavery, undertook to defend slavery....We are obliged to reject such words because they are a "A profanation of God's name."[592]

Of the humanity of the African:

> Does the Negro have less ability to think, to feel, to will? Does he have less of a desire to happiness? Was he born not to be entitled to all these? Does the Negro have an iron neck that does not feel a burdensome yoke? Does he have a stiffer heart that does not bleed when...his beloved child is torn away from him?[593]

On the institution of slavery:

> [It is designed] to reduce defenseless human beings to a condition of merchandise [which] relentlessly [tears] them away from the hearts of husbands, wives, parents, and children...

---

[590]Kaganoff and Urofsky, p. 29.
[591]Fein, "Baltimore Jews," p. 332.
[592]Fein, "Baltimore Jews," p. 332.
[593]Fein, "Baltimore Jews," p. 333.

Of the moral condition:

> There are enough churches, synagogues and temples, but there is very little religion, little morality...here [among the Jews]. Everything is empty, everything is glimmer....Here, too, rules the golden eagle rather than the cherubim....Here, too, all feelings of the heart and dreams are concentrated only on acquiring [things]....There is only one thought: to make as much as possible.[594]

Rabbi Einhorn was even prophetic in his view on the racial foundation of America:

> The old world is fast crumbling and a new world seeks to rise from its ruins....All men possess one and the same natural and spiritual origin, the same native nobility, and are, therefore, entitled to the same rights, the same laws....To achieve this goal we need only indomitable courage in our battle against the forces of darkness....
>
> America of the future will not rest on slave chains or belittling its adopted citizens. It will also give up its disinterestedness in the fate of other peoples of the world....[T]he next battles will leave a real blood bath, but slavery will be drowned in that bath.[595]

With Rabbi Einhorn's life in danger, he was forced to flee the city in 1861, amid riots between rival factions. According to his version, he was "requested" by his congregation to leave town.[596] In his correspondence with a supporter, Reuben Oppenheimer, Einhorn points an accusing finger against his opponents at his own temple: "[T]here is nothing so loathsome, indeed, than this riffraff of bacon reformers. The light of the Rabbis becomes a destroying torch in the hands of such people."[597]

Other rabbis who opposed slavery, such as Sabato Morais in Philadelphia and Bernhard Felsenthal in Chicago, were prevented from speaking out "by the timid leaders of their congregations....But a great many Jews stood on the side of the

---

[594]Fein, "Baltimore Jews," p. 333.

[595]Fein, "Baltimore Jews," pp. 331, 336, 341.

[596]Feldstein, p. 99; Fein, "Baltimore Jews," p. 339; Cunz, p. 306. Ismar Elbogen, *A Century of Jewish Life,* trans. Moses Hadas (Philadelphia: Jewish Publication Society of America, 1953), pp. 118-19, suggests that rather than being "requested to leave," Einhorn escaped being lynched. The *Sinai* also succumbed due to Einhorn's inability to collect debts owed to him by Southern Jews. See Albert M. Friedenberg, "American Jewish Journalism to the Close of the Civil War," *PAJHS,* vol. 26 (1918), p. 273.

[597]Fein, "Baltimore Jews," p. 340. See also Feuerlicht, p. 75.

South and sacrificed political and civic positions in order to join the Confederacy."[598]

With characteristic understatement William Toll, writing for the American Jewish Historical Society, said of Jewish clergy, "They were not conspicuous for their support of Black freedom."[599]

The Jewish Press

The Jewish press weighed in with its opinion on the matter of Black slavery and of the character of the African as well. Again, the abolitionists were bitterly disappointed. The *Jewish Record* of January 23, 1863:

> We know not how to speak in the same breath of the Negro and the Israelite. The very names have startlingly opposite sounds – one representing all that is debased and inferior in the hopeless barbarity and heathenism of six thousand years; the other, the days when Jehovah conferred on our fathers the glorious equality which led the Eternal to converse with them, and allow them to enjoy the communion of angels. Thus the abandoned fanatics insult the choice of God himself, in endeavoring to reverse the inferiority which he stamped on the African, to make him the compeer, even in bondage, of His chosen people.
>
> There is no parallel between such races. Humanity from pole to pole would scout such a comparison. The Hebrew was *originally* free; and the charter of his liberty was inspired by his Creator. The Negro was never free; and his bondage in Africa was simply duplicated in a milder form when he was imported here....The judicious in all the earth agree that to proclaim the African equal to the surrounding races, would be a farce which would lead the civilized conservatism of the world to denounce the outrage.[600]

It lamented, "Alas, that the holy name and fame of the prophet Moses should be desecrated by a comparison with the quixotic achievements of President Lincoln!"[601] Writes Korn, "The *Record* had no faith in the ability of the Negro to take his place in the ranks of the civilized....Compare the achievements of Jews...with the failure of freed Negroes in the North to demonstrate any potentialities whatever, said the *Record*, and it would be clear that

---

[598]Elbogen, pp. 118-19.

[599]Toll, "Pluralism and Moral Force," p. 89.

[600]Hugh H. Smythe and Martin S. Price, "The American Jew and Negro Slavery," *The Midwest Journal*, vol. 7, no. 4 (1955-56), p. 318; Korn, *Civil War*, p. 27; Feuerlicht, p. 76.

[601]Korn, *Civil War*, p. 28; *Jewish Record*, January 23, 1863.

the Negro did not deserve freedom."[602]When Rabbi Heilprin challenged Raphall's official view of slavery, "the most prudent and typical Jewish response" to their debate was that of *The Jewish Messenger*, which refused to print Heilprin's remarks because they had "no desire to take part in a controversy of this nature."[603]

The Jewish newspaper of Baltimore, *Der Deutsche Correspondent*, defended slavery on a "rational" basis. The paper called upon its readers, immigrants in a new land, "never to forget that the Constitution of the United States in support of which every adopted citizen of the Republic has sworn an oath of loyalty, sanctions and protects the institution of slavery." From this, wrote the eminent Jewish historian Dr. Isaac M. Fein,

> the immigrant was to draw the only possible conclusion: Beware, live up to your oath, defense of slavery means good citizenship....Most of the Jews, like the non-Jewish Germans, were for the status quo on the issue of slavery.
> At the two extremes were the German elite and the 48'ers. The elite was economically and socially related to the South. This group was outspoken for slavery without any reservations, and later it became secessionist.[604]

Important Jewish literary figures like Isaac Harby, Edwin DeLeon and Jacob N. Cardozo expressed their full support for slavery in their writings.[605] Robert Lyon's *Asmonean* newspaper had already committed itself to a pro-slavery position in 1850 - 1851, by defending the wisdom of the Fugitive Slave Law.[606] Said Lyon:

> Let our citizens, one and all, resolve this day, to put down Abolitionism, in whatever shape and form it may present itself, to discountenance it, by whomsoever its principles may be advocated, and to crush out at once and forever this attempt to plunder our Southern citizens of their property....Once more, Down with Abolitionism! Let us stand by the Union, and nothing but the Union.[607]

---

[602]Korn, *Civil War*, p. 28; *Jewish Record*, March 24, 1865.

[603]Sokolow, p. 35.

[604]Fein, "Baltimore Jews," p. 324. The term 48'ers refers to the immigrants who arrived en masse in 1848, primarily from Germany, and many of whom were Jewish.

[605]Karp, *Haven and Home*, p. 80.

[606]Korn, *Civil War*, p. 253, note 76.

[607]Korn, *Civil War*, p. 253, note 76.

Major Mordecai Manuel Noah (1785-1851) was a journalist, judge, playwright, politician and was considered the most distinguished Jewish layman until 1840. He was such a prolific proponent of slavery that the first Black American periodical, *The Freedom's Journal*, was launched in response to Noah's racist propaganda.[608] In 1846, he offered to put up two-thirds of the money to publish a racist newspaper.[609] He actually defended slavery by calling it liberty:

> There is liberty under the name of slavery. A field negro has his cottage, his wife, and children, his easy task, his little patch of corn and potatos, his garden and fruit, which are his revenue and property. The house servant has handsome clothing, his luxurious meals, his admitted privacy, a kind master, and an indulgent and frequently fond mistress.[610]

He argued that "the bonds of society must be kept as they now are" and that "To emancipate the slaves would be to jeopardize the safety of the whole country." The *Freedom's Journal* called Noah the Black man's "bitterest enemy" and William Lloyd Garrison, the leading white abolitionist, called him the "lineal descendant of the monsters who nailed Jesus to the cross."[611]

Jewish Public Opinion

Those Jews who took a stand stood with slavery, while other Jewish organizations vacillated, taking no forthright position in the midst of the national crisis. Rabbi Korn:

> The Independent Order of B'nai B'rith and other fraternal groups appear to have ignored the South-North turmoil in pre-war years, tolerated the enforced separation of the war years, and continued as before once the war had been ended; indeed, in 1866, the Memphis Lodge of B'nai B'rith urged that the annual district convention be held in a Southern city because "it would tend greatly to the extension of our beloved Order in the South." The Board of Delegates of American Israelites discussed only

---

[608]Jonathan D. Sarna, *Jacksonian Jew: The Two Worlds of Mordecai Noah* (New York: Holmes and Meir Publishers, 1981), pp. 111 and 197 note 52; Bernard Postal and Lionel Koppman, *Guess Who's Jewish in American History* (New York: Shopolsky Books, 1986), p. 19; *EJ*, vol. 12, p. 1198; Joseph R. Rosenbloom, *A Biographical Dictionary of Early American Jews: Colonial Times through 1800* (Lexington: University of Kentucky Press, 1960), p. 134.

[609]Sarna, p. 110.

[610]Sarna, p. 110.

[611]Sarna, p. 111.

> Jewish subjects during its few pre-war years, and hardly even met during the period of the war. It was a weak, incomplete organization, altogether, but its leaders were moderates who would not for an instant have injected into its proceedings.[612]

Presumably, the Civil War divided the country, "pitting brother against brother" in a bitter ideological battle. Not so among the country's Jews, who carried on lively interaction—social and commercial. Northern Jewish congregations "responded generously" to the call for help from their brethren in the Confederacy. In 1865, says Feingold,

> the Jewish communities of Philadelphia and New York shipped two-and-a-half tons of Matzohs, the special unleavened bread required for the Passover holidays, to the Jewish congregations in Columbia and Charleston in South Carolina.[613]

In the West, Jewish loyalties were questioned. One editor reported confidentially on the composition of a local secessionist movement. They were mostly "Mormons, Mormon Apostates (who are even worse), gamblers, English Jews and the devil's own population to boot." A Union major was dispatched to San Bernadino and reported that of the approximately 1,500 inhabitants of the town about 1,000 were Mormons. "The remainder consisted of a few respectable Americans, and a good many Jew merchants who control the business of the town and go along with any side that pays best for the time being."[614]

In Los Angeles, the elections in the fall of 1861 fulfilled the Unionist's fears as the Secessionists swept to victory. The *News* (September 6, 1861), appalled at the outcome, turned in anger upon Jewish Democrats:

> The Union party has been utterly defeated in this country. Secession and disunion have carried the day and years of repentance cannot wash away the stain....Nearly the whole of the Jewish population of this city voted the secessionist ticket, and we sincerely believe many of them will live to rue the day they did so. That a foreigner should come from a land where he is no better than a serf, having no choice in the selection of his rulers; should come here and give his vote and influence against our government and in favor of the same state of affairs he left behind in the old world, seems passing strange.[615]

---

[612]Korn, *Civil War*, p. 30.

[613]Feingold, *Zion*, p. 92.

[614]Max Vorspan and Lloyd P. Gartner, *History of the Jews of Los Angeles* (San Marino, California: Huntington Library, 1970), p. 29.

[615]Vorspan and Gartner, p. 30.

The Jewish community responded by branding the newspaper "anti-Semitic," drawing from the *News* an angry rebuke:

> It is not denied that nearly the whole of the Jewish population voted the disunion ticket....How strange does it seem then, that foreign born citizens should give their newly acquired vote and influence against the free and liberal government now in existence, and favor the schemes of Davis and his co-conspirators....The charge that we have desired to awaken religious persecution against those of the Jewish faith is false. We mention them because, comprising so large a body of our voting population, they had nearly all voted the disunion ticket. We chronicled the fact and it has not been nor cannot be denied. We advocate the rights of all men under the Constitution and Government of the United States but when the foreign born citizen violates his most solemn oath; when he turns against the Constitution which he has solemnly sworn to support, then he is to be despised.[616]

Jews and the Confederacy

> *"Some Southern Jews...were particularly fervent in their advocacy of slavery and of the rights of the South. In the defense of a cause that was holy to them, they were willing to sacrifice their lives — and they did."* [617]

The Jews served in disproportionately large numbers and with distinction to maintain the slavocracy from which they had grown so wealthy.[618] To these Jews, a free Black was a simply unbearable, intolerable and mortally resistible concept. Simon Wolf's *The American Jew as Patriot, Soldier and Citizen* and Harry Simonhoff's *Jewish Participants in the Civil War* detail the Jewish involvement in the physical conflict.[619] The Confederate army had 23 Jewish staff officers, including David De Leon who was Surgeon General, A. C. Meyers who was Quartermaster General,

---

[616]Vorspan and Gartner, pp. 30-31.

[617]*JRM/Memoirs1*, p. 21.

[618]Wiernik, p. 229.

[619]Simon Wolf, *The American Jew as Patriot, Soldier and Citizen* (Philadelphia: Levytype Company, 1895); Simonhoff, *Jewish Participants in the Civil War* (New York: Arco Publishing, 1963).

and the Secretary of War, Judah P. Benjamin. The *Memphis Daily Appeal* editorially commented on September 27, 1861, that "The Israelites of Memphis are behind none in showing their devotion to the South, both by liberal contributions and by taking up arms in her defense." Rabbi Korn says quite directly:

> The Jews of the Confederacy had good reason to be loyal to their section. Nowhere else in America – certainly not in the antebellum North – had Jews been accorded such an opportunity to be complete equals as in the Old South. The race distinctions fostered by slavery had a great deal to do with this, and also the pressing need of Southern communities for high-level skills in commerce, in the professions, in education, in literature, and in political life. But the fact of the matter is that the older Jewish families of the South, those long settled in large cities like Richmond, Charleston and New Orleans, but in smaller towns also, achieved a more genuinely integrated status with their neighbors than has seemed possible in any other part of the United States then or now. Political recognition, social acceptance, and personal fame were accorded to Jews of merit.[620]

"Whatever their status may have been in the South," noted Lewis Killian, "Jewish Southerners were loyal to the Confederacy and supported slavery with greater unity than their northern coreligionists opposed it."[621] Even the women were passionate in their pro-slavery views, as Albert Mordell observed: "The Jewish female population of the South were more virulent in their hatred of Lincoln and more fanatical in upholding the Confederacy than the men."[622] The Jewish Ladies of Charlotte sent $150 to the families of the soldiers of the Confederacy "with our prayer to Almighty God for their safety, and that He will bless our glorious cause with victory and success."[623] Eugenia Levy Phillips, the wife of a Confederate colonel, was jailed for espionage and is described by Korn as "the first to rebel and the last to succumb."[624]

---

[620] Korn, "The Jews of the Confederacy," pp. 4-5.

[621] Killian, p. 73.

[622] Albert Mordell, "Jewish Participants in the Civil War," review in *Jewish Quarterly Review* (October 1963), p. 175.

[623] Korn, "The Jews of the Confederacy," p. 37.

[624] Korn, "The Jews of the Confederacy," pp. 42-43 (picture on p. 36).

Some notable Jewish families wearing the Confederate gray were the six Cohen brothers from North Carolina, the five Moses brothers from South Carolina, Raphael Moses and his three sons from Georgia, three Moses brothers from Alabama, three Cohen brothers from Arkansas, three Levy brothers from Virginia, four Jonas brothers from Mississippi, and many more. Other Jews who contributed in various substantial ways were[625]:

[625]The following figures are provided by Simon Wolf in his book *The American Jew as Patriot, Soldier and Citizen* (Philadelphia, 1895).

Jewish Confederate Soldiers by State as Recorded by Simon Wolf

State	Number
Alabama	135
Arkansas	53
Florida	2
Georgia	144
Kentucky	22
Louisiana	224
Mississippi	158
Missouri	86
North Carolina	58
South Carolina	182
Tennessee	38
Texas	103
Virginia	119
Total	**1324**

Also, according to Wolf, there were 834 Jewish Civil War veterans whose state was unclassified. The exact proportions of Jews taking up arms for the Confederacy is unknown. A count performed by Wolf found fewer Jewish soldiers on the Confederate side than on the Union side. According to Learsi (pp. 97-98):

> In all likelihood, however, Simon [Wolf's] findings are far below the number of Jewish soldiers and sailors in the Confederate forces, at least. In 1864 application was made to James A. Seddon, the Confederate Secretary of War, to grant Jewish soldiers leave for the approaching High Holy Days. He denied the request on the ground that such leave might disrupt some commands, since there were ten to twelve thousand Jewish soldiers in the Confederate Armies.
>
> It may also be assumed that the ratio of Jews who bore arms to defend the South was larger than the corresponding ratio in the North; there was a much larger proportion of native born among them, whose roots lay deep in the history and traditions of the land.

In his article "Identifying the Jewish Serviceman in the Civil War: A Re-appraisal of Simon Wolf's *The American Jew as Patriot, Soldier and Citizen*," *AJHQ*, vol. 59 (1969-70), p. 358, Dubow claims that Wolf's book contains "many errors."

> Many of the names are incompletely listed with the initials or surnames only. Organizations are improperly identified, and no distinction is made between state volunteer and Regular Army organizations. In some cases, no military organization of any kind is indicated. There is also no separation of Union and Confederate units under those states which furnished troops to both sides.

Albert Lucia Moses
Dr. Marx E. Cohen, Jr.
Max Frankenthal
Moses Ezekial
Captain Harby
Adolf Proskauer
Dr. Simon Baruch
Edward Rosewater
Benjamin Franklin Jonas
David Cohen Labatt
Dr. Joseph Bensadon

Jewish Confederate Army Staff Officers:

Jewish Officer	Assignment
Jacob Abrams	Staff of General Elzey
Dr. I. Baruch	Assistant Surgeon-General
Marcus Baum	Staff of General Kershaw
Captain H. L. Benjamin	General Staff
Judah P. Benjamin	Secretary of War
General David De Leon	Surgeon General
Edwin De Leon	Special Envoy to Court of Napoleon III
Captain Joseph Frankland	Assistant Provost Marshall
Edward Kauffman	Staff of General Bagly
N. Kraus	Staff of General Miller
Lt. Alexander Levy	Staff of General Magruder
Capt. M. Levy	Staff of General Braxton
*Lt. M. J. Marcus	Staff of General Benning
Victor Meyer	Staff of General Barksdale
Assist. Adj. Gen. J. Randolf Mordecai	Staff of Gens. White and Taliaford
Captain A. J. Moses	Staff of General Hannon
Major Alfred T. Moses	Staff of General Taylor
Altamont Moses	Military Telegraph Service
F. J. Moses	Assistant Surgeon
Colonel Raphael J. Moses	Staff of General Longstreet
General A. C. Myers	Quartermaster General
Major Isaac Scherck	Staff of General Hardee
Morris Straus	Staff of General Jenkins

Jewish Confederate Navy Officers:

Louis P. Levy, Gunboat *Chicora*
Midshipman Randolph Lyons
Z. P. Moses, Navy Department
Captain Levi Charles Harby[626]
Lieutenant Barnham
Perry De Leon
Lazarus Weil
Simon Weil
Isaac Moise
Paymaster I. C. Moses
Lieutenant R. J. Moses, Jr.

[626]Simonhoff, *Jewish Participants in the Civil War*, p. 261: Harby commanded the *Neptune* and a fleet of gunboats and in his naval capacity engaged in attacks on "Moslem pirates" and Seminole Indians.

Proud to Murder Black Men

Captain Madison Marcus of the 15th Georgia Infantry died defending Fort Gilmer in Virginia from a force of Blacks and whites of the Union on October 13, 1864. London's *Jewish Chronicle* printed an account of this "Hebrew hero" and "Gallant officer" in their December 16th edition of that same year.[627]

> [Captain Marcus] instructed his men to reserve their fire until the enemy were almost upon them; at which time he gave the order, and more terrible fire from cannon and ringing rifle never greeted any foe. The Negroes, leaping down to the ditch immediately beneath the work, endeavored to hoist up one another on their shoulders; but no sooner did the whites of a Negro's eyes gleam over the embankment than they were sealed in death....[The hand grenades] exploded before reaching the bottom of the ditch, and many of the Negroes were so mangled by this proceeding as to render their features undistinguishable.[628]

Jews and the Economics of the Civil War

> *"[The Jewish peddler] received a hearty welcome from the planter on the balcony and the grinning servants on the lawn."*[629]

The Jews became the focus of the suspicions of other white Americans when they were perceived to be profiting from the turmoil. Many Jewish merchants, it was claimed, were trading between the warring factions in violation of the laws. As the Union tried to cripple the Confederate economy, Northern Jewish merchants were allegedly trading Southern goods, such as cotton and tobacco, in exchange for much needed gold. Confederates used the gold to buy weapons and ammunition, food and medical supplies, which, in addition to strengthening the rebels, fueled their economy and prolonged the war.[630]

---

[627]"Review," *AJA*, vol. 4 (April 1961), pp. 28-29.

[628]Wolf, *Patriot, Soldier and Citizen*, p. 424; Feingold, *Zion*, p. 91; Martin Rywell, *Jews in American History: Their Contribution to the United States, 1492-1950* (Charlotte, North Carolina: Henry Lewis Martin Co., 1950), p. 172; Leo Shpall, *The Jews in Louisiana* (New Orleans: Steeg Printing & Publishing, 1956), pp. 12-13.

[629]*JRM/Memoirs 1*, p. 7.

[630]Joseph H. Parks, "A Confederate Trade Center Under Federal Occupation: Memphis, 1862 to 1865," *Journal of Southern History*, vol. 7, no. 3 (August 1941), p. 295.

Certainly, the Jews were well placed in the regional economy to engage in this activity. Jews in the South were of the merchant class, having developed "a separate and distinctive accommodation to the plantation economy." The Southern planters depended upon these merchants to move their produce to market as well as for a source of supplies and financing. Jews had become commission merchants, brokers, auctioneers, cotton wholesalers, slave clothing dealers, and peddlers, keeping the slave economy oiled with money, markets, and supplies.[631] These rural merchants, "a disproportionate number of whom were Jews," bought much of their inventory from the cities, and the credit they extended to their customers likewise rested on financial sources in the city, including the Jewish wholesalers and moneylenders in the North.[632]

This middleman positioning of the Jewish merchants gave them immense influence and leverage within the Southern economy. It was also the primary reason why Jews—North and South—almost unanimously supported the proslavery interests. In the Midwest and in the border states, Jewish wholesale houses had many customers in the South and they were not ready to interrupt their cash flow for Negro freedom.[633] When the war broke out and the Union embargo made trade with the South illegal, prices for the restricted but essential items skyrocketed in the South.[634] Opportunities for immense profits from the

---

[631]Feingold, *Zion*, pp. 59-60. *MUSJ1*, p. 216: "Jews were needed there because fewer able whites turned to commerce. As the Gentile elite of the region became engrossed in politics and in the nursing of social status, competent Jews moved into the economic vacuum." See the example of this in Frederic Bancroft, *Slave Trading in the Old South* (Baltimore: J. H. Furst Co., 1931), pp. 105-6, where he describes a merchant in Richmond, Virginia: "A Jew named Levy [probably Lewis B. Levy], who had a clothing-store for negroes in the basement of the City Hotel, would gladly have explained how much such outfits enhanced the selling price of slaves. He made a specialty of supplying clothes for just such occasions. He 'particularly solicited the attention of traders' and 'persons bringing their servants [!] to the city for hire or sale.' Did he prosper? How could it be otherwise when seven leading traders vouched for him!"

[632]Ashkenazi, p. 104; Raphael, p. 15; Herbert Weaver, "Foreigners in Ante-Bellum Mississippi," *Journal of Mississippi History*, vol. 16, no. 1 (January 1954), p. 153.

[633]A. Hertzberg, p. 123.

[634]An example of this is found in *The Memphis Daily Appeal*, which reported (June 11 and 18, 1862): "Landings which had been quiet for months became scenes of bustling activity in less than two weeks as more than two hundred newly arrived merchants, the majority of whom were Jews, spread out their 'immense cargoes' for display."

"The Israelites have come down upon the city like locusts," wrote a correspondent of the Chicago *Times*. "Anything in the line of trade, up to a box of cigars, or a dozen papers of needles, may be obtained of these eager gentlemen at

smuggling and contraband trade with the Confederate states enticed many to partake. Author and historian Isaac M. Fein's review of the evidence includes this analysis from the memoirs of a Jew, Simeon Hecht:

> Fortunes were made quickly in these days....[T]here were a great deal of speculators notably some of our leading coreligionists. Money...became plentiful. Some men arose from obscurity and became multimillionaires in a very short time....[There were] great opportunities to commit excessive frauds....It was a noted saying at the time, and according to my opinion, a very true one, that the war could have been ended in two years if it had not been for the Wall Street speculators....The pie was too full of plums to be eaten at one sitting. Among the speculators were some of our coreligionists.[635]

There was no shortage of observers of this phenomenon who incriminated the Jewish traders. The *New York Tribune, Herald,* and *Commercial,* the *Patterson Press,* the *Missouri Republican,* the *Chicago Tribune,* and the *Detroit Commercial Advertiser* were only a few of the papers which alleged that Jews were responsible for the speculation in gold: "all Jews are gold speculators"; "the Jews are engaged in destroying the national credit, in running up the price of gold"; "those hook-nosed wretches speculate in disasters; the great majority of those engaged in gold speculation are of the Jewish race." The *New York Dispatch* reported that if you walked

---

ruinous prices, for the purchaser." See Parks, "A Confederate Trade Center," p. 293.

[635]Fein, "Baltimore Jews," p. 348. See the observations of Albert D. Richardson, *The Secret Service* (Hartford: American Publishing Co.,1865), p. 264:

> But stores were soon opened, and traders came crowding in from the North. Most of them were Jews. Everywhere we saw the deep eyes and pronounced features of that strange, enterprising people. I observed one of them, with the Philistines upon him, marching to the military prison. The pickets had caught him with ten thousand dollars' worth of boots and shoes, which he was taking to Dixie. He bore the miscarriage with great philosophy, bewailing neither his ducats nor his daughter, his boots nor his liberty – smiling complacently, and finding consolation in the vilest of cigars. But in his dark, sad eye was a gleam of latent vengeance, which he doubtless wreaked upon the first unfortunate customer who fell into his clutches after his release. Glancing at the guests who crowded the dining-hall of the Gayoso, one might have believed that the lost tribes of Israel were gathering there for the Millennium.

Even prior to the hostilities, others became resentful of business practices they attributed to Jews as a class. See Frederick Law Olmsted, *A Journey in The Seaboard Slave States [1856]* (New York: G.P. Putman's Sons, 1904), p. 70, and cited in Korn, *Civil War,* p. 292, note 132 (according to Korn "in the glib language of prejudice"):

> ...a swarm of Jews, within the last ten years, has settled in nearly every southern town, many of them men with no character, opening cheap clothing and trinket shops; ruining or driving out of business, many of the old retailers, and engaging in an unlawful trade with the simple negroes, which is found very profitable.

A. Hertzberg, p. 132: "Smuggling was a well-established, even major, economic enterprise during the four years of the war....Jews were involved."

to the corner of Williams Street and Exchange Place, all you would see were the "descendants of Shylock," and all you would hear would be "Up to shixty-five, up to sheventy-one! Mine God, it vill go up to von hundred (*sic*)!"[636] A writer in *Harper's Weekly* denounced all Jews as "secessionists, copperheads, and rebels," while Southerners accused them of being "merciless speculators, army slackers, and blockade-runners across the land frontiers to the North."[637] A soldier newspaper (*Corinth War Eagle*, August 7, 1862), published in the town that held Gen. Ulysses S. Grant's headquarters, called Jews "sharks, feeding upon the soldiers."[638]

Even Union Army officials began to lodge frequent complaints about the Jewish traders. In 1861, Treasury agent William P. Mellen and Lt. S. Ledyard Phelps denounced the Jews of Paducah, Kentucky. As United States forces advanced southward in 1862, Brig. Gen. Leonard F. Ross blamed Jews for the illegal cotton trade. Maj. Gen. William T. Sherman, Maj. Gen. Samuel R. Curtis, Brig. Gen. Alvin P. Hovey, and Maj. Gen. Stephen A. Hurlbut—all registered complaints against the illicit trade, and specifically, that of the Jews. Col. C. C. Marsh even expelled a dozen Jewish cotton buyers "for dealing in southern money, and depreciating United States Treasury notes." James Grant Wilson summed up their complaint against the smugglers.

> This business was carried on in good part by Jews, desperate for gain, who often succeeded in passing our pickets under cover of night. Many a midnight chase [we have] had after the Memphis smugglers, and many an ambulance, drawn by a pair of horses or mules, and loaded down with well-filled trunks, containing medicine and other contraband articles, did [we] capture, which were endeavoring to escape to the Confederates, after evading the cavalry and infantry pickets posted around Memphis.[639]

The charges persisted but so did the profits. Jews "were denounced as extortionists, speculating on the necessities of the people while many of their breadwinners were at the front."[640] The Godchaux brothers, Leon and Mayer, were involved in the

---

[636] Korn, *Civil War*, p. 161.

[637] Dinnerstein, *Uneasy at Home*, p. 87.

[638] John Y. Simon, ed., *The Papers of Ulysses S. Grant*, vol. 7 (Southern Illinois University Press, 1979), p. 52.

[639] James Grant Wilson, *General Grant* (New York, 1897), p. 149.

[640] Feldstein, pp. 110-11, quotes from the diary of a Confederate businessman named Isador Straus.

trade in Mississippi; Abraham Levi speculated in cotton through the Clinton firm of Bloom, Kahn & Co.[641]

Grant's Order #11

Those Gentiles losing their lives at the battle fronts were unimpressed with the newfound Jewish prosperity. Observers of the inter-regional economy, including some of Lincoln's own staff, complained that Jews were "taking large amounts of gold into Kentucky and Tennessee."[642] But not only was this speculation a problem, it soon was suspected that the cotton agents themselves were going from behind the Union lines to the Confederate areas and coming back and spreading information that should not have been put in the hands of the enemy. These agents, writes U. S. Grant, III, "seem to have been mostly Jews and to have been generally spoken of as such, although there were undoubtedly some who were not Jews."[643]

It was this perception, and after the issue of warnings against the illicit trade, that Ulysses S. Grant issued what became known as Order #11 on December 17, 1862:

> Hdqrs. 13th A.C., Dept. of the Tenn., no. 11
> Holly Springs, December 17, 1862
>
> The Jews, as a class violating every regulation of trade established by the Treasury Department and also department orders, are hereby expelled from the department within twenty-four hours from the receipt of this order.
>
> Post commanders will see that all of this class of people be furnished passes and required to leave, and anyone returning after such notification will be arrested and held in confinement until an opportunity occurs of sending them out as prisoners, unless furnished with permit from headquarters.
>
> No passes will be given these people to visit headquarters for the purpose of making personal application for trade permits. – By order of Maj. Gen. U.S. Grant.
>
> Jno. A. Rawlins,
> Assistant Adjutant General[644]

---

[641]Ashkenazi, pp. 83, 121.

[642]Simon, vol. 7, p. 51.

[643]U. S. Grant, III, *Ulysses S. Grant* (New York: William Morrow & Company, 1969), pp. 171-72.

[644]Korn, *Civil War,* p. 122. For other discussions on Order #11 see Joseph Lebowich, "General Ulysses S. Grant and the Jews," *PAJHS,* vol. 17 (1909), pp. 71-79, and Isaac Markens, "Lincoln and the Jews," *PAJHS,* vol. 17 (1909), pp. 116-23; Learsi, p. 106. For a review of the warnings issued prior to Order #11, see Rev. P. C. Headley, *The Life and Campaigns of General Grant* (New York: Derby & Miller Publishing Co., 1866), pp. 198-99.

Some controversy surrounds the issuance of the order and its actual source,[645] but it nonetheless remains an example of "anti-Semitism" to many Jews. Lincoln soon repealed the order but another one issued by Colonel John W. Dubois in Holly Springs and Oxford, Mississippi, and Paducah, Kentucky, was actually carried out. It read: "On account of the scarcity of provisions all cotton speculators, Jews, and other vagrants, etc....having no permission from the Commanding General, will leave town within twenty-four hours."[646] In some Southern towns resolutions were passed denouncing Jews and there were raids on Jewish stores.[647]

These edicts, though lacking due process, are indicative of the tensions between Jews and their Gentile neighbors. Some Jews spoke out admitting the criminal actions of profiteering Jews. Rabbi Simon Tuska of Memphis called these Northern Jews "greedy birds of prey." Jacob Peres of Memphis wrote to Isaac Leeser in Hebrew: "Some time ago over 20 Jews were in jail for smuggling. It is a great [profanation of the name of God.]" Leeser wrote in the *Occident* of

> the crowd of needy [Jewish] adventurers, who travel of glide rather through the highways and byways of the land in quest of gain, often we fear unlawful, who in their material labors are perfectly indifferent to the duties of their religion, and not rarely conceal it by a pretended conformity.[648]

David Einhorn urged American Jewry to "make war upon the Amalek in our own midst!! Let us meet them that bring shame and disgrace upon us and our religious faith, with the fulness of our moral indignation."[649]

Though Lincoln repealed the order it was not because the problem did not exist. Maj. Gen. Henry W. Halleck wrote to Grant in explanation of the repeal: "The President has no objection

[645]Lee M. Friedman, "Miscellanea: Something Additional on General Grant's Order Number 11," *PAJHS*, vol. 40 (1950-51), pp. 184-86. See also Elbogen, pp. 119-20.

[646]Feingold, *Zion*, p. 94; James G. Heller, *Isaac M. Wise, His Life and Work and Thought* (New York: Union of American Hebrew Congregations, 1965), p. 351. Simon, vol. 7, p. 53: "U.S. Senator Lazarus W. Powell stated that he had documents showing that about thirty Jewish male citizens of Paducah were expelled on twenty-four hour notice along with their wives and children."

[647]Killian, p. 74.

[648]Korn, *Civil War*, p. 152. A. Hertzberg, p. 133: "The rabbis of that time seem to have felt that Jews were 'overrepresented' in smuggling, but that they were not the major figures in this trade."

[649]Korn, *Civil War*, p. 152.

to your expelling traders & Jew pedlars, which I suppose was the object of your order, but as it in terms prescribed an entire religious class, some of whom are fighting in our ranks, the President deemed it necessary to revoke it."[650] Even the Congress rejected resolutions condemning the order by a vote of 56-53 in the House, and 30-7 in the Senate. Representative Elihu B. Washburne wrote to Lincoln that General Order No. 11 was "the wisest order yet made....That construed as it was undoubtedly intended — that is, to exclude Jew peddlars, &c. it would be all right, but to apply it to all the Jew residents, would be a hardship." He said, further, "if you would only express precisely in your order what you meant (as he supposed) to exclude these Jew traders it would be all right."[651]

As the country picked up the pieces from the bloody clash, Jews had actually made money and moved measurably ahead of the rest of the population. In Feingold's *Zion In America*, he makes a remarkable observation:

> It is...something of a paradox to note that for Jews in the North, where most Jews lived, the war actually proved to be something of a boon. They had avoided the open breach of the troubled decade of the fifties and now during the war an acceleration of German Jewry's headlong leap into affluence could be noted.[652]

The immense profits were parlayed into legitimate endeavors. Dr. Fein continues:

> Some of the Baltimore Jews became big real estate men, bankers, railroad magnates, and manufacturers of ready-clothes, which grew tremendously as a result of Government orders for uniforms. The economic situation, indeed, improved so much that a local Jewish correspondent wrote: "The Jews on the whole, by their intelligence and their activity, have acquired some wealth....They are not sorry that they have left their Polish and German villages....The Poles are numerous here."[653]

---

[650]Simon, vol. 7, p. 54. According to Washburne, "his order so much harped on in Congress was issued on express instruction from Washington." Friedman, "General Grant's Order Number 11," p. 185.

[651]Simon, vol. 7, pp. 55-56.

[652]Feingold, *Zion*, p. 91. Dutch Jews experienced this phenomenon when, in the mid-eighteenth century, and during the decline of Amsterdam as an economic and military power, the overall wealth of the Jews increased "considerably." See *EAJA*, p. 214. In Maryland, wrote Isaac M. Fein in "Baltimore Jews during the Civil War," p. 352: "The Jewish community emerged from the Civil War crisis much stronger and more integrated." *MUSJ2*, p. 29: The Jews of Alexandria, Virginia, established a congregation in 1850 and they owe their "growth and prosperity to the Civil War."

[653]Fein, "Baltimore Jews," pp. 348-49.

Barry E. Supple, writing in the *Business History* journal, concurred: "For most of them the Civil War brought prosperity—at least to some degree. Even where, as in the case of Straus and the Lehman brothers, operating within the southern economy, they had to bear the brunt of commercial dislocation and general insecurity, there might be some counterbalancing benefits."[654] He called the period "one of relatively uncomplicated prosperity" for the Jews. Those whose business was in clothing such as the Seligmans, and whose principal economic activity was in buying and selling, found their wartime profits extraordinary.[655] Other Jewish historians, such as Arnold Shankman, saw similarly:

> After the Civil War, Jews controlled the dry-goods stores of the South to a remarkable extent. In virtually every important Southern town, one or more Jewish peddlers leased a store and began to sell notions, farm equipment, clothing, and groceries to the local population....So completely did Jews appear to dominate the Southern retail trade that a sociologist studying Indianola, Mississippi, during the 1930s alleged that one could not purchase a pair of socks locally on a Jewish holiday.[656]

The public's perception of Jewish profiteering in the midst of a divisive conflict was only confirmed by these facts. Some historians have gone to great lengths to justify the actions of these profiteers, but few have ventured to explain in legitimate business terms the disproportionate advantage realized by them. In any event, Jews were measurably wealthier but public ire was strong and growing more pronounced, even within the Southern haven in which the Jews thrived so freely. It was this image that had to be repaired and was cause for concern among the Jewish leadership. Once again their motives were questioned and once again they planned their defense.

---

[654]Supple, "A Business Elite," p. 154.

[655]Supple, "A Business Elite," p. 155. Mary Elizabeth Massey, *Ersatz In The Confederacy* (Columbia, South Carolina: University of South Carolina Press, 1952), p. 19, quotes a Richmond woman: "The war was a harvest to that class....Many of them were...the future Rothschilds of the South."

[656]Arnold Shankman, "Friend or Foe? Southern Blacks View the Jew," in *Voices of Jacob, Hands of Esau: Jews in American Life and Thought,* by Stephen J. Whitfield (New York: Archon Books, 1984), pp. 106-7.

Reconstruction, Blacks and Jews

> *"Everywhere the serfs, the majority of the population, constituted an enormous oppressed class with the least rights and the greatest obligations. The Jews belonged to the three upper classes and the position of the bulk of the Jews resembled that of the burghers whose function it was to control the economic life of the country."*[657]

The Jews faced the Reconstruction era without having markedly changed their attitude or behavior toward the ex-slave. In Louisiana, writes Moses Rischin, Jews typically "were not in visible opposition to slavery. The point is a significant one in that throughout the history of [the town of] Opelousas, Jews supported the white side of a racial conflict that began with Reconstruction and which continues to be the major line of ethnic demarcation in the present-day community."[658]

In the North, the Jews parlayed their substantial war-time profits into new markets and industries. "In the age of the great industrial expansion," Eric Hirshler writes of the German Jews,

> their role was outstanding in three particular economic areas: in the textile and clothing field; in banking and finance; and in the development of a new kind of merchandising such as the department store and mail order business.[659]

This move into legitimate markets left them with control of 90% of all wholesale clothing in New York and 80% of all retail clothing stores.[660] Investment banking was the domain of a remarkable group of German Jews based in New York whose names are synonymous with high finance to this day.[661]

---

[657]George Horowitz, *The Spirit of Jewish Law* (New York: Central Book, 1963), p. 78. See also Abrahams, p. 102-3.

[658]Moses Rischin, ed., *The Jews of North America* (Detroit: Wayne State University Press, 1987), p. 227.

[659]Hirshler, pp. 59-60. A. Hertzberg, p. 137: "By 1880, about half of the Jewish business firms in the country were in clothing and allied occupations both in manufacturing and retail sales. Three-quarters of all the clothing businesses of all kinds were controlled by Jews. They owned an even higher proportion of the department stores that were then being opened on the 'main street' of almost every city in the country."

[660]Hirshler, pp. 60, 61. See also Raphael, p. 17, and Rudolf Glanz, "Notes on Early Jewish Peddling in America," pp. 125-26, on this point.

[661]Barry E. Supple, "A Business Elite: German-Jewish Financiers in Nineteenth-Century New York," *Business History*, vol. 31 (1957), pp. 142-77: Semon Bache, August Belmont, Marcus Goldman, Meyer Guggenheim, Lazarus Hallgarten, Philip Heidelbach, Isaac Ickelheimer, Abraham Kuhn, Henry Lehman, Emanuel Lehman,

Blacks emerged from the Civil War dominating the skilled crafts and construction trades as masons, carpenters, bricklayers, and painters,[662] but before they were forced out by white laborers, their money was of particular interest to the Jewish merchants. For this reason alone Jews tolerated the Black consumer to a greater extent than did their Gentile counterparts,[663] and their businesses "were crammed with Negroes."[664]

This post-slavery direct contact between Jewish merchant and Black consumer marked the beginning of the modern era relationship and its subtle duality. Jewish establishments, on one hand, were the primary outlet whose doors were open to Blacks but, on the other hand, the feigned friendship was frequently counteracted by bitter, one-sided hostility.[665] After all, says Feingold, "there was a concealed advantage in living in a society which reserved most of its fear and rancor for its blacks."[666]

The Jews "virtually monopolized peddling and controlled the dry-goods stores of the South to a remarkable extent."[667] They sold to Blacks on credit keeping ledger sheets for them—a custom called keeping "a book on schwartzers"—with endless payment terms.[668] Fyodor Dostoevsky wrote in 1877 of the Southern American Jews:

Mayer Lehman, Leonard Lewisohn, Solomon Loeb, Joseph Sachs, Jacob Schiff, William Scholle, 7 brothers Seligman, Philip Speyer, Lazarus Straus, Ernst Thalmann, Felix Warburg, Baruch Wertheim, among them.

[662]Feuerlicht, pp. 188-89. Brenner, p. 245: "Most of the craft work on the plantations was done by slaves. Between the Civil War and the end of the 19th century, Blacks predominated in many trades in the South. But they were then driven from them. Similarly, they were excluded from many skilled craft unions in the North until the 1960s and even later."

[663]Feingold, *Zion*, pp. 59-60.

[664]Arnold Shankman, *Ambivalent Friends: Afro-Americans View the Immigrant* (Westport, Connecticut: Greenwood Press, 1982), p. 114; Feingold, *Zion*, pp. 59-60.

[665]According to Bertram W. Korn, "The Jews of the Confederacy," pp. 36-37, the Black freedmen, placed in legislative roles, pursued an open, fair and equal society even for the oppressive Jews. A statute that denied every one who was not a Christian the right to hold public office was removed in 1868, when "the Reconstructionist legislature—aided by its Negro members—adopted a new constitution omitting all religious tests except a belief in Almighty God."

[666]Feingold, *Zion*, p. 61.

[667]Shankman, p. 111.

[668]Harry Golden, *Our Southern Landsman* (New York: G. P. Putnam's Sons, 1974), p. 157. "Schwartzers" is a Jewish term for "nigger."

> [They] have already leaped en masse upon the millions of liberated Negroes, and have already taken a grip upon them in their, the Jew's own way, by means of their sempiternal; "gold pursuit" and by taking advantage of the inexperience and the vices of the exploited tribe...the Negroes have now been liberated from the slave owners [but] they will not last because the Jews...will jump at this new little victim.[669]

In 1913, one observer recalled that after the Civil War, "the Jews invaded the Southern States...with their merchandise in packs on their backs and began to open stores in the cities, towns, and crossroads as fast as their wholesale Jewish merchant connections in Baltimore, Philadelphia, and New York could ship the goods they ordered."[670]

Economic Exploitation

The "free Blacks" were a new consumer class who needed food, shelter and clothing just like the slave. While others were revulsed by the sheer thought of a "free nigger" in their midst, the Jews' revulsion was mitigated by the ready money in the ex-slave's pockets. After all, Jews had handsomely profited by supplying the slave's needs through the plantation, and now that same money source was re-routed through the hands of the ex-slave in the form of wages. Business was now directly retail. Jewish shops offered an open, if not entirely welcome, market for the Black consumer. Says Ashkenazi, "The free black population of New Orleans was a significant economic group, and even urban slaves had funds at their disposal not available to their plantation counterparts."[671]

---

[669]Whitfield, *Voices of Jacob*, pp. 241-42.

[670]Shankman, *Ambivalent Friends*, pp. 111, 113. Thomas D. Clark, "The Post-Civil War Economy in the South," *PAJHS*, vol. 55 (1965-66), pp. 425, 428:

> [T]here appeared the wholesale merchants in Louisville, St. Louis, Baltimore, Charleston, Cincinnati, New Orleans, and Mobile. Many of these houses were operated by Jewish merchants who had either survived the war or were quick to see the opportunity for trade on a new basis of merchandising in the post-war South....They searched for just the right spots to open stands, and when they located them they emptied their packs onto store shelves and went into business in permanent locations....Almost every town had one or more of these merchants who made modest beginnings and advanced his mercantile career as the South moved further away from the reconstruction years. Possibly a major portion of the dry goods and clothing sold in the southern small towns were sold by these merchants. The smaller retailers really clothed the South either by the sale of cloth or ready-made clothing.

[671]Ashkenazi, p. 126.

The Southern merchant now had to subtly coax what could no longer be forcibly extracted. Jews were pioneers in this new brand of Black consumer exploitation, while still maintaining the supplier role with the plantation owner, who had developed a new form of slavery called *sharecropping*—a system barely discernible from chattel slavery.[672]

Meanwhile, the terror that characterized legal slavery was paired with a contempt for the ex-slave to maintain a psychological slavery, and again the Jews could be seen as beneficiaries. The Jews "imbibed generously of its pervasive racist sentiment," admits Feingold, "and participated in the ritualized violence formalized in its 'code duello.'"[673] They were free from the pervasive "anti-Semitism" because Southerners "were so deeply prejudiced against Negroes and Catholics that they had little room to hate the Jews."[674] In fact, Jews became firmly rooted in the social and economic fabric of the region. A report by the American Jewish Historical Society concluded that "contrary to popular notion the Jewish merchant found the South almost as good a base of operation as the East."[675] It said that Southern Jews "were members of the lodges, served on all sorts of boards and committees, were sources of advice, and oftentimes gave a sound leadership in the organization of banks. To a great

---

[672]Ashkenazi, p. 68:

> Planters had lost direct control of the labor force when their slaves were freed. A sharecropping system had taken root in the Felicianas by 1865, under which freedmen worked parcels of land and shared a portion of the crop with the landowners. Freedmen could work their parcels without the supervision attendant upon their position as slaves, and they could dispose of some of the fruits of their labor as their own. The planters and farmers (those who tilled between fifty and one hundred acres) lacked funds and, after 1867, credit. They viewed sharecropping as a way to keep their land planted and harvested while their former slaves remained tied to the land in some fashion. The planters with whom the Meyers traded remained on their land and actively pursued cotton growing along with their sharecroppers. Relations between the landowner and his sharecroppers were little changed from those before the end of slavery.

[673]Feingold, *Zion*, p. 61; Harry Golden, *Our Southern Landsman* (New York: G. P. Putnam's Sons, 1974), pp. 108-9. See also Janowsky, pp. 185-86.

[674]Clark, p. 430. See also Leonard Reissman, "The New Orleans Jewish Community," *Jewish Journal of Sociology*, vol. 4 (1962), p. 121. According to Weisbord and Stein, pp. 22-23:

> Race consciousness in Dixie resulted in benefit to the Jew as a white man. Differences between whites were submerged in a society that was preoccupied with maintaining the subordinate status of blacks....[And as Bertram Korn wrote], "The Negroes acted as an escape valve in Southern society. The Jews gained in status and security from the very presence of this large mass of defenceless victims who were compelled to absorb all of the prejudices which might otherwise have been expressed more frequently in anti-Jewish sentiment."
>
> North as well as south Jewish racial views were not appreciably different from those of Christians.

[675]Clark, p. 432.

extent they set the styles of their communities because they had the outside purchasing contacts from which they imported new goods and styles into their trade."[676]

The Land and the Lien

In the midst of this assault and the hardening of Jim Crow, the Black man tried to maintain a foothold on the American dream but found the Jewish merchant class unwilling to offer a hand. The Jews were charged with "overpricing their goods, of selling cheap and shoddy merchandise, of charging exorbitant rates of interest, of discriminating among their customers, and generally of driving the Southern farmer into complete failure [and some] of these charges in specific instances no doubt were true."[677] These merchants engaged in a form of legal land theft that secured thousands of acres in the name of debt service. The lien laws of the South were the credit instrument that allowed the poor farmer to purchase planting supplies on credit until the harvest. A tool, a mule, a seed—in exchange for a lien on the farm. When the payment was late or if the crop failed, the entire farm could be foreclosed and taken by the merchant—all for a fraction of its actual worth. Jews were the prevalent wholesalers, and as such extended credit, and were represented in "substantial numbers" in banking throughout the South.[678] Some of these bankers and merchants abused the opportunity by actually speculating in foreclosures. Thomas D. Clark apologetically explains the process:

---

[676]Clark, pp. 428-29.

[677]Clark, p. 431.

[678]According to Clark, p. 432: "His [the Jew's] safe bulged with thousands of liens and mortgages." Rubin, p. 166. See Larry Schweikart, "Southern Banking and Economic Growth in the Antebellum Period: A Reassessment," *Journal of Southern History*, vol. 53, no. 4 (1987), p. 35. See also Allison Davis, Burleigh B. Gardner, Mary R. Gardner, *Deep South: A Social Anthropological Study of Caste and Class* (Los Angeles: University of California, Center for Afro-American Studies, 1941), p. 264:

> In Rural County, however, where there are no large towns, the functions of the buyer, the ginner, and the advance merchant have often been performed by one individual or firm. Such a merchant-ginner-buyer exerted a dominant economic control over the tenants and planters to whom he furnished credit.
>
> The wholesale merchants in Old County who once rivaled the banks as credit agencies for planters were, with one exception, Jews. Most of them were socially middle class in Old City, but a few had risen into the upper class.

> There was involved in land dealing, however, the exceedingly delicate question of foreclosure, and not even the hardest-hearted furnishing merchant relished the opprobrium which was likely to result from the public sale of chattel goods and land for debt. It was much simpler to secure the transfer of ownership of property in quiet private negotiations than to stand exposure to criticism by public sale. It was in this way that many furnishing merchants accumulated large tracts of land, and sometimes men who started out as merchants became larger farmers who gradually came to run their stores as adjuncts to their farming activities. Doubtless many merchants insured the future success of their stores by building up a controlled trade upon their private domains. So prevalent did the custom of giving land as security become that it was common practice in much of the South to speculate on the amount of mortgage every man had on his farm and as to the probable date on which he would have either to secure an abundance of providential assistance or be foreclosed.[679]

As farmers absorbed the inherent risks of producing a successful crop, many a Jewish merchant became the direct beneficiary of the failure of the family farm. Clark presents these merchants as unwilling victims of a law with which they were forced to comply. Contrarily, he points out that these Jews gave the "sound advice" that produced these laws and it was they whose businesses stood to benefit the most. The abuses became rampant, leading to the system's demise:

> When the boll weevil reduced the cotton crop, and when competition of cash stores developed an expansion of industry, the old line furnishing business went into eclipse in the South. Its end came only after merchants had committed countless sins against real Southern agricultural progress, and had been properly criticized for it in the newspaper and periodical press, and even in books.[680]

Struggling whites and Blacks fell victim to this sophisticated land snatch, just as the Red man had fallen prey to an earlier version. As today, the Black ex-slave was scapegoated by white victims who had lost land and who were left in economic travail—and the lynchings increased. Jews such as Isaac Hermann (1838-1917) encouraged this rancor:

> In the Reconstruction period, Hermann was a leader in the movement to organize the [Civil War] veterans into an association whose primary aim, it would seem, was to protect the whites against the Negro freedmen....He worked to restore white

---

[679]Clark, pp. 431-32.

[680]Clark, p. 432.

> supremacy and to resist what he believed to be the encroachments of the Negroes.[681]

The Jewish Press: Creating a Black Image

The Jewish press actually encouraged resentment toward the Black, portraying him as unfit for citizenship. Since the war, the preferred Jewish image of the diligent and humble immigrant striving to be a model American citizen had given way to a hostile skepticism. Jews were now seen by a growing number of observers as having produced wealth for themselves at the expense of the American people. As the anti-Jewish sentiment became audible, the Jewish press turned on the most vulnerable and easy target. The *Jewish Sentiment* editorialized in 1898:

> The laws of nature cannot be reversed by "an act of Congress" and the white man is not only superior to the black man but will assert his supremicy (sic) at the proper time and in the proper manner...[682]

The *Sentiment's* editor Frank Cohen wrote of a lynching in November of 1899:

> North Carolina has recently done herself proud while several other states have had dignified hanging bees — provoked by the usual cause....Those negroes who conduct themselves properly, are respected and protected, but the lawless brute who violates the sanctity of the white man's home deserves death and usually receives it with electrical swiftness.[683]

Jewish Sentiment, August 11, 1899:

> The primary needs of the negro race is [*sic*] obedience to the law and recognition of the rights of others....If law abiding and worthy, every opportunity will be accorded him short of social equality and this no self-respecting white man can endure. If the unmentionable crime against womanhood is persisted in mobs in the future will deal with him as they have in the past.[684]

---

[681] *JRM/Memoirs 3,* p. 236; Schappes, pp. 495-98.

[682] *Jewish Sentiment,* December 31, 1897, p. 3; August 24, 1900, p. 3; October 28, 1898, p. 3, reported in Steven Hertzberg, "The Jewish Community of Atlanta," *AJHQ,* vol. 62, no. 3 (March 1973), p. 280.

[683] *Jewish Sentiment,* November 11, 1899, p. 3, reported in S. Hertzberg, p. 280.

[684] *Jewish Sentiment,* August 11, 1899, p. 3, reported in S. Hertzberg, p. 281.

The *Jewish Sentiment* was aptly named and represented its constituency well. The Jewish/Black relationship had shifted from slaveowner/slave to merchant/consumer but with the same effect: Jews continued to exploit, at first the manpower and then the economic power of their former slaves. This duality became the foundation of the modern relationship between Blacks and Jews as the tumultuous 19th century came to a close.

The Holocaust

Black men, women, and children fell victim by the tens of millions to the slave traders and slave makers. As chattel, the African was unaccounted for in many a transaction and hidden within a substantial smuggling commerce. Given the evidence presented of the mercantile capabilities of the Jews and their concurrent indifference to African humanity, one might fairly assert that they are responsible for innumerable deaths and murders. Certainly, one could justifiably argue that in places such as Surinam, Curaçao, Barbados and other slave depots under their control, a majority of the murders of Black hostages were committed by Jews or their agents. To quantify, however, is a most difficult proposition. Tens of millions suffered and died—how many tens of how many millions is the question.

Philip D. Curtin, author of *The Atlantic Slave Trade*, traced the most circulated slave importation figure, of 15 million, back to a most unlikely source—an American publicist of the 1860s.[685] Of the trail of miscalculations, Curtin says: "[O]n closer examination, the vast consensus turns out to be nothing but a vast inertia, as historians have copied over and over again the flimsy results of unsubstantial guesswork."[686] Other writers of English language textbooks on the history of the slave trade estimate in percentages the rate of the loss of African life in the trade[687]:

- Robert Rotberg sets the loss of life during the maritime leg of the journey into slavery at 25 to 33 per cent.
- J. D. Hargreaves says it was about one-sixth.

---

[685]Philip D. Curtin, *The Atlantic Slave Trade: A Census* (Madison: University of Wisconsin Press, 1969), pp. 6-7. Curtin tracks the use of a fallacious guess through the works of a series of historians, all basing their figures on those of a previous "expert" in the field with each adding a new degree of authority. The publicist Edward E. Dunbar passed his guesstimate to DuBois to Kuczynski to Fage to Davidson to Davis. Another faulty trail (see pages 9-10) commences with George Bancroft to W. E. H. Lecky to Eric Williams to E. D. Morel to Melville J. Herskovits.

[686]Curtin, p. 11.

[687]Curtin, pp. 275-76. See also Boogaart and Emmer, "The Dutch Participation in the Atlantic Slave Trade, 1596-1650," in *The Uncommon Market*, eds. Gemery and Hogendorn.

- J. D. Fage says it was "at least" one-sixth.
- Donald L. Wiedner says mortality reached about 12 per cent in French ships, contrasted with 17 per cent in Dutch and British ships; Portuguese losses in the early centuries ran about 15 per cent, but when pressure from the nineteenth-century abolitionists forced the slave traders to take evasive actions, the casualty rate rose to 25 to 30 per cent.
- Westergaard's archival survey of the Danish slave trade, for example, showed that individual voyages between 1698 and 1733 had mortality rates as low as 10 per cent and as high as 55 per cent.

Curtin's exhaustive review of the mortality data, including the assumptions above, brings him to this assertion:

> The cost of the slave trade in human life was many times the number of slaves landed in the Americas. For every slave landed alive, other people died in warfare, along the bush paths leading to the coast, awaiting shipment, or in the crowded and unsanitary conditions of the middle passage. Once in the New World, still others died on entering a new diseased environment.[688]

It is generally agreed that the oft repeated figure of 15 million via the publicist is "conservative." But even if that figure were true, Curtin's claim that "many times" that number of Africans killed would place the number closer to 100 million murder victims. The actual figures are staggering; and as key operatives in the enterprise, Jews have carved for themselves a monumental culpability in slavery—and the holocaust.

The Count

To what extent Jews used the African is a difficult determination to make. Dr. Bertram Korn reasons:

> Jews who were more firmly established in a business or professional career, as well as in their family relationships, had every reason to become slave-owners, although, of course, some socially prominent families took pride in employing white servants in their homes.[689]

---

[688]Curtin, p. 275.

[689]Korn, "Jews and Negro Slavery, p. 181.

Colonial Jews were rarely to be found in the ranks of the impoverished, being "securely ensconced in the middle class."[690] Historian Jacob Marcus counts slaves in his description of the Jewish households:

> Merchants who were prosperous owned their own homes, occasionally some farm or uncultivated lands, perhaps some urban real estate, and a slave or a bond servant. Most Jewish shopkeepers and merchants were "comfortable." That is to say, they made a good living and lived comfortably. Many of them owned their own homes, while practically all had at least one domestic slave and could afford to lose twenty shillings at cards — once a week — at the club.[691]

Marcus again:

> Jews who had come up in the world patterned themselves most carefully on their cultured and often wealthier Christian compatriots. Their well-appointed homes boasted silver, fine linens, expensive glassware, good cutlery, rugs, carpets and slaves to wait upon them...[692]

"The possession of one or two house servants," says Henry Feingold, "was fairly widespread. As many as a quarter of the South's Jews may have fallen into this category," which was "slightly above that of other Southern merchants." Slave ownership among Jews was an indication of wealth and social status.[693] Roberta Strauss Feuerlicht counts Jews as having an even greater role in slavery:

> Just as a disproportionately large number of Jews were slave owners, a disproportionately large number of Jewish merchants sold slaves as they would any other goods. Several of these merchants were prominent in their communities: an acting rabbi, the president of a congregation.[694]

To quantify these assertions of inordinate Jewish slaveholding and dealing could not be accurately done until the census of 1820 — America's first attempt to count and segment her population by ethnic origin. It must be stressed that the figures represent only what the Jewish population would admit to, and, as taxable commodities, slave holdings would likely be underreported. The

---

[690] *MCAJ2,* p. 820.
[691] *MCAJ2,* pp. 819, 821.
[692] *MCAJ3,* p. 1178.
[693] Feingold, *Zion*, p. 60.
[694] Feuerlicht, p. 73.

brisk slave-smuggling trade operated by the Jews of the Caribbean after the ban on the legal trade makes it difficult to assign definitive numbers to their slave commerce. Also, the high turn-over wholesale trade, in which Jews were numerous, would not have identified Jews as owners of the Black stock temporarily in their hands. Ira Rosenwaike analyzed the 1820 data that indicates the number of domestic slaves held by Jews:

> The Jewish population in 1820 is concentrated in a few principle towns, in particular the five centers which then had functioning congregations[:] New York, Philadelphia, Charleston, Richmond and Savannah....In Charleston, Richmond and Savannah the large majority (over three-fourths) of the Jewish households contained one or more slaves; in Baltimore only one out of three households were slaveholding; in New York, one out of eighteen....Among the slaveholding households the median number of slaves owned ranged from five in Savannah to one in New York.[695]

Rosenwaike, whose Jewish population studies have been published in the major Jewish historical journals, has recently analyzed the 1971 population studies of Lee Soltow. Rosenwaike does not dispute Soltow's startling findings:

> Soltow estimates that 36 percent of the 625,000 families in the South in 1830 were slaveholders. Of the 322 household heads identified in the present study as [Jewish] residents of the same states at this enumeration, a considerably larger proportion — 75 percent — were owners of one or more slaves.[696]

"In Charleston, Richmond, and Savannah," he continues, "the overwhelming proportion (over four-fifths) of the Jewish households contained one or more slaves; in New Orleans over three-fifths were slaveholders; in Baltimore, less than one-fifth."[697] Nationwide, "Probably close to two-fifths of the Jewish families of 1820 owned slaves..."[698]

---

[695]Rosenwaike, "The Jewish Population in 1820," pp. 2, 17, 19.

[696]Rosenwaike, *Edge of Greatness*, p. 66. Also Lee Soltow, "Economic Inequality in the United States in the Period from 1790 to 1860," *Journal of Economic History*, vol. 31 (1971), pp. 825-26. Korn, "Jews and Negro Slavery," p. 183: "The proportion of Jewish slave-owners, then, was possibly even larger than that of non-Jews, since the overwhelming majority of Southern Jews lived in the towns and cities."

[697]Rosenwaike, *Edge of Greatness*, p. 66.

[698]Rosenwaike, "Jewish Population of 1820," p. 18. These figures correspond to data collected seventy years later by the Bureau of the Census which surveyed American Jews. See Raphael, p. 17: "Even more striking: two-thirds of all the Jewish families in the United States had at least one servant! Jews had clearly achieved a comfortable position in American society."

Ira Rosenwaike, Bertram W. Korn and Malcolm Stern are among the Jewish scholars who have studied American Jewish population data. All of their results confirm the pervasive involvement of Jews in Black slavery. Dr. Korn analyzes the available census data:

> In the 1820 manuscript census records for New Orleans, it has been possible to identify only six Jews. Each of these owned at least one slave, and the six owned twenty-three slaves altogether. By 1830, twenty-two Jews can be identified in the census returns — a very low number, since there were about sixty-six Jews in the area when the newly established congregation published its list of contributors in 1828, although some of the donors were not permanent residents. More than half of these twenty-two did not own slaves, but ten of them owned a total of seventy-five slaves. Obviously some of the newly arrived Jewish settlers could not afford to own slaves. By 1840, when sixty-two Jews can be identified in the census returns — again a very small number, since there must have been at least several hundred Jewish families in the community by that time — the newcomers had prospered to so great a degree that only seven reported that they owned no slaves. The fifty-five identifiable Jewish slave-owners of New Orleans in 1840 held a total of three hundred and forty-eight Negroes in bondage, an index to growing prosperity....Yet, according to the Mobile 1850 census, which lists seventy-two identifiable Jewish heads of family, thirty-one Jews were owners of slaves, to a total of ninety slaves. The proportion is even higher in view of the fact that we include in the figure for heads of families, nineteen young clerks and peddlers who lived in the homes of relatives, and fourteen Jewish bachelors who lived in a single boarding-house.[699]

[699]Korn, "Jews and Negro Slavery," pp. 182-83.

Census Data of Jews and Black Slaves

The following tables have been published by Jewish scholars who have researched and analyzed the available population data. These 1790 Census figures are included because they are the only "official" data available. Dr. Korn comments:

> Seventy-three Jewish heads of households have been identified as Jewish; of these, at least thirty-four owned one or more slaves, to a total of 151 slaves. The only large holdings of slaves were possessed by Jacob Jacobs of Charleston (11), and Abraham Cohen (21), Solomon Cohen (9), and Esther Myers (11), all of the Georgetown District.[700]

Many families did not participate in this census and still more would not have revealed their identity as slaveholders or as Jews, having emerged so recently from the era of Inquisition.[701]

Area	# of Jewish Heads of Households	Jewish Slave Holders	Slaves
New England	23	5	21
New York	60	20	43
Pennsylvania	31	3	6
Maryland	8	3	3

The Census of 1830 provides another "official" tally of the slave holdings of Jews. The chart below lists records of slave holdings of Jews in areas outside of major Jewish communities.[702]

Jewish Heads of Households in All Other Places, Census of 1830

Head of Household	Number of Blacks			
	Slave		Free	
County	M	F	M	F
ALABAMA				
Mobile				
George Davis Jr.		1		
George Davis Sr.	4	3		
Henry Lazrus	2	1		
ARKANSAS				
Hempstead				
Abraham Block		2		

[700]Korn, "Jews and Negro Slavery," p. 182.
[701]Korn, "Jews and Negro Slavery," p. 182.
[702]Rosenwaike, *Edge of Greatness*, pp. 134-38, Table A-12.

DISTRICT OF COLUMBIA

Washington				
Raphael Jones				2

FLORIDA

Alachua				
David Levy for his father	9			7

GEORGIA

Augusta				
B. Abrahams		1		
Jacob Abrahams	2	2		
Levi Florance	3	7		
Isaac Hendricks	1			
Isaac Henry	9	4		
Jacob Moise	2	4		
Burke				
Joseph Bush	6	6	3	3
Camden				
G. P. Cohen		1		

ILLINOIS

St. Clair				
John Hays	4	2		

INDIANA

Knox				
Samuel Judah			1	1

KENTUCKY

Lexington				
Benjn Gratz	5	4		
Louisville				
Henry Hyman	1	1		
Jacob Levin		2		
Grant				
Abraham Jonas	1	1		

LOUISIANA

Pt. Coupee				
Widow of Ben Jewel Sr.	26	16		

MARYLAND

Frederick				
Isaac Lyon		1		

MISSISSIPPI

Natchez				
Jacob Soria	1	1		

MISSOURI

Lincoln				
Emanuel Block	1	2		
Pike				
Pheneas Block	1	2		
Washington				
Jacob Phillips(on)	1	2		

NORTH CAROLINA

Mecklenburg				
Nathan Cohen		2		
New Hanover				
A. Lasarus		2		

Malcolm Stern published some additions and corrections to Rosenwaike's analysis that included a slave count. See Malcolm H. Stern, "Some Additions and Corrections to Rosenwaike's 'An Estimate and Analysis of the Jewish Population of the United States in 1790,'" *AJHQ*, vol. 53 (1964), pp. 285-89; Ira Rosenwaike's original article is in *PAJHS*, vol. 50, no. 1 (March 1961), pp. 23-67.

Jews/Location	slaves
Newport, Rhode Island	
Sarah Lopez	6
Abraham Rivera	4
Moses Seixas	6
Boston, Massachusetts	
Moses Michael Hays	2
New York, New York	
Solomon Myers Cohen	1
Isaac Gomez, Jr.	7
Isaac M. Gomez	1
Rebecca Gomez	1
Uriah Hendricks	2
Abraham Isaacs	1
Joshua Isaacs	2
Benjamin S. Judah	2
Elizabeth Judah	2
Eleazar Levy	1
Isaac H. Levy	3
Joshua Levy	2
(E)Manuel Myers	3
Simon Nathan	3
Rachel Pinto	1
Solomon Simpson	1
Alexander Zuntz	2
Bedford, New York	
Benjamin Hay(e)s	5
David Hay(e)s	1
Mt. Pleasant, New York	
Michael Hay(e)s	2
Philadelphia, Pennsylvania	
Myer Hart	3
Jonas Phillips	1
Lancaster, Pennsylvania	
Joseph Simons	2
Baltimore, Maryland	
Moses Jacobs	1
Elkin Solomon	1
Isaac Solomon	1
Jews/Location	**slaves**
Charleston, S. Carolina	
Joseph Abendanon	4
Emanuel Abrahams	4
Jacob Abrahams	1
Jacob Cantor	1
Gershom Cohen	6
Isaac De (Da) Costa	6
Sarah De (Da) Costa	5
Isaac De Lyon	2
Simon Hart	1
Jacob Jacobs	11
Jacob Jacobs	3
Israel Joseph	1
Mark(s) Lazarus	2
Moses Levey (Levy)	2
A(a)ron [Lopez]	2
Mordica(i) Lyon	1
Barnet Moses	2
Isaac Moses	1
Lyon Moses	4
Abraham Seixas	5
Samuel Simons	2
Joseph Tobias	3
Rachel Woolf	6
Cheraw Dist., S. Carolina	
David Azariah	1
Georgetown, S. Carolina	
Wolf A(a)ronson	1
Abraham Cohen	21
Solomon Cohen	9
Daniel Hart	6
Hyman Hart	6
Nathan Hart	5
Esther Myers	11
Berkeley Cty, S. Carolina	
Joseph [Solomons]	4
Total Enslaved Africans	209

Census of 1820[703]							
	Charleston	New York	Philadelphia	Richmond	Baltimore	Savannah	TOTAL
Households	109	74	58	32	21	21	315
Slaveholding Households	92	4	-	25	7	17	145
Slaves	481	5	-	88	11	116	701
Free Colored in Household	11	27	8	2	15	7	70

Absentee Jewish Owners of Slaves, 1830 Census[704]			
Name of Absentee Slaveholder	**County or City**	**State**	**Number of Slaves**
Isaac Abraham	Glynn	Georgia	5
Gratz and Bruce	Lexington	Kentucky	75
Isaac Hyams & Co.	Mecklenburg	N. Carolina	13
[Gershom] Lazarus	New Hanover	N. Carolina	5
W. Lazarus	New Hanover	N. Carolina	30
Jacob Barrett	Lexington	S. Carolina	45
David D. Cohen	Berkeley	S. Carolina	23
Mordecai Cohen	Berkeley	S. Carolina	27
Jacob Dela Motta	Charleston	S. Carolina	4
Hetty Moses	Charleston	S. Carolina	5
Isaih Moses	Berkeley	S. Carolina	35
Rachel Myers	Charleston	S. Carolina	10
I.J. (J.I.) Cohen	Richmond	Virginia	4
J.J. (J.I.) Cohen	Richmond	Virginia	1
Mordecai Marx	Richmond	Virginia	1
Samuel S. Myers & Co.	Richmond	Virginia	82

[703]Rosenwaike, "Jewish Population of 1820," pp. 19A-B.
[704]Rosenwaike, *Edge of Greatness*, p. 70, Table 22.

Slaves in Jewish Wills

> *"[Isaiah] Isaacs stipulated that the men and women to be freed were to receive a generous supply of clothing; [Jacob I.] Cohen left money to these servants but specified that if any of them preferred to remain in bondage, they were free to choose their own masters. The money from the sale was to be invested by the municipal authorities and the interest used to buy bread for the poor on the Fourth of July."*[705]

Another indication, but still incomplete accounting, of Jewish slaveholdings are the references to slaves in the wills of Jews. Professor Jacob R. Marcus assembled 129 Jewish wills from the American Jewish Archives for the period of 1789 to 1865. Of those, 33 refer to ownership and disposition of 132 slaves. In many of these wills, however, the African children are not enumerated, and many refer to groups of slaves of unspecified numbers. In 19 of the 33 wills, the slaves were bequeathed to relatives to be used as they saw fit, and in 5, the executors were instructed to sell them. Professor Marcus adds that "It is quite likely that some of the 97 remaining decedents owned slaves and lumped them together with all other types of property..."[706]

The section of this volume entitled "Jews of the Black Holocaust" details the slave dispensation in some of these wills.

Anti-Semitism ?

> *"Before the Civil War some Jews admittedly had been slaveholders and slave traders, and one wonders whether they skipped the passages in the Passover Haggadah that extol freedom after the torment of Egyptian bondage."*[707]

Some Jewish historians have claimed that Jews only participated in slavery to defer anti-Jewish sentiment that would

---

[705] *MUSJ1*, p. 586.
[706] Korn, "Jews and Negro Slavery," p. 183.
[707] Whitfield, *Voices of Jacob*, p. 241.

have resulted if they had taken a moral stand.[708] But throughout the historical record there appears no hint of moral indignation on the part of Jews. Dr. Korn states, "There is no iota of evidence, no line in a letter, no stray remark which would lead us to believe that these Jews gave conscious support to the slave system out of fear of arousing anti-Jewish sentiment."[709]

Many Jewish historians concur, including Oscar I. Janowsky, who believes that Jews had little to fear:

> One fact stands out clearly — the people of the United States have never been infected with the violent forms of European anti-Semitism. The very first settlers, it is true, were not wholly free of anti-Jewish prejudice. But even this milder form of intolerance generally remained dormant in the liberalizing atmosphere of the New World.[710]

Oscar Straus wrote that when his father was peddling through the rural areas of Georgia, he was "treated by the owners of the plantations with a spirit of equality that is hard to appreciate today."[711] A host of Jewish authorities have discounted the suggestion that anti-Semitic oppression was significant in early American Jewish history:

- Dr. Marcus contends that "Colonial Jews suffered no egregious civil or economic disabilities; they were not packed into overcrowded ghettos, nor humiliated by narrow-minded civil servants and bureaucrats."[712]

- Richard Tedlow reasons that "Perhaps the key is that neither Southern nor Northern anti-Semitism at that time had extensive institutional props; neither was organized."[713]

- Jewish author/lecturer Julius Lester maintains that "While individual Jews were subjected to anti-Semitic incidents and insults, on the whole the Jewish community was free to pursue its life."[714]

- David Brener: "It was a fact that many colonies had legal restrictions against the Jews, but in reality such laws were generally ignored....Very little of the traditional anti-Jewish medieval legislation took root in British North America, and so

---

[708]See *MUSJ1*, p. 587.

[709]Korn, "Jews and Negro Slavery," p. 217; Harry Golden, *Our Southern Landsman* (New York: G. P. Putnam's Sons, 1974), p. 108.

[710]Oscar I. Janowsky, ed., *The American Jew: A Composite Portrait* (New York: Harper & Bros., 1942), p. 184.

[711]Korn, "Jews and Negro Slavery," p. 218.

[712]*MCAJ2*, p. 799.

[713]Richard S. Tedlow, "Judah P. Benjamin," in Kaganoff and Urofsky, p. 50.

[714]Julius Lester, lecture at Boston University, January 28, 1990.

there were fewer laws that hampered Jews. The Colonies possessed no feudal heritage, developed no guilds; knew no prohibitions in the purchase of land. The only truly effective barriers here were nature herself, her savage Indians, and man's own personal incapacity....The Jews could make progress here because there were no bounds to his freedom of movement, his freedom to settle where he wished and marry whom he would. Capital went further in America than in Europe and competition was less keen. Additionally the American Jew's strong family ties in Europe were a boon to the import and export industry in which they would engage."[715]

- Charles Stember writes that even with its reputation for bigotry and intolerance, "The South has traditionally been one of the least anti-Semitic regions in the nation, and a considerable body of data suggests that it remained so until the 1940s."[716]
- Roberta Strauss Feuerlicht's analysis concludes that "anti-Semitism has been malignant in other places and other times, but in America it has been benign or virtually non-existent."[717]
- Eric Hirshler maintains that during the Civil War era, "there was no discrimination in public institutions."[718]
- Barry E. Supple: "Jews were no longer a harassed minority [and] the community promised a relatively unhindered advance to business talent..."[719]
- Stanley Chyet: "Religious liberty was never an especially great problem for the Jew in America." Almost from the beginning, "[he] found little trouble securing religious freedom [and] no colony drove him out because he was a Jew."[720]
- Raphael Mahler: Those who laid the foundation for the largest Jewish community in the world "had already attained a level of social and legal equality unprecedented in the history of the Diaspora."[721]
- Max I. Dimont: "At the time of the Revolution, 50 percent of the American people were slaves or indentured servants. But the Jews were neither. They were all free. Though most were shopkeepers and craftsmen, many were manufacturers, importers, exporters, wholesalers, and slave traders. They dealt in coffee,

---

[715]Brener, pp. ix, 2.

[716]Charles Herbert Stember et al, *Jews in the Mind of America* (New York: Basic Books, 1966), p. 390.

[717]Feuerlicht, p. 189.

[718]Hirshler, p. 59.

[719]Barry E. Supple, "A Business Elite: German-Jewish Financiers in Nineteenth-Century New York," *Business History*, vol. 31 (1957), p. 162.

[720]Quoted in Andrea Finkelstein Losben, "Newport's Jews and the American Revolution," *Rhode Island Jewish Historical Notes*, vol. 7, no. 2 (November 1976), p. 261.

[721]Raphael Mahler, *A History of Modern Jewry: 1780-1815* (New York: Schocken Books, 1971), p. 1.

sugar, tobacco, and molasses. They paid the same taxes non-Jews paid, and, by and large, suffered no more disabilities than other minorities did. And these disabilities, such as the lack of franchise in some of the colonies, did not affect their other freedoms. Anti-Semitism was almost nonexistent in Colonial America."[722]

- Jacob J. Weinstein: "Then, too, the issue of slavery dominated American politics and offered a safety valve for latent prejudices and subconscious frustrations. Thus, anti-Semitism did not enter the consciousness of the average American very deeply. There were, it is true, some anti-Semitic undertones during the Civil War. But it is interesting to note that the leading role played by Judah P. Benjamin in the Confederacy aroused no perceptible resentment toward the Jews in the North or South during the worst days of the Civil War and Reconstruction animosities."[723]

Jews were not only citizens of high standing, they were also respected figures in public life and "pillars of local authority."[724] They held office and shaped political and economic policy.

Though there were incidents attributable to "anti-Semitism," the problem was not pervasive. Jews enjoyed, by all accounts, a greater freedom to pursue their social and economic interests than at any other time and place to date—freedom even to deny the same to others.

---

[722]Dimont, p. 55.

[723]Janowsky, pp. 185-86. See also Feingold, *Zion*, p. 61.

[724]Toll, "Pluralism and Moral Force," p. 89. See "Reconstruction" section of this volume and the Jewish contribution to Southern economic structure.

Slave Ships and Jews

> *"As a slave entrepreneur he gambled on the hazards of the voyage, the African supply, losses by death in the middle passage and the fluctuating West India markets."*[725]

During the 14th and 15th centuries, European Jews were dominant as shippers, navigators, cartographers and traders, piloting the seas and exploring for new trade routes and sources of commerce. Their money backed many exploratory forays and their equipment and supplies filled many of the ships' holds. By the time they settled in the New World, they had acquired hundreds of vessels to ferry their goods through the Caribbean and South American settlements and on to Europe. The Jews, in fact, were the largest ship chandlers in the entire Caribbean region and owned warehouses with inventories to outfit the largest sailing vessels and to make ship repairs. It was written of the Curaçao traders that "nearly all the navigation...was in the hands of the Jews."[726]

Sugar was exchanged for kidnapped Africans—an extremely profitable arrangement for the Jews involved in the trade. Slave shipping itself brought an immense return and there was no comparable endeavor for the profiteer.[727] "It was generally agreed," says historian Philip S. Foner of the 19th-century American trade, "that it was possible to gain almost $175,000 on a single successful voyage, and even if this averaged one out of four

---

[725]*MEAJ2*, p. 539.

[726]*Emmanuel HJNA*, p. 83. *Ibid*, vol. 2, p. 681: "According to a letter of the Curaçoan Jews to the Amsterdam Parnassim, February 17, 1721, the shipping business was mainly a Jewish enterprise." Liebman, *New World Jewry*, p. 183: "The ships were not only owned by Jews, but were manned by Jewish crews and sailed under the command of Jewish captains."

[727]Philip S. Foner, *Business and Slavery* (Chapel Hill, North Carolina: University of North Carolina Press, 1941), pp. 166-67, discusses the profits of the 19th century trade. The slave ship *Espoir* made a profit of $436,200 on one trip. Banker's son and kidnapper C. A. L. Lamar [not known to be a Jew] estimated that his African expedition would bring a $480,000 profit. He wrote in July of 1860, "The trade cannot be checked while such great percentages are made in the business. The outlay of $35,000 often brings $500,000....No wonder Boston, New York and Philadelphia have so much interest in the business." With the introduction of steamers in the trade, the profits were even greater, for these vessels were able to carry many more slaves than even the terrifically overcrowded sailing ships.

There are references to the profits made from the voyage of the slave ship *La Fortuna* in Daniel P. Mannix (in collaboration with Malcolm Cowley), *Black Cargoes* (New York: Viking Press, 1962), p. 199, and Captain Theophilus Conneau, *A Slaver's Log Book* (Howard S. Mott, 1976), pp. 92-93.

trips, the reward was worth the risk."[728] This profit potential was readily apparent to the Jews, who concentrated their talents in the shipping trades. According to Rufus Learsi:

> In each of the five towns in the original thirteen colonies—Newport, New York, Philadelphia, Charleston and Savannah—where organized Jewish communities existed in 1776, the Jews were only a small fraction of the population; but in the economic life of each, especially in maritime commerce, their share was considerable.[729]

Jews had a natural inclination toward this maritime commerce, having been masters of the trade, by this time, for centuries. And it was, continues Learsi, "their place in shipping and ocean commerce that made the Jews a factor in the economic growth of colonial America."

> Their ships carried the yield of American fields and forests to Europe and brought back to the colonies the textiles, implements and luxuries of the Old World. The complicated steps involved in disposing of cargoes abroad and obtaining return cargoes were greatly facilitated by their friends and relatives in Amsterdam, London, Lisbon and other European ports, who served as their partners and agents – an advantage which an international people would naturally enjoy. A few ventured into the hazards of preying on enemy merchant ships as licensed privateers; and to some extent the importation of Negro slaves, nearly all of whom were sold in the West Indies, figured in their transactions. The unspeakable traffic, alas, was not in disrepute: the royalty and nobility of England amassed fortunes from it.[730]

The holds of the holocaust ships were indescribably filthy and the ship owners assumed a high death rate in transport—indeed, some of the survivors were close to death upon arrival. Lenni Brenner has written that "Countless thousands of Africans were brought here in colonial times as slaves by Sephardi [Jewish] merchant-shippers..."[731] But Abram Vossen Goodman assures us that "that was before the sufferings of the unhappy blacks had excited compassion."[732]

---

[728]Foner, pp. 166-67.
[729]Learsi, p. 34.
[730]Learsi, p. 35.
[731]Brenner, pp. 221-22.
[732]Goodman, p. 50.

Jewish-Owned Slave Ships

The following is a partial listing of ships that are recorded as having Jewish owners and are known to have transported slaves. This list, it must be emphasized, is indeed a *partial* list. It excludes, for instance, evidence of the transport of slaves by Southern Confederate Moses Cohen Mordecai, who was described as "a prominent merchant and probably the largest ship owner in the United States."[733] There can be no serious doubt that as a Southern shipper from Charleston he engaged extensively in slave shipping. Also excluded from this list are Abraham Gradis and the Gradis family, who are the recorded owners of at least 26 ships that they used to ship Africans around the Caribbean and the world.[734] The Jessurin family of Curaçao alone "owned over one hundred ships sailing the seven seas in the 1800s," when Jews were masters of the slave trade.[735]

Certainly, much more research is required to assemble a truly representative list which, when complete, would be expanded manifold.[736]

Abigail	Aaron Lopez, Moses Levy, Jacob Franks
Active	Aaron Lopez
Africa	Jacob Rivera, Aaron Lopez
Albany	Rodrigo Pacheco
Ann	Aaron Lopez
Anne & Eliza	Justus Bosch, John Abrams
Antigua	Nathan Marston, Abram Lyell
Betsy	Jacob Rivera, Aaron Lopez
Caracoa	Moses and Sam Levy
Charlotte	Moses and Sam Levy, Jacob Franks
Cleopatra	Jacob Rivera, Aaron Lopez
Crown	Isaac Levy, Nathan Simpson
De Vrijheid	David Senior, Jacob Senior

[733]Simonhoff, *Jewish Participants in the Civil War*, p. 260.

[734]Korn, *Jews of New Orleans*, p. 5.

[735]Liebman, *New World Jewry*, p. 183.

[736]*JRM/Docs*, pp. 392, 416, 448; Schappes, pp. 58, 334, 569, 583, 627; Jay Coughtry, *The Notorious Triangle: Rhode Island and the African Slave Trade, 1700-1807* (Philadelphia: Temple University Press, 1981); Donnan, *passim*; Virginia Bever Platt, "And Don't Forget the Guinea Voyage": The Slave Trade of Aaron Lopez of Newport," *William and Mary Quarterly*, vol. 32, no. 4 (1975), p. 603; Emmanuel, vol. 2, *passim*; Kohler, "Newport," p. 73; Jonathan D. Sarna, Benny Kraut, and Samuel K. Joseph, *Jews and the Founding of the Republic* (New York: Markus Wiener Publishing), p. 45.

Eagle	Moses Seixas
Elizabeth	Mordecai and David Gomez
Fortunate	Aaron Lopez
Four Sisters	Moses Levy
George	Aaron Lopez
Greyhound	Jacob Rivera, Aaron Lopez (later by Moses Levy)
Hannah	Jacob Rivera, Aaron Lopez
Hester	Mordecai, David Gomez, also Rodrigo Pacheco
Hetty	Mordecai Sheftall
Hiram	Moses Seixas
Hope	Aaron Lopez (also owned by Myer Pollack)
Juffr. Gerebrecht	Philippe Henriquez, David Senior & Co.
Juf Gracia	Raphael Jesurun Sasportas (captain)
Leghorn	Rodrigo Pacheco
Mary	Jacob Rivera, Aaron Lopez
Nancy	Myer Pollack
Nassau	Moses Levy
Nina	Luis de Santagel, Juan Cabrero
Pinta	Luis de Santagel, Juan Cabrero
Prince George	Isaac Elizer, Samuel Moses
Prudent Betty	Jacob Phoenix
Royal Charlotte	Aaron Lopez
Sally	Saul Brown (Pardo) & Bros.
Santa Maria	Luis de Santagel, Juan Cabrero
Sherbo	Jacob Rivera
Shiprah	Naphtali Hart
Spry	Jacob Rivera, Aaron Lopez
Three Friends	Jacob Rivera & Co.
Union	Moses Seixas

The below-listed ships were owned by Jews who are known to have participated in the slave trade[737] (*asterisk means ownership is presumed):

Year	Owner	*Ship Name (tons)*
1702	Moses, Joseph, and Samuel Frazon	*Joseph & Rachel* (130)
1713	Abraham de Lucena and Justus Bosch	*Mary & Abigail*
1720	Mordecai Gomez and Rodrigo Pacheco	*Young Catherine , Young Adrian*
1737	Rachel Marks, and others	*Lydia* (54)
1743	Joseph Marks	*Barbadoes Factor* (50)
1743	Joseph Marks	*Charming Sally* (60)
1746	Joseph Marks	*Hannah* (40)
1747	Joseph Marks	*Polly* (40)
1748	Joseph Marks	*Dolphin* (50)
1749	Joseph Marks	*Prince Orange* (70)
1751	Joseph Marks	*Charming Polly* (50)
1743	Nathan Levy and David Franks	*Drake*
1745	Nathan Levy and David Franks	*Sea Flower* (30), *Myrtilla* (100), *Phila* (105), *Parthenope* (95)
1758	Naphthali, Isaac, and Abraham Hart	*General Well, Defiance, Perfect Union, Dolphin, Confirmation, Diamond, Rising Sun, Lord Howe, Rabbit*
1759	Naphtali Hart and Company	*General Webb**
1760	Naphtali Hart	*Peggy**
1760	Samuel Levy	*Charming Betsey* (80)
1760	John Franks	*Two Sisters* (30)
1771	Aaron Lopez	*New York**
1771	Samson Levy and another	*Deborah* (40)
1772	Moses & David Franks, Isaac Levy	*Gloucester* (230)
1773	Moses and David Franks	*Delaware* (300), *Belle* (170), *Mars* (400)
1774	Aaron Lopez	*Lark**

[737]Freund, pp. 35, 75-76; Samuel Oppenheim, "Jewish Owners of Ships Registered at the Port of Philadelphia, 1730-1775," *PAJHS*, vol. 26 (1918), pp. 235-36; Broches, pp. 12, 14; Kohler, "New York," p. 83; Libo and Howe, p. 46; Lee M. Friedman, *Jewish Pioneers and Patriots*, p. 90; Korn, *Jews of New Orleans*, p. 93; Irwin S. Rhodes, *References to Jews in the Newport Mercury, 1758-1786* (Cincinnati: American Jewish Archives, 1961), pp. 3, 13, 15; Kohler, "Newport," p. 73, lists Myer Pollack as owner of a ship *Nancy*; Hershkowitz, "Wills of Early New York Jews, 1743 - 1774," *AJHQ*, vol. 56 (1966-67), p. 168; Leo Hershkowitz, "New York," p. 27; Feingold, *Zion*, p. 45; *MEAJ1*, 204. See also Emmanuel, vol. 2, Appendix 3, pp. 681-738, for lists of Jewish-owned ships.

Jewish Ship Owners List, continued.

Year	Owner	*Ship Name*
1783	Abraham Gradis	*Polly, David, Patriarch Abraham, le Parfait, l'Alliance, le Vainqueur*
1806	David G. Seixas	*Jane*
1806	David G. Seixas & Benjamin S. Spitzer	*Nancy*
	Joseph Bueno	*Rebecca*
1806	James DeWolf	*Ann*
	Isaac Levy, and others	*Crown Gally*
		Postillion
	Hayman Levy	*Orleans*
		Dreadnought
	Judah Hays	*Duke of Cumberland*
	Jacob Franks	*Duke of York*
	Samuel Jacobs	*Betsey*
	Emanuel Alvares Correa, Moses Cardozo Abraham Hart	*Pearl* [738]
	Moses Levy	*Mary and Ann*
	Moses Levy	*General Well*
	Moses Lopez	*Rebecca*
	Naphthali Hart	*King George*

Seized Slave Ships

Ownership of some vessels, as well as the financial backers and insurers of slave expeditions, is difficult to trace until a seized vessel is reclaimed[739]:

- The *Braman* was taken into custody on June 9, 1856, and the owners charged with being engaged in the slave trade. It was bonded by John Levi and Henriques da Costa.
- The *Orion* was seized on June 21, 1859, and bonded by Rudolph Blumenberg.
- The *Charlotte E. Tay* was arrested on April 24, 1860, and bonded by Fred K. Myer.
- The *Josephine* was arrested on May 28, 1860, and was bonded by Benjamin Isaacs.

---

[738] S. Broches, p. 11: "When privateers seized the ship *Pearl* two West Indies Jews, Emanuel Alvares Correa and Moses Cardozo, the well known merchant, Abraham Hart of Newport, appeared in court to guarantee the lawful sailing of their vessel and demand that it be turned over to him."

[739] From Senate Executive Document 53, 37th Congress, 2nd Session. See also Pollins, p. 53: "...And there was an overlap with finance, with some Jews providing marine insurance. It is not all uncommon to come across Jews as insurers and ship-owners, whether plaintiffs or defendants, in court cases."

On December 14, 1722, Louis and Mordecai Gomez "petitioned concerning merchandise and negroes imported in the ship *Greyhound* as they were the agents for the several owners of the cargo saved by the *Greyhound.*"[740]

Jews and the Rape of Black Women

> *The female slave was a sex tool beneath the level of moral considerations. She was an economic good, useful, in addition to her menial labor, for breeding more slaves. To attain that purpose, the master mated her promiscuously according to his breeding plans. The master himself and his sons and other members of his household took turns with her for the increase of the family wealth, as well as for satisfaction of their extra-marital sex desires. Guests and neighbors too were invited to that luxury.*[741]

Jews engaged in the widespread practice of the sexual exploitation of dependent female slaves. Such was the practice of Jews since the Middle Ages—a practice that required religious legislation to abate. Slave women were employed primarily for domestic and agricultural service in the households of the Jewish upper classes. The Jews of Spain and Portugal, for instance, used their house servants and slaves as concubines, and in seventeenth-century Amsterdam they did the same even though the practice of polygamy was then against the law.[742] Jewish marriage contracts from the Middle Ages include the condition that the husband promise not to buy a female slave without his wife's consent, parallel to his promise not to take a second wife against his first wife's will.[743]

Once out of the realm of direct civil or religious authority, the Black woman became open game. Dr. Henry L. Feingold has confirmed that

> There are some recorded cases of illicit cohabitation between Jews and Negro slaves but this is undoubtedly only the tip of the

---

[740]Freund, p. 34.

[741]Louis M. Epstein, *Sex Laws and Customs in Judaism* (New York: KTAV Publishing House, 1967), pp. 173-74.

[742]Liebman, *The Jews in New Spain*, p. 59.

[743]*EHJ*, pp. 271-72; S. D. Goitein, *A Mediterranean Society*, vol. 1, pp. 134-38.

> iceberg. Isolated Jewish peddlers are known to have sometimes chosen Negro or Indian women as common-law wives. Sometimes generous bequests to Negro housekeepers in wills hint at deeper involvements. In one case in 1797, Moses Nunes of Savannah, acknowledged his concubine and the children he had with her, by willing her several of his remaining slaves. Similarly, land and money were willed by Isaac H. Judah to his two mulatto sons. The most renowned product of such a union is Francis Lewis Cardozo, Jr., who...was sired by either Jacob N. Cardozo, a well-known Southern journalist or his brother Isaac, grandfather of the Supreme Court justice.[744]

When Feingold refers to the "tip of the iceberg," he is undoubtedly considering the so-called "mulatto" Jews who were never officially recognized as Jews, but were the offspring of Jewish rapists of African women.[745] Marcus asserts that some Jews,

> late in getting a good start in life, did not marry until they had made some progress on the ladder of success, and these late marriages very likely help account for Negro concubinage. Many of the Jewish settlers affranchised Negro and mulatto women who were obviously their mistresses, and occasionally they made some provision for the children as well. One can only speculate as to the reactions of white wives forced to share their estates with the children of slaves but, although there is little indication of their attitude toward this social condition, its very prevalence would suggest they tolerated it as part of the prevailing mores.[746]

The Nunez brothers lived in the backwoods and were said to have "traded with the Indians among whom they lived and fathered a brood of half-breeds."[747] Abram Mordecai, who in 1785 carried on extensive trade with the Indians, had his house burned by Indians "because of an intrigue with an Indian squaw."[748] In his will, Isaac Pinheiro left most of a very substantial estate to Vinella Pinheiro, a "free" Black woman. David Da Costa left most

---

[744]Feingold, *Zion,* p. 61; see also for brief reference *MCAJ1,* p. 155.

[745]*MCAJ1,* p. 166.

[746]*MCAJ1,* pp. 121-22. In Marcus' subsequent book, *United States Jewry, 1776-1985,* p. 586, he restates the same: "Many of the women emancipated had obviously been their owner's mistresses; some of them had borne their master's children; in a few instances, testators acknowledged their parentage. Two educated and cultured blacks, Francis Louis Cardozo, Sr., and his brother Thomas Y., may have been the children of a scion of this Charleston clan. Not infrequently, the mistress, the common-law wife, was a freedwoman, often a mulatto."

[747]*MCAJ2,* p. 732.

[748]Rabbi Alfred G. Moses, "The History of the Jews of Montgomery," *PAJHS,* vol. 13 (1905), pp. 83-84. According to Dimont, pp. 58-59, "such intermarriages also took place in the lower social ranks; Jewish peddlers, cowboys, and adventurers who often married Indian women or servant girls. Others lived with slave women in common law marriages."

of his estate to a "free" mulatto woman on condition that she maintain Da Costa's mother for life.[749] The first Jew living in New England, named Sollomon, is described as a "Malata Jue," perhaps born of an African slave mother and a Jewish father.[750]

In another case, Marcus describes a "cultured Jew" as having "a Negro concubine who reared their numerous children in the Dutch Reformed faith."[751] Americans in the Caribbean were "shocked" when Nathan Levy cohabitated with a Black woman and was "frequently seen promenading with her, arm in arm."[752] Jacob Monsanto, son of Isaac Rodrigues Monsanto, one of the very first known Jews to settle in New Orleans and owner of a several-hundred-acre plantation at Manchac, reportedly "fell in love with his slave, Mamy or Maimi William. Their daughter Sophia, grew up to be a lovely quadroon."[753] Rabbi Korn saw a trend:

> [I]t is likely that some of these Negroes [received] their names either from Jewish owners or Jewish fathers. This is probably also true of Sheldon Cohen of St. Petes Parish, South Carolina, Constance Herschell of New Orleans, Levy Jacobs of Fayetteville, North Carolina, George and Samuel Kauffman of King and Queen County, Virginia, Affey Levy of Charleston, Justine Moise of New Orleans, Harry Mordecai of Frankfort, Kentucky, Betty Rosenberg of Charleston Neck, and Catherine Sasportes of Charleston.[754]

The crime of rape was so widespread that significant portions of the Jewish population were its result. A Jewish historian reported that in 1791, "Portuguese Jews number 834 and the German Jews 477, besides 100 Jewish mulattoes, constituting in all more than one-third of the white population of the Colony [of Surinam]."[755]

---

[749]*MCAJ3*, p. 1409.

[750]Goodman, p. 16.

[751]*MCAJ1*, p. 156. Concubinage among Jews has deep historical roots. See Louis M. Epstein, "The Institution of Concubinage Among the Jews," *American Academy for Jewish Research, Proceedings*, vol. 6 (1934-1935), pp. 153-88, for a detailed account. Genovese and Foner, eds., *Slavery in the New World* (Englewood Cliffs, New Jersey: Prentice Hall, 1969), p. 39, confirmed the practice: "The Portuguese not only took Negro and mulatto women as mistresses and concubines, but they sometimes spurned their white wives in order to enjoy the favors of duskier beauties."

[752]*MUSJ1*, p. 91.

[753]Sharfman, pp. 187-88.

[754]Korn, "Jews and Negro Slavery," p. 201.

[755]P. A. Hilfman, "Further Notes on the Jews in Surinam," *PAJHS*, vol. 16 (1907), p. 12; Wiernik, p. 49. Herbert S. Klein, *African Slavery in Latin America and the Caribbean* (New York: Oxford University Press, 1986), p. 133: "There even developed a small free mulatto Jewish community which in 1759 formed their own synagogue. But both white and mulatto Jews declined at the end of the 18th century, and by 1791 they were an insignificant element in the society." John Gabriel Stedman, p. x, "The population in [Surinam] included a relatively large

It is hardly possible that any of these 100 could have been products of a Black African male slave and a Jewess.

In Jamaica, the rape of captive Black women reached epidemic proportions. There developed a large free "colored" population, all of whom "were deprived of almost all civil rights."[756] The concubinage system was considered the "norm" in Jamaican society, and Black women "were universally maintained by white men of all ranks and conditions as kept mistresses." Even as late as 1843, an observer could find no improvement: "No one who has ever visited Jamaica will attempt to speak with pleasure on the morals and domestic relations of the country."[757]

Jean Laffite, the Jewish pirate operating in the Caribbean, bred Black women for sexual purposes. Rabbi Sharfman in *Jews on the Frontier*:

> Most desired were the females from French Senegal. They were priced even higher than prized males. These possessed fine figures with silky black hair that flowed to their waists and knees. French and Spanish plantation owners in Santo Domingo, by selective breeding, had produced an exotic type they called "Les Sirenes." These, whom Southerners called "Serpent Women," had remarkably exquisite facial features, lithe bodies, small hands and feet. These above all were sought as mistresses....Laffite maintained a number of tantalizing "Serpent Women" at Grand Isle, across Barataria Pass from Grand Terre. He turned Grand Isle into an island of pleasure—saloons for drinking and gambling and bordellos lavishly outfitted. "Les Sirenes" were among as many as two hundred alluring females of all nations. These beauties offered guests a combination of Laffite's Lucullan delights and orgies of the renowned New Orleans Swamp.[758]

Dr. Feingold assumes that "Such mulatto progeny could not have fared too well in the Jewish community which shared fully in the prohibition against miscegenation."[759] But in New Orleans:

> Crescent City Jews blended into their environment to become morally and religiously adrift. Samuel Kohn['s]..."housekeeper" Delphine Blanchard Marchegay arrived as a slave from Santo Domingo, served him well by day and by night....Since

number of unmarried male persons, who took concubines out of the slave group; married men also lived with slave girls as concubines." See also Hartog, *Curaçao*, p. 173.

[756]Hurwitz and Hurwitz, pp. 45-46.

[757]Hurwitz and Hurwitz, p. 46.

[758]Sharfman, p. 153. See Hartog, *Curaçao*, pp. 175-76, for other evidence of breeding.

[759]Feingold, *Zion*, p. 61. Liebman, *The Jews in New Spain*, p. 260: Diego Nunez Pacheco "sired a daughter born to a mulatto, Catalina, who was a slave of Catalina Enriquez in Veracruz."

> interracial cohabitation was illegal though quite common, "housekeeper" was actually a euphemism for "concubine." Some of the most prominent New Orleanians preferred to mate with their "housekeepers" rather than legally marry according to civil if not religious law.[760]

Among these men was the Jew Daniel Warburg. Warburg of New Orleans had two "mulatto" sons named "Eugene" and "Daniel" as products of the rape of a Cuban Black woman named "Marie Rose."[761] Dr. Bertram Korn has speculated that Samuel Myers may have purchased an African woman named "Alice" as a concubine "in view of his first wife's death just four months before. The relevant dates are as follows: Sarah Judah Myers died on Oct. 12, 1795; Myers bought Alice on Jan. 4, 1796; Myers married Judith Hays on Sept. 27, 1796; he sold Alice on Oct. 2, 1797."[762] Rabbi Sharfman acknowledges the social/racial hierarchy:

> The full-blooded Negro slave had no social status. When a white man cohabited with a black slave, their mulatto offspring was elevated on the social ladder. The offspring of a white and a mulatto was a quadroon (one-fourth Negro blood), and offspring of a white and a quadroon was an octaroon (one-eighth Negro blood) — the more white blood the higher the rung on the social ladder. Wealthy whites were therefore especially desirous to take octaroon or quadroon girls as mistresses. Under Louisiana law, they could never live as man and wife, nor could they cohabit. Nonetheless "Quadroon Balls" were openly and publicly held in New Orleans.[763]

"By far the greatest profits from mulatto or quadroon girls was derived from their sale to brothels," writes Sean O'Callaghan in his study of international prostitution. "White men preferred them to their white sisters in the profession, who were mainly 'white trash,' ignorant, unkempt and ugly. Many of the quadroon girls, on the other hand, were very beautiful, and did their best to please their customers. The hope in the breast of every quadroon prostitute was that one of her clients might set her up in an apartment as his mistress."[764] As legal slavery came to a close, Black women remained as the sexually exploited product of

---

[760]Sharfman, pp. 186, 187: "One of the better known of these meeting places was the Washington Ballroom operated by Simon Sacerdote (Latin for 'priest'), his surname originally Kohn (Hebrew for 'priest')."

[761]Korn, *Jews of New Orleans*, p. 181.

[762]Korn, "Jews and Negro Slavery," p. 188.

[763]Sharfman, p. 187.

[764]Sean O'Callaghan, *Damaged Baggage: The White Slave Trade and Narcotics Traffic in America* (London: Robert Hale, 1969), p. 160.

Jewish brothel owners. Jews soon thereafter moved into and, in fact, dominated the international "white slave trade," marketing their own and other Caucasian women to the highest bidders.[765]

There are actually only five instances in which documentary evidence indicates cohabitation of Jews with Black women,[766] says Rabbi Korn, and they are indeed "only the tip of the iceberg." Undocumented are the Jewish Indian traders "consorting with red women and begetting children by them,"[767] and the intensely sexual plantation life as described by Freyre and others. It is certain that with the buying and selling of Black women, Jews raped and exploited them with abandon.[768]

---

[765]Edward J. Bristow, *Prostitution and Prejudice* (New York: Schocken Books, 1983), p. 1; Peter Y. Medding, ed., *Studies in Contemporary Jewry, II* (Bloomington, Indiana: University Press, 1986), p. 310.

[766]Korn, "Jews and Negro Slavery," p. 202.

[767]*MEAJ2*, p. 320. See also Jack Benjamin Goldmann, *A History of Pioneer Jews in California, 1849 - 1870* (thesis, University of California, 1939), p. 51, for brief reference to Nathan Tuck, who came to Los Angeles from Cleveland in 1853 and "soon married a full-blooded squaw."

[768]Gilberto Freyre, a Brazilian scholar, describes the plantation owners of this New World period in his book *The Masters and the Slaves: A Study in the Development of Brazilian Civilisation.* There were no penalties for such behavior; in fact, it was not even considered rape—it was *recreation* in the *leisure time* sense. Current criminal statistics that chart the frequency of rape do not account for the pervasive brutal assault on Black women in American history. The irrefutable proof is in the collective face of the current Black population, which retains little of their original and bountiful pigmentation.

Slavery in Jewish Law

> *"Both biblical and rabbinic law permitted Jews to own slaves in all ages wherever slavery was in general practice....[L]iving in a society where slavery was an established institution, the Jews could hardly be expected to eliminate it."*[769]

The guardians of the holy laws of Judaism have never prohibited slavery or prevented all of its associated crimes and abuses. Black Africans were made brutally aware of this fact as their relationship with Jews developed. According to Jewish law, a Jew who buys an adult "heathen" male slave must have him circumcised. If the slave refuses after a year of attempts, the Jew must sell the slave to a "heathen." In order to keep an uncircumcised slave, the slave must agree to obey the seven commandments of the descendants of Noah.[770] New World Jews, however, made no attempt to convert their slaves to Judaism.[771]

In addition to slavery, Jewish law permitted the exploitation and oppression of the Gentile. For example, according to Rabbi Ishmael, paraphrased by Rabbi Henry Cohen in his book *Justice, Justice:*

> [A] Jew was legally bound to restore a lost article he had found only if its owner were Jewish, but not if the article had belonged to a Gentile. Other kinds of talmudic "discrimination" against the non-Jew included: He could not serve as an agent for a Jew in a legal transaction; he could not buy cattle from a Jew; he could be charged an exorbitant price (termed: ona'ah or over-reaching),

---

[769]Cohen, *Justice,* p. 49. There are 613 *mitzvot* or commandments included in the Jewish holy book, *The Torah.* Numbers 232-235 permit and regulate slavery. In Anita Libman Lebeson's *Jewish Pioneers in America: 1492-1848* (New York: Behrman's Jewish Book House, 1938), p. 202, she states: "Their religion did not prevent Jews from owning slaves. They were known to have imported slaves in 1661. In 1720, a Jew exchanged merchandise for slaves he had brought in his own ship from Guinea." Brenner, p. 226: "Every Jew knows that Hebrews were slaves in Egypt. That never stopped Aaron Lopez or Judah P. Benjamin or Simon Baruch from owning Blacks." See herein, the chapter entitled "Jews of the Black Holocaust."

[770]Reznikoff and Engelman, pp. 77-78; Sharfman, p. 190.

[771]*MCAJ2,* p. 963. There are records of "Jewish mulattoes" (discussed previously), the offspring of the rape of Black slave women by Jewish men, who set up a Jewish community. They were, however, shunned by the white Jewish community.

> while a Jew could not be so charged....The early mishnaic law forbidding Jews to sell cattle to non-Jews was considered no longer binding, since such a ruling would, under new conditions, entail an economic loss for the Jew....For example, in the Sefer Chasidim, a book of rules written by a Rav Judah for the pietists of the twelfth century, a Jew, who was commanded to desecrate the Sabbath to save the life of a fellow-Jew, was prohibited from committing even a minor violation of the Sabbath to save the life of a Gentile![772]

Jewish slave-dealing in the American frontier appeared to be in direct conflict with Old Testament doctrine,[773] but it is also the misinterpretation of the Old Testament that offered the holy justification for oppression on purely racial grounds. It suggested that "Ham was smitten in his skin" and that Noah told Ham that his "seed will be ugly and dark skinned."[774] It was this interpretation of the scripture that the New World Jews chose to embrace. Even though slavery—more accurately described as an apprenticeship system—was Biblically permitted, the brutality of the system practiced by the European upon the African was unprecedented. Dr. Feingold has found that Biblical slavery

> was of a precapitalist variety and had virtually no commerce connected with it. Unlike the situation in the plantation South, it did not shape the pastoral economy of ancient Israel which in any case found little use for masses of slaves. Rather than being considered an animated tool, as he was in the South, the slave in ancient Israel was merely a member of society in dependent status. He was entitled to the full protection of the laws of the community.[775]

Philip Birnbaum stated plainly in his work *A Book of Jewish Concepts* that there is no evidence that slave markets ever existed in Israel. "Kidnapping a man or selling him as a slave was a capital offense. A fugitive slave law, that once permitted in America the act of tracking runaway slaves by bloodhounds, would have been unthinkable in ancient Israel, where the relationship between master and slave was often cordial."[776] In fact, to the rabbis, the stealing of a human being was so heinous a crime that they interpreted "Thou shalt not steal" in the Ten Commandments as referring to that crime in particular.[777]

---

[772]Cohen, *Justice*, pp. 50-51; Horowitz, pp. 235-36.

[773]Cohen, *Justice*, p. 49.

[774]Feingold, *Zion*, p. 86.

[775]Feingold, *Zion*, p. 87.

[776]Birnbaum, p. 453; S. D. Goitein, *Jewish Letters of Medieval Traders*, p. 13; Seminario, p. 24.

[777]Horowitz, p. 196.

The slave, as defined in scripture, sometimes inherited the property of his master and was sometimes admitted into the family as a son-in-law.[778] According to a statement in the Talmud, the rabbinical interpretation of the law of God, the Hebrew slave was to be regarded as his master's equal:

- "You should not eat white bread, and he black bread; you should not drink old wine, and he new wine; you should not sleep on a featherbed, and he on straw. Hence, it has been declared that whoever acquires a Hebrew slave acquires a master."
- "A son or pupil may, but a Hebrew slave may not wash his master's feet or help him put on his shoes..."
- "Though the Torah permits us to impose hard work on a Canaanite (non-Jewish) slave, piety and wisdom command us to be kind and just." "Freed slaves were considered proselytes, converts to Judaism, in every respect."[779]
- "'Mercy is the mark of piety,' says the Shulchan Aruch, quoting the language of far earlier authorities, 'and no man may load his slave with a grievous yoke. No non-Jewish slave may be oppressed; he must receive a portion from every dainty that his master eats; he must be degraded neither by word nor act; he must not be bullied nor scornfully entreated; but must be addressed gently, and his reply heard with courtesy.'"[780]

There is no evidence yet uncovered that would suggest that Jews who colonized the West adhered to these principles of Jewish law with regard to the Black African. Even the Jewish laws that governed the treatment of the beasts of the field,[781] when applied to the African, were violated in every respect:

- It was prohibited to slaughter an animal and its mother on the same day. And if "the paternity was definitely known or could be easily ascertained" the father could not be slaughtered on that day.
- It was prohibited to take a mother bird from her young while she was sitting on them.
- "It is forbidden to tie the legs of cattle, wild beasts or fowl merely to cause them suffering."
- "If horses are pulling a wagon and they come to a bad spot or to a high mountain and they cannot go on without help, one is bound to help even an alien in order to avoid pain to living things; lest the alien driver should beat them excessively to make them pull beyond their strength."
- "Not only was cruelty forbidden, but positive acts of kindness were commanded."

---

[778]Birnbaum, p. 453.
[779]Birnbaum, p. 453.
[780]Abrahams, p. 101.
[781]Horowitz, pp. 111, 113, 117, 118-19.

- If an animal falls into a body of water on the sabbath, one may bring cushions and bolsters and put them under it to help it get a footing so as to get out and to bring food to the animal in order to keep it alive.
- "One should provide food for his animal, says the Talmud, even before sitting down to one's own meal. Some even held that one was not permitted to buy animals if he was not able to support them."

The practice of Judaism did, at times, include the assistance of the Black slaves. In seventeenth-century Mexico, the Jews had a curious religious ritual: "A Negro was dressed in a red suit and went through the streets playing a tambourine. This was the signal to congregate for a special community meeting or for prayer."[782]

The brutality of the slave system, with the participation of the Jewish people, shows that whatever humane guidance Jewish law provided had never established itself as custom among the Jews in the New World.

Blue Laws

The religious laws that reflected the superstitions of America's founders may have had more to do with Blacks and Jews than with the propagation of any religious order. The Blue Laws seem, in at least some cases, to be legislative reactions to illicit commerce between Black slaves and Jews during Sundays, when some slaves of Christians had a day off and Jewish businesses were open. The slaves were permitted to congregate in the commercial districts where Jews invited their business. A frequent accusation leveled against the Jewish businessmen was that they encouraged the slaves to steal goods from their plantation masters for sale to the Jews, who would then resell the item back to the planter.[783] "It is doubtful," wrote Myron Berman, "that religious concerns alone

---

[782]Liebman, *The Jews in New Spain*, p. 254.

[783]Frederick Law Olmsted, *A Journey in The Seaboard Slave States [1856]* (New York: G.P. Putman's Sons, 1904), p. 69, refers to the practice, as does Arkin, *AJEH*, p. 94. Abrahams, pp. 107-8, refers to a sixteenth-century code-book, which still largely regulates Jewish life: "It is forbidden to purchase stolen goods, for such an act is a great iniquity. It encourages crimes and causes dishonesty. If there were no receiver there would be no thief....Any article concerning which there is even a presumption that it is stolen, must not be purchased. Sheep from a shepherd, household goods from servants, must not be accepted, for the probability is that the property belongs to their masters."

motivated the passage of the Sunday blue laws." Richmond's city fathers

> disclaimed any intention of legislating religious belief but some favored the adoption of the Sunday blue laws to prevent a disturbance of the peace. The fear of large congregations of slaves and of the encouragement given to possible larceny motivated Richmond's mayor to observe in 1806 concerning the stores open on Sunday. "These shops afford to the slaves of the city, an opportunity on Sunday, of disposing of the plunder of the week; and also holds out an invitation to country negroes to bring to town on that day, what they can plunder from their master and mistresses which they can safely dispose in these shops."[784]

In Charleston, South Carolina, a grand jury issued a statement condemning Jews for opening their shops and selling goods on Sunday, thus profaning the Lord's Day. What seemed to worry these Christians, wrote Dr. Marcus, "was not so much the violation of the closing law but the fact that Jews were employing their black slaves as clerks."[785] One incident illustrates the brutality of the slave system: "Jewish apprehensions soared at Charleston in 1773 when a Sephardic Jew was convicted of receiving stolen money from a slave. The Negro was executed, and the Jew was flogged, fined heavily, and pelted with rotten eggs as he was locked in the pillory."[786] These Black–Jewish transactions were the subject of concern even in the Caribbean, where laws were established to discourage the practice. In late seventeenth-century Jamaica, Jews were accused of "inciting the slaves to rob their masters so that the Jewish merchants could buy stolen goods." In 1694, an act was passed, pointing specifically to Jews as primary participants in this trade, entitled *An Act against Jews ingrossing Commodities imported in the Leeward Islands, and trading with the Slaves belonging to the Inhabitants of the same.*[787]In mid-seventeenth-century Brazil, the Jews were charged by Inquisitional authorities with leaving their stores open, letting

[784]Bermon, p. 158; *MUSJ1*, p. 520. A similar charge was made against the Jews in Barbados, prompting a legislative response. See George Fortunatus Judah, "The Jews' Tribute in Jamaica," *PAJHS*, vol. 18 (1909), pp. 170-71.

[785]The Sunday closing law was defended as a police measure, not as a religious necessity. See Reznikoff and Engelman, p. 112; "The Sunday Law and the Jews," *Judaism*, vol. 20, no. 4 (1971), p. 491. Jews protested these laws and in one of these cases, Commonwealth *v.* Wolf, a Pennsylvania case decided in 1817, Wolf contended that Biblical law required that he work six days. The court rejected this argument by pointing out that because of numerous Jewish holidays which fell on weekdays, Jews were often permitted to work less than six days.

[786]*MCAJ3*, p. 799.

[787]Goodman, pp. 9-10; Friedenwald, p. 100.

their slaves work, and sending their children to school on Sundays. As a result, the elders of the Jewish community appeared before the Supreme Council and promised that they would henceforth close their stores and refrain from making their slaves work on Sundays.[788] Here, as with the Inquisition, the charges exhibit more concern over the contact with the slaves than with the practice of "Judaism." Once again, the use or misuse of the Black slaves seemed to be an underlying theme of this "religious legislation." Even as religious liberty became a favorite campaign theme, these kinds of targeted acts persisted. The very year that James Madison and his associates secured the passage of Thomas Jefferson's Bill for Establishing Religious Freedom, this same Madison sponsored a Sunday closing law under the guise of punishing "Disturbers of Religious Worship and Sabbath Breakers."[789]

Jews, Blacks, and the Law

> *He who is escaped from his master unto thee shall dwell with thee...thou shalt not oppress him.*[790]

Much like the Nazis at the concentration camps of Auschwitz, Treblinka or Buchenwald, Jews served as constables, jailers and sheriffs, part of whose duties were to issue warrants against and track down Black freedom-seekers. They assiduously enforced the slave codes designed to safeguard against the possibility of rebellion.[791] Once the Black runaways were apprehended, many

---

[788]Wiznitzer, *Jews in Colonial Brazil*, pp. 100-101.

[789]*MUSJ1*, p. 520.

[790]Cohen, *Justice*, p. 49.

[791]Feingold, *Zion*, p. 62. Feldstein, p. 96: "...Jews engaged in the domestic slave trade, bought and hired slaves to be used on their farms, and treated their chattels in the same manner as their Christian neighbors. One wonders if Benjamin Davis, who in 1838 placed an ad in the Columbus (Georgia) *Enquirer* offering for sale 'sixty likely Virginia negroes' was reminded of the similar plight of his own people who were enslaved by the Egyptian Pharaohs." Korn, "Jews and Negro Slavery," p. 190: "From testifying against Negroes in court, to apprehending a runaway slave, to inflicting punishment upon a convicted Negro, these Jews were thoroughly a part of their society." For one example see Korn, *Jews of New Orleans*, p. 171.

Jews issued punishment as well. Lashing and branding were part and parcel of the Jewish slave-making regime and were liberally employed. As Stanley Feldstein put it in his book *The Land That I Show You*, "Jews also engaged in the dehumanization process—the making a thing of a human being."

In Philip Birnbaum's *A Book of Jewish Concepts*, he provides the framework for slaveholding within the Jewish tradition:

> When a man strikes his male or female slave with a rod so hard that the slave dies under his hand, he shall be severely punished (Exodus 21:20). Rest on the Sabbath and the privilege of participating in the religious life of the family circle were not to be denied by an Israelite owner. Fugitive slaves were given asylum, and were not to be surrendered to their owners. The slave went free, if the master destroyed his eye or tooth. Freed slaves had the status of proselytes in every respect.[792]

This, of course, had nothing to do with the New World Jewish tradition of brutal subjugation of the Black African by any means necessary.[793] Mordecai Shetfall of Georgia oversaw his district as the constable, whose official occupation was to enforce the slave

---

[792]Birnbaum, p. 452.

[793]Kohler, "Settlement of the West," pp. 34-35, reports that the treatment of Blacks was improved by a most unlikely source. Louis XV was then on the French throne, and in March 1724, he resurrected and put into effect the old edict of Louis XIII, expelling the Jews and improving the lot of the Black slaves. These edicts were known as the *Code Noir* or Black Codes, here described by Kohler:

> The articles of the edict, treating on slavery, add interest to the instrument. Louis XV was not in favor of slavery. The Spaniards had introduced the negro from Africa and were selling him to the French settlers on three years' time. It was found, as an official report has it, that "one negro could do the work of four white men in the new country." On this ground, and on the argument that by converting the negroes to Christianity he would be doing the Lord a great service, after much persuasion, Louis XV finally consented to servitude in the colonies and recognized it in this edict. Up to that time there had been no restrictions thrown upon the slave owner, and even the rack had been introduced as punishment and other barbarities practiced. Though some of his measures seem at this day to have been harsh, the edict worked a great improvement in the treatment of slaves. First of all the requirement was that all slaves must be educated in the rites of the Catholic church and be baptized. The edict also prohibited rites other than Catholic; labor on church holidays and Sunday; inter-marriage of whites and blacks, concubinage, marriage of slaves except on consent of owners, and forbade owners to force marriage. Slaves were interdicted from carrying arms, and masters from poorly feeding, or torturing, or mutilating slaves. It specified that the condition of the mother – be she free woman or slave – should decide the free or slave state of the child. It required masters to bury slaves in holy ground, and bury them at night if not baptized. For run-away slaves it provided that masters cut off one ear for the first offense, brand and hamstring for second, and inflict death for the third.

Another article of this very same edict ordered the expulsion of all Jews from French colonial territories. Of the 300 Jews estimated to be in the Mississippi valley at the time, it was claimed that all were driven out and returned with the British after the fall of Quebec. But Harry Simonhoff, *Under Strange Skies* (New York: Philosophical Library, 1953), p. 268, wrote that "Evidently Jews did not take this 'Black Code' too seriously."

codes; Moses Levy was Charleston's most successful detective; Moses N. Cardozo was a plantation owner and jailer of Richmond's Powhatan Courthouse; J. S. Cohen was city marshal of Mobile in 1841, where he supervised the sale of Africans who were impounded through the bankruptcy of their captor. Jews advertised for "nee'r do well" runaway slaves and offered rewards in the local newspapers. In the Mobile *Daily Adviser and Chronicle*, Cohen offered ten Blacks for immediate cash, including "a first rate mantua maker, and several good cooks, washers and ironers," made available through bankruptcy.[794]

In Charleston, the following Jews[795] were officially responsible for the apprehension and punishment of African Black people who wanted freedom more than slavery:

---

[794]Korn, "Jews and Negro Slavery," p. 190. A *mantua* is a woman's gown.

[795]Korn, "Jews and Negro Slavery," p. 190. Jewish peddlers travelling throughout the countryside frequently encountered fleeing Black slaves, and some apparently saw the commercial potential. Frederick Law Olmsted, the 19th century traveller and park designer, described an incident in 1822 where an unnamed Jew, returning from a peddling excursion, observed a man's footprints in the banks of a stream. He perceived them to be those of a runaway African slave for which he presumed there to be a reward (*A Journey Through Texas* [Austin: University of Texas Press, 1978], pp. 330-31):

> The trail soon left the road, and he followed it cautiously, to an overgrown gully, where he found his fugitive, overcome with sleep. The poor wretch yielded without a word, only begging for something to eat. But the Jew was too wise to keep the muscular advantage he had over a negro faint and sick with hunger, and tying his hands behind him, drove him before him to the road. The prostration of the fellow was so extreme, however, that the task of driving him in to settlements would be tedious; and, after a short distance, the Jew mounted his feeble prize behind him, joining his ankles firmly together by a handkerchief, beneath the mule's belly. For a time, all went well – the Jew vigilant and merry, revolver in hand. But there came the Nueces [River] to cross; the mule would drink; the bridle goes loose; the spark of liberty suddenly kindles, and headlong, over the mule's head, goes Jew, revolver, and all, floundering under the feet of the frightened animal. Up the bank goes a stampede of mule and crouching runaway, securely tied together, the bags of dollars and provision not even left to the dripping speculator. The Jew is the only one of the party that has ever again been heard from.

It should be noted that some Jewish writers have claimed that Olmsted displayed bias against Jews in some of his observations of American culture. They cite examples such as below (*ibid*, p. 329):

> There are a few Jew-Germans in Texas, and, in Texas, the Jews, as everywhere else, speculate in everything – in popular sympathies, prejudices, and bigotries, in politics, in slavery. Some of them own slaves, others sell them on commission, and others have captured and returned fugitives. Judging by several anecdotes I heard of them, they do not appear to have made as much by it as by most of their operations.

Lewis Gomez	1802	Turnkey of Jail
Elisha Elizer	1802	Deputy Sheriff
Moses Solomon	1802	Constable
Nathan Hart	1821	Constable
Solomon Moses	1822	Constable
Samuel Hyams	1822	Keeper of Jail
Mark Marks	1822	Deputy Sheriff
Solomon Moses, Jr.	1822	Deputy Sheriff
Moses Levy	?	Detective

Jews in the towns and cities appear to have been content to abide by the excessively cruel punishments meted out to Blacks who were caught by "the law." These are a few examples of the testimony of Jews against Blacks taken from the Richmond court records.

- In 1798, "Polly, a mulatto slave," was tried for taking a loaf of white sugar worth two dollars from Benjamin Solomon's home, and was sentenced to five lashes on her bare back and ordered to be branded on her left hand.
- A "free" Black man was accused of stealing two silver watches valued at $32 from Myer Angel in 1832, and was sentenced to five years imprisonment, six months of which was to be spent in solitary confinement.
- Benjamin Wolfe's store was broken into in 1797, and $500 in merchandise was claimed stolen. Three slaves were tried for the crime, but only one was convicted. He was sentenced to be hanged.

These examples from Korn's article on Jews and slavery precludes the unofficial cruelty meted out at the whim of the slave master. Jews, acting both as private citizens and as public officials, brought their Black slaves to court in legal actions where the outcome was all but guaranteed.[796] The most extreme case on record was the murder of a slave by Joseph Cohen of Lynchburg, Virginia, in 1819, a crime for which he was indicted, tried and convicted—"although of course the penalty for the murder of a Negro by a white was much less severe than the penalty for a trivial misdemeanor committed by a Negro."[797]

[796]Korn, "Jews and Negro Slavery," pp. 189-90. See Schappes, p. 597, for evidence of the manumission societies acting in behalf of Blacks mistreated by Jewish masters.

[797]Korn, "Jews and Negro Slavery," pp. 189-90; Feingold, *Zion*, p. 62.

Jews and the Great Nat Turner

The great Nat Turner's 1831 revolt against the slave masters of Virginia was put down with the help of at least two Jewish militiamen. Dr. Henry Myers and Sam Mordecai were mobilized to repel the revolt, and Jewish writer Emma Mordecai described the lynching of Turner's men:

> If the conduct of the Blacks was outrageous, that of the whites was most barbarous towards many of them who were arrested; for instance, they burned off the foot of a negro whom they had taken upon suspicion and found out that he was innocent. They had one of the ears cut off of another (who had to be sure been guilty of murdering his master in a most barbarous manner) and after rubbing the wound with sand, they tied him to a horse, had the horse mounted and rode, and then turned loose into the woods. Certainly, this negro deserved to be punished in the most severe manner warranted by civilized society, but this Indian-like treatment casts a great reflection on the troops by whom it was authorized.[798]

Jews assisted in crushing other slave uprisings, especially, as in New York, when the rebellious slaves belonged to them. Lebeson writes:

> When in 1741, it was discovered that New York Negroes had conspired against the white population, and had planned to burn the city, a large number of Negroes were arrested and transported or condemned to death. Some of these slaves belonged to Jewish owners. Cuffee, belonging to Lewis Gomez, had planned to burn his masters house. Machado's house was burned by his Negroes. A few were acquitted, among them servants belonging to Judah Hays and Samuel Myers Cohen.[799]

---

[798]Bermon, p. 167.

[799]Lebeson, *Jewish Pioneers in America*, pp. 202-3.

Black Slave Owners and Jews

Rabbi Bertram Korn makes reference in his essay "Jews and Negro Slavery in the Old South" to the likelihood that some Blacks with Jewish names may have received them "either from Jewish owners or Jewish fathers."[800] The list Dr. Korn uses is drawn from Carter G. Woodson's *Free Negro Owners of Slaves*. He finds eight of "these Negroes" with Jewish names who own a total of 39 slaves. Like their fathers and owners, brought up in the Jewish tradition, they apparently felt quite comfortable participating in such Jewish family traditions as slave holding.[801]

It should also be stated that many of these purchases of Blacks by Blacks cited by Woodson were for the purpose of freeing the slave from bondage, as in the case of Meir Josephson, who stated in a letter that "A free nigger wants to court her [Josephson's slave] and to buy her from me."[802]

---

[800] Korn, "Jews and Negro Slavery," p. 201.
[801] Korn, "Jews and Negro Slavery," p. 201 note 83; Feingold, *Zion*, p. 61.
[802] *JRM/Docs*, pp. 359-60; Rosenbloom, pp. 77-78.

Jews of the Black Holocaust

> *"What is hateful to you, do not do to your neighbor."*[803]

All of the following "Chosen People" are confirmed to have participated in the Black African slave trade. According to *their* own literature, each one is a prominent historical figure and most are highly regarded and respected by Jews themselves. Even the most prominent of Jewish Americans never voiced any reservation whatsoever about this practice.[804] Writes Rabbi Bertram W. Korn, "it is realistic to conclude that any Jew who could afford to own slaves [and needed them] would do so."[805] In fact, "Jews participated in every aspect and process of the exploitation of the defenseless blacks."[806] Here, in alphabetical order, is an annotated list of just a *few* of those.

---

[803]Babylonian Talmud, Shabbat 8; Albert Vorspan, *Great Jewish Debates and Dilemmas* (New York: University of American Hebrew Congregations, 1980), p. 3.

[804]Bertram Wallace Korn, *The Early Jews of New Orleans* (Waltham, Massachusetts: American Jewish Historical Society, 1969), pp. 201, 319.

[805]Bertram W. Korn, "Jews and Negro Slavery in the Old South, 1789-1865," in *Karp, JEA3*, p. 184.

[806]Korn, "Jews and Negro Slavery," p. 189.

Mordecai Abraham of Virginia placed this advertisement in the *Virginia Gazette or American Advertiser* on January 12, 1783:

> THIRTY DOLLARS REWARD
>
> RAN AWAY from the subscriber, in King William County, on Saturday the 5th instant, a large Mulatto Man named OSBOURN, late the property of William Fitzhugh, Esq; he is about five feet ten inches or six feet high, almost white enough to pass for a white-man, he has grey, or rather white eyes, which appear very weak, with a kind of blemish in the right one, occasioned by his shutting it when a person addresses him. His dress is uncertain, though I believe he went off with a blue suit of cloathes, and likewise a coarse upper jacket, and soldier's under jacket and breeches of buff, with buttons marked USA. I am informed he lately lived in Mecklenburg, under Col. Mounford, near Taylor's Ferry on Roanoke. Whoever will apprehend the said fellow and secure him, so that I may get him again, shall receive TWENTY DOLLARS reward, or if delivered to me in King William County, the above reward. All masters of vessels and other persons are hereby forbid to carry the said fellow out of the state, or to employ him in any craft whatever.[807]

Joseph Abrahams, a Jewish businessman of Charleston, South Carolina, placed this advertisement in the *Gazette of the State of South-Carolina* on August 25, 1779:

> RUN away from the subscriber, a young negro fellow, named Brutus, this country born, about 18 years old; he had on when he went away, an Osnabrugs shirt, brown fustian breeches and Osnabrugs coatee with red cuffs and collar; he was formerly the property of the estate of Mr. Stanyarne: He has a mother in Dorchester. Whoever takes up said negro and delivers him to me, shall receive a reward of one hundred Dollars, and charges paid.[808]

Simon Abrahams of Richmond, Virginia, was fined $3.33 in 1834, "for allowing a hired slave to go at large contrary to the Act of Assembly."[809]

---

[807]Lathan A. Windley, comp., *Runaway Slave Advertisements: A Documentary History from the 1730s to 1790*, 4 volumes (Westport, Connecticut: Greenwood Press, 1983), vol. 1, p. 346 and vol. 3, p. 559. Abraham may have owned a slave he called "Brutus." See also Barnett A. Elzas, *Jews of South Carolina* (Philadelphia: J.P. Lippincott Co., 1905), p. 103.

[808]Windley, vol. 3, p. 371.

[809]Herbert T. Ezekiel and Gaston Lichtenstein, *History of Jews of Richmond 1769-1917* (Richmond, 1917), p. 91.

David De Acosta, described as "a gentleman of Spain," owned a forty-one-acre plantation on Barbados in 1680 "worked by sixty-one black slaves...seven white servants and three bought ones (felons), apparently all Christians." His will dated February 1684-1685 dispenses his Africans:

> The two former to enjoy and possess my plantations negroes, &c. each paying half of debts owing, and sharing proceeds and expenses each year. No negroes or anything to be sold, & should Daniel B. Henriques sell anything he will forfeit his inheritance in favour of my wife, & the sale shall be deemed null & void.[810]

Jacob Adler. In 1863, he and his partner, Herman Cone of Jonesboro, Tennessee, purchased two African men they named "Friendly" and "Joe William," for $4,500.[811]

Charity Adolphus (d. 1773). When her house was burned down, "she escaped with her life, only by being carried out of the burning house by her faithful Negro slave, Darby."[812]

J. Adolfus of Jamaica despised the Black man so much that in 1812, when a Jamaican assemblyman advocated the equality of the "free colored," Adolfus and two other Jews, L. Spyers and J. Da Silva, physically attacked him at his home.[813]

Samuel Alexander was one of the founders of Congregation *Beth Shalome* of Richmond in 1791. He and his brother **Solomon** (listed herein) were also slave owners who are considered to be humanitarians because they arranged to have their hostages "manumitted." They reserved the right, however, to keep them as indentured servants.[814]

---

[810]Wilfred S. Samuel, *A Review of The Jewish Colonists in Barbados in the Year 1680* (London: Purnell & Sons, 1936), pp. 13, 92.

[811]Korn, "Jews and Negro Slavery," p. 193.

[812]David De Sola Pool, *Portraits Etched in Stone: Early Jewish Settlers, 1682-1831* (New York: Columbia University Press, 1952), p. 478.

[813]Samuel J. Hurwitz and Edith Hurwitz, "The New World Sets an Example for the Old: The Jews of Jamaica and Political Rights, 1661-1831," *AJHQ*, vol. 55 (1965-66), p. 46.

[814]Edwin Wolf and Maxwell Whiteman, *The History of the Jews of Philadelphia* (Philadelphia: Jewish Publication Society of America, 1957), p. 191; Joseph R. Rosenbloom, *A Biographical Dictionary of Early American Jews: Colonial Times through 1800* (Lexington: University of Kentucky Press 1960), p. 7.

Solomon Alexander was a one-time acting mayor of Richmond, Virginia, who enslaved a Black woman named "Esther."[815]

Jorge de Almeida owned and operated a silver mine in Taxco. In about 1585, at the height of the Inquisition, he and a friend are alleged to have "strangled a Negress who had called a friend of their's a Jew."[816]

Myer Angel, of Richmond, Virginia, accused "Walter Quarles, colored," of stealing two silver watches of the value of $40 each in 1832. Quarles received a sentence of five years confinement in the public jail and penitentiary house "on low and coarse diet, one-tenth part of the time to be spent in solitary confinement."[817]

Juan De Araujo (or **Arauxo**) "had been a minor slave trader who had travelled widely through the Spanish Indies, between Puebla, Vera Cruz, Cartagena, Havana and, possibly even, Angola."[818]

Issack Asher of New York was charged with "selling an unhealthy Negro" in 1863.[819]

Solomon Audler of New Orleans was listed as the "owner" of four Africans in the census of 1830.[820]

Maurice Barnett of Baton Rouge, Louisiana, "owned" at least eleven African citizens. He was such a prolific slave dealer and auctioneer that twentieth-century picture postcards of the "Old Slave Block" depict his office at 40 St. Louis Street. He was one of the closest associates of the slave-breeding and slave-smuggling Jewish pirate Jean Laffite. Below is an example of the Black–Jewish relationship of the time:

---

[815]Myron Bermon, *Richmond's Jewry 1769-1976: Shabbat in Shockoe* (Charlottesville, Virginia: Jewish Community Federation of Richmond; University Press of Virginia, 1979), p. 163.

[816]Seymour B. Liebman, *The Jews in New Spain: Faith, Flame, and the Inquisition* (Coral Gables, Florida: University of Miami Press, 1970), p. 173.

[817]Ezekiel and Lichtenstein, p. 91.

[818]Daniel M. Swetschinski, "Conflict and Opportunity in 'Europe's Other Sea': The Adventure of Caribbean Jewish Settlement," *AJHQ*, vol. 72 (1982-83), p. 214.

[819]Earl A. Grollman, "Dictionary of American Jewish Biography in the 17th Century," *AJA*, vol. 3 (1950), p. 4.

[820]Korn, *Jews of New Orleans*, p. 167.

SALES AT AUCTION

By M. Barnett, Sen., Auctioneer Cornelius Hurst vs. His Creditors — Syndic Sale.

On Monday, the 2d Dec, 1839, at 12 o'clock noon, at the City Exchange, St. Louis street between Chartres and Royal streets, by order of Alexander Grant, syndic of said estate, and by virtue of an order issued by the honorable the first judicial district court of the state of Louisiana, dated the 26th day of October, 1839, the following slave surrendered to his creditors by said insolent, viz:

DICK, about 28 years of age, a well disposed man.
OSBORN, about 26 years of age, mulatto; a good carriage driver and waiter, active and handy at anything he is put to.
LUCINDA, about 22 years of age, Osborn's wife, very intelligent, good cook, washer and ironer. Lucinda's Children:
COMMODORE, about 6 years of age,
JOSEPHINE, about 4 years of age,
HENRY, about 2 years of age,
OSBORN, about 1 year of age.
NED, about 19 years of age, accustomed to work in a brick yard.
LOUIS, about 17 years of age, accustomed to work in a brick yard.
MINGO, about 28 years of age, brick moulder, stout able bodied man.
WINNEY, about 37 years of age, worked in a brick yard.
PRISCILLA, about 24 years of age, stout able bodied woman.
SERENA, about 21 years of age, a good off-bearer in a brick yard, and her child.
MATILDA, about 25 years of age, cook, washer and ironer, and her three children, viz:
THOMAS, about 10 years of age.
TONEY, about 6 years of age.
WILLIAM, an infant.
SALLY, about 22 years of age, mild and well disposed woman; cook, washer and ironer.
JULIANNA, about 21 years of age, and her child; accustomed to work in a brick yard.
MARY, about 23 years of age, also accustomed to work in a brick yard.
JACOB, about 25 years of age, stout man, accustomed to work in a brick yard.

> Terms – Six months credit for all but Jacob, who will be sold at six and twelve months, for notes drawn and endorsed to the satisfaction of the syndic, who reserves to himself the privilege of refusing names as endorsers, until he is satisfied therewith, without assigning any cause therefor; the notes to bear an interest at the rate of ten per cent per annum (if not met at maturity) until paid – without this however giving the parties thereto the right of prolonging the payment after due. The purchasers will be allowed forty-eight hours after a notification from the notary that the titles are completed, to arrange the settlements, and if not effected within the period, the slave or slaves to be resold at auction, for cash, on the account and risk of the said original purchasers, without delay or public notice; and said parties held responsible for said loss that may accrue thereon, with all expenses, costs, & c.. Acts of sale before Edward Barnett, notary public, at the expense of the purchasers. The slaves not to be delivered until the terms of sale are complied with.[821]

Jacob Barrett of Columbia, South Carolina, and a later resident of Charleston, was a merchant who once traded twenty Black human beings "...at very large profits, keeping for his own use Armistead Booker, a good-looking, active carriage driver and barber, who attended to his horses and in the store, and Aunt Nanny, a first rate cook." He was the cousin of one of the era's biggest Jewish slave dealers named Jacob Ottolengui.[822]

Hester Barsimon's family of five had "only one black attendant."[823]

Abraham Baruch (d. 1701) household at Bridgetown consisted of three Jews and three slaves. In 1685, "one of his negroes was concerned in a native rebellion and was executed by the Island authorities, whereupon a sympathetic legislature voted his master a sum of £17 10s. O*d*. by way of compensation!"[824]

Dr. Simon Baruch (b. 1840) was a surgeon and captain in the Confederate Army and, according to Harry Simonhoff, "He went through the terrors of Reconstruction, and as a secret member of the *original* Ku Klux Klan he wore at night its long white flowing robes emblazoned with a scarlet cross."[825]

---

[821] Korn, *Jews of New Orleans*, pp. 107-9: "Auction," p. 208, plate 12; I. Harold Sharfman, *Jews on the Frontier* (Chicago: Henry Regnery Company, 1977), p. 151.

[822] Korn, "Jews and Negro Slavery," p. 194.

[823] Samuel, p. 43.

[824] Samuel, p. 33.

[825] Harry Simonhoff, *Jewish Participants in the Civil War* (New York: Arco Publishing, 1963), p. 225. See the discussion of, and justification for, Baruch's Klan

Rebecca Baruh lived alone with one slave in seventeenth-century Barbados.[826]

Daniel Becker was convicted of illegal liquor sales to Black slaves in South Carolina in 1836.[827]

Diego Nunes Belmonte and other Portuguese Jewish merchants were partners in the slave trade between Luanda and the West Indies.[828]

Don Manuel Belmonte of Amsterdam was, according to Drs. Emmanuel,

> a Spanish-Jewish nobleman of culture and refinement, high in royal and religious circles, [who] had no qualms about carrying on the slave trade. He and a gentile associate conducted it on an extensive scale, of course with Company participation.[829]

He formed an association with Jean Cooymans, ex-sheriff of Amsterdam, to ship slaves in large quantities to Curaçao.[830]

Judah Phillip Benjamin (1811-1884) was born in the British West Indies and brought up in Charleston. He was a rabid pro-slavery senator from Louisiana in the Civil War era who led the call for secession of the southern states from the Union in order to maintain the profits of free slave labor. He owned a plantation called *Bellachasse* and used 140 African slaves in its operation.[831]

---

membership in Margaret L. Coit, *Mr. Baruch* (Boston: Houghton Mifflin Company, 1957), pp. 1-32.

[826]Samuel, p. 43.

[827]Korn, "Jews and Negro Slavery," p. 191.

[828]Ernst van den Boogaart and Pieter C. Emmer, "The Dutch Participation in the Atlantic Slave Trade, 1596-1650," *The Uncommon Market*, eds., Henry A. Gemery and Jan S. Hogendorn (New York: Academic Press, 1975), p. 354.

[829]*Emmanuel HJNA*, p. 75. Belmonte was count palatine and representative of her Catholic Majesty before the High States General of Holland. Also known as Isaac Nunez, he, jointly with Moseh Curiel, represented the Jews before the Dutch government. In 1658, Belmonte was ambassador-extraordinary of Holland to England; see note no. 55. See also Swetschinski, p. 236.

[830]*Emmanuel HJNA*, p. 76; Johannes Menne Postma, *The Dutch in the Atlantic Slave Trade: 1600-1815* (Cambridge: Cambridge University Press, 1990), pp. 38-46.

[831]Harry Simonhoff, *Jewish Notables in America: 1776-1865* (New York: Greenberg Publisher, 1956), p. 370; *EJ*, vol. 4, pp. 529-30; Henry L. Feingold, *Zion in America: The Jewish Experience from Colonial Times to the Present* (New York: Twayne Publishing, 1974), p. 60; Simon Wolf, *The American Jew as Patriot, Soldier and Citizen* (Philadelphia: Levytype Company, 1895), p. 114. Whereas most references have confirmed 140 slaves, Feingold has reported the number to be as high as 740.

Benjamin's slavery-supporting career started when he argued the "Creole Case" representing an insurance company with an interest in a slave cargo.[832] He was described by Richard S. Tedlow as:

> The most important American-Jewish diplomat before Henry Kissinger, the most eminent lawyer before Brandeis, the leading figure in martial affairs before Hyman Rickover, the greatest American-Jewish orator, and the most influential Jew ever to take a seat in the United States Senate...[833]

But it was Benjamin the senator who supported the institution of slavery, contending that it was more humane to whip and brand the Black man than to imprison or transport him. Ohio's abolitionist senator, Benjamin F. Wade, denounced Benjamin as "[a]n Israelite with the principles of an Egyptian."[834]

Benjamin was born on Saint Croix in the West Indies on August 6, 1811. His father was a drifter who has been described as "that rara avis, an unsuccessful Jew," and his mother was of Portuguese descent. The family moved to Charleston, South Carolina, in 1822, and soon thereafter Benjamin attracted the attention of a wealthy Jew who sent him first to private school and then to Yale. He left without taking a degree, he claimed, because of financial straits, but there is considerable evidence that he was dismissed for disciplinary reasons.[835]

He was elected to the federal senate in 1852, where he neglected no opportunity to defend the institution of slavery. Confederate president Jefferson Davis chose Benjamin to be attorney general, but in nine months transferred him to the most important of the Confederacy's cabinet positions, Secretary of War. It soon became common knowledge that, next to Davis, Benjamin was the most influential man in the rebel government.[836]

---

[832]Max J. Kohler, "Judah P. Benjamin: Statesman and Jurist," *PAJHS*, vol. 12 (1904), pp. 70-71, 73.

[833]Richard S. Tedlow, "Judah P. Benjamin," in *Turn to the South: Essays on Southern Jewry*, by Nathan M. Kaganoff and Melvin I. Urofsky (Charlottesville: American Jewish Historical Society, University Press of Virginia, 1979), p. 44.

[834]Sharfman, pp. 189-90.

[835]Tedlow, p. 44.

[836]Tedlow, p. 45.

Bertram W. Korn pointed out the irony that Benjamin's honors were "in some measure dependent upon the sufferings of the very Negro slaves he [and others] bought and sold with such equanimity....Few politicians are as consistent in anything as Benjamin was in support of the 'peculiar institution.' Indeed, there was truth in Ben Wade's clever slur..."[837] Even Jewish historian Morris U. Schappes has written that "history has found Benjamin guilty and his cause evil."[838]

Dr. Joseph Bensadon of Louisiana was devoted to the Confederacy and the preservation of the slave system. He served as a surgeon in the Civil War.[839]

Francisco Lopez Blandon (b. 1618) was imprisoned by the Inquisitional authorities for practicing Judaism from 1643 - 1649, but "had a Negro slave who brought him food and messages from the outside. This slave also eavesdropped in the office of the head jailer and reported all that he heard."[840]

Abraham Block of Richmond, Virginia, owned a Black woman named "Matilda Drew." In 1826, she was before the court on the charge of "carrying off two pounds of cheese, valued at 25 cents; 2 $^{1}/_{2}$ pounds of sugar, valued at 30 cents; one bottle of cordial, $1; and five tumblers, 37 cents, the goods and chattels of Grace Marx. She was found not guilty. For defending her from the charge of stealing $1.62 of property the court allowed her counsel $10."[841]

Simon Bonane (or Bonave). In 1699, he was aboard the pirate ship *Adventure of London* and according to Max J. Kohler: "In August, 1720, we read that 'Simon the Jew don't expect his [slave] ship from Guinea before the fall (sic).'"[842]

Jacob Bortz, of Georgia, who is believed to be Jewish, placed this ad in the Savannah *Georgia Gazette*, July 27, 1774:

---

[837]Tedlow, p. 49.

[838]Morris U. Schappes, *Documentary History of the Jews in the United States* (New York: Citadel Press, 1950), p. 429.

[839]*EJ*, vol. 11, p. 519; Leo Shpall, *The Jews in Louisiana* (New Orleans: Steeg Printing & Publishing Co., 1956), pp. 12-13.

[840]Liebman, *The Jews in New Spain*, p. 262.

[841]Ezekiel and Lichtenstein, p. 90.

[842]Max J. Kohler, "Phases of Jewish Life in New York Before 1800," *PAJHS*, vol. 2 (1894), p. 84.

> RUN AWAY from the subscriber in Goshen, A NEGROE FELLOW, named FRANK, has some white spots on his legs occasioned by burns, had on a jacket and trowsers of blue negro cloth, and took also with him check trowsers. A reward of 10 s. will be given on delivering him to JACOB BORTZ.[843]

Stephen Boyd was a Dutch Jew of Baltimore who employed a Jewish indentured servant named **Wolf Samuels** to oversee his 94 Black slaves on his 4,000-acre plantation.[844]

Domingo da Costa Brandau and his wife, **Maria Henriques Brandau**, lived in Amsterdam in 1639 and had an *engenho* or plantation in "Arrerippi" (possibly Recife, Brazil), where African citizens were forced to labor without pay.[845]

David Perayra Brandon of Charleston, South Carolina, left instructions to his relatives in his 1838 will:

> I recommend my faithful Servant and friend Juellit or Julien free Negro, to my dear Rachel [his stepdaughter] and W.C. Lambert [her husband] my friend and request them to take him under their protection to treat him as well as they would do me and to give him Such portion of my Cloths as they will think useful to him and never forsake him being the best friend I ever had.[846]

Saul Brown (a.k.a. **Pardo**, d. 1702) was a Newport merchant involved in the business of African human import/export. In 1695, he was the first *hazan* (minister) of the *Shearith Israel* congregation.[847]

Benjamin Bueno was a slave owner in seventeenth-century Barbados.[848]

---

[843]Windley, vol. 4, p. 54.

[844]Joseph L. Blau and Salo W. Baron, eds., *The Jews of the United States, 1790-1840*, 3 volumes (New York: Columbia University Press, 1963), vol. 3, p. 799. The authors claim that Boyd "was neither a Jew nor a Dutchman," but Samuels describes him as such in a letter to his family in 1819. See also Isaac M. Fein, *The Making of An American Jewish Community* (Philadelphia: Jewish Publication Society of America, 1971), p. 11.

[845]Isaac Emmanuel, "Seventeenth Century Brazilian Jewry: A Critical Review," *AJA*, vol. 14 (1962), p. 37.

[846]Korn, "Jews and Negro Slavery," pp. 186-87.

[847]*EJ*, vol. 4, p. 1411; Schappes, p. 569; Rosenbloom, p. 14.

[848]Samuel, pp. 14, 90.

Joseph Bueno (a.k.a. **Joseph Bueno de Mesquita**, d. 1708) purchased a cemetery for Jews in New York in 1682 with the proceeds from his Caribbean Black flesh shipping business. He left to his wife, Rachell, "all the slaves now belonging to me..."[849]

Rachael Burgos had a household of six persons and a couple of slaves in Bridgetown in 1680.[850]

Mathias Bush, a member of Lancaster, Pennsylvania, Jewish merchantry, placed this advertisement in the summer of 1765:

> Was committed to my Custody, on the 22d Day of this instant July, the following Negroes, viz. a Negroe Man, named Jack, alias Tobias, and a Negroe Woman, Named Jane, Wife to the said Jack, alias Tobias, and her two Children, a Boy, five years old, or thereabouts, and a girl about four years old. The man is about thirty-four years of age, and the woman about thirty; they have sundry good clothes with them; they say they belong to James Campbell, in Conegocheague, near Fort Loudoun. The said Campbell is hereby desired to come and pay the charges, and take them away, or they will be sold for the same, in four weeks from this day, by me.
>
> Matthias Buch, Goaler.[851]

Samuel De Campos, a Barbados merchant in 1720, left to his daughter Sarah "a negro boy by name Scipio and a mulatto girl named Debora." To his daughter Hester, "a negro boy by name Joe and a girl by name Jenny."[852]

Moses Nunez Cardozo (1755-1818) was a Virginia plantation owner and jailer at Richmond's Powhatan Courthouse whose responsibilities included the apprehension and punishment of runaway Africans.[853]

Luis Rodriguez Carvajal became a businessman in New Spain and "perhaps shared with the rest of his family in the lucre of the slave trade."[854]

---

[849]Leo Hershkowitz, *Wills of Early New York Jews (1704-1799)* (New York: American Jewish Historical Society, 1967), p. 15; Rosenbloom, p. 14.

[850]Samuel, p. 40.

[851]Billy G. Smith and Richard Wojtowicz, *Blacks Who Stole Themselves: Advertisements for Runaways in the Philadelphia Gazette 1728-1790* (Philadelphia: University of Pennsylvania Press, 1989), p. 78.

[852]Samuel, p. 59.

[853]Korn, "Jews and Negro Slavery," p. 190; *EJ*, vol. 5, p. 162; Rosenbloom, p. 18.

[854]Martin A. Cohen, "The Religion of Luis Rodriguez Carvajal," *AJA*, vol. 20 (April 1968), p. 39.

Raquel Nunez Carvallo left to her son Jacob Frois "one negro woman by name Abbah." To son Isaac Frois "now of the Island of Jamaica...one negro girle by name Rose."[855]

The Cohens of Baltimore were considered the "outstanding" Jewish family in the city and one of the leading Jewish families in the country. They were important bankers, industrialists, and professionals and one of them, **Mendes I. Cohen**, "belonged to the Peace Party, a camouflaged secessionist group, and was a delegate to the State Peace Convention, another, Edward, went one step further and served in the Confederate army."[856]

Abraham Cohen (c. 1739-1800) of the Georgetown district of South Carolina was a Postmaster General and a slave-dealing auctioneer who held 21 African citizens against their will.[857]

Abraham Cohen financed **David Nassi** (also **Nassy**), who was a founder of the Jewish colony at Cayenne, now French Guiana, in 1662. Nassi used countless captive Black people to establish the colony.[858]

Barnett A. Cohen (1770-1839) and his wife **Bella**, of the Barnwell District of Kings Creek, South Carolina, held more than twenty Africans as slaves.[859]

Benjamin Cohen was a well-known Savannah, Georgia, merchant who believed:

> that the institution of slavery [is]...the only human institution that would elevate the Negro from barbarism and develop the small amount of intellect with which he is endowed.[860]

---

[855]Samuel, p. 84.

[856]Isaac M. Fein, "Baltimore Jews during the Civil War," in Karp, *JEA3*, p. 348.

[857]Korn, "Jews and Negro Slavery," pp. 181, 195; Ira Rosenwaike, "An Estimate and Analysis of the Jewish Population of the United States in 1790," *PAJHS*, vol. 50 (1960), p. 47; Rosenbloom, p. 20.

[858]Emmanuel, "Seventeenth Century Brazilian Jewry, p. 62.

[859]Ira Rosenwaike, "The Jewish Population of the United States as Estimated from the Census of 1820," *Karp, JEA2*, p. 18; Korn, "Jews and Negro Slavery," p. 180; Rosenbloom, p. 21.

[860]Feingold, *Zion*, p. 89. See the entry for **Solomon Cohen**, who is also reported to have expressed a similar sentiment.

J. S. Cohen was the Mobile, Alabama, City Marshal in 1841. His responsibilities included tracking and apprehending freedom-seeking Africans.[861]

Jacob Cohen's plantation worked 294 slaves at no pay.[862]

Jacob I. Cohen (c. 1744-1823) was born in Germany and operated as a slave maker in the South and then in Philadelphia. He was a land speculator who hired Daniel Boone, the "noted Kentucky pioneer and Indian fighter," to survey his land. Cohen was president of his Jewish Congregation *Mikveh Israel* from 1810-1811. He and his partner, Isaiah Isaacs of Richmond, enslaved Blacks they named "Tom," "Dick," "Spencer," "Mieshack," "Fanny," "Eliza," and their children of an unspecified number. As a demonstration of good will, Cohen ordered that they be freed *after* his death and each given $25.[863]

Joseph Cohen of Lynchburg, Virginia, was convicted in 1819 of the murder of one of the many African citizens he enslaved. As a policy, the penalty received was comparable to that of a trivial misdemeanor of today.[864]

Levi Cohen is named on a Georgia receipt for slaves.[865]

Mordecai Cohen (c. 1763-1848) was born in Poland and owned a plantation at St. Andrews, South Carolina, where twenty-seven Africans provided the free field labor. He was one of the wealthiest planters in South Carolina and a commissioner of markets in Charleston from 1826 to 1832. When the twenty-three Black house servants are added, the resulting total is fifty, a number sufficient to place him third among Jewish

---

[861]Korn, "Jews and Negro Slavery," p. 190.

[862]Ira Rosenwaike, *On the Edge of Greatness: A Portrait of American Jewry in the Early National Period* (Cincinnati: American Jewish Archives, 1985), p. 69.

[863]*EJ*, vol. 5, p. 662; Schappes, pp. 101, 593; Korn, "Jews and Negro Slavery," pp. 185-88; Rosenwaike, "Jewish Population in 1790," p. 63; Charles Reznikoff and Uriah Z. Engelman, *The Jews of Charleston* (Philadelphia: Jewish Publication Society of America, 1950), p. 77; "Acquisitions," *AJA*, vol. 5 (January 1953), p. 58; Bermon, pp. 163-64; Rosenbloom, p. 24.

[864]*EJ*, vol. 12, p. 1085; Feingold, *Zion*, p. 62; Korn, "Jews and Negro Slavery," p. 189.

[865]"Acquisitions: Material Dealing with the Period of the Civil War," *AJA*, vol. 12 (1960), p. 117.

slave owners in South Carolina.[866] His sons, **Marx** and **David**, owned farms and likewise terrorized and exploited Black people.[867]

Samuel Myers Cohen (c. 1708-1743) was a New York City shopkeeper, elected constable of the Dock Ward and high official (*shohet* and *bodek*) of Congregation *Shearith Israel.* In his will he bequeathed to his wife Rachel "all those negroe Slaves I have which I shall die possessed of." Two of his captives named "Windsor" and "Hereford" were implicated in a failed rebellion known as the "Negro Plot" of 1741, but later released.[868]

Simon Cohen (1781-1836) came to New Orleans from Amsterdam in 1810 and eight years later bought a Black woman and her two-month-old baby. This sale was annulled when it was discovered that the woman had already been mortgaged to someone else. By 1820, Cohen owned a tobacconist's shop, a billiard parlor and held four African people as hostages.[869]

Solomon Cohen (1757-1835) was a distinguished merchant and civic leader of the Georgetown district of South Carolina and held nine African citizens against their will. Cohen expressed his anti-Black sentiment in a letter to his sister-in-law **Emma Mordecai**:

> [I] believe that the institution of slavery was refining and civilizing to the whites – giving them an elevation of sentiment and ease and dignity of manners only attainable in societies under the restraining influence of a privileged class – and at the same time the only human institution that could elevate the Negro from barbarism and develop the small amount of intellect with which he is endowed.

Dr. Korn commented, "Perhaps no more concise and self-deceptive rationalization of slavery was ever written than the observations which were recorded by Solomon Cohen."[870]

---

[866]Rosenwaike, *Edge of Greatness*, pp. 69-70.

[867]Korn, "Jews and Negro Slavery," p. 180; Rosenbloom, p. 25.

[868]Leo Hershkowitz, "Wills of Early New York Jews (1743-1774)," *AJHQ*, vol. 56 (1966), p. 66; Pool, p. 229; *EJ*, vol. 12, p. 993; Lee M. Friedman, "Wills of Early Jewish Settlers in New York," *PAJHS*, vol. 23 (1915), pp. 151-52; Anita Libman Lebeson, *Jewish Pioneers in America: 1492-1848* (New York: Behrman's Jewish Book House, 1938), p. 203; "Acquisitions," *AJA*, vol. 7 (1955), p. 158; Kohler, "New York," p. 84; *MCAJ2*, p. 822; Rosenbloom, p. 26.

[869]Korn, *Jews of New Orleans*, p. 156.

[870]Korn, "Jews and Negro Slavery," p. 182; *EJ*, vol. 16, p. 533; Roberta Strauss Feuerlicht, *The Fate of the Jews: A People Torn Between Israeli Power and Jewish Ethics*

Solomon Cohen possibly from Augusta, Georgia, is named on an 1863 receipt as the seller of two Black African slaves to Bernhard Phillips for $3,000.[871]

Herman Cone and his partner, **Jacob Adler** of Jonesboro, Tennessee, purchased two African Black men in 1863 for $4,000. They named them "Friendly" and "Joe William."[872]

Jacob De Cordova (1808-1868) was a Texas real estate promoter and newspaper editor. He started Jamaica's first daily newspaper, and in 1850 he organized Houston's first Jewish place of worship. In 1858, he "wished it distinctly understood that our feelings and education have always been pro-slavery." He said of Texas in a lecture in Philadelphia in 1858:

> By a wise provision of our state constitution, the institution of slavery has been guaranteed to Texas. Such being the case, Texans are proverbially jealous of this right and will not allow any intermeddling with the subject directly or indirectly.[873]

Jacob Cardozo was a conservative Democrat and in his view slavery was economically and morally justified: "The Negroes were often better off than white wage-slaves; the black bondsmen are morally and intellectually inferior." In regard to the ethical question, he placed the responsibility squarely on God: "The reason the Almighty made the colored black is to prove their inferiority." In his *Reminiscences of Charleston*, he lamented the plight of the poor former slave masters:

> The owner of two hundred to five hundred slaves, with a princely income, has not only to submit to the most degraded employments, but he frequently cannot obtain them. In some instances he has to drive a cart, or attend a retail grocery, while he may have to obey the orders of an ignorant and coarse menial. There is something unnatural in this reverse of position—something revolting to my sense of propriety in this social degradation.[874]

(New York: Times Books, 1983), p. 74; Rosenwaike, "Jewish Population of 1820," p. 18; Rosenbloom, p. 27. See the entry for **Benjamin Cohen** above, who is also reported (Feingold, *Zion*, p. 89) to have expressed a similar sentiment.

[871]"Acquisitions," *AJA*, vol. 2 (January 1950), p. 32.

[872]*EJ*, vol. 5, p. 868; Korn, "Jews and Negro Slavery," p. 193.

[873]*EJ*, vol. 5, p. 1455, and vol. 15, p. 1035; "Trail Blazers of the Trans-Mississippi West," *AJA*, vol. 8 (June 1952), p. 76; Korn, "Jews and Negro Slavery," pp. 210-11.

[874]*MUSJ1*, p. 425; *MEAJ2*, p. 218; Korn, "Jews and Negro Slavery," p. 211.

Emanuel Alvares Correa (1650-1717) was active in the Curaçao slave trade for many years and in 1699 served as an intermediary between the Dutch and Portuguese West Indies companies for the transfer of a shipment of slaves from Africa to Mexico via Curaçao.[875]

Isaac Da Costa (1721-1783) was a merchant and shipping agent of Charleston, South Carolina, and "probably the most outstanding Jew of Charleston before the Revolution." Born in England, he helped to found Congregation *Beth Elohim* in 1749 and was its first *hazzan*. He was also active as a Mason. Da Costa was in partnership with Thomas Farr, Jr.,[876] handling imports and exports of merchandise including African men, women, and children. He was said to be a "large scale" hostage importer, and in 1760 he brought to South Carolina 200 African people as slaves; in 1763 he brought 160 more.[877]

Joseph D'Acosta came to New Amsterdam in 1655. He was a leading merchant in Amsterdam and was a principle shareholder of the slave-dealing Dutch West India Company.[878]

Nemias Daniel, "a Jew," of the Parrish of Christchurch, Barbados, was listed as the owner of 20 acres and twelve "negroes" in 1679.[879]

Aaron Daniels (1776-1862) was a storekeeper in New Orleans who enslaved eight Black people in 1830.[880]

---

[875]*EJ*, vol. 14, p. 1663; *EHJ*, p. 273; S. Broches, *Jews in New England* (New York: Bloch Publishing, 1942), p. 11; "Jews in the Vice-Admiralty Court of Colonial Rhode Island," *PAJHS*, vol. 37 (1940), p. 392; Rosenbloom, p. 28.

[876]Farr advertised on at least three occasions for the return of runaway slaves. Advertisements were placed in the Savannah *Gazette of the State of Georgia*, on February 24, 1785, for the return of "A Negro Fellow named Abram"; in the *Gazette of the State of South-Carolina*, on October 21, 1777, for "a negro man named London, a Bricklayer by trade"; and in the *South-Carolina and American General Gazette* on November 4, 1780, for a "LIKELY mustee woman named ISABELLA" and her two children. In the same ad he sought "a thick clumsy made negro woman, named BETSY, of a very black complexion, full face and flat nose, about 28 years of age." See Windley, vol. 4, p. 123, and vol. 3, pp. 354, 571-72.

[877]Feingold, *Zion*, p. 42; *JRM/Docs*, pp. 272, 353; *EJ*, vol. 5, p. 1220 and vol. 14, p. 1663; *MEAJ2*, p. 322; Rosenbloom, pp. 28-29.

[878]Schappes, p. 567.

[879]Samuel, p. 90.

[880]Korn, *Jews of New Orleans*, p. 316.

Joseph Darmstadt (died c. 1820) was born in Germany and then moved to Richmond, Virginia. In 1800, he founded the *Beth Shalome* Congregation, and he was active in Masonry and owned a Black man named "George." He once accused a "free" Black man named Daniel Clayton of stealing "a bag and lot of beeswax, valued at 50 shillings." This accusation was, of course, a conviction, for which the Black man was sentenced to 39 lashes to his bare back.[881]

Ansley, Benjamin, George, and **Solomon Davis** were reputed to be the largest Jewish slave-dealers. They travelled throughout the South selling gangs of Black men, women, and children, including infants, starting in 1838. Based in Richmond and Petersburg, Virginia, the four brothers "did not hesitate to go at lengths to obtain slaves, advertising their supply throughout the south." This advertisement placed by Ansley Davis was recounted in 1830s testimony against the domestic slave trade:

> The subscriber wishes to purchase one hundred slaves of both sexes, from the age of ten to thirty, for which he is disposed to give much higher prices than have heretofore been given. He will call on those living in adjacent counties, to see any property.[882]

They announced in the Columbus, Georgia, *Enquirer:* "Sixty likely Virginia Negroes – house servants, field hands, blow boys (buglers), cooks, washers, ironers and three first rate seamstresses." The Davises kept their source of supply secret and assured everyone that they would continue to receive slave shipments by every arrival in Columbus.[883]

They were even mentioned in Harriet Beecher Stowe's *A Key to Uncle Tom's Cabin*:

> The Davises, in Petersburg, are the great slave-dealers. They are Jews, who came to that place many years ago as poor peddlars; and, I am informed, are members of a family which has its representatives in Philadelphia, New York, &c. These men are always in the market, giving the highest price for slaves. During the summer and fall they buy them up at low prices, trim, shave and wash them, fatten them so that they may look sleek, and sell

[881]Korn, "Jews and Negro Slavery," p. 190; Ezekiel and Lichtenstein, p. 79; Rosenwaike, "Jewish Population in 1790," p. 63; *EJ*, vol. 5, p. 1307; Rosenbloom, p. 31.

[882]Theodore D. Weld, *Slavery and the Internal Slave Trade in the United States* (New York: Arno, 1969), p. 51.

[883]Sharfman, pp. 146-47.

> them to great profit. It might not be unprofitable to inquire how much Northern capital, and what firms in some of the Northern cities, are connected with this detestable business.[884]

Benjamin owned a "colod woman named Elsey," and the Davises even gave warranties on their slaves, as seen in a receipt for a fifteen-year-old Black girl named "Savry" who was "warranted Sound and Healthy."[885] According to the Bibb County, Georgia, records, Benjamin Davis was the seller, and Elisha Davis the buyer, of sixteen Black Africans (listed below [sic]) for $7000 on April 16, 1852:

Peter Davis (man, dark compliction)
Tom (man, dark compliction)
Charles (man, dark compliction)
Prince (man, dark compliction)
Peter Griffin (man, dark compliction)
Sarah (woman, dark compliction)
Florah (woman, dark compliction)
Milly (woman, dark compliction)
Melvina (woman, yellow compliction)
Francis (woman, yellow compliction)
Lucy (girl, dark compliction)
Fanny (girl, dark compliction)
Henry (boy, dark compliction)
Loi (boy, dark compliction)
Sandy (boy, dark compliction)
Munroe (boy, 6 mos.)[886]

George Davis, Sr., called himself "the Original George Davis" in 1824, in order to differentiate from the others. He acted as the local agent for a New Orleans Jewish slave-dealer named **Levy Jacobs**. He was an auctioneer and property speculator and was prepared to sell:

> Negroes, horses, mules, cows, asses, quadruped and biped, and all other animals in the Catalog of Creation...for cash down and no grumbling. (adv. Oct 15, 1840).

Delinquent tax lists of April 1826 and May 1828 indicate Davis owned and owed: 1826, 7 slaves — $2,500; 1828, 8 slaves — $3,000. He owned 7 slaves according to 1830 census data.[887]

Rachel D'Azevedo of Charleston held Blacks whom she named "Rose," "Flora," "Dinah" and "Maria," and whom she gave to her daughter, Sarah A. Motta. Another Jew, **Abraham Moise**, conspired with them to maintain the Blacks as hostages.[888]

---

[884]Harriet Beecher Stowe, *A Key to Uncle Tom's Cabin* (1853; reprint, Salem, New Hampshire: Ayer Publishing Company, 1987), p. 297.

[885]Korn, "Jews and Negro Slavery," pp. 198-99; *EJ*, vol. 14, p. 1664; *EHJ*, p. 274; Sharfman, p. 147.

[886]African-American Family History Association, *Slave Bills of Sale Project,* vol. 1 (Atlanta, Georgia, 1986), p. 0407.

[887]Bertram Wallace Korn, *The Jews of Mobile, Alabama, 1763-1841* (Cincinnati: Hebrew Union College Press, 1970), pp. 23-24.

[888]Korn, "Jews and Negro Slavery," p. 186; *EJ*, vol. 3, p. 1006; Reznikoff and Engelman, p. 77.

David Dearosto was listed as the owner of 41 acres of St. Thomas, Barbados, with 61 Black slaves, 7 "Hired Servants," and 3 "Bought Servants," in a survey of 1670.[889]

Moses Deazevedo, of Barbados, registered his feeling toward his sons in his will dated October 6, 1715:

> To my son Jacob I remit his debt & since he has been disobedient I give him 1/- for whatever claim he may raise against my estate. To son David Eliahu I remit the considerable sum of money paid out for him as appears in my books & since he has been disobedient I give him 1/- in cash. To son Abraham 10/- & my worn clothes and my white linen....To grandaughter Lebanah Mendes for her & her heirs the gift of a mulatto named Mary & of my Cormanty negress named Esperanto....To son Solomon a negress named Zabelina with her mulatto daughter Bashe & her son Cain & her daughter Maria & all their issue & I confirm the deed of gift of my Madagascar (negress) named Diana for him and his heirs mad 29 June 1715.[890]

Mathias Dellyon of the Parish of St. Peter, Barbados, left to each of his daughters Ester and Deborah "a negro woman."[891]

Isaac Delyon, of Charleston, placed this advertisement in the *South-Carolina and American General Gazette*, on January 19, 1780:

> Five Hundred Dollars Reward
>
> RUN away some time past, from the subscriber, a negro boy, named Harry, about 17 years of age, about 5 feet 7 inches high, round visage, had on when he went away, a Bath coating close bodied coat, leather breeches, green cloth Jacket and breeches; he is a very likely country born fellow, and speaks good English. The above reward will be paid on his being delivered to the Warden of the Work house, or to me in Charlestown; and One Thousand Pounds on conviction of any white person harbouring him. The said fellow formerly belonged to Boone's estate on John's Island, and has been seen by negroes lurking about said plantation.[892]

DePas Family of Martinique held much property and many slaves. The French Minister of Foreign Affairs and War, the Duke of Choiseul, enumerated some of their holdings:

---

[889]Samuel, p. 91.
[890]Samuel, p. 83.
[891]Samuel, p. 60.
[892]Windley, vol. 3, p. 566. May be the same as **Isaac Lyon[s]**. See entry herein.

M. DePas – 3 estates and 280 slaves.
M. DePas, Jr. – 4 estates with one of them having 100 slaves.
Jean DePas – a plantation with 30 slaves.
Michel DePas – ("he is a mulatto and a bastard") one "great estate" with 120 slaves; one estate with 30 slaves.
Others in the family include M. S. J. DePas, Antoine DePas and Lewis DePas.[893]

Abraham Depeza, one of the Barbados Hebrew Nation "being sick & weake in body," wrote his will dated August 11, 1716. He left to his youngest son Isaac on his 21st birthday "a negro girl named Obbah." To his daughter Sarah Depeza, "A negro girl named Peggy." To his wife, Hester Depeza, "my negro woman by name Mary..."[894]

DeWolf Family. From 1790 onward, the slave trade of Rhode Island was chiefly in the hands of the brothers DeWolf,[895] who were considered "the most active slave traders in Bristol."[896] The Jewish historians have not explicitly identified the DeWolfs as members of their "race," though others have traced them to apparently Jewish roots. In James Pope-Hennessy's *Sins of the Fathers: A Study of the Atlantic Slave Traders 1441-1807*, he states the following:

> Miss Abigail married one of her brother's supercargoes, Marc Antoine de Wolfe, a Jew from the French island of Guadeloupe. De Wolf settled down in his wife's home town of Bristol, Rhode Island, and sent several of their eight sons into the slave trade.[897]

The most famous of these, **James DeWolf**, was tried before a Newport grand jury in 1791, and found guilty of murder for having thrown into the sea a Black woman who had contracted small-pox while on board his ship. By the time the verdict was reached he had already left the state; he was later elected to the United States Senate.

---

[893]Lee M. Friedman, *Jewish Pioneers and Patriots* (Philadelphia: Jewish Publication Society of America, 1942), p. 91.

[894]Samuel, p. 58.

[895]James Pope-Hennessy, *Sins of the Fathers: A Study of the Atlantic Slave Traders 1441-1807* (New York: Alfred A. Knopf, 1968), p. 239; Wilfred H. Munro, *The History of Bristol, Rhode Island: The Story of the Mount Hope Lands* (Providence: J. A. & R. A. Reid, 1880), pp. 322-25, 350-52, 370-71.

[896]William G. McLoughlin, *Rhode Island: A History* (New York: W. W. Norton & Company, 1978), p. 107.

[897]McLoughlin, p. 107.

Politically, James and his brother **John DeWolf** embraced the Republican party and Thomas Jefferson. Jefferson appointed James' brother-in-law, Charles Collins, the reputed part-owner of at least two slavers, to the post of tax collector in two of the busiest slaving ports of Bristol and Warren, Rhode Island.[898] Working in collusion with Collins, **George DeWolf** dispatched slaver after slaver on illicit voyages—duty-free.[899] The DeWolfs were not beyond dealing in drugs and are recorded as having invested in hemp, more commonly known as marijuana.[900] James issued these instructions to Jonathon Dennison, the captain of his slaver *Ann,* in July of 1806:

> Your having engaged to go a Voyage to Africa in my ship *Ann,* my instructions are that you proceed with all possible Dispatch direct to Cape Coast, and make Trade at the Place and its Vicinity, and purchase as many good, healthy young slaves as may be in your power to purchase, by bartering away your present Cargo with the Natives; and after compleating your Business in Africa, you will proceed to Mount Video in South America, and there dispose of your slaves, and purchase a return Cargo of Ox Hides and dried beef, and some Tallow and other produce of that Country, such as you may judge will pay a handsome Profit, and after compleating your Business there, you will return home to this Port with all possible Dispatch.
>
> I am sir, Your Friend and Owner, Jas. De Wolf [901]

When the Rhode Island colonial government tried to pass an act which included outlawing the slave trade, John Brown (the founder of Brown University) and John DeWolf, among others, worked to delete that part of the bill. Neither state nor national prohibition could prevent DeWolf—who was still sending slaves to South Carolina—from continuing the trade.[902]

---

[898]Peter T. Coleman, *The Transformation of Rhode Island, 1790-1860* (Providence: Brown University Press, 1969), pp. 55-56.

[899]Peter T. Coleman, p. 57.

[900]Peter T. Coleman, p. 43.

[901]George Francis Dow, *Slave Ships and Slaving* (Salem, Massachusetts: Marine Research Society, 1927), p. 261.

[902]McLoughlin, p. 106. See Peter T. Coleman, pp. 51-52, for a brief description of the legislation. Also, Lorenzo Greene, *The Negro in Colonial New England* (New York: Atheneum, 1974), pp. 30-31 note.

Luis Dias, of Barbados, left to his family equal shares of "all my Estate, horses, Negroes, Gold, Silver, Jewells, Pearles, Goods, Household stuffe [and] at their pleasure...one piece of gold & another of silver as also 2 negroes small or great."[903]

John Drayton advertised on September 9, 1774, for *"an indigo overseer"* to look after about 30 Africans.[904]

Elisha Elizer was the Deputy Sheriff in Charleston, South Carolina, in 1802, whose job it was to punish runaway Black people. This may be the same Elizer (Eleazer) listed as a postmaster general in Greenville in 1784 and as a justice of the peace in 1813 by other sources.[905]

Isaac Elizer (1720-1807) owned the slave ship *Prince George* with **Samuel Moses.** He outfitted slave ships with bondage hardware and rewarded the crews of his profitable ships with African citizens. "He was a merchant-shipper and, like many of his friends and associates, occasionally engaged in the slave traffic." He was called a "notable and respected businessman" and was active in his Newport, Rhode Island, Jewish congregation.[906] Elizer and Moses wrote to their Captain John Peck, to sail to Africa and sell the liquor

> for the most possible [that] can be gotten, and invest the neat proceeds into as many good merchantable young slaves as you can....As soon as your business there is compleated, make the best of your way from thence to the island of New Providence [Bahamas] and there dispose of your slaves for cash, if the markets are not too dull....And also we allow you for your commission, four slaves upon the purchase of one hundred and four, and the privilege of bringing home three slaves, and your mate, one....But further observe, if you dispose of your slaves in Providence [Bahamas], lay out as much of your neat proceeds as will load your vessel in any commodity of that island, that will be for our best advantage, and the remainder of your effects bring home in money.
>
> Isaac Elizer, Samuel Moses [907]

---

[903]Samuel, pp. 78-79.

[904]Elzas, p. 71.

[905]Korn, "Jews and Negro Slavery," p. 190; Rosenbloom, p. 34.

[906]Schappes, p. 38; Feingold, *Zion*, p. 42; quotes are from *JRM/Docs*, pp. 359-61; Feldstein, p. 12; Rosenwaike, "Jewish Population in 1790," p. 48; James A. Rawley, *The Transatlantic Slave Trade, A History* (New York: W. W. Norton & Company, 1981), p. 370.

[907]*MEAJ1*, pp. 127-28; *MUSJ1*, p. 211.

In May of 1769, Elizer ran a newspaper advertisement: "Notice: Reward $5, return of runaway negro woman, Bina, threat of prosecution of harborer."[908]

Marie Emeronthe (d. 1851) was a banker and associate of **Samuel Hermann**. She died owning at least five African hostages.[909]

Daniel Bueno Enriques (b. 1637), also known as **Daniell Boyna**, owned a ten-acre plantation in St. Michael's Parish, Barbados, and "worked it with fourteen negroes and a white overseer."[910]

Solomon Etting (1764-1847), a prominent Maryland Jew, son-in-law of **Barnard Gratz**, and member of Philadelphia's *Mikveh Israel*, held four Black people as slaves in Baltimore. Etting was a merchant in partnership with **Joseph Simon** and founder of the Masonic lodge in Lancaster, Pennsylvania. In 1826, he became the first Jew to serve in public office when he was elected to the Baltimore city council and later became its president. He served on the board of the Maryland State Colonization Society which raised $300,000 in 1831 to send Blacks back to Africa. Less than two percent of the state's Black population showed interest in the project.[911]

Sam Fechheimer owned a large plantation in Rogersville, Kentucky, with many slaves. His niece and nephew, **Alfred** and **Emily Seasongood**, described the setting:

> [There were] log cabins, in which the colored help lived...built side by side some distance from my Uncle Sam's home, and we enjoyed going there and watching the little pickaninnies play and their mammies comb and wash them....In this cabin lived a handsome young darkey who was my uncle's valet, and was quite out of the ordinary; he used to sing and play most divinely. The mammies were called aunts, and I remember one especially, very black and fleshy, but the dearest, most affectionate woman....And my Aunt Delia would often bring some of the

---

[908]Irwin S. Rhodes, *References to Jews in the Newport Mercury, 1758-1786* (Cincinnati: American Jewish Archives, 1961), p. 11.

[909]Korn, *Jews of New Orleans*, pp. 110, 301.

[910]Samuel, p. 15.

[911]Rosenwaike, "Jewish Population of 1820," p. 18; Isaac M. Fein, *The Making of an American Jewish Community*, pp. 17-18; Wolf and Whiteman, p. 192; David Brener, *The Jews of Lancaster, Pennsylvania: A Story With Two Beginnings* (Lancaster: Congregation Shaarai Shomayim, 1979), p. 8; Rosenwaike, "Jewish Population in 1790," p. 48; *EJ*, vol. 6, p. 951; *MUSJ1*, p. 586; Rosenbloom, p. 36.

> black babies into the house and comb, wash, and dress them by the open grate fire.[912]

And of the impact of emancipation, Emily wrote:

> The slaves were all set free, and there were trying times, as most of the Southern people were so dependent upon them and were unable to do things for themselves. Many young ladies were helpless....Many slaves who had kind masters refused to be set free and wanted to remain with them.[913]

Jacob Fonseca (d. c. 1729) was a New York merchant who belonged to the Congregation *Shearith Israel.* He held African citizens named "Sarah," "Faba," "Betty," and "Gnatto." Upon his death, he willed them to his wife Rebecca, "to have and to hold for proper use and behoof for and during her life." The congregation paid his widow "for the hire of two Negros."[914]

Jacob Franco owned "Negroes" named "Clarina," "Anthony," "Johnny," and "Jack." He bequeathed to his son Moses "the house wherein I now dwell with the yard together with all my negroes goods chattels wares merchandises Jewells money."[915]

David Franks (1720-1793) was a member of one of colonial America's most active merchant families. David Franks dealt regularly with **Joseph Simon**, the **Harts**, the **Gratz** brothers and the Newport gang of slave dealers. He traded heavily with the Indians but supplied weapons to the English against them in Pontiac's War of 1761-1764. In 1761, he, with a group of Philadelphia merchants, signed a petition against a tax on slave imports. On October 6, 1778, Franks petitioned New York authorities "for a pass to New York for himself, daughter, man-servant, and two maid-servants," but was granted one only for himself, daughter, and one maid-servant, "provided she be an indented servant." Franks' daughter, Mrs. Hamilton, owned a slave named "Sam," who was offered for sale at £45 cash or £50 trust.

Franks was eventually run out of Pennsylvania and exiled to England for his alleged shady dealings with his uncle **Nathan Levy** and brother **Moses**. He managed to find refuge

---

[912]*JRM/Memoirs 3,* p. 68; Sharfman, p. 152; Jacob Rader Marcus, *The American Jewish Woman: A Documentary History* (New York: KTAV Publishing House, 1981), pp. 174-75.

[913]Marcus, *The American Jewish Woman,* p. 176.

[914]Leo Hershkowitz, "Wills of Early New York Jews (1704-1740)," *AJHQ,* vol. 55 (1966), p. 351; Rosenbloom, p. 37.

[915]Samuel, pp. 85-86.

in New York and Philadelphia, where he died in a yellow fever epidemic.[916]

Henry Benjamin Franks (d. 1758) of Trenton, New Jersey, identified a "Negro Wench Prisula" as his property in his 1758 will.[917]

Isaac Franks (1759-1822) of Philadelphia "sold slaves from time to time" and owned a young female child named "Bell." The son of **Moses Benjamin Franks** and an active Mason, he once rented his Germantown house to George Washington. He was a land speculator and held many prominent positions, including lieutenant colonel, quartermaster, and foragemaster in the military, and justice of the peace and chief clerk of the Pennsylvania Supreme Court in the judiciary.

Franks advertised in the *Pennsylvania Journal* on January 4, 1786: "For Sale. A young likely Negro-Wench. About eight years old; has twenty years to serve. Enquire of Isaac Franks."[918]

Jacob Franks (1688-1769) was a New York City merchant born in London who arrived in the city in 1708 and married the daughter of **Moses Levy**. He and his sons, **Moses**, **David**, and **Naphtali**, all worked with Levy and **Nathan Simpson** in the liquor business and the Black flesh trade. According to Jacob Rader Marcus,

> Jacob Franks was engaged in general commerce and shipping. On occasion he imported household servants, Negro slaves. Over a period of years, from 1717 to 1743, he brought twelve, mostly from the West Indies.

Franks was a founder and president of the *Shearith Israel* Congregation and enslaved at least one African named "Cato." He was said to have gotten his share of business during Queen Anne's War (1702-13), which gave Britain a monopoly on the

---

[916]Schappes, p. 575; *EJ*, vol. 7, p. 106, and vol. 14, p. 1663; *EHJ*, p. 273; Wolf and Whiteman, p. 47; Irving J. Sloan, ed., *The Jews in America: 1621-1970* (New York: Oceana Publications, 1971), p. 2; Edward D. Coleman, "Jewish Merchants," p. 285; Rosenbloom, pp. 38-39; Herbert Friedenwald, "Jews Mentioned in the Journal of the Continental Congress," *Karp, JEA1*, p. 328; Morris Jastrow, Jr., "Notes on the Jews of Philadelphia, from Published Annals," *PAJHS*, vol. 1 (1902), p. 57.

[917]Lebeson, p. 203; Samuel Oppenheim, "The Will of Henry Benjamin Franks, December 13, 1758, and Inventory of his Estate," *PAJHS*, vol. 25 (1917), p. 27; Rosenbloom, p. 39.

[918]Wolf and Whiteman, p. 192; *EJ*, vol. 16, pp. 359-60; Herbert Friedenwald, "Some Newspaper Advertisements of the Eighteenth Century," *PAJHS*, vol. 6 (1897), p. 56; *Karp, JEA1*, p. 236; Tina Levitan, *The Firsts of American Jewish History* (Brooklyn: Charuth Press, 1957), pp. 74-75; Rosenbloom, p. 39.

slave trade. He was the major supplier of British weaponry and the most prominent shipper of New York.[919]

The Frazons—Moses, Joseph, and **Samuel**—of Charlestown, Massachusetts, held Black slaves and "shipped almost anything from a piece of iron to a biscuit." Samuel Frazon "was once haled into a Boston court for beating a colored servant...not his own (sic)." He held at least one African as his own.[920] In 1702, the Frazons owned their own boat, the *Joseph and Rachel* (130 tons), and participated in the West Indies trade.

It was once reported that Samuel Frazon had "fallen into the hands of Indians, who had released him when he paid a ransom of '18 pistols.' The same report says that the Indians, however, refused to release his colored servant. This is possibly the same negro, Cypia, mentioned in a trial of Thomas Cooper against the Frazons, where it is shown that Frazon paid over forty two pounds for him in 1704."[921]

Minger Goldsmith. According to the 1840 census, Goldsmith claimed to be the owner of "1 female slave w/4 children."[922]

The Gomez Family. The patriarch **Lewis** (or Luis, 1660-1740) was born in Madrid and then moved to New York in 1703. He raised five sons: **Mordecai** (1688-1750), **Daniel** (1695-1780), **David** (1697-1769), and **Isaac** (1705-1770). They variously traded with Indians, distilled liquor and retailed in New York. Another son, **Benjamin** (1711-1772), was a New York liquor dealer and pawn broker who enslaved Blacks named "Ishmael" and "Jenney," whom he bequeathed to his daughter "and her heirs forever." Other Black Africans he owned were "John St. John" and a "Mustie wench Kattey," whom he likely raped until his death. She was "to be made free from the Yoke of Slavery, as a reward for her fidelity"—after his daughter's death.[923]

---

[919]*MEAJ1*, pp. 58, 64-65, and *MEAJ2*, p. 293; *EJ*, vol. 7, p. 107; *MCAJ2*, p. 771; Rosenbloom, p. 39.

[920]*MEAJ1*, p. 105; *MCAJ2*, p. 771; Rosenbloom, p. 41.

[921]Broches, p. 14. It is more plausible that "Cypia" would have considered himself *rescued* by the Indians rather than kidnapped as a hostage as this passage suggests.

[922]Korn, *The Jews of Mobile, Alabama*, p. 51.

[923]Hershkowitz, "Wills (1743-1774)," p. 113; Friedman, "Wills," p. 156. Friedman reports that the Gomez will says "trustee" rather than "mustie" in reference to the African woman named "Kattey."

All of the Gomezes were considered to be the original founders and trustees of *Shearith Israel* congregation and purchased land that was to be a Jewish cemetery. The elder Gomez was its president in 1730. Benjamin served as *parnass* four times and the others all served at least once. All were notorious slave merchants and yet highly respected in the Jewish community.[924] They owned the Black man named "Cuffee," who, in the "Negro Plot" of 1741, allegedly planned to burn down the house of his captors.[925]

References to the Gomezes' exploitation of Black Africans are many. Lewis and Mordecai were the agents of the owners of the ship *Greyhound* that imported "merchandise and negroes" into New York in late 1722.[926] On May 4, 1752, the following advertisement was inserted in the *Gazette*: "To be sold by Abraham Pereira Mendes, a Parcel of likely young Negroes, Pimento, old Copper, Coffee etc....If any one person has a mind to purchase any of the goods mentioned, they may enquire of Mr. Daniel Gomez."[927] Also in 1752, Gomez had a number of slaves making wax and tallow candles.[928]

Lewis, in his will, left his wife "with as many of my slaves as are necessary to attend her." Mordecai bequeathed to his sons **Isaac** and **Jacob** "Equally to be divided between Them my Two Negro Men Slaves called Levant and Frank and my Negro Woman Slave called Perla..."; and to his wife, sons and daughters, "To be divided between Them my Negro Woman Slave called Hannah my Negro Boy Slave called Pascual and my Negro girl Slave called Celia."[929]

Lewis Gomez. In 1802, Lewis Gomez was the turnkey of the jail of Charleston, South Carolina. Part of his responsibilities included the tracking and punishment of freedom-seeking Blacks.[930]

---

[924] *EJ*, vol. 7, pp. 768-69; Hershkowitz, "Wills (1743-1774)," pp. 62-63; Pool, pp. 223, 236, 238, 477; Lebeson, p. 203; *MEAJ1*, pp. 64-65; Rosenbloom, p. 45.

[925] Lebeson, pp. 202-3.

[926] Kohler, "New York," p. 81.

[927] Miriam K. Freund, *Jewish Merchants in Colonial America* (New York: Behrman's Jewish Book House, 1939), p. 35.

[928] *MCAJ2*, p. 695.

[929] Hershkowitz, "Wills (1743-1774)," pp. 80-81. Compare with Friedman, "Wills," p. 154, who states that Mordecai's sons will divide three "negro slaves," and that they, with his wife and daughters Hester and Rachel, will inherit "certain negro slaves." See also Pool, p. 236; Lebeson, p. 203; Rosenbloom, p. 45.

[930] Korn, "Jews and Negro Slavery," p. 190.

Rebekah Gomez (d. 1801) held a Black hostage as a slave.[931]

Rev. Bernhard Henry Gotthelf, a Jew of Louisville, Kentucky, was a chaplain in the Confederate Army.[932]

Edward Gottschalk operated a commission brokerage firm that was one of the largest in the city. He bought and sold African citizens and personally held at least nine Blacks as hostage/servants. He owned 65,000 acres of land in Texas with an undetermined, though likely massive, number of African people.[933]

Abraham Gradis (c. 1699-1780) and the Gradis family owned at least 26 ships that they used to ship African hostages to such French colonies as San Domingo, where they "owned extensive territory." Abraham accepted payment for his debts in Black human beings. He devised a strategy, though never implemented, for the development of Louisiana.[934] Rabbi Bertram Korn wrote that, if acted upon, his vision "might have stimulated the kind of growth the colony sorely required." The plan?

> The key to the problem, as Gradis saw it, was the massive importation of Negro slaves into the colony under the auspices of the King — he suggested ten thousand slaves over a period of five years. These slaves would be utilized primarily for the clearing and cultivation of land.[935]

The Gratz Family of Philadelphia was one of the most distinguished families in Jewish American history. They were the leaders of that city in the colonial period, speculators in western Indian lands, and they were closely connected with the **Hays**es, **Moses**es and **Franks**es in their slave shipping businesses. **Michael Gratz** (1740-1811) "owned personal slaves," one of whom operated his kosher kitchen. Michael's wife **Miriam** wrote a letter to him dated June 2, 1777, that reminded: "Donte forget your promess in getting me a Grego

---

[931]Pool, p. 286.

[932]Bertram W. Korn, "Jewish Chaplains During the Civil War," *AJA*, vol. 1 (June 1948), p. 6.

[933]Korn, *Jews of New Orleans*, pp. 174-75.

[934]*EJ*, vol. 7, p. 844; *EHJ*, p. 273; *JRM/Docs*, pp. 326-29; Wolf, p. 482.

[935]Korn, *Jews of New Orleans*, p. 5.

[Negro] boy or girl if to be had, as servants is very [scarce]." The Gratzes funded western expeditions for the purpose of taking Indian lives and land for their personal wealth. More evidence of their slavemaking mentality is in a casual letter written to Michael Gratz by a relative named Josephson (see **Meir Josephson** entry).[936]

Moseh Hamis, a Jew residing in Barbados, prepared a will in Portuguese dated March 26, 1684, in which he and his wife directed that 2,000 lbs. of sugar be paid after their death to his son Simon Massiah "to help in the purchase of a young negress."

> It is my last wish that our slaves named Consciencia continue serving my said Wife all her life, & if she serves her faithfully, & with love and due respect as if I had been living, I desire & direct that on the death of my said wife she shall become free, without any person or persons, heirs of myself or my wife, having the right to keep her captive; this being a reward for her good service to me, and as I hope to my wife.[937]

Isaac Harby (1788-1828) was a Charleston, South Carolina, dramatist and political essayist and president of the Reform Society of Israelites. He regularly wrote in opposition to "the abolitionist society and its secret branches," as early as 1824. He edited the *Quiver*, the *Investigator*, and the *Southern Patriot*, and contributed to the *Mercury* and the *Courier*.[938]

Aaron Hart, in his will of 1762, bequeathed to his servant "a mourning gown."[939]

Ephraim Hart (1747-1825). A wealthy New York stockbroker, land speculator, and state senator (in 1810), Hart enslaved at least one Black woman named "Silvia." He was an official of Congregation *Shearith Israel*, and founder of its burial society *Hebra Hesed ve Emet*, as well as a member of the Philadelphia Synagogue.[940]

---

[936]Schappes, p. 574; Wolf and Whiteman, pp. 36-64, 192; *EJ*, vol. 7, p. 858; Marcus, *The American Jewish Woman*, p. 12; Irving J. Sloan, ed., *The Jews in America; 1621-1970* (New York: Oceana Publications, 1971), p. 4.

[937]Samuel, pp. 71-72.

[938]Korn, "Jews and Negro Slavery," p. 211; *EJ*, vol. 7, pp. 1332-33; Sloan, p. 5; Rosenbloom, p. 49.

[939]Friedman, "Wills," p. 155.

[940]*EJ*, vol. 7, p. 1355; Schappes, pp. 595, 599; Rosenwaike, "Jewish Population in 1790," p. 46; Rosenbloom, pp. 51-52.

Henry Hart, a "Jew Tailor" of Arundel County, Maryland, was accused in 1752 of an illicit relationship with a maid. He was sentenced to serve a man named McNamara for six months "for the Damage Sustained...on Acct. of the said Henry Hart begetting a Bastard child on the body of Susanna Talome, a Servant belonging to the said McNamara."[941]

Isaac Hart (d. 1780) was a founder and member of Newport's Touro Synagogue. His firm, Naphtali Hart & Co., shipped and traded in Black slaves and cultivated their New England property with hired hands and slaves.[942] He sided with and supplied the British during the Revolutionary War and was shot to death by the Continental army.[943]

Jacob Hart (b. 1781) came to New Orleans from New York in 1804 and traded in slave ships and African people. In 1808, Hart advertised in Saint Dominigue for the sale of Black people, including a cook, two fishermen and a tailor who spoke English and French fluently. In 1810, he bought two Africans in Florida. The 1820 census reports that he imprisoned seven African people as slaves. He became the owner of a number of vessels, including the schooner *Celestine,* and he brokered the sale of four African citizens. At the time of his bankruptcy in 1823, he held fourteen Black hostages.[944]

Levy Hart owned a general merchandise business firm in Savannah, Georgia, in the early 1800s. "Unlucky in 'chattel,' he was exasperated by a very valuable slave, Sandy, who functioned as a butcher, and was prone to 'take off' now and again."[945]

Michael Hart (d. 1813), an Easton, Pennsylvania, Indian trader, "never acquired wealth" but he owned a stone house, collected some silverplate, owned a slave, and sold whiskey to the Indians "in hundreds of gallons."[946]

Michael Hart (d. 1861). Though Hart was from New York, he owned a Virginia plantation. When he feared that Richmond

---

[941]Isaac M. Fein, *The Making of An American Jewish Community,* p. 10.

[942]Feldstein, p. 13.

[943]*EJ*, vol. 7, p. 1356; Rosenbloom, p. 52.

[944]Korn, *Jews of New Orleans*, pp. 96, 100-101, 296; Sharfman, p. 153.

[945]Saul Jacob Rubin, *Third to None The Saga of Savannah Jewry 1733-1983* (Savannah, 1983), pp. 86-87.

[946]*MUSJ1*, p. 151.

would be taken by the Union Army in the Civil War, his son escaped with "most of the slaves belonging to the estate."[947]

Moses Hart, son of **Aaron**, was sent to Albany in 1786, where his mother:

> wanted him to buy a good Negro wench for houseworke [because the] last one had died — and if the price was right [his] father wanted a Negro hand who knew something about farming, could handle an ax, and work in the garden.[948]

Myer Hart, of Easton on the Delaware, was the richest man in town and one of the founding fathers. In 1768, he owned "two houses, a bond servant, six lots, a horse, a cow, and his stock in trade."[949]

Nathan Hart of Newport informed the community by newspaper advertisement on March 18, 1765, that among other things, he "also wants to purchase a negro."[950]

Nathan Hart was the constable of Charleston in 1821, whose job it was to punish runaway slaves. In October of 1827, he sold five slaves to **Sophie Monsanto**, and he was listed as enslaving fifteen Blacks in the census of 1830.[951]

Philip Hart (1727-1796) was a Charleston Jew with at least one African captive named "Flora."[952]

Samuel Hart came to Louisiana via England, and by 1823 he owned half of the steamboat *United States* and "four Negro slaves," $20,000 in bank stock and two lots in Louisville, Kentucky. He had a "slave mistress," named "Polly," with a "mulatto child." Hart cut them from his will and added "Cecilia Beni," "a woman of color," and her four children, presumably all his.[953]

---

[947]Korn, "Jews and Negro Slavery," p. 188 note.
[948]*MEAJ1*, p. 277.
[949]*MCAJ2*, p. 821.
[950]Rhodes, p. 7.
[951]Korn, "Jews and Negro Slavery," p. 190; Korn, *Jews of New Orleans*, pp. 103, 296; Rosenbloom, p. 55.
[952]Korn, "Jews and Negro Slavery," p. 185; Reznikoff and Engelman, p. 77; Rosenbloom, p. 55.
[953]*MUSJ2*, p. 68.

David Hays (1732-1812). A farmer and storekeeper and son of **Jacob Hays**, David Hays fought against the Indians in the French and Indian War. One of his Black captives was named "Darby." The inventory of his estate, valued at $3,658.98, included the following items all valued greater than or equal to his Black humans.[954]

An inventory of the Goods, Chattels & Effect belonging to the Estate of David Hays of the Township of Mount Pleasant, Deceased.

6 Cows @ $15	$90	1 Lott wheat in the Sheaf	15
1Colt	12.50	1 Lott Rye	15
1 Yoke Oxen	50	1 Lott Oats	10
3 Calves @ $3.50	10.50	1 Lot Hay in the Barn	10
1 fat Steer	18	8 Stacks Hay @ $5	40
2 fat Cows @ $18	36	1 Mare & yearling Colt	14
1 Bay Horse	10	14 Hogs @ $5	70
1/2 field Rye	25	1 Ton of plaster	15.75
1/2 field Corn	15	1 Waggon & Harness	25
1 field Corn	15	4 feather beds	25
1 field Wheat	15	1 Lot silver Plate	15
1 Lott Buckwheat	17.50	1 Silver Watch	20
1 Windfan	12	**1 Black Girl**	**10**
10 Sheep @ $1	10	**1 Black Woman**	**10**

Grace Hays (d. 1740) conveyed in her will "fifty ounces of sterling wrought silver plate and the best negro slave which I should be possessed of..."[955]

Judah Hays (1703-1764) was a New York merchant and ship owner who was elected constable in 1736. His Black captives were allegedly part of a foiled 1741 plot to burn the city and escape from their Jewish captors. "Like other well-to-do men of his period," wrote Harold Korn, "he bought negroes and the time of indentured servants. He paid £80 for a negro man named Aaron and £20 for four years' service of an indentured boy named John Camble."[956]

---

[954]Lebeson, p. 203; Pool, pp. 330-31; Solomon Solis-Cohen, "Note Concerning David Hays and Esther Etting His Wife and Michael Hays and Reuben Etting, Their Brothers: Patriots of the Revolution," *PAJHS*, vol. 2 (1894), p. 65; *MCAJ3*, p. 1295. Will is in "Items Relating to the Hays family of New York," *PAJHS*, vol. 27 (1920), pp. 323-25. Rosenbloom, p. 57.

[955]Pool, p. 226.

[956]Lebeson, pp. 202-3. The Blacks held by **Samuel Myers Cohen** were allegedly also involved (see Cohen's entry, p. 226). Harold Korn, "Receipt Book of Judah and Moses M. Hays, Commencing on January 12, 1763 and Ending on July 18, 1776," *PAJHS*, vol. 28 (1922), p. 228; Rosenbloom, p. 59.

Hays had some apparent difficulties tracking his runaway slave "Sarah" when he ran this ad in February of 1751:

> Run away last Sunday night, from Judah Hays, a Negroe wench, named Sarah, aged about 30 years; she is a likely wench, of a Mulatto complexion, was brought up at Amboy, in Col. Hamilton's family, and has had several Masters in the Jerseys: She dresses very well, has a good parcel of cloaths, and speaks good English. Whoever takes up the said wench, and brings her to her said master, or secures her in any county goal, so that he may have her again, shall receive Forty Shillings reward, and reasonable charges. Whoever entertains said wench, shall be prosecuted with the utmost rigour of the law. All masters of vessels, boat-men, &c. are forewarned of conveying said wench away, as they shall answer the same.
>
> Judah Hays
>
> N.B. Said wench has robb'd her said master, in apparel, &c. upwards of Fifty Pounds.

And this one in May of 1751:

> Whereas the subscriber hereof, has great reason to apprehend that his Negroe wench Sarah, formerly advertised in this paper, has been and is now harboured and concealed by some white person in this town; this is to give publick notice, that whoever brings said wench to me, or has her confined in goal, shall immediately receive from me Five Pounds as a reward: And farther, that whoever will give information upon oath, who it is that harbours and detains said Negroe wench, shall have Ten Pounds reward.
>
> N.B. All masters of vessels, boatmen and others, are cautioned against taking said wench on board, as she has lately been seen in sailors dress.
>
> Judah Hays."[957]

Samuel Hays (1764-1838) of Philadelphia was a slave owner and active Mason who is remembered as a humanitarian because he arranged to have his slaves liberated. He reserved the right, however, to keep them as indentured servants.[958]

---

[957]Smith and Wojtowicz, pp. 33, 34.

[958]Wolf and Whiteman, p. 191; Rosenwaike, "Jewish Population in 1790," p. 51; Rosenbloom, p. 60.

Abraham Baruch Henriques, a Portuguese Jew of Barbados, bequeathed to his family the "liberty to sell houses, slaves or plantations..."[959]

David Henriques was a Jamaican Jewish slave-marketing "specialist" in the late eighteenth century.[960]

Manuel Dias Henriques (probably the same as **Manuel Diaz Enriquez**) "lived in New Spain during the early 1620's where he had been a representative of Portuguese slave traders."[961] He was accused of being a Jew by Inquisitional authorities in early 17th century New Spain. Though unnamed in the historical record, his uncle was described as "a broker or dealer in Negro slaves."[962]

Jacob Henry held a seat in the House of Commons of North Carolina in 1808. He was the son of **Joel** and **Amelia Henry**, who in 1810, held ten Black African slaves. Jacob's household consisted of twelve Black hostages, according to the census of 1810; in 1820 that number is believed to have increased to fifteen.[963]

Isaac Hermann (1838-1917). Author Jacob R. Marcus described Isaac Hermann as follows:

> In the Reconstruction period, Hermann was a leader in the movement to organize the veterans into an association whose primary aim, it would seem, was to protect the whites against the Negro freedmen....[H]e worked to restore white supremacy and to resist what he believed to be the encroachments of the Negroes.[964]

Samuel Hermann was a New Orleans merchant and banker and partner of Asher Moses Nathan, and, according to census data of 1810, he enslaved four Blacks—ten in 1820 and seventeen in 1830. His dealings in Blacks were "extensive." In 1825, he sold 16 Black Africans to various farmers.[965]

---

959 Samuel, p. 79.

960 *EJ*, vol. 14, p. 1663; *EHJ*, p. 273.

961 Swetschinski, p. 238.

962 Liebman, *The Jews in New Spain*, p. 210.

963 Leonard Dinnerstein and Mary Rale Palsson, eds., *Jews in the South* (Baton Rouge: Louisiana State University Press, 1973), pp. 48-49.

964 *JRM/Memoirs 3*, p. 236.

965 Korn, "Jews and Negro Slavery," p. 183 note; Korn, *Jews of New Orleans*, pp. 111-13, 300; *EJ*, vol. 4, p. 138; *MUSJ1*, p. 178.

Solomon Heydenfeldt (1816-1890) of California gave up his judgeship because his position automatically bound him to the Union but his sympathies were with the Confederacy.[966] Jewish historians have claimed that he was against slavery, and yet, contrarily, he wrote in a pamphlet of the "unjust and bitter crusades of the Northern Abolitionists." He was a "passionate secessionist" and thought Lincoln's slave emancipation plan of 1861 to be "tyranny." He opposed the importation of slaves into Alabama in 1849 not for any humanitarian reason, but because of "the unproductiveness of slave labor, and its gradual, but certain, impoverishment of our State, is a sufficient reason for limiting its farther propagation among us." He felt that when other states recognized the uneconomic character of slave labor they would dump the freed Africans on Alabama.[967]

Aaron Hirsch (1829-1911) was a French Jew who settled in New Orleans and later became a resident of Mississippi and Arkansas. He was a strong Confederate, who expressed the Jewish sentiment of his time when in the 1860s he stated that

> the institution of slavery as it existed in the south was not so great a wrong as people believe. The Negroes were brought here in a savage state; they captured and ate each other in their African home. Here they were instructed to work, were civilized and got religion, and were perfectly happy.[968]

Hirsch spoke in favor of slavery because the plantation owners were his customers. He owned slaves and bought and sold them in his Batesville, Arkansas, business, Hirsch & Adler. During the Civil War he bought six Blacks and later exchanged them for a farm. He was against the proposal to free the slaves who had fought for the Confederacy, reasoning that the war was fought to keep them enslaved.[969]

---

[966]George Cohen, *The Jew in the Making of America* (Boston: Knights of Columbus, Stratford Company, 1924), p. 87.

[967]Simonhoff, *Jewish Participants in the Civil War*, pp. 175-77; Schappes, pp. 293-301; *EJ*, vol. 8, p. 448. Korn, "Jews and Negro Slavery," p. 210: Heydenfeldt first published his *Communication on the Subject of Slave Immigration, Addressed to Hon. Reuben Chapman, Governor of Alabama*, in the Huntsville *Democrat* on Jan. 31, 1849, and subsequently in pamphlet form.

[968]Korn, "Jews and Negro Slavery," p. 214; Feldstein, p. 101.

[969]*JRM/Memoirs 2*, pp. 135, 142; *JRM/Memoirs 1*, p. 20; Simonhoff, *Jewish Participants in the Civil War*, pp. 278-81.

Haham Jeossuha His advertised in the *Royal Gazette* of Kingston, Jamaica, for the return of a runaway slave on December 15, 1792.[970]

Uriah Hyam (d. 1740) was a New York merchant, member of *Shearith Israel* and slave maker. He held Black people against their will and one, named "Cavandro," he bequeathed to his son, **Andrew Israel**, in his 1740 will.[971]

Henry Hyams was a staunch supporter of slavery, Jewish leader and lieutenant governor of Louisiana in 1859.[972]

Samuel Hyams, of Charleston, had more than twenty African hostages. As the 1822 keeper of the jail, his job was to incarcerate freedom-seeking Blacks.[973]

Levi Hyman was a merchant and landowner, who lived at his plantation estate in St. Andrew, Jamaica, called "Hyman's Delight." In 1811, he held 32 African citizens, 46 in 1821 and 45 in 1830.[974]

Rev. Bernard Illowy, (1812-1871) of Baltimore, was a Jewish spiritual leader and vocal supporter of the American slave system. He said that the Abolitionists had "thrown the country into a general state of confusion" and called them "ambitious aspirants and selfish politicians."[975]

Abraham Isaacks paid a £700 debt to **Nathan Simson** with "feathers, flour, cider, negro slaves and cash."[976]

Jacob Isaacks was a Newport merchant who frequently bought and sold Black human beings even from his home on Broad Street. One 1777 advertisement offered "Foodstuffs, pork,

---

[970]Bertram W. Korn, "The Haham DeCordova of Jamaica," *AJA*, vol. 18 (1966), p. 148.

[971]Friedman, "Wills," p. 151; Hershkowitz, "Wills (1704-1740)," p. 357; Lee M. Friedman, *Early American Jews* (Cambridge, Massachusetts: Harvard University Press, 1934), p. 72.

[972]Feingold, *Zion*, p. 89; *EJ*, vol. 11, p. 519.

[973]Korn, "Jews and Negro Slavery," p. 190; Rosenwaike, "Jewish Population of 1820," p. 18.

[974]Hurwitz and Hurwitz, p. 47.

[975]Feingold, *Zion*, p. 90; Bertram Wallace Korn, *American Jewry and the Civil War* (Philadelphia: Jewish Publication Society of America, 1951), p. 26; Isaac M. Fein, *The Making of an American Jewish Community*, p. 95; *EJ*, vol. 8, p. 1257.

[976]*MCAJ2*, p. 612.

negro man and woman." He placed ads in the *Newport Mercury* over the next seven years for the sale of "negroes" at least five times.[977]

Isaiah Isaacs (1747-1806). Born in Germany, Isaiah Isaacs was the first Jew in Richmond, Virginia, and a founder of the Congregation *Beth Shalome*, grantor of its cemetery land, and slave driver. In 1788, he was elected to the Common Hall. He was in slave-making alliance with **Jacob I. Cohen** and held Black Africans named "Lucy," "James," "Polly," "Henry," and "Rachel," and her children "Clement Washington" and "Mary." His business firm once took a Black captive as security for a debt.

Isaacs placed this advertisement in the *Virginia Gazette or American Advertiser* on June 1, 1782:

> TWENTY DOLLARS REWARD
>
> RAN AWAY from the subscriber, living in the town of Richmond, a very likely Negro woman named MOLLY, lately the property of Mr. Edward Busbel, of Gloucester-town; she is much pitted with the small-pox, about twenty-two years old, and about five feet six inches high; had on when she went away, a Virginia cloth vest and petticoat, checked; she had with her a checked apron, a callico petticoat, and a pair of leather high-heeled country made shoes. I expect she will make towards Williamsburg or Gloucester-town, as she came from those parts a few days ago. She had four horse-locks fastened on her legs when she went away. Whoever apprehends and delivers the said Negro to me, shall receive the above reward and reasonable charges, paid by ISA[I]AH ISAACS.[978]

Referring to the words of Isaacs, the great Jewish scholar Jacob R. Marcus wrote that "the following phrases [are] redolent of the spirit of the great Virginians of [Isaacs'] generation":

> Being of the opinion that all men are by nature equally free, and being possessed of some of those beings who are unfortunate[ly], doomed to slavery, as to them I must enjoin my executor a strict observance of the following clause in my will. My slaves...are hereby manumeted and made free, so that after [30 years] they shall enjoy all the privileges and immunities of freed people....Each one of my slaves is to receive the value of twenty dollars in clothing on the days of their manumission.[979]

---

[977]Rhodes, pp. 18, 19. The ads were placed on September 7, 1782; November 9, 1782; September 13, 1783; June 12, 1784; and September 11, 1784.

[978]Windley, vol. 1, pp. 338-39.

[979]Schappes, pp. 99-102, 593; *EJ*, vol. 9, p. 41; Korn, "Jews and Negro Slavery," p. 187; Rosenwaike, "Jewish Population in 1790," p. 63; Bermon, pp. 2, 163-64; *MEAJ2*, p. 183; Rosenbloom, p. 67. See also the listing for **Jacob I. Cohen** on p. 225.

Samuel Isaacs (Isaaks), from one of the original 300 families to populate Texas (comprised of 1,800 persons and 443 slaves), was allotted "a Spanish Grant of one league (4,428.4 acres grazing land) and one labor (177.13612 acres farming land)," situated about midway between the Gulf Coast and the upriver settlement of Washington-on-the-Brazos.[980]

Solomon Isaacs of the New York family of that name imported some slaves into Charlestown in 1755.[981] In his will, probated in 1757, he left "a substantial inventory of goods, a house, books, mahogany furniture, colored prints, silver plate, several Negro slaves — three of whom were children — two horses and a chaise, and a quarter ownership of a sloop."[982]

David Israel, Jewish inhabitant of Barbados, wrote his will in Portuguese dated May 24, 1689, "revoking all previous Wills made if it should please God to take me to a better world I ask pardon for all my sins & that my soul may be rec'd in mercy." Then, to his wife Sarah he left "a negress named Betty, and the use of two negresses named below to go (eventually) to my daughter Esther when 21, or on her previous marriage."

> To my son Isaac a male negro named Antonio....Also my two negresses Maria Ibo and Esperansa they to be delivered by my wife unto Esther when she marries or attains 21 years....To my daur. Rahel, wife of David Judah Rodriques £25 sterling payable by executors and 2 *moreques* (=*negro-boys* (moliques)) for my grand-daughter Ester Zinha. To grandson Jacob son of David and Rahel Judah Rodrigues a *moliques* named Robin....Also 2 negroes named Vallenty and Macaco which I sent him for the service of the business.[983]

Rabbi George Jacobs of Richmond, Virginia, held Black hostages and rented them for a fee.[984]

Gerrit Jacobs (d. 1754) from the Netherlands was a storekeeper and planter with a plantation in Surinam called *Nieuw Meerzorg*, with 100 Black African slaves. He later ordered that

---

[980]Sharfman, pp. 236-37.
[981]Feldstein, p. 14; *MEAJ2*, p. 322.
[982]*MCAJ2*, p. 823. Lee M. Friedman, "Early Jewish Residents of Massachusetts," *PAJHS*, vol. 23 (1915), p. 84: Isaacs owned a ship named *Sarah* in 1737.
[983]Samuel, pp. 75-76.
[984]Korn, *Civil War*, p. 29.

number to be increased to more than 200. To his wife **Haija Sadoks**, he bequeathed "ten domestic slaves," which he stipulated could not be sold. To his stepson went "the Negro boy Present."[985]

Israel Jacobs (c. 1741-1810) of Philadelphia held Black hostages but was, nevertheless, well respected in his synagogue.[986]

Jacob Jacobs of Charleston, an auctioneer, left an estate that included ten slaves, horses, carriages, notes and bonds.[987] He advertised in the *Gazette of the State of South-Carolina* November 24, 1779:

Four Hundred Dollars Reward

> RUN away from the Subscriber, on Sunday Night last, two Negro Fellows named Hercules and Romeo, the former is about five Feet two or three Inches high, very black, speaks good English, and had on when he went away a blue Coat and Jacket with a red Cape, and white metal buttons: The latter is about five Feet high, of a yellowish Complexion, speaks good English, and had on a great Coat, red Jacket and black or Osnabrugs Breeches. They both had hats, and may perhaps change their Dress, having carried all their Cloathing with them: The above Reward will be given for the taking of the said two Negroes, and the half for either of them. All Masters of Vessels are forbid carrying off the Negroes at their Peril.[988]

John Jacobs, possibly a Jew, placed this advertisement in the *Virginia Gazette* on February 7, 1771:

> RUN away from the Subscriber, in Amherst county, on or about the 5th of October last, a new Negro man slave who calls himself CHARLES, which is every word of English he can speak, he is a black fellow, with a smooth skin, of a middle size, well made for strength, appears to be about 18 years of age, and has a good set of teeth. He was purchased from the Yanimerew the 14th of last September, and was one of the number judged to have had the small pox. Had on when he left me a Negro cotton Jacket with buttons (both top and bottom) of brass, a pair of cotton breeches, very long, with flat metal buttons to the waistband, cotton boots, and a coarse linen cap. Whoever will deliver him to me, or secure him so that I may get him again, shall receive a reward of

---

[985]Fredrik Oudschans Dentz, "The Name of the Country Surinam as a Family-Name: The Biography of a Surinam Planter of the Eighteenth Century," *PAJHS*, vol. 48 (1958-59), pp. 21, 24, 25.

[986]Wolf and Whiteman, pp. 190-91; Rosenbloom, p. 73.

[987]*MUSJ1*, pp. 158, 210.

[988]Windley, vol. 3, p. 377.

> FIVE POUNDS; and if he is taken out of the colony and brought home to me TEN POUNDS current money.[989]

Joseph Jacob, of Newport, ran an advertisement in December of 1769: "Notice: Reward $3 South Hampton, Long Island runaway Indian servant."[990]

Levy Jacobs was a New Orleans and Mobile liquor- and slave-dealer who advertised to "buy and sell Negroes" in 1819. In September of 1828, he notified the public that he was expecting about 100

> prime, Virginia slaves, selected expressly for this market — among which are Ostlers, Carriage Drivers, Mechanics, Field Hands and Cooks, House Servants, seamstresses and washer women.

As proprietor of one of the leading auctioneer houses of New Orleans, Jacobs was reported to have "paraded blacks on the slave block that was operated by **Levy Jacobs** and his Christian partner, George Asbridge."[991] When he was accused of selling Kentucky slaves and not the advertised Virginia slaves he posted this notice:

> Notice — A report being circulated that I have for sale no other than Kentucky slaves, I beg leave to state to the public that all the Negroes which I have on hand, and shall hereafter keep for sale are and will be Virginia born Negroes, of good character; that the person who has stated to the contrary, with the view of injuring me, I call upon in this public manner to come forward and support this charge if he can, or hereafter hold his peace. All Negroes sold and bought by me from traders (excepting at my own house) will be free of commission.
>
> L. Jacobs[992]

Manis Jacobs (c. 1782-1839) was the rabbi and president of the New Orleans Jewish congregation *Shanarai Chasset* and a leading Jewish citizen, even though he held eleven Black people as slaves. Rabbi Sharfman writes of Jacobs: "Though

---

[989]Windley, vol. 1, p. 310.

[990]Rhodes, p. 11.

[991]Sharfman, p. 152.

[992] *EHJ*, p. 274; Korn, *Jews of New Orleans*, pp. 163-64; *EJ*, vol. 14, p. 1664. The state of Virginia is reputed to have been the most prolific breeder of Black people for the purpose of slavery in the United States. For reference to the value and quality of bred slaves, see Sharfman, pp. 152-53.

unordained, he felt his ability to recite Hebrew prayers qualified him. He proudly signed his name in Hebrew on bills of sale, as a cachet or seal — some on his transactions involving the purchase of slaves still exist."[993]

Samuel Jacobs, in 1761, "ordered a Negro girl from New York—domestic slaves were popular because hired help was scarce." Jacobs was the owner of the slave schooner *Betsey*.[994]

Solomon Jacobs (1777-1827) was acting mayor of Richmond, Virginia, in 1818-1819, president of *Beth Shalome* Congregation, and the first Jew to become grand master of the Masons of Virginia. He was an agent for the French government's tobacco interests and the Richmond representative for the Rothschild banking house. He owned a slave named "Esther," and when he died his tombstone epitaph read:

Fond as a Husband.
Indulgent as a Father.
Kind as a Master...

His widow, **Hetty**, then successfully lobbied the Virginia House and Senate to allow the sale of a number of Black female captives and children because of the "conduct of said slaves toward their mistress...was so very malevolent and very objectionable."[995]

L. Jacoby. In 1830, Jacoby held thirty Africans against their will in the New Orleans area.[996]

Joseph Jonas, in an address to the Ohio House of Representatives on February 25-26, 1861, said, "I am not in favor of slavery, and would not own a slave on any account. But this is not the question. Slavery in the South is an institution, and the framers of the Constitution guarded their rights and their property."[997]

---

[993]Korn, *Jews of New Orleans*, pp. 199-201, 319; Sharfman, p. 191.

[994]*MEAJ1*, pp. 204, 208.

[995]Korn, "Jews and Negro Slavery," pp. 187, 193; Ezekiel and Lichtenstein, p. 85; Bermon, p. 166; *EJ*, vol. 9, p. 1237; Rosenbloom, p. 75.

[996]Korn, "Jews and Negro Slavery," p. 183.

[997]Jonathan D. Sarna and Nancy H. Klein, *The Jews of Cincinnati* (Cincinnati: Jewish Institute of Religion, 1989), p. 51.

Israel I. Jones (1810-1877) of Mobile, Alabama, was leader of the Jewish community in the mid-1800s, as well as a slave-trading auctioneer. President of Congregation *Shaarai Shomayim* from 1844-1873, he was on the Board of Delegates of American Israelites, the first national Jewish organization. On Feb. 6, 1841, he advertised in the Mobile *Daily Advertiser and Chronical* that he had "Negroes at Auction," including a "Man Alfred, 25 years old, field hand; Boy Isaac, 7 years old; Woman Judy, 30 years old and two work horses."[998]

Samuel Jones (c. 1737-1809) was a Charleston Jew who ordered that his survivors free two of his eight Black hostages named "Jenny" and her son "Emanuel." This selective manumission of an African woman indicates that she was the victim of rape by the Jew and that her son may have been the result of that crime.[999]

J. Joseph advertised for the return of a runaway African female child in the *Quebec Gazette* on July 28, 1791.[1000]

Meir Josephson, a Pennsylvania trader, informed **Michael Gratz** in a letter written in Yiddish:

> ...that I may sell my nigger wench at a profit. So if a ship with niggers should arrive, or a ship with [indentured] Germans you will let me know, because I cannot manage without a servant. The wench I now have has two virtues, both bad ones. First, she is drunk all day, when she can get it, and second, she is mean so that my wife cannot say a word to her. She is afraid of her. How did all this happen? A free nigger wants to court her and to buy her from me. I don't want to give her away for less than 110 pounds with her bastard, because I bought the bastard too. At present she costs me 90 pounds. So if I can make out with her, I think it is best to let her go and get another. So if you have occasion to hear of a good nigger wench or of a good servant, you will inform me.[1001]

Baruch H. Judah "hired" a Black African woman named "Mary" who was tried in 1820, and acquitted, for setting fire to the house of her employer.[1002]

---

[998]*EHJ*, p. 274; Korn, "Jews and Negro Slavery," p. 185; *EJ*, vol. 2, p. 505.
[999]Korn, "Jews and Negro Slavery," p. 185; Rosenbloom, p. 76.
[1000]"Acquisitions," *AJA*, vol. 7 (January 1955), p. 167.
[1001]*JRM/Docs*, pp. 359-60; Brener, pp. 77-78.
[1002]Ezekiel and Lichtenstein, p. 88.

Isaac H. Judah (1761-1827) of Richmond, Virginia, was a merchant and *Beth Shalome's* first minister. He fathered two "mulatto" children named "Philip Norbourne" and "Benjamin Wythe," the products of the rape of an African woman. Judah's slave "Harry" was charged on March 13, 1815, with "going at large and hiring himself to Paul Christian, was remanded to jail and Judah summoned to appear the next day and show cause why he should not be fined for allowing the said slave to go at large and hire himself out."[1003]

Manual Judah owned a Black slave named "Shadrach," who was tried in the Richmond courts in 1805 for stealing a hog. He was found guilty, and given nine and thirty lashes on his bare back.[1004]

Samuel Judah was the most prominent of the Jewish slave-traffickers in Canada.[1005]

David S. Kaufman of Texas was a notable proponent of the spread of the slavocracy.[1006]

Betsy Levi Kokernot and her son **Louis** of New Orleans operated a retail store in the 1830s. In 1832, the sheriff seized part of their stock to pay bills and found that:

> Betsy and Louis seemed to have caught an inordinate number of runaway Negroes, or stopped Negroes carrying money without proper identification; probably much of their trade was with slave owners.[1007]

David Cohen Labatt of Louisiana was devoted to the Confederacy and the preservation of the slave system.[1008]

Joseph Lasalle was active in the Louisiana militia and local politics. He owned four female slaves in 1830.[1009]

[1003]Bermon, p. 39; Ezekiel and Lichtenstein, p. 86; Blau and Baron, vol. 1, pp. 206-9; Rosenbloom, p. 80.

[1004]Ezekiel and Lichtenstein, p. 81.

[1005]B. G. Sack, *The History of Jews in Canada* (Montreal: Harvest House, 1965), pp. 52-53.

[1006]Korn, "Jews and Negro Slavery," p. 209; *EJ*, vol. 15, p. 1034.

[1007]Korn, *Jews of New Orleans*, p. 171.

[1008]Shpall, pp. 12-13.

[1009]Korn, *Jews of New Orleans*, pp. 177, 319.

Benjamin D. Lazarus sold "A Negro named Sam, about Eighty Years of age, diseased, and a Negro Woman named Sylvie about seventy five years of Age," for ninety dollars. Dr. Bertram W. Korn comments on the cruelty of this act:

> Perhaps the estate required cash, and undoubtedly the slaves were too old for any useful purpose, but what future could they have at the hands of a purchaser who would be compelled somehow to regain his investment?[1010]

Jacob Lazarus, Jr., from Charleston, South Carolina, enslaved more than twenty African hostages.[1011]

Rachel Mordecai Lazarus was "fully aware of the evils of slavery, but, after a fashion, defended this institution in her correspondence with Maria Edgeworth. Rachel contended that the black under chattel slavery was no worse off than the European who suffered under wage slavery."[1012]

Sampson Lazarus of Lancaster, Pennsylvania, "had a female slave and a horse and was a shopkeeper," in 1782.[1013]

Ishak Gabay Letob, probably of Speightstown, Barbados, prepared his will in Portuguese, dated August 24, 1698:

> To son Jacob Gabay Lettob my slave-girl Juana, so that she may look after him, he being ill, and she is not to be disposed of by him but at his death she is to go to whichever one of his brothers she prefers. To grand-dau. Ribca Ulloa the daur. named Peggy, of said Juana and for her heirs at her death but not otherwise.[1014]

Edwin De Leon (1828-1891) considered those who opposed slavery to be guided by a "mistaken philanthropy" with a disregard for "Providence" or "God." He was one of the chief Confederate propaganda agents and vehemently supported slavery with the belief that Blacks are the "bearer of burdens; never a conqueror or a king." In 1862, he was sent abroad by Jefferson Davis and **Judah P. Benjamin** on a secret mission to persuade Britain, France and other countries to grant

---

[1010] Korn, "Jews and Negro Slavery," pp. 192-93.
[1011] *Karp, JEA2*, p. 18.
[1012] *MUSJ1*, p. 588.
[1013] Brener, p. 8.
[1014] Samuel, p. 54.

diplomatic recognition to the Confederacy. He failed after nearly two years and expenditures of $30,000.[1015]

Lewis Leon was a Confederate Jew who said retrospectively: "I still say our Cause was just, nor do I regret one thing that I have done to cripple the North." Author Charles Segal says that this statement "is indicative of Jewish loyalty to the Southern cause."[1016]

Abraham Levi was in partnership with Edward Newman in New Orleans. Levi's assets at the outbreak of the war were said to be in the range of $300,000. Records of some of Levi's transactions for the year 1860 indicate that in January, A. Levi & Co. advanced $7,000 to James Bogan, a planter in East Baton Rouge Parish. In return, Bogan signed a series of promissory notes that gave A. Levi & Co. a mortgage on his 746-acre plantation and his slaves.[1017]

Jacob Levin of Columbia, South Carolina, was the leader of his Jewish community in the mid-1800s and a slave-trading auctioneer. An acting rabbi, he was quoted in prestigious Jewish periodicals, and his wife was director of the Columbia Hebrew Sunday School. He was also the secretary and treasurer of the Hebrew Benevolent Society of Columbia and a grand master of the Masons. On December 17, 1852, he advertised in the *Columbia Daily South Carolinian* the sale of:

> 22 Likely Negroes, the larger number of which are young and desirable. Among them are Field Hands, Hostlers and Carriage Drivers, House Servants, & c., and of the following ages: Robinson 40, Elsey 34, Yanaky 13, Sylvia 11, Anikee 8, Robinson 6, Candy 3, Infant 9, Thomas 35, Die 38, Amey 18, Eldridge 13, Charles 6, Sarah 60, Baket 50, Mary 18, Betty 16, Guy 12, Tilla 9, Lydia 24, Rachel 4, Scippio 2.
>
> The above Negroes are sold for the purpose of making some other investment of the proceeds, the sale will therefore be positive.[1018]

[1015]*EJ*, vol. 5, p. 1471; Schappes, pp. 398-401; Simonhoff, *Jewish Notables*, p. 378.

[1016]Charles M. Segal, *Fascinating Facts About American Jewish History* (New York: Twayne Publications, 1955), p. 82.

[1017]Elliott Ashkenazi, *The Business of Jew in New Orleans, 1840-1875* (Tuscaloosa: University of Alabama Press, 1988), p. 82.

[1018]*EHJ*, p. 274; Korn, "Jews and Negro Slavery," p. 196; *EJ*, vol. 14, p. 1664.

Arthur Levy of New York owned at least one Black woman named "Cresie."[1019]

Ash Levy worked with the notorious **Davis** brothers in their slave dealings.[1020]

Benjamin Levy (c. 1650-1704) was a New Orleans printer and publisher who bequeathed to his African hostage, "Richard White," the chance to buy his freedom for $500 from Levy's son, **Alexander**. The deception was that, as a slave, "Richard White" was unpaid. Additionally, "White" was "never to be sold, Mortgaged, or hired out for a longer term than one Year at a time, and never to be hired out of the State of Louisiana."

The elder Levy also instructed that each of his eight remaining hostages named "Harry," "Samuel," "Joseph," "Ellen," "Martha," "Horace," "Millie" and "Richard" be given a token trinket as a "small memorial of their old master."

In 1761, Levy joined coreligionists **David Franks** and **Joseph Marks** in the signing of a petition protesting a duty on imported Blacks.[1021]

Chapman Levy (1787-1850) was born in Camden, South Carolina, and elected to the state legislature and served as a colonel in the War of 1812. He was a prominent Jewish lawyer who held 31 Black human beings as slaves. He moved to Mississippi and operated a plantation until his death. Levy's will manumitted some of his hostages and retained others. His mother, **Sarah**, sold her Black hostage "Kennedy" and an African woman to Levy for $300.[1022]

Eugene Henry Levy of New Orleans was an official in the Confederate Army who said: "The slaves are in their proper sphere as they are at present situated within the boundaries of the Confederacy." The day before General Robert E. Lee surrendered, Levy was captured and soon released. He made his post-Civil War sentiments known when he declared that "Negroes are among the masters and have the inclination to be

---

[1019]Schappes, p. 99.

[1020]Bermon, p. 167.

[1021]Korn, "Jews and Negro Slavery," p. 186; Korn, *Jews of New Orleans*, p. 152; *EJ*, vol. 11, pp. 156, 1551; Edward D. Coleman, "Jewish Merchants," p. 285; Rosenbloom, pp. 88-89.

[1022]Rosenwaike, "Jewish Population of 1820," p. 18; Korn, "Jews and Negro Slavery," pp. 185-86; *EJ*, vol. 11, p. 156; *MUSJ1*, p. 210; Rosenbloom, p. 89.

tyrants. The extermination of this race is a necessary consequence of this state of affairs."[1023]

Gershon Levy and **Hyam Myers** did business with the notorious Indian murderer Sir Jeffrey Amherst.[1024]

Hayman Levy (1721-1789) was born in Germany and came to New York City in 1748. He made his fortune fur-trading with the Indians and in the Black Holocaust as owner of several ships. His *Shearith Israel* congregation voted him its president six times.[1025]

Hyman Levy was a Jamaican Jewish "specialist" in the Black flesh trade in the late eighteenth century.[1026]

Isaac Levy was the brother of **Nathan Levy** (see entry herein) and partner with **David** and **Moses Franks** in African flesh dealing. He worked in New York, Philadelphia, Boston, and London and was part owner of the slave ship *Crown Gally.* He once brought 117 Africans into bondage.[1027]

Israel Levy, a merchant of Charlestown, sold an African man named "Thomas (H)Eskett" to John Evans in 1759.[1028]

J. Levy (may be the same as John B. Levy) owned a Louisiana plantation at Ascension Parish with forty-one Black people working his fields at no wage.[1029]

Jacob Levy, Jr., (d. 1837) was active in the Congregation *Shearith Israel* of New York and owned slaves named "George Roper," "Mary Mundy," "John Jackson," "Samuel Spures," "Edwin Jackson," "Elizabeth Jackson" and "James Jackson," among others. One of his daughters married **Moses Seixas**, another

---

[1023]Korn, "Jews and Negro Slavery," p. 212; Simonhoff, *Jewish Participants in the Civil War*, pp. 253-54.

[1024]"Acquisitions," *AJA*, vol. 16 (1964), p. 94.

[1025]*EJ*, vol. 11, p. 157; Simonhoff, *Jewish Notables*, pp. 33-36; Jacob R. Marcus, *Studies in American Jewish History* (Cincinnati: Hebrew Union College Press, 1969), p. 233; Rosenbloom, p. 91.

[1026]*EHJ*, p. 273; *EJ*, vol. 14, p. 1663.

[1027]*EJ*, vol. 11, p. 162; Leo Hershkowitz, "Wills of Early New York Jews (1784-1799)," *AJHQ*, vol. 56 (1966), p. 168; Wolf and Whiteman, p. 24.

[1028]"Acquisitions," *AJA*, vol. 14 (1962), p. 93; Rosenbloom, p. 92.

[1029]Korn, "Jews and Negro Slavery," p. 180.

married **Moses Hays,** and another married **Joseph L. Joseph**, all of whom were slave dealers or owners.[1030]

John B. Levy came to New Orleans in 1828 with 37 Africans on the schooner *Transport*.[1031]

Joseph Israel Levy, in his 1786 will, left to the mother of his child Jabica "five hundred Rupees, and two slave girls and the garden and the house, with everything belonging unto her to be paid to her by my executors..."[1032]

Levy Andrew Levy, described as a "gentleman," participated in the extermination plot against the Indians by providing them with blankets deliberately laced with smallpox. He is listed as a resident of Lancaster, Pennsylvania, with "two female slaves and one house." Levy once had a slave "who preferred freedom with the Indians to servitude under Levy. The slave ran off with a local tribe."[1033]

Lewis B. Levy of Richmond, Virginia, was a "manufacturer [of] all kinds of servant's clothing." He sold rags to such slave dealers as the Davis brothers.[1034]

M. C. Levy of Charleston, South Carolina, had more than twenty African hostages.[1035]

Moses Levy (c. 1665-1728) was a New York merchant, distiller, real estate investor, ship and land owner. He became probably the most prominent and wealthiest New York Jew of the 18th century terrorizing Black humans. He was elected constable of his municipal district in 1719 but declined to serve. He was president of his Jewish congregation and died holding that office. Levy's slave-trading profits were used to help build the *Shearith Israel* on Mill Street.[1036]

[1030]Schappes, pp. 134, 599.
[1031]Korn, *Jews of New Orleans*, p. 161.
[1032]Friedman, "Wills," p. 161.
[1033]Brener, pp. 8-9.
[1034]Korn, "Jews and Negro Slavery in the Old South,"*PAJHS*, vol. 50 (1960), p. 184 (plate).
[1035]Rosenwaike, "Jewish Population of 1820," p. 18.
[1036]*EJ*, vol. 11, p. 161; *MEAJ1*, p. 51; Rosenbloom, p. 94.

Moses Levy of Charleston, South Carolina, was the most successful detective on the Charleston police force. Part of his responsibility was to pursue runaway Blacks.[1037]

Moses Elias Levy (1782-1854) was a plantation owner in Florida, Saint Thomas, Virgin Islands, and Havana, Cuba. While in England, Levy attacked the evils of slavery in public forums and written pamphlets. In Florida, he used dozens of Black Africans to try to establish a Zionist homeland.[1038]

Nathan Levy (1704-1753) came to Philadelphia from London on the same ship (*Myrtilla*) that brought the Liberty Bell. He established an indentured servant placement service with his brother **Isaac**, and on January 3, 1738, they advertised in Benjamin Franklin's *Gazette* for buyers for "A likely young Negroe Man to be sold by Nathan and Isaac Levy, fit for Town and Country."

In 1741, they teamed up with **David** and **Moses Franks** to ship their Black victims in from Africa. Levy was a founder of the Jewish community in Philadelphia and bought land for the Jewish cemetery in 1740. He was "undoubtedly the city's richest Jew at the time of his death in 1753."[1039]

Uriah Phillips Levy (1792-1862) was a ship captain in the navy before he was twenty, and later a commodore. He held title to Thomas Jefferson's famous estate *Monticello*, and to the Virginia plantation *Washington Farm*, where Black Africans were imprisoned as slaves. He was a member of Congregation *Shearith Israel* in New York and a charter member of Washington's Hebrew Congregation. Jacob R. Marcus has written of the contradiction:

> Jews in the South knew full well that there was a slave problem, but like the people about them, they did nothing to come to grips with this evil. Though Captain Uriah P. Levy wanted to abolish slavery, his wish did not deter him from running his Virginia plantation with slave labor.[1040]

[1037]Korn, "Jews and Negro Slavery," p. 190.

[1038]*EJ*, vol. 11, p. 162; Korn, "Jews and Negro Slavery," p. 180. The area of Levy's land holdings amounted to 36,000 acres, which is equivalent to two and a half times the area of Manhattan Island. See Elfrida D. Cowen, "Notes: Moses Elias Levy's Agricultural Colony in Florida," *PAJHS*, vol. 25 (1917), pp. 132-34.

[1039]*EJ*, vol. 11, p. 162; Wolf and Whiteman, p. 24; *MCAJ2*, p. 825; Rosenbloom, p. 95.

[1040]Korn, "Jews and Negro Slavery," p. 188 note; *EJ*, vol. 11, p. 164; *MUSJ1*, p. 587; Rosenbloom, p. 97.

Rabbi Max (Menachem) Lilienthal (1815-1882) of Cincinnati was a major Jewish leader and ardent supporter of the Southern state's right to kidnap and enslave African people.[1041]

Alexander Lindo (1753-1812) was a "major importer of slaves" in the late eighteenth century. He admitted to being responsible for the deaths of over 150 African slaves in the Middle Passage and 20 more upon their arrival in Jamaica, though he was never punished.[1042]

Moses Lindo (1712-1774) of South Carolina was a wealthy planter and enslaver of Africans, according to the *Jewish Encyclopaedia.*[1043] He ran an advertisement stating that "If any person is willing to part with a plantation of 500 acres with 60 or 70 Negroes, I am ready to purchase it for ready money." Lindo imported 49 slaves from Barbados in the 1750s, and in 1756 he bought 2 African male children from John Gordon, according to a bill of sale. One of his slave ships was named *Lindo Packett.*

Lindo was reputed to be one of the best judges of indigo in America or Europe. He was largely responsible for the growth of that industry from 300,000 pounds yearly to over 1,200,000 pounds. "Lindo himself handled millions of pounds of it. He lived to see the indigo industry employ 10,000 slaves," according to Jacob Rader Marcus.[1044]

Aaron Lopez (1731-1782) was the most notorious of the slave-dealing Jews. He was Newport's leading participant in the Black Holocaust, largest taxpayer, and the epitome of the Newport slave-dealing Jewish culture. His son-in-law, **Abraham Pereira Mendes**, carried on the murderous trade and built massive wealth in his own right.[1045] Born in Portugal

---

[1041]Korn, *Civil War,* p. 28; *EJ*, vol. 11, p. 243.

[1042]*EHJ*, p. 273; *EJ*, vol. 14, p. 1663.

[1043]*Jewish Encyclopaedia*, vol. 8 (New York and London: Funk and Wagnalls Company, 1905 - 1916), p. 93.

[1044]Elzas, p. 50; *EJ*, vol. 11, p. 259; "Acquisitions," *AJA*, vol. 14 (1962), p. 93; *MEAJ2*, p. 243; *MCAJ2*, p. 618; Kenneth Libo and Irving Howe, *We Lived There Too* (New York: St. Martin's/Marek, 1984), p. 60; Rosenbloom, p. 97.

[1045]*EJ*, vol. 11, p. 488; Simonhoff, *Jewish Notables*, pp. 5-8; *EHJ*, p. 273; Feingold, *Zion*, p. 42; *JRM/Docs*, pp. 384, 416, 446; Bruce M. Bigelow, "Aaron Lopez: Colonial Merchant of Newport," *New England Quarterly*, vol. 4 (1931), p. 757. Also in *Rhode Island Jewish Historical Notes*, vol. 2 (June 1956-April 1958), pp. 4-18; Virginia Bever Platt, "And Don't Forget the Guinea Voyage: The Slave Trade of Aaron Lopez of Newport," *William and Mary Quarterly*, vol. 32, no. 4 (1975), p. 601. Copies of some

Lopez moved to Newport, Rhode Island, in 1752, renounced his Marrano past and built an extensive trans-Atlantic slave-dealing empire. "What can be said about this most attractive figure," writes Dr. Marcus, "is that he lived on a baronial scale, maintained an entourage of over thirty persons, including the necessary slaves and hired servants, and had his own stable and two chaises."[1046] He was engaged extensively in smuggling and the owner of between 30 and 40 ships.[1047] By 1749, Lopez was generally considered to be one of the largest merchants in the country, shipping every marketable item including molasses, Blacks, rum, pork and bottled beer.[1048] He owned a wharf, arranged for building, chartering, and outfitting the vessels, hired captains and crews, and kept detailed accounts.[1049]

Lopez reportedly launched his career as a slave merchant late in 1761 when he and **Jacob Rodriguez Rivera** began to outfit their jointly owned brigantine *Grayhound* for an African voyage.[1050] On January 7, 1763, William Pinnegar captained a Lopez ship that delivered 134 Africans to Lopez's Jewish

---

original Lopez slave papers are in the *Newport Historical Society Bulletin*, no. 62 (July 1927); Rosenbloom, pp. 97-98.

[1046] *MCAJ3*, p. 826; Broches, p. 16.

[1047] *MCAJ2*, pp. 789, 793; Stanley F. Chyet, "Aaron Lopez: A Study in Buenafama," *Karp, JEA1*, p. 197. According to Bigelow, Lopez had thirty vessels: "there are 24 vessels in which Lopez was chiefly concerned and which remained in his possession during those years. These consisted of 9 sloops, 3 schooners, 7 brigantines, and 5 ships." The below list of 26 ships, owned wholly or partially by Lopez, was derived from the available historical record including Bigelow, pp. 760-61, 766; Platt, pp. 602, 603, 607-8 and 608 note; Elizabeth Donnan, *Documents Illustrative of the Slave Trade in America*, 4 volumes (Washington, D.C.: Carnegie Institution of Washington, 1930), vol. 3, pp. 226, 265 note, 272-76; Marc Lee Raphael, *Jews and Judaism in the United States: A Documentary History* (New York: Behrman House, 1983), p. 28; "Items Related to the Jews of Newport," *PAJHS*, vol. 27 (1920), p. 213. Of these, only the ones definitively recorded as having transported slaves are included in the section of this report entitled "Slave Ships and Jews."

Ships Owned by Aaron Lopez

Active	*Coaxel*	*Grayhound*	*Ocean*
Africa	*Diana*	*Hannah*	*Ranger*
America	*Dolphin*	*Hope*	*Royal Charlotte*
Ann	*Eagle*	*Industry*	*Sally*
Betsy	*Friendship*	*Jacob*	*Spry*
Charlotte	*George*	*Mary*	*Venus*
Cleopatra		*Newport Packet*	

[1048] Broches, p. 13; Rhodes, p. 9.

[1049] Platt, p. 602.

[1050] Rawley, p. 368.

agents in South Carolina, Da Costa and Farr.[1051] Four captains made thirteen of the voyages, two of whom died in Lopez's service.[1052] Below are the recorded slaving voyages of Aaron Lopez in the years 1764 through 1774[1053]:

Sloop *Spry*, Capt. Willaim Pinneger, July 16, 1764 - May 22, 1766, stopping at Barbados, Jamaica, and New York on the return voyage. The cargo included iron hoops, iron chains and slave shackles.[1054] Slaves sold: 57.

Brig *Africa*, Capt. Abraham All, May 3, 1765 - July 11, 1766. Slaves sold at Kingston: 45.

Sloop *Betsey*, Capt. Nathaniel Briggs, July 22, 1765 - August 21, 1766. Slaves sold at Kingston: 40.

Brig *Sally* (the *Spry* rerigged), Capt. Nathaniel Briggs, August, 1766 - July 1767. Slaves sold at St. Kitts: est. 33.

Brig *Africa*, Capt. Abraham All, October 20, 1766 - January 9, 1768. Slaves sold at Kingston: 69.

Brig *Hannah*, Capt. Nathaniel Briggs, May 3, 1768 - May 4, 1769. Slaves sold in South Carolina and Barbados: 63.

Sloop *Mary*, Capt. William English, June 4, 1770 - spring 1771. Slaves sold in Barbados: est. 57.

Ship *Cleopatra*, Capt. Nathaniel Briggs, July 1770 - 1771. Slaves sold in Barbados: 96.

Ship *Cleopatra*, Capt. Nathaniel Briggs, June 16, 1771 - May 27, 1772. Slaves sold in Barbados: 230.

Brig *Ann*, Capt. William English, November 27, 1772 - winter 1773-74 (arrived in Jamaica October 8, 1773). Slaves sold at Kingston: 104.[1055]

[1051]*MCAJ3*, p. 1504; Platt, p. 603.

[1052]Rawley, p. 369.

[1053]Platt, pp. 603, 608. See also Rawley, p. 371: "As in the case of Lopez, the slave ships were small; 70 Negroes for the first voyage, 94 for the second, 58 for the third, and 50 for the last, in all 265. Mortality was low on these voyages. Captain Rogers buried 2 slaves on the African coast and another after arrival at Barbados. On the second voyage only one death occurred, and on the third voyage only four deaths were recorded, 3 men and 1 woman."

As a smuggler of slaves he would not have reported or kept records of such transactions and Lopez's bookkeeping was notoriously unconventional. See Chyet, p. 199.

[1054]Chyet, p. 199.

[1055]"Some Old Papers Relating to the Newport Slave Trade," *Newport Historical Society Bulletin*, no. 62 (July 1927), pp. 14-15: "When the Brigantine was thus ready to sail her owners gave to Captain English the following orders:

Newport, November, 1772
Capt. William English

Ship *Africa*, Capt. Nathaniel Briggs, April 22, 1773 - August 1774. Slaves sold in Jamaica: est. 49.

Ship *Cleopatra*, Capt. James Bourk, June 30, 1773 - August 1774, Cargo consigned to Briggs. Slaves sold in Jamaica: est. 77.

Brig *Ann*, Capt. William English, spring 1774 - March 1775. Slaves sold in Jamaica: 112.

Sir:

...When please God you arrive there safe convert your cargo into good slaves; on the best term you can; You are not insensible that lying any considerable time on the Coast, is not only attended with a very heavy expense, but also great risk of the Slaves you may have on board. We therefore would recommend to you dispatch, even if you are obliged to give a few gallons more or less on each slave....We here enclose you David Mill Esq. of Cape coast Castle's receipt for twenty seven men and thirteen women Slaves, left in his hands by Capt. Briggs the last voyage on our accounts payable to his or our order, which we have made payable to you; When you have finished the sales of your Cargo, apply to the said Mr. Mill and receive from him the above mentioned slaves, which from his universal character, we are confident he will not only immediately comply but will also deliver you slaves to your satisfaction; To these slaves we desire you'll put some particular mark that may distinguish them from those of the Cargo, so that their sales in the West Indies may be kept by itself, for the Insurance on these is not blended with the Cargo.

You are to be particularly careful, that as soon as you have got your slaves on board, and before you leave the Coast you are to fill up two Sets of bills of lading; The one mentioning the number of Slaves you have on board, bought with your Cargo, which are two-thirds on acct. of Aaron Lopez and the other third on account of Jacob Rod Rivera; And another set for the forty slaves you receive from Mr. Mill, those are one-half on each our Acct., and remit us by two different Oppts, One of each of these bills of lading, and the third carry with you; for in case of accident (which God forbid) we have no other way of proving our interest, than by a bill of lading.

When thus you have finished your trade on the Coast, you are to proceed directly to the Island of Jamaica when if you arrive in any time between the first of December and the first of July, you are to go directly to Savanah La Mar, and there deliver your whole quantity of slaves on our Acct. to Capt. Benjamin Wright, in whose hands we shall lodge whatever future orders we may have occasion to give you; But if you arrive off of Jamaica in any time between the month of July and the first of December, than you are not to proceed to Savanah La Mar, but to Kingston in that Island, and there apply to Mr. Thomas Dolbeare merchant there, to whom you are to deliver your slaves on our Accts and in whose hands we shall also lodge, whatever orders we may find necessary further to give you, and if on inquiry you find when you arrive at Kingston, that Capt. Wright is in any part of the Island, you are desired to send him immediate intelligence of your arrival, but this is not to prevent the delivery of the Slaves to Mr. Dolbeare as aforesaid, and should Capt. Wright not be at Savanah La Mar when you arrive there, nor in any part of Jamaica, in that case dispatch an express to Mr. Dolbeare at Kingston, and follow what orders you may receive from him. Either Capt. Wright or Mr. Dolbeare will have orders to load our Brig with the produce of the Island if the season of the year will permit it. Therefore as soon as you have delivered your slaves, and your vessel ready, proceed directly back to this port.

The experience you have in the Guinea trade and the raised opinion we have of your integrity and care render it unnecessary for us to give you any particular charge in respect to the sales, and purchase of your Cargo, nor to remind you that you keep a watchful eye on the slaves during the time you may have them on board. We expect you [to] embrace every opportunity to let us hear from you at any of the ports you may be at, Not in the least doubting, but your conduct will fully answer all our expectations. We conclude wishing you a pleasant prosperous voyage and safe return to your family in health, we are

Your friends and owners,
Jacob Rod Rivera,
Aaron Lopez

Mortality on these voyages was extremely high, as this passage from the *William and Mary Quarterly* suggests:

> Captain Briggs had taken aboard twenty-one slaves at the Windward Coast south of Cape Verde, ten at Cape Mount on the Grain Coast, and sixty-seven along the Gold Coast—a total of ninety-eight. However, as Lopez informed his London correspondent, William Stead, there was severe loss of life at sea, and much sickness among the survivors forced a hurried sale at St. Kitts. *Sally*'s log records the burial of six slaves at sea, dead "with the feaver and flox"; the loss was doubtless much heavier, as the log does not cover a four-month period of coasting southward and eastward from the Windward Coast to Cape Coast Castle....The figure, given above, of thirty-three slaves sold is calculated from the sum realized on the sale of the survivors, who may have been more numerous than this but of low value because of their debilitated condition.[1056]

The *Cleopatra* was assumed to have experienced very heavy mortality, according to Lopez biographer Virginia Bever Platt, because the ship had carried a "much higher number of 230 blacks to Barbados on her next voyage."[1057] Using this reasoning and simple mathematics, one could conclude that as many as, or more than, 287 Black Africans may have lost their lives in these two voyages of the *Cleopatra* alone.

In the last recorded voyage of the *Ann*, "[Captain] English reached Kingston on October 7, having lost five slaves on the voyage but with his people apparently healthy. By the time the sale could be made, two more had died and the prevalence of 'the Swelling' among the remainder caused a drastic reduction in their value..."[1058]

Lopez's other commercial ventures were sometimes called into question. One Caribbean trader bitterly complained in a series of letters about the quality of the lumber, flour, and fish cargoes dispatched from Newport—consignments that often arrived out of season or in leaky vessels to which he had to give time and attention. Flour too often was of low grade, staves and hoops for the making of molasses hogsheads were often worm-eaten, and fish was putrid from being packed in insufficient brine. Lopez found it difficult to dispose of such

---

[1056]Platt, p. 605, and on p. 614: "The price of slaves was high, amounting to 210 to 220 gallons of rum per slave."

[1057]Platt, p. 608. Another reference to a slave dying while in bondage to Lopez occurs in a news item in the *Newport Mercury* on September 16, 1771, reporting on the "drowning of Negro boy of Lopez at his wharf." See Rhodes, p. 12.

[1058]Platt, p. 614.

cargoes and implied that slave cargoes were easier to handle and more profitable.[1059]

Dr. Marcus discusses the household and business of Lopez and his utter dependency on free Black labor:

> Lopez always maintained a staff of Negro domestics and in addition often hired Negro slaves from their masters, though in his papers such laborers were always referred to as servants, never as slaves. At least half a dozen negroes were usually employed at one time at the Lopez shop, storehouse and wharf. For his living quarters, Lopez supplemented his Negro domestics by hiring an Indian woman to wash and scrub and a white seamstress to sew and make garments for the family and the Negro household servants.[1060]

Lopez took 27 of these slaves to Leicester, Massachusetts, when fleeing the British attack on Newport.[1061]

It was also Lopez who was identified as the primary Newport merchant who ignored the non-importation protest of British tax policies organized by the Revolution-era colonists. The man who fingered Lopez was Ezra Stiles, a leading clergyman and President of Yale University. He referred to Lopez in his Diary as "a Merchant of the first Eminence; for Honor and Extent of Commerce probably surpassed by no Merchant in America."

Journeying to Rhode Island with his wife and family on May 28, 1782, he passed Scott's Pond, near Providence, and was thrown by his horse into quicksand, where he drowned.[1062]

[1059]Platt, p. 611.

[1060]*MCAJ2*, p. 574. For Lopez's and Rivera's ownership of slaves see *Census of the Inhabitants of the Colony of Rhode Island and Providence Plantations, Taken by Order of the General Assembly in the Year 1774* (Providence, Rhode Island, 1858). According to Platt, p. 607: "Both Lopez and Rivera owned slaves – Lopez held five, Rivera twelve in 1774 – and employed them, with those of other owners, in the unpleasant work of 'trying' or rendering the whale head matter for the making of candles."

[1061]*MCAJ3*, p. 1289.

[1062]See herein "Jews and the American Revolution" for more on the activities of the Newport Jews concerning the non-importation protests of the colonists leading to the Revolutionary War. Also Jankowsky's *The American Jew*, p. 13; *MEAJ1*, pp. 142-43; Rawley, p. 368, states that "Aaron Lopez, within a few years stood in the forefront of Newport slave merchants"; "An Historical Review of New England Life and Letters," *The New England Quarterly*, vol. 4 (1931), p. 776; and *Rhode Island Jewish History Notes*, vol. 2 (June 1956-April 1958), pp. 4-18. See also Dexter, *The Literary Diary of Ezra Stiles*, vol. 3, pp. 24-25.

Haham Eliahu Lopez, the spiritual head of the Barbados Jews of the late seventeenth century, said that he "would certainly continue in enjoyment of his own two negro attendants."[1063]

Moses Lopez purchased a Black woman from John Roosevelt. The sale was witnessed by **Judah Hays** and **Jacobus Roosevelt**.[1064]

Rachel Lopez lived in Bridgetown, Barbados, with a family of four and "one negro."[1065]

Aaron Baruch Louzada lived with his family in Broad Street, Bridgetown, Barbados, attended by five Black slaves.[1066]

Rachell Baruh Louzada's will in Portuguese, dated October 29, 1703, required her sons **Solomon** and **Jacob** to "sell everything in the house, goods, jewels, silver, gold & copper, also slaves, & to pay all my debts, funeral expenses, & doctors bills....To my daughter Hannah Baruh Louzada a negress named Esperansa, & a diamond ring, also £25 current money with which to commence seeking a livelihood, & that she may live in sisterly harmony with her brothers...as God commands."[1067]

James Lucena was a Portuguese cousin of **Aaron Lopez** who found revenue as a shipper in the African slave trade. A refugee from the Portuguese Inquisition, he came to Rhode Island in the early 1750s claiming to be a Catholic. In June of 1768, he wrote to Lopez asking instructions as he prepared for a voyage to Africa to kidnap innocent Africans. In the letter he establishes that it was customary for ship owners to pay their captains with slaves.

Lucena reportedly enslaved at least nine and as many as twenty Africans and owned 750 acres in Georgia when the trustees of that colony introduced slavery in 1749. He was a justice of the peace in 1766, and in 1771 he owned 1000 more acres and "sent a vessel to Jamaica for a parcel of Negroes."[1068] On March 21, 1770, he placed the following advertisement in the Savannah *Georgia Gazette*:

1063 Samuel, p. 7.
1064 "Acquisitions," *AJA*, vol. 13 (1961), p. 117; Rosenbloom, p. 99.
1065 Samuel, p. 43.
1066 Samuel, p. 23.
1067 Samuel, pp. 80-81.
1068 *MEAJ2*, pp. 321-24; *MCAJ3*, pp. 1242, 1467.

> RUN AWAY from the subscriber, on Friday last, A NEGROE FELLOW, named SAM, about 22 years old, and about 5 feet 6 inches high, is well known in and about Savannah, has his country marks on each side his face thus | | |, his teeth remarkably wide apart, and speaks very good English, had on when he went away a dark grey cloth double breasted waistcoat and a white negroe cloth under jacket, a pair of green negroe cloth long trowsers, and a round sailor's cap. Whoever delivers him to me at Savannah shall have a reward of twenty shillings, and all reasonable charges.
>
> James Lucena
>
> N.B. Said negroe is suspected to be concealed on board some vessel, and I forewarn the masters of vessels from carrying him off, as they may depend on being prosecuted to the utmost rigour of the law.[1069]

Abraham De Lyon, Sr., arrived in Savannah, Georgia, in 1733, and later held eighteen Black hostages against their will.[1070]

Abraham De Lyon (may be the same as above) left his Savannah, Georgia, wine-making business because of "the want of Negroes...whereas his white servants cost him more than he was able to afford."[1071]

Isaac Lyons of Columbia, South Carolina, owned a plantation and held numerous African citizens against their will. He imported eight Blacks in 1763.[1072]

Samuel Maas of Charleston, according to Professor Marcus, took

> only four weeks to be convinced that blacks had to be watched, disciplined, and, if necessary, ruthlessly punished. Slavery he agreed, was a sound institution; the Southern economy was built on black labor. The black made an ideal workhand, for only he, stemming from the torrid African lands, could tolerate the humidity, intense heat, and backbreaking labor of the Carolina lowlands. Undoubtedly, Maas was influenced in his views by his uncle and by the luxury of the well-appointed home with its

---

[1069] Windley, vol. 4, p. 44.

[1070] Rosenwaike, "Jewish Population of 1820," p. 19; *EJ*, vol. 7, p. 429; Rosenbloom, p. 102.

[1071] Brener, p. 4; Edward D. Coleman, "Jewish Merchants in the Colonial Slave Trade," *PAJHS*, vol. 34 (1938), p. 285.

[1072] Korn, "Jews and Negro Slavery," p. 180; *MEAJ2*, p. 322.

massive silver service and numerous, obsequious slaves ready to respond to his slightest nod – all this impressed Maas mightily.[1073]

Esther Marache sent her "mulatto wench" out to peddle cakes, but "[did] not want her admitted into anyone's home."[1074]

A. J. Marks (This may be Alexander Marks; 1788-1861) was the acting rabbi in New Orleans in the 1830s, and owned eleven Africans according to the 1840 census.[1075]

Joseph Marks signed a petition from a group of Philadelphia merchants against a tax on Negroes in 1761. Joining him were Jews **David Franks** and **Benjamin Levy**.[1076]

Mark Marks was deputy sheriff of Charleston in 1822, part of whose job was to punish runaway Blacks.[1077]

Mordecai Marks (1739 or 1740-1797) was a merchant and farmer "who owned his own trotting and pacing mares, a Negro slave, and a small library."[1078]

Isaac Rodrigues Marques (d. 1706 or 1707) was a New York merchant, importer, and ship owner from Denmark who dictated in his will that a "good serviceable negro woman" be purchased to serve his "dear mother" after his death.[1079]

Joseph Marx (1771 or 1772-1840) was born in Hanover, Germany, and moved to Richmond, Virginia, where he engaged in large real estate transactions. He was an associate of Thomas Jefferson and active in the Jewish community while holding 11 Blacks against their will to perform hard labor at no pay.[1080]

Abraham Pereira Mendes (1825-1893) was a Jamaican rabbi, the son-in-law of **Jacob Rodriguez Rivera**, and made his money as a slave trader. On May 4, 1752, he advertised the following:

[1073]*MUSJ1*, p. 588.

[1074]*MCAJ3*, p. 1505.

[1075]Korn, "Jews and Negro Slavery," p. 196 note; *EJ*, vol. 8, p. 125; Rosenbloom, p. 106.

[1076]Edward D. Coleman, "Jewish Merchants," p. 285.

[1077]Korn, "Jews and Negro Slavery," p. 190; *EJ*, vol. 5, p. 161.

[1078]Marcus, *Studies in American Jewish History*, p. 79; Jacob Rader Marcus, "Light on Early Connecticut Jewry," *AJA*, vol. 1 (January 1949), p. 26.

[1079]Friedman, "Wills," p. 149. See also Libo and Howe, pp. 46-47; Rosenbloom, p. 109.

[1080]Rosenwaike, "Jewish Population of 1820," p. 19; Rosenbloom, p. 109.

> To be sold by Abraham Pereira Mendes, a Parcel of Likely young Negroes, Piemento, Old Copper, Coffee, etc....If any Person has a Mind to purchase any of the Goods mentioned, they may enquire of Mr. Daniel Gomez.[1081]

In 1767, when on a mission to Jamaica, Mendes reported back to his father-in-law that a consignment of Negroes was "in such poor order" because of the storage conditions that he could not do anything but sell them off cheaply:

> To my great surprise I found the negroes nothing to what I expected....Captain All's small cargo, however, turned out as we see to consist almost entirely of "refuse slaves," and Captain All himself fell ill.[1082]

Joseph Mendes, of the town of Speights in the Parish of St. Peters, Barbados, prepared his will in English dated February 17, 1700:

> To my dear & loving wife Rachel M. 3 Negro Slaves, Mary, Astor she & her boy Matte & the Issue or Offspring of their bodies for ever....To son Moses M. £1000 on marriage or 21st birthday (which shall first happen) & for ever one Negro Woman named Hagar & the issue or offspring of her body & 2 negro boys named Jack Coger & Tom. To daughter Sarah £1000 on marriage or 18th birthday (which shall first happen) & for ever one negro woman named Mary & a Negro girl named Evare & the issue...of their bodies. To daughter Luna £1000 on marriage or 18th birthday (which shall first happen) & £40 [so] that 2 young negroes be bought for her forever....Ex'ors may sell all such Lands houses & Negroes as I have in this Island for the better adjusting their Accounts.[1083]

Jacob Defonseca Meza of Barbados owned "a certain Molatto woman Isabella."[1084]

Abraham Bueno DeMezqueto (**Mesquita**). Probably a son of **Benjamin Bueno de Mesquita**, who, with two sons, was banished from Jamaica on August 16, 1665. Abraham owned a plantation at Barbados in 1692, and was recorded as a slave owner in the census of 1707.[1085]

[1081]**Daniel Gomez** was also Jewish (see entry). Feldstein, p. 12; *EJ*, vol. 11, p. 1343, and vol. 12, p. 1043; Kohler, "New York," p. 82.

[1082]Pope-Hennessy, p. 240; Donnan, vol. 3, pp. 225-26. See discussion of white mortality in the slave trade in Philip D. Curtin, *The Atlantic Slave Trade: A Census* (Madison: University of Wisconsin Press, 1969).

[1083]Samuel, pp. 54-55, 57.

[1084]Samuel, p. 80.

[1085]Malcolm H. Stern, "Some Notes on the Jews of Nevis," *AJA* (October 1958), p. 156.

Gustavas Meyers was a staunch supporter of slavery and a Jewish leader.[1086]

Moses Michal (or **Michaels**, c. 1685-1740) was born in Germany and was a New York merchant in partnership with **Michael Asher** of Boston. By 1730, he was the largest importer among the Curaçaoan Jews. He was a member of *Shearith Israel* and enslaved at least two Blacks named "Tham" and "Prins."[1087]

Abigail Minis (1701-1794). In 1740, many Jews left Savannah, Georgia, because of the restriction against slavery. Ms. Minis and family stayed, waited for the law to change, and then forced at least 17 Blacks to work her 2,500-acre farm. Her son **Philip** was president of Savannah's Congregation *Mikveh Israel*. Minis named three of the Africans "Sue," "Lizzy," and "Sandy."[1088] He advertised in the Savannah *Georgia Gazette* on June 28, 1775:

> RUN AWAY, A CREOLE NEGROE FELLOW, named Charles, well known in Savannah. Ten shillings reward will be given on delivery of him to Philip Minis.[1089]

Isaac Miranda was an active trader and land owner in Lancaster County in 1720. In 1730, the Indians filed a formal complaint against Miranda, who they claimed defrauded them. According to historian David Brener, "In all probability it was the gullibility and childish wants of the Indians which made them give their valuable furs in exchange for trinkets, mirrors, rum and blankets. Such was the nature of Indian traders."[1090]

Moline Family was run out of San Domingo in 1793 when the Africans revolted against the white man's slave society. They brought with them some African captives, branded with the Moline name, to work for them in Pennsylvania. Another source lists a **Solomon Moline** from Cape Francois, who fled to Philadelphia in 1792 with his family and slaves.[1091]

[1086]Feingold, *Zion*, p. 89.

[1087]Hershkowitz, "Wills (1704-1740)," p. 360; Rosenbloom, p. 112.

[1088]*MEAJ2*, pp. 357-61; *EJ*, vol. 12, p. 32; *MCAJ3*, p. 1467; Simonhoff, *Jewish Notables*, pp. 17-20; Korn, "Jews and Negro Slavery," p. 180; Marcus, *The American Jewish Woman*, p. 26; *MUSJ1*, p. 210; Rosenbloom, p. 113.

[1089]Windley, vol. 4, pp. 66, 195.

[1090]Brener, p. 2.

[1091]Wolf and Whiteman, p. 191; Rosenbloom, p. 116.

Manoel Rodrigues Monsancto of Brazil was charged with openly professing Judaism by Inquisitional authorities in 1646. He held a woman from Guinea named "Beatriz" and her "mulatto" daughter "Rachel" as slaves.[1092]

Monsanto Family of Louisiana included **Benjamin**, **Isaac**, **Manuel**, **Eleanora**, **Gracia**, and **Jacob**. They made frequent purchases of Blacks, including twelve in 1785, thirteen and then thirty-one in 1787, and eighty in 1768. In 1794, Benjamin sold "Babet," a Black woman, to Franco Cardel. Manuel sold two Blacks from Guinea named "Polidor" and "Lucy" to James Saunders for $850 in silver. As individuals they were owners of Africans, whom they named "Quetelle," "Valentin," "Baptiste," "Prince," "Princess," "Ceasar," "Dolly," "Jen," "Fanchonet," "Rozetta," "Mamy," "Sofia," and many others. Isaac repeatedly mortgaged four of these when in financial trouble.

Benjamin Monsanto of Natchez, Mississippi, entered into at least 6 contracts for the sale of his slaves, which would take place *after* his death. Gracia bequeathed nine Africans to her relatives in her 1790 will, and Eleanora also held Blacks as slaves. Manuel Jacob Monsanto entered into at least 12 contracts for sale of slaves between 1787 and 1789 in Natchez and New Orleans, Louisiana.[1093] "His family consists of himself and seven Negroes."[1094] Later, "Jacob Monsanto, son of Isaac Rodrigues Monsanto, one of the very first known Jews to settle in New Orleans, owner of a several-hundred-acre plantation at Manchac, fell in love with his slave, Mamy or Maimi William. Their daughter, Sophia, grew up to be a lovely quadroon."[1095]

An excerpt of one of Benjamin's many slave contracts follows:

[1092]Arnold Wiznitzer, *Jews in Colonial Brazil* (Morningside Heights, New York: Columbia University Press, 1960), p. 60.

[1093]*EHJ*, p. 274; *JRM/Docs*, p. 456; Korn, *Jews of New Orleans*, pp. 10, 17, 18, 21, 26, 27, 36-40, 44, 47-49, 57-66; *EJ*, vol. 14, p. 1664, and vol. 12, p. 1041; Blau and Baron, vol. 3, p. 799; "Acquisitions," *AJA*, vol. 3 (1951), p. 43; Libo and Howe, p. 63; Rosenbloom, p. 116.

[1094]Korn, *Jews of New Orleans*, p. 59.

[1095]Sharfman, p. 187.

> Be it known to all to whom these presents shall come, that I Benjamin Monsanto do really and effectually sell to Henry Manadu a negro wench named "Judy," aged Eighteen years, native of Guinea, for the sum of four hundred Dollars in all the month of January in the year one thousand Seven hundred and ninety one; and paying interest at the rate of ten per cent for the remaining two hundred and fifty Dollars until paid; said negro wench being and remaining mortgaged until final payment shall have been made; wherewith I acknowledge to be fully satisfied and content, hereby renouncing the plea of non numerata pecunia, fraud, or others in the case Whatsoever; granting formal receipt for the same. For which said consideration I do hereby resign all right, title, possession and claim, in and to the said Slave, all of which I transfer and convey to the Said Purchaser and his assigns, to be, as his own, held and enjoyed, and when fully paid for, Sold, exchanged, or otherwise alienated at pleasure in virtue of these presents granted in his favor in token of real delivery, without other proof of property being required, from which he is hereby released, binding myself to maintain the validity of this present sale in full form and right in favor of the Purchaser aforesaid, and granting authority to the Justices of his Majesty to compel me to the performance of the same as if Judgment had already been given therein, renouncing all laws, rights, and privileges in my favor whatsoever. And I the said Henry Manadu being present, do hereby accept this Instrument in my favor, receiving said negro Wench as purchased in the form and for the consideration therein mentioned and contained, wherewith I am fully satisfied and content, hereby renouncing the plea of non numerato pecunia, *fraud*, or other considerations in the case Whatsoever; granting formal receipt for the same. Done and executed, in testimony thereof, at the post of Natchez, this nineteenth day of the month of February in the year one thousand seven hundred and ninety...[1096]

Benjamin Monsanto sold land and "a Dwelling House, Store, and two other buildings, for which I have received payment in a negro, named 'Nat;' to my full satisfaction." Another contract stipulated "that Don Louis Faure is bound to defend the said sale in case the negro shall be claimed by any other Person."

In a 1792 contract, Benjamin mortgaged his Black slaves:

> I do hereby specially mortgage three slaves to me belonging, namely Eugene and Louis, aged twenty four years each, the first named of the Senegal nation and the second of the Congo nation; and a Negro Woman named Adelaide, aged twenty eight years, also of the Congo nation; which said slaves I warrant free from

[1096] Blau and Baron, vol. 3, pp. 847-48.

> mortgage or other incumbrance, as I have made appear by certificate from the Recorder of mortgages; and which said slaves I promise and engage shall not be sold nor otherwise alienated during the term of this obligation...[1097]

Major Alfred Mordecai. Born in Warrenton, North Carolina, Mordecai completed West Point and in 1861 was assigned to the army arsenal at Watervliert, New York. He resigned his commission rather than fight against the Confederates and made these observations of the African and slavery:

> [I have] a sort of repugnance to the Negroes which has increased upon me as I have been less and less associated with them. Therefore, I have never wished to make a home among them. This feeling is, naturally enough, much stronger on the part of my family; we have seldom spoken of it, but I am sure that it would be utterly repugnant to the feelings of my wife and daughters to live among slaves, and if it can be avoided, I should be extremely loathe to oblige them, by residence and habit, to overcome this repugnance, even supposing it possible....I have no doubt that the race is in a better condition here than they are as savages in Africa, or than they would be as free men, from all the experience we have seen. But I never wished to be one of the agents in thus bettering their condition...and I am utterly averse to any participation in the schemes for destroying or weakening the hold of the masters on their slaves, unless they themselves are willing to abandon it.[1098]

In his letter of March 17, 1861, to brother **Samuel**, Mordecai defended slavery as a constitutional right:

> ...it appears to be sufficient to know that at the formation of our government slavery existed all over the land and was expressly protected by the Constitution from being interfered with by any authority but the states themselves; that therefore the people who have retained it are entitled to the enforcement of their constitutional rights with regard to it both in the letter and the spirit.[1099]

Furthermore, Mordecai firmly believed that the maintenance of slavery was the result of the activities of Northern abolitionists and condemned abolitionism, which had "grown

[1097]Blau and Baron, vol. 3, p. 850.

[1098]Bertram W. Korn, "The Jews of the Confederacy," *AJA*, vol. 13 (1961), pp. 29-30; Bermon, p. 165.

[1099]Korn, "The Jews of the Confederacy," pp. 16-19.

to a fearful extent within a few years."[1100]

Mordecai's Southern relatives had been slaveholders as far back as he could remember; indeed, his brother **George**, a wealthy Raleigh businessman, owned about one hundred slaves.[1101]

Augustus Mordecai, brother of **Emma**, owned a plantation called *Rosewood* in North Carolina, with many slaves.[1102]

Benjamin Mordecai of Charleston dealt in huge sales of Blacks and penned them up like livestock next to his warehouses. At least one of his captives was named "Abram" or "Abraham." Of his participation in the Civil War the *Boston Transcript* reported that Mordecai "has presented to his belligerent state and city $10,000, to aid the purpose of secession, with the offer besides of a large number of negroes to work in the cause..."[1103]

In 1857, he advertised in the *Charleston Courier* "Prime Field Negros and House Servants" for sale.[1104] They included:

Coachmen and House Servants	**Cooks, Seamstresses, Washers and Ironers**
Tom, 25 years of age	Elvy, 18
John, 21	Amelia, 22
Lilburn, 24	Lydia, 40
Isaac, 22	Louisa, 40
	Patsy, 19; Nurse

Field Hands and Laborers

Caroline,17	Moses, 33; woodworker	Nancy, 20; with 2 children
Betsy, 17	Henry, 20	Susan, 30
Catherine, 16	Lawrence, 45	Caroline, 18
Octavia, 16	Dave, 25; laborer	Benjamin, 25
Mary, 28	Henry, 22; tailor	Sam, 16; ploughboy
Sarah, 30; w/ child	Lucy, 19	Lindsay, 27
Sarah, 18	Margaret, 16	Isaac, 18
Saunders, 22	Milly, 17	Byron, 22
Sampson, 30	Salina, 16	Nat, 30; laborer and sailor

[1100] Stanley L. Falk, "Divided Loyalties in 1861: The Decision of Major Alfred Mordecai," *PAJHS*, vol. 48 (1958-59), pp. 148-49.

[1101] Falk, pp. 149-50.

[1102] *JRM/Memoirs 3*, p. 324.

[1103] Korn, *Civil War*, p. 159; Segal, *Fascinating Facts*, p. 84; Harry Golden, *Our Southern Landsman* (New York: G. P. Putnam's Sons, 1974), p. 223.

[1104] *EHJ*, p. 274; Korn, "Jews and Negro Slavery," p. 198 note; *EJ*, vol. 14, p. 1664.

Mordecai regularly shipped slaves to New Orleans between 1846 and 1860 and bought at least 102 slaves at Charleston district judicial sales of the 1850s.[1105]

Emma Mordecai was a Jewish relative of the **Gratz** and **Hays** families who enslaved several Black Africans. She described in her journal how the Jews participated in the lynching of Nat Turner's rebel forces by burning off the foot of an innocent Black man and cutting off the ear of another. They then rubbed sand into their wounds and horse-dragged them to their death.[1106]

The slaves of Emma Mordecai included "George," "Cyrus," "Massie," "Mary," "Georgiana," and possibly "Phil," "Lizzy," and "Elick." She said of the freed Blacks: "They are as ill-bred as old Lincoln himself....They will now begin to find out how easy their life as slaves had been, and to feel the slavery of their freedom."[1107]

George Washington Mordecai was a wealthy Raleigh, North Carolina, plantation owner, bank president, and slave driver who owned at least one hundred Black Africans. He wrote to a northern Republican in 1860: "I would much sooner trust myself alone on my plantation surrounded by my slaves, than in one of your large manufacturing towns when your labourers are discharged from employment and crying aloud for bread for themselves and their little ones."[1108]

Jacob Mordecai of Henrico County, Virginia, held more than twenty African hostages.[1109]

Mordecai Moses Mordecai, a Russian Jewish businessman in Pennsylvania, helped **Joseph Simon** to buy a slave.[1110]

Rebecca Mordecai, of Richmond, Virginia, was fined $3.33 in 1839, "for allowing a hired slave to go at large contrary to the Act of Assembly."[1111]

[1105]Michael Tadman, *Speculators and Slaves: Masters, Traders and Slaves in the Old South* (Madison: University of Wisconsin Press, 1989), p. 257.

[1106]Simonhoff, *Jewish Participants in the Civil War*, p. 298; Bermon, p. 167.

[1107]*JRM/Memoirs 3*, pp. 328-43.

[1108]Korn, "Jews and Negro Slavery," p. 212; *EJ*, vol. 12, p. 1218; Falk, p. 149.

[1109]Rosenwaike, "Jewish Population of 1820," p. 18; *MUSJ1*, p. 130; Bermon, p. 166.

[1110]*MCAJ2*, p. 806.

[1111]Ezekiel and Lichtenstein, p. 92.

Samuel Mordecai (1786-c. 1865) was a journalist from Richmond who derived part of his income from his articles in the pro-slavery journal *The Farmer's Register*. He regarded slavery as a natural and desirable condition of society and helped to put down Nat Turner's 1831 rebellion and assisted in the lynch mob that followed.[1112]

Barnard Moses of Charleston, South Carolina, placed the following advertisement in the *South-Carolina Gazette and General Advertiser* on November 4, 1783.

> RUN away from the subscriber, a Negro Wench called HAGAR, and her daughter called MARY, Hagar is about 40 years of age, speaks very good English. Mary about 12 years of age, speaks good English, had on when she went away a green frize habit. Whoever apprehends and secures said negroes, so that the owner may get them, shall receive a Guinea reward for each. Any person or persons harbouring said negroes, many depend on being prosecuted according to law; a farther reward of Five Guineas will be given to any person who shall give information of either of the said negroes being harboured by any white persons, on conviction.
>
> Barnard Moses.
>
> N.B. I was since informed the above negroes crossed Ashley River a few days ago, and suppose they are gone to Mr. William Stoutenburg's plantation, as her relations belong to him. All masters of vessels are forbid to harbour, or carry them off.[1113]

Isaac Moses of Philadelphia enslaved "a certain Negro named Bill of the age of thirty or thereabouts."[1114]

Isaiah Moses enslaved thirty-five Black Africans, whom he forced to work his farm at St. James, Goose Creek, South Carolina.[1115]

J. F. Moses of Lumpkin, Georgia, was a slave dealer who once advertised:

> **NEGROES, NEGROES**
>
> The undersigned has just arrived in Lumpkin from Virginia, with a likely lot of negroes, about 40 in number, embracing every

---

[1112]Korn, "Jews and Negro Slavery," p. 212; Bermon, p. 167; Rosenbloom, p. 118.

[1113]Windley, vol. 3, p. 722.

[1114]Wolf and Whiteman, p. 191; Rosenbloom, p. 120.

[1115]Korn, "Jews and Negro Slavery," p. 180.

> shade and variety. He has seamstresses, chamber maids, field hands, and doubts not that he is able to fill the bill of any who may want to buy. He has sold over two hundred negroes in this section, mostly in this county, and flatters himself that he has so far given satisfaction to his purchasers. Being a regular trader to this market he has nothing to gain by misrepresentation, and will, therefore, warrant every negro sold to come up to the bill, squarely and completely. Give him a call at his mart.[1116]

Major Moses was a Jew who gave the name "London" to one of his Black captives.[1117]

Meyer Moses advertised in the *South-Carolina Gazette* for a runaway slave on September 19, 1771:

> RUN AWAY from the Subscriber about a week past, a negro man named JACK, had on when he went away a soldier's coat, and petty coat trowsers; he is a square well set fellow, about five feet six inches high, much pock marked in the face; one of his feet is frost bitten; speaks good English. Any person that will apprehend and bring him to me, or deliver him to the warden of the work-house, shall receive FIVE POUNDS reward, and if discovered to be harboured by a white person TWENTY POUNDS reward, and if by a negro, TEN POUNDS, on conviction. Masters of vessels are cautioned against carrying him off, as they must answer the consequence: I have been informed he gives himself out for a freeman, lately from England and wants to ship himself.[1118]

Myer Moses (1779-1833) of Charleston, South Carolina, had a long record of civic leadership as a state legislator, a commissioner of schools, a director of the Planters and Mechanics Bank, a major in the War of 1812, and a major slave dealer. The following is an excerpt of an advertisement placed in *The Southern Patriot* of Charleston on August 14, 1815:

> **Sales at Auction by Myer Moses**
>
> On Tuesday, 22d August, at 10 o'clock, will be exposed to public sale, at the North side of the Exchange, the following Valuable property:
>
> That well settled farm, on Charleston Neck, situated but one mile from the Lines, fronting on King and Russel-streets. On the

---

[1116]Korn, *Civil War*, p. 16; Korn, "Jews and Negro Slavery," p. 186.
[1117]Korn, "Jews and Negro Slavery," p. 185.
[1118]Windley, vol. 3, pp. 304, 442.

premises is a comfortable Farm House [with] two very convenient Negro Houses....At the same time will be sold THE FOLLOWING VALUABLE SLAVES

BOOMA, (an African) about 22 years of age, an excellent jobbing carpenter, and a prime field hand, has been emply'd several years as a market man, in selling vegetables.
MARIA, (a country born) about 22 or 23 years old, an excellent market wench, speaks French remarkably well, is a plain cook and tolerable washer, but prefers the attendance of market, or working in the field, and is a prime field hand.
SARAH, (a country born) about 20 years old, a prime field hand.
BEN, (an African) about 20 years old Born in Africa, a prime field hand and a good boatman.
ANDREW, (an African) age unknown, a prime field hand, possesses an uncommon good disposition.
PHILLIS, (a country born) a cook, washer and ironer.
JOHN, (ditto) her son, a mullatto boy, about 16 or 17 years old, a smart house servant, understands the management of horse, drives a chair.
ROBERT, (ditto) her son, a mullatto boy, about 5 years old.
This family will be sold together or separate.

Conditions – For Lots and Farm, one half cash, balance payable in 12 months, by Note with two approved endorsers; for the Negroes, cash, or Notes with two approved endorsers, at 60 days, with discount added.

Indisputable titles will be given, and the Negroes warranted sound and agreeable to description.[1119]

Raphael J. Moses (1812-1893) was a lawyer, orator, leader of the Columbus, Georgia, Jewish community, and a staunch supporter of slavery. At one time he held title to at least 47 Black people, whom he forced to tend his 20,000 fruit trees. He helped lead Georgia out of the Union and then joined the Confederate army with his three sons. He was a Florida delegate to the 1847 Democratic convention, where he teamed with Alabama secessionist William L. Yancey to include in the platform the right to carry slaves into the Northwest

[1119] *EJ*, vol. 12, p. 414; Schappes, pp. 611-12; Rosenbloom, pp. 121-22.

territories. When this failed he protested and withdrew his delegation from the convention.[1120]

Samuel Moses was a ship owner who formed a partnership with **Isaac Elizer** and **Jacob Rivera**. He rewarded the crews of his profitable ships with Black men and women.[1121]

Solomon Moses (c. 1734-1828). Born in Amsterdam, Moses was Charleston's constable in 1822, whose job was to punish Africans who sought freedom.[1122]

Solomon Moses, Jr., (1783-1857) was Charleston, South Carolina's deputy sheriff in 1822, whose job, like his father's (above), was to punish runaway Blacks.[1123]

Clara la Mota purchased a female slave and married **Benjamin Monsanto** in 1787.[1124]

Sarah A. Motta was the daughter of **R. D'Azevedo**, from whom she inherited at least four Blacks and was given an option in the will to free or keep them. She continued to force them to labor for her without pay.[1125]

Isaac Motta was a South Carolina resident who, acting possibly as a legal agent or bounty hunter, placed this advertisement in the *South-Carolina Gazette* on March 29, 1770:

> RUN AWAY from the Honourable WILLIAM DRAYTON, Esq; at St. Augustine, in East-Florida, two NEGRO MEN; Anthony, about 25 Years of Age, very black, near six Feet high, has lost part of the first Joint of his left Thumb; Frank, about 22 Years of Age, yellow Complexioned, and pitted with the Small-pox. They were born on the Estate of the late THOMAS DRAYTON, Esq; at Indian-Land, and are supposed to have attempted to return thither. Ten Pounds Currency will be paid for each, on being delivered to the Warden of the Work-House.[1126]

[1120]Feingold, *Zion,* p. 89; Simonhoff, *Jewish Participants in the Civil War,* p. 193; *EJ,* vol. 12, p. 1114; Korn, "Jews and Negro Slavery," p. 179.

[1121]Feingold, *Zion,* p. 43; Feldstein, p. 12.

[1122]Korn, "Jews and Negro Slavery," p. 190; Rosenbloom, p. 122.

[1123]Korn, "Jews and Negro Slavery," p. 190; Rosenbloom, p. 122.

[1124]Korn, *Jews of New Orleans,* p. 42.

[1125]Korn, "Jews and Negro Slavery," p. 186.

[1126]Windley, vol. 3, pp. 284-85.

Dr. Jacob De La Motta (1789-1845) of Charleston enslaved Africans named "Ann Maria Simmons" and her son "Augustus," who were transferred to his sister Rachel after his death. He also held two other African citizens whom he called "Sam" and "Sylvia." A physician who was active in politics, he served as minister at the Jewish congregations in Savannah and Charleston. He was also involved in Masonry and was the secretary of the South Carolina Medical Society, the assistant commissioner of health, and the founder and president of his orthodox congregation.[1127]

Esther Myers (1748-1826) of the Georgetown district of South Carolina was the wife of **Mordecai** and enslaved 11 African citizens.[1128]

Dr. Henry Myers. According to Jewish writer **Emma Mordecai**, Myers joined the militia and helped to put down the 1831 rebellion of Nat Turner.[1129]

Hyam Myers did business with Sir Jeffrey Amherst, the infamous Indian exterminator. Myers wrote to **Samuel Jacobs** on September 27, 1761:

> I take this opportunity to inform you that [I] have shipp'd you on board a schooner bound to Quebeck, which will sail in a day or two, your Negro girl, seal, and blank paper.

A subsequent letter identifies the "Negro Girl" as "Jenny," whose price was £65.[1130]

Joseph Myers, of Lancaster, Pennsylvania, owned a slave, age 25, in 1773.[1131]

Manuel Myers (d. 1799) was a New York merchant, distiller, and high official of Congregation *Shearith Israel*. To his wife, Judith, he left: "my mulatto boy slave, named Harry, during the term of her natural life, and upon the decease of my said

---

[1127]Korn, "Jews and Negro Slavery," pp. 186 and 192; *EJ*, vol. 5, p. 1467; Reznikoff and Engelman, p. 77; Rosenbloom, p. 124.

[1128]Korn, "Jews and Negro Slavery," p. 181; Rosenwaike, "Jewish Population in 1790," p. 56.

[1129]Bermon, p. 167.

[1130]"Acquisitions," *AJA*, vol. 16 (1964), p. 94; *MEAJ1*, pp. 220-21; *MCAJ3*, p. 1503, also indicates that an earlier "sale of Negroes" occurred between these two on September 9, 1761.

[1131]Brener, p. 8.

wife, I do manumit set free and release from slavery my said slave named Harry." His wife died 33 years later.[1132]

Mordecai Myers' plantation housed sixty-four slaves.[1133] Based on regional records, it may be that he or his relatives are responsible for the following advertisement in the *South-Carolina Gazette* of October 24, 1770:

> ABSENTED herself from the Subscriber, on Thursday last, a tall stout NEGRO WENCH, named LUCY, well known in and about Jacksonburgh; formerly the Property of Francis Oldfield, on Ponpon Neck. She had on when she went away a Callico Petticoat and Jacket: But as she took other Cloaths with her, may probably appear in other Dresses. TEN POUNDS Currency Reward will be paid to any Person who will give Information of her being harboured by a white Person, and ONE DOLLAR if by a Negro, on Conviction of the Offender; and FIVE POUNDS like Money to any one who will deliver her to Mordecai Myers.[1134]

Years later he still sought his slave through an advertisement in the Savannah *Georgia Gazette*, on May 17, 1775:

> RUN AWAY from the subscriber, A NEGROE WENCH, named Lucy, from Ponpon, formerly the property of Francis Oldfield, said wench supposed to have gone to George Galphin, Esq.'s or harboured by horse thieves, &c. either Joseph or Brukins Prine. Whoever brings said wench to me shall have one hundred pounds reward South-Carolina currency; if harboured by white persons, and the same prosecuted. I hereby promise a reward of five hundred pounds South-Carolina currency.
>
> Mordecai Mires.
>
> N.B. The wench has been absent four years.[1135]

Moses Myers (1752-1835) of Philadelphia held an African named "David Anderson" against his will.[1136]

Samuel Myers (1755-1836) of Petersburg, Virginia, enslaved Blacks named "Isaac," "Judah," "Maria," and "Betsy," and in 1796 bought an African woman named "Alice," probably to sexually violate at his will, due to the loss of his wife four months earlier. He sold "Alice" shortly after his next

---

[1132]Hershkowitz, *Wills*, p. 208; Pool, p. 280; Rosenbloom, p. 127.
[1133]Rosenwaike, *Edge of Greatness*, p. 69.
[1134]Windley, vol. 3, pp. 293-94.
[1135]Windley, vol. 4, p. 63.
[1136]*EJ*, vol. 12, pp. 724, 1215; Wolf and Whiteman, p. 191; Rosenbloom, p. 128.

marriage.[1137] The Samuel S. Myers & Co. in Richmond held 82 African citizens as slaves in 1830. The Virginia capital was the center of the nation's tobacco industry, an industry in which slaves were owned by manufacturing enterprises. Samuel S. Myers & Co. was one of Virginia's leading tobacco manufacturers.[1138]

David Naar (1800-1880) was born in St. Thomas, Danish West Indies, to **Joshua Naar** and **Sarah D'Azevedo**. According to an island census in 1830, his family, including himself, numbered "2 men, 1 woman, 2 sons and 1 daughter, his domestic staff 5 colored women and his stock of slaves still 1 full-grown."[1139] Soon thereafter, the increasing threat of slave insurrections in the Caribbean and the decline of trade caused a considerable number of Jews, including the Naars, to begin to emigrate to continental North America.

"David Naar wielded a powerful influence as owner and editor of the *Daily True American*," writes biographer Rabbi S. Joshua Kohn: "It became the organ of the Democratic party in central New Jersey" and was edited for more than half a century, from 1853 to 1905, by David Naar and by his nephew, **Moses D. Naar**, and by David's son, **Joseph L. Naar**. He was politically rewarded with several prominent positions:

- Appointed as one of the lay Judges of the Court of Common Pleas of Essex County.
- 1843: appointed Mayor of the Borough of Elizabeth by the New Jersey Legislature.
- 1844: elected a Delegate from Essex County to the State Constitutional Convention.
- 1844: campaigned for James K. Polk as President and in 1845 was rewarded with the appointment as Commercial Agent of the United States to Saint Thomas.

[1137]Korn, "Jews and Negro Slavery," pp. 187, 188 note; Bermon, p. 164; Louis Ginsberg, *History of the Jews in Petersburg, 1789 - 1950* (Petersburg, Virginia: 1954), pp. 7-9; *EJ*, vol. 12, p. 726; "Acquisitions," *AJA*, vol. 7 (1955), p. 167; Rosenbloom, p. 129.

[1138]Rosenwaike, *Edge of Greatness*, pp. 69-70.

[1139]S. Joshua Kohn, "David Naar of Trenton, New Jersey," *AJHQ*, vol. 53 (1963-64), p. 375; *cf* Wolf, pp. 462-73, section entitled "Suppression of Negro-Revolts by the Jews of Surinam (1690-1772)." It is quite likely that this family may have been related to a Captain Moses Naar (Wolf, p. 468), who is described as having led the wholesale pogrom against the freedom-seeking Black slaves of Surinam's Jews in which countless Africans were tracked and murdered by the Jewish militia. See also herein section entitled "Surinam," and Albert Friedenberg, "The Jews of New Jersey From the Earliest Times to 1850," *PAJHS*, vol. 17 (1909), pp. 42-43.

- 1848: returned to Elizabeth, New Jersey, where he was soon elected Recorder of the Borough and a member of the Borough Council.
- 1851-1852: chosen Clerk of the General Assembly for two successive terms.[1140]

Naar used his influence in these positions to promote his white supremacist ideology. As a member of the committee on the new bill of rights, he played a prominent part in its deliberations and conclusions. In the new constitution of 1844, the word "white" was inserted into the text concerning suffrage, effectively disfranchising Blacks. It was not until the enactment in 1870 of the Fifteenth Amendment to the Constitution of the United States that the right of suffrage was restored. Furthermore, the word "white" was not struck out of the New Jersey constitution by amendment until the year 1875.[1141]

Naar was appointed to a committee to prepare an address and resolutions at the Democratic convention held on December 11, 1860, in Trenton. The resolutions passed:

> RESOLVED, That we see no remedy for this deplorable state of public affairs unless the North, in the most prompt and explicit manner, shall avow its determination to remove all political agitation for the abolition of slavery; shall repeal all acts designed to nullify or embarrass the faithful execution of the Fugitive Slave Law; shall consent to the citizen of the South enjoying the services of his domestic while temporarily sojourning here on business or pleasure...[1142]

Rabbi Kohn described Naar as one who "espoused the cause of the South and was a strong and irreconcilable exponent of states' rights and pro-slavery." In the election of November 7, 1860, with Naar's help, New Jersey was the only Northern state to vote against Lincoln. Among the examples of his anti-Black wisdom: "Is it 'freedom' to destroy the peace, happiness and prosperity of thirty millions of white freemen, in order to give a nominal freedom and bring into a condition of actual misery, four million of negroes? Is it 'freedom' of the 'higher law' which ignores the laws of God and man, and seeks to substitute for the will of madmen and fanatics?"[1143]

[1140]Kohn, pp. 377-78.
[1141]Kohn, p. 377.
[1142]Kohn, p. 380.
[1143]Kohn, p. 381.

The Emancipation Proclamation, promulgated on September 25, 1862, brought forth a vigorous denunciation from Naar:

> The injustice of this measure is only exceeded, we think, by its impolicy, and will serve, we fear, to aggravate the difficulties of our position. What is to be gained by the emancipation of the slaves in any point of view, we have never been able to discover; but to the contrary, we can perceive that, if successful, it will be of great harm to the population of the non-slave holding States, both white and colored. In anticipation of this project, we have more than once admonished our readers of the pernicious effect which must follow, in a social and industrial point of view, the influx in their midst of a body of Negro slaves, unaccustomed to voluntary habits of industry or self-control, and we do not propose now to repeat what we have said.[1144]

To Naar, the forthcoming Proclamation "will witness the most stupendous act of folly and usurpation on the part of the occupant of the Executive Chair that has ever been perpetuated by the ostensible representative of the American people." In a speech at a mass meeting in Trenton, on March 4, 1863, he voiced the opinion that Americans were "cutting each other's throats" for the sake of a few Negroes and that the abolitionists had wanted to place the Negro above the white man. Says Rabbi Kohn: "Naar was against Negro suffrage because it would mean that Negroes could hold office. This was too difficult a thought for him to accept." He condemned the proponents of freedom for Blacks with a curious logic:

> This is the case with the fanatical Zealots, who unfortunately for the country, now hold the reins of Government....They have determined that Negro slavery shall be abolished and that determination they are bent upon adhering to even at the cost of Constitutional liberty and of the Union itself. Failing in that they have resolved to have no Union at all.[1145]

When Lincoln was assassinated, it was Naar who objected to the recitation of the *Escaba* (Memorial Prayer) in the synagogues of Philadelphia. Finally, in an editorial entitled "Treason," the *Daily Gazette & Republican* expressed its view of Naar:

[1144] Kohn, pp. 386-87.
[1145] Kohn, p. 387.

> ...a West India Jew, whose very being is made of low cunning, craftiness, meaness, and deception, is less to be wondered at, and merely shows to what perfection the animal can be brought when put under proper training. That future historians will link the name of Naar with those of Arnold and Judas there is but little doubt, judging from the present course of events.[1146]

David Namias was a Barbados planter in 1680 "with a dozen negroes and twenty acres of land." His household in St. Michaells housed "nine persons (Jews) and five further slaves."[1147]

David De Isaac Cohen Nassy, of Philadelphia, held two "personal slaves" (which is synonymous with "sexual slave"). His Jewish ancestors built a whole colony in Surinam based on African slave labor.[1148]

Asher Moses Nathan of Baton Rouge, Louisiana, was a businessman who loaned money to plantation owners for slave buying and was himself a slave dealer. He owned an eighty-year-old Black male whom Nathan attempted to sell when he fell ill in 1807. This practice, in another instance, netted his estate $72 when he sold a 70-year-old Black woman named "Lucretia."[1149]

Nathan Nathans was the president of the *Beth Elohim* Congregation in Charleston, South Carolina, and owned and operated a plantation on the Cooper River using the forced labor of African hostages.[1150]

Aaron Navarro's household comprised seven Jews "and no less than eleven black slaves....Other Navarros, **Samuel** and **Judith**, also owned slaves.[1151] He dispensed his Black slaves in his will of July 4, 1685:

[1146]Kohn, p. 383.

[1147]Samuel, p. 14.

[1148]Wolf and Whiteman, p. 191; *EJ*, vol. 12, p. 843; Rosenbloom, p. 131. The Dutch family of Nassys were probably the most notorious of the slave-dealing Jews of colonial South America and the Caribbean. Much of the history of the settlements in these regions refer to a Nassy in a leadership role within the Jewish community. See the section of this document entitled "The Jews in Colonial South America." Also see R. Bijlsma, "David de Is. C. Nassy, Author of the *Essai Historique sur Surinam*," in *The Jewish Nation in Surinam: Historical Essays*, by Robert Cohen (Amsterdam: S. Emmering, 1982), pp. 65-74.

[1149]Korn, *Jews of New Orleans*, pp. 139-40.

[1150]Korn, "Jews and Negro Slavery," p. 180.

[1151]Samuel, pp. 40-41.

> I say that Entitta & her daughter Hannah are mine, being the daughter & grand-daughter of my slave (negress) Maria Arda; if they wish to free themselves, they can come to an arrangement with my wife, & no one may prevent or contradict them; this is my order & desire.[1152]

Major Mordecai Manuel Noah (1785-1851) was a journalist, judge, politician and "was probably the most distinguished Jewish layman until 1840." A prolific proponent of slavery, he felt that "the bonds of society must be kept as they now are." To emancipate the slaves, he said, "would be to jeopardize the safety of the whole country." The first Black American periodical, *The Freedom's Journal*, was launched in response to Noah's racist propaganda—it characterized him as the Black man's "bitterest enemy."[1153]

Benjamin Nones (1757-1826). Born in France, Nones moved to Philadelphia and enslaved two African people to build his business. They regularly ran away and by 1793 he manumitted them. He was an active Mason and president of Philadelphia's *Mikveh Israel* synagogue for eight years.[1154]

Jacob Franco Nunes' household of four used "only one negro slave."[1155]

Moses Nunes (1705-1787 or 1797) of Savannah, Georgia, enslaved at least thirteen and possibly twenty Africans. He admitted to repeatedly raping one Black woman named "Mulatta Rose," who bore his children, named "Robert," "James," "Alexander," and "Frances." He was a landowner and merchant and was a prominent Mason. His grandson Joseph had five children by the rape of a Black woman named "Patience." He tried to sell these children but was legally challenged when their race was questioned.[1156]

[1152]Samuel, p. 73.

[1153]*EJ*, vol. 12, p. 1198; Jonathan D. Sarna, *Jacksonian Jew: The Two Worlds of Mordecai Noah* (New York: Holmes and Meir, 1981), *passim*; Rosenbloom, p. 134.

[1154]Wolf and Whiteman, p. 190; Rosenbloom, p. 135.

[1155]Samuel, p. 35.

[1156]Korn, *Civil War*, p. 181; *MEAJ2*, pp. 333-34; Rosenbloom, p. 136; *MCAJ3*, p. 1467; Korn, "Jews and Negro Slavery," p. 203.

Abraham Nunez left to his granddaughter Hester Lopez "the following negroes viz. – Old Katy, Old Flora & Katy Casandar & John her children (& the children thereafter to be born of her body) Ishmael a negro boy....To great grand daughter Ester N. (daur. of my son Morducoy & my grand daur. Rebecca) my negro woman slave called Casander & Sammy her child & the children she shall have at the time of my decease."[1157]

Joseph Ottolenghe, a Jew, emigrated from London in 1752 for the purpose of teaching Black people a false version of Christianity while he himself held slaves and owned plantations.[1158]

Jacob Ottolengui was a Charleston Jew who claimed to hold about 1000 Black African men, women, and children, who worked his rice plantation near the Savannah River. An 1857 advertisement placed by Ottolengui in the *Charleston Courier* offered for sale the below listed:

Valuable Negros...

November, aged about 65, a carpenter
Jane, aged 30, a market woman
Jane, aged 25, a cook and house servant
Joseph, aged 30, a drayman (horse carriage driver)
Billy, aged 26, a drayman
Sandy, aged 26, a drayman
The above negros can be seen at my office, 22 Broad street, and treated for at private sale, previous to the day of sale...[1159]

Esther Pachecho of St. Michael, Barbados, owned and bequeathed "one negro woman named Quasheba & her increase" to her daughter & her heirs "forever."[1160]

Rebecca Pachecho owned four slaves in 1680 in Barbados.[1161]

Rodrigo Pacheco. In May of 1732, Pacheco instructed his partner to load their vessel (probably the *Albany* or the *Leghorn*) in New York with "choice flour, bread, pork, pease, tarr, staves and what more else is proper"; to proceed then to Jamaica to

[1157]Samuel, p. 62.
[1158]See this document, "A Jew Teaches A Slave Religion."
[1159]Korn, "Jews and Negro Slavery," p. 194.
[1160]Samuel, p. 83.
[1161]Samuel, p. 43.

sell the cargo and take "Sugar, Rum, Limejuice, Negros and Cash to the value of about £800"; then on to South Carolina to exchange for rice to then sail to Lisbon.[1162] Ann Evits bequeathed a "negro girl" to him in her will.[1163]

Joseph de Palacios of New Orleans, Louisiana, bought a plantation called *Lis Loy* near Mobile, Alabama, in or around 1765 in partnership with two other Jews, **Samuel Israel** and **Alexander Solomons**, using three of their Black captives as collateral.[1164]

David Pardo of New York purchased five Africans at a public auction in Curaçao in June of 1701.[1165]

Sara Lopez [also **Sarra Lopes**] **Pardo** of New Orleans owned an African, whom she named "Martine."[1166]

Moses Petaete was noted as the owner of a "negro."[1167]

Moses H. Penso left 403 slaves, including 53 house slaves, to his Jewish wife.[1168]

Thomas Nunez de Peralta owned a slave named "Sebastion Domingo," alias "Munguia."[1169]

Manuel Bautista Perez was arrested in Lima in 1639 by the authorities of the Spanish Inquisition. Historian Frederick Bowser wrote that Perez

> may well have been the wealthiest merchant in Peru at the time of his arrest and who certainly dominated the colony's slave trade....At the time of his arrest Perez had accumulated a fortune of close to half a million pesos and had begun diverting his assets from trade to more gentlemanly pursuits, including silver mines in Huarochiri and plantations around Lima.[1170]

[1162]Leo Hershkowitz, "Some Aspects of the New York Jewish Merchant and Community, 1654-1820," *AJHQ*, vol. 66 (1976), p. 20; *MEAJ1*, pp. 64-65; *MCAJ2*, p. 639.

[1163]*MCAJ3*, p. 1160.

[1164]Korn, *Jews of New Orleans*, pp. 25-27; Korn, *The Jews of Mobile, Alabama*, p. 13; Rosenbloom, p. 138.

[1165]Hershkowitz, *Wills*, p. 6, note 4; *EJ*, vol. 13, p. 94.

[1166]Korn, *Jews of New Orleans*, p. 72; Rosenbloom, p. 138.

[1167]Samuel Oppenheim, "Early Jewish Colony in Western Guiana," *PAJHS*, vol. 16 (1907), p. 133.

[1168]*MCAJ1*, p. 180.

[1169]Liebman, *The Jews in New Spain*, p. 259.

Isaac Pesoa (1762-1809) of Philadelphia is considered by Jews to be a humanitarian. Although he arranged to have his captives liberated, he reserved the right to keep them as indentured servants.[1171]

Alexander Phillips (d. 1839) of Baton Rouge, Louisiana, held captive four Blacks in 1820 and ten in 1830, according to the United States census. At the time of his death he held 3 Africans valued at $900.[1172]

Jonas Phillips (1736-1803) was born in Germany and moved to Philadelphia, where he was an advocate of religious equality at the Constitutional Convention while enslaving an African woman named "Phillis." He was a fur trader, auctioneer and Mason and was the first president of the reorganized Congregation *Mikveh Israel* in Philadelphia.[1173]

Isaac Pinheiro (d. 1710). A prominent New York merchant and plantation owner in Charleston, Pinheiro enslaved at least 14 Black humans, including some whom he named "Bastiano," "Andover," "Sharlow," "Tom," "Mingo," "Piero," "Ventura," "Toby," "Peter," "Manuel," "Will," "Jack," "Cattoc," "Lewisa," "Doggu," "Fanshow," "Black Sarah," and "Maria." On February 13, 1707, his wife Elizabeth [Esther] purchased from Lord Cornbury for £40 "a Negro woman called Bastiana." Pinheiro stipulated in his will that no one should disturb his heirs "from the quiet peaceable possession and enjoyment of the said Negroes."

> To my son Moses £100 when 18 years of age and a negro boy....I leave to my sons Jacob and Moses a certain Plantation...also a cafemill now standing on the Plantation...with 14 negroes...and by a deed of gift some years past, I gave to my son Jacob and my son Abraham, 7 negroes, 3 of whom are dead and lost by the late French invasion, and the other 4 are now in my possession....I leave to my wife Elizabeth [Esther] the use of all the above named Plantation and negroes and mill until my son Moses is of age.[1174]

[1170]Frederick P. Bowser, *African Slave in Colonial Peru: 1524-1650* (Stanford, California: Stanford University Press, 1974), p. 59.

[1171]Wolf and Whiteman, p. 191; Rosenbloom, p. 140.

[1172]Korn, *Jews of New Orleans*, pp. 143-44.

[1173]Wolf and Whiteman, p. 191; Sloan, p. 4; *EJ*, vol. 13, p. 405; Rosenbloom, p. 141.

[1174]Hershkowitz, *Wills*, pp. 21-24; Pool, p. 454; Lebeson, p. 203; Friedman, "Wills," pp. 157-58; Rosenbloom, p. 144; *MCAJ1*, p. 99.

Jorge Homen Pinto was a Brazilian planter and one of the settlement's wealthiest Jews. He owned nine sugar mills in 1650 with at least 370 Black African slaves.[1175]

Myer Pollack of eighteenth-century Newport, Rhode Island, was, according to Jewish historian Max J. Kohler, "heavily interested in the West India trade in molasses, which was brought from there to Newport, manufactured into rum in the latter place, and exported to Africa, the vessels commonly returning to the West Indies with slaves."[1176]

Solomon Polok was a member of a prestigious Philadelphia family, and worked as an overseer on a Mobile, Alabama, plantation in the late 1830s.[1177]

Diogo Dias Querido, of Amsterdam, was reportedly involved in "large-scale operations on the west coast of Africa," employing 10 ships and "many smaller ships and boats." He held "several Negro slaves," whom he trained to be interpreters of African languages for his operation. In 1611, the authorities of the Inquisition charged Querido with instructing the Africans in, and converting them to, Judaism.[1178]

B. L. Ramirez owned Indian slaves and was *factotum* of his Mexico City synagogue.[1179]

Moses Raphael was a commercial lawyer and owner of a plantation called *Esquiline Hill* near Columbus, Georgia. Forty-seven Blacks raised peaches and plums for him in chattel slavery.[1180]

Solomon Raphael of Richmond held Blacks captive named "Pricilla," "Sylvia," and her child "Nelly."[1181]

[1175]Arkin, *AJEH*, p. 205; Herbert I. Bloom, "A Study of Brazilian Jewish History," *PAJHS*, vol. 33 (1934), p. 76.

[1176]Max J. Kohler, "The Jews in Newport," *PAJHS*, vol. 6 (1897), p. 73.

[1177]Korn, "Jews and Negro Slavery," p. 180; *EJ*, vol. 15, p. 412.

[1178]Wiznitzer, *Jews in Colonial Brazil*, pp. 46-47.

[1179]Seymour B. Liebman, "The Mestizo Jews of Mexico," *AJA*, vol. 19 (April 1967), p. 168.

[1180]Feingold, *Zion*, p. 60; Korn, "Jews and Negro Slavery," p. 180; Feldstein, p. 82.

[1181]Korn, "Jews and Negro Slavery," p. 187; Ezekiel and Lichtenstein, pp. 78, 80; Bermon, p. 163; *MUSJ1*, p. 133; "Selected Acquisitions," *AJA*, vol. 19 (April 1967), p. 94.

Rabbi Morris Jacob Raphall of Congregation *B'nai Jeshurun* in New York was America's most prominent rabbi. He gave a sermon on January 4, 1861, which was used extensively by Jews and Christians in their defense of slavery. Raphall said, in part:

> ...it remains a fact which cannot be gainsaid that in his own native home, and generally throughout the world, the unfortunate negro is indeed the meanest of slaves. Much had been said respecting the inferiority of his intellectual powers, and that no man of his race has ever inscribed his name on the Parthenon of human excellence, either mental or moral.[1182]

Samuel Reese worked with the notorious **Davis brothers** in their slave dealings.[1183]

Zalma Rehine (1757-1843), of Richmond, "became the nucleus around which the first Jewish congregation in the state was formed." According to the 1830 census, he owned 2 slaves.[1184]

Pedro Gomez Reinal was granted the exclusive right to import slaves into the colonies by King John IV of Portugal. The contract contained a clause permitting Gomez to have two Portuguese on his ship who would be in charge of the sale of the Africans and do anything else necessary "among the people of the sea."[1185]

Judith Risson, of Barbados, owned two slaves in 1680.[1186]

Jacob Rodriguez Rivera (1717-1789) was the president of the Newport, Rhode Island's Congregation *Jeshuat Israel* in 1760, a notorious African slave dealer, and was considered to be the second wealthiest Jew behind his son-in-law **Aaron Lopez**. His diverse connections included work with the **Monsantos** of New Orleans, as well as with **Samuel Moses** and **Isaac Elizer** to outfit slave ships with leg irons and handcuffs and other

---

[1182]Simonhoff, *Jewish Notables*, p. 327; Robert V. Friedenberg, *"Hear O Israel," The History of American Jewish Preaching, 1654-1970* (Tuscaloosa and London: University of Alabama Press, 1989), pp. 42-58. See this document's section entitled "Jews, Slavery and the Civil War."

[1183]Bermon, p. 167.

[1184]Ira Rosenwaike, "The Founding of Baltimore's First Jewish Congregation: Fact vs. Fiction," *AJA*, vol. 28 (1976), p. 124.

[1185]Seymour B. Liebman, *New World Jewry, 1493 - 1825: Requiem for the Forgotten* (New York: KTAV, 1982), p. 170.

[1186]Samuel, p. 43.

hardware of bondage. At his home he had twelve slaves serving six people.[1187]

Gaspar de Robles was born in Portugal and was raised by his aunt and uncle. When he was fourteen:

> his uncles, Vicente Enriquez and Gaspar Mendez, took him to Angola, from where they brought Negroes and transported them to Brazil, Jamaica, and New Spain. While in Angola, his uncles taught him about Judaism and persuaded him to leave the Christian faith. His uncles taught him...many details of how to live as a Jew.[1188]

Ruben Levin Rochelle was a prominent Louisiana Jew whose estate included "some slaves." There is one recorded sale of an African man in 1807. Dr. Korn described an incident at the commission brokerage house in New Orleans, operated by Rochelle and **Hart Moses Shiff**, in which a slave working there (but owned by a Louisiana judge) had escaped. The judge demanded the slave's return and Rochelle & Shiff placed the following notice in the *Louisiana Gazette* of January 18, 1812:

> 20 Dollars Reward. Absconded from the house of the subscribers, on the night of the 16th inst. a mulatto boy, named Ovid, (the property of Judge A. Trouard, of the German Coast) about 17 years of age, about five feet high, he had a grey coloured coate, with black velvet collar and plated buttons, a grey waistcoat, white nankeen pantaloons, and short boots. Whoever will deliver him to the subscribers, or to his owner, or secure him in any Jail, shall receive a reward of twenty dollars, besides all reasonable charges. Masters of vessels are forewarned from harboring or carrying off said boy at their peril.[1189]

Fernando Rodriguez was the leader of the Veracruz Jewish community. "He was a broker and trader of Negro slaves."[1190]

Sam Rothschild's Jewish partner, **Philip Sartorius**, recalled that in 1850, Rothschild

---

[1187]*JRM/Docs*, p. 446; Feldstein, p. 12; Korn, *Jews of New Orleans*, p. 9; *MCAJ3*, p. 1529; Rhodes, p. 8. See also Jacob Rader Marcus, *Jews and the American Revolution: A Bicentennial Documentary* (reprinted from *AJA*, November 1975), pp. 231-32, for a letter from Rivera to his ship captain, Nathaniel Briggs, in 1785, informing him of a profitable slaving voyage by an associate; Rosenbloom, p. 149.

[1188]Liebman, *The Jews in New Spain*, p. 226.

[1189]Korn, *Jews of New Orleans*, pp. 128, 133; Sharfman, p. 150.

[1190]Liebman, *The Jews in New Spain*, p. 256.

gambled all our money off and sold [our trading] boat and stock to another flat boat man for a Negro girl, took her to New Orleans and traded her off for tobacco.[1191]

Philip Moses Russell (c. 1745-1830) held Blacks as slaves in Philadelphia, was a surgeon, merchant, and prominent member of his synagogue.[1192]

Hyman Samuel, a watch and clockmaker from London, resettled in Petersburg, Virginia, and in 1792 he is listed as the owner of "1 negro over 16 years of age."[1193]

Francis Salvador (1747-1776) was born in London to a wealthy Jewish family. In 1773, he left his wife and four children and came to South Carolina, where he owned a 6- or 7-thousand-acre indigo plantation with "at least thirty slaves." He was the first Jew to hold a South Carolina State office and was considered one of "the foremost men of the Commonwealth." In 1776, "Salvador was shot and falling among the bushes was discovered by the Indians and scalped."[1194]

Philip Sartorius (1830-1913). Between 1853 and 1857 Sartorius owned several slaves. He once joined a posse of slave hunters in pursuit of a dozen Africans who had run from the Jeffries plantation in Jefferson county. When they found the Blacks the 12 bloodhounds severely attacked them. Sartorius claimed to be repulsed by the sight.[1195]

Abraham Sarzedas (d. c. 1779) lived in Newport, New York, the West Indies, and Georgia, where his plantation was absolutely dependent upon the forced labor of kidnapped Africans. He claimed that he owned just three slaves to tend his 500-acre farm and in 1774 he and his wife Caty enslaved four Blacks while living in Newport, Rhode Island.[1196]

[1191]Korn, "Jews and Negro Slavery," p. 193.

[1192]Wolf and Whiteman, pp. 190-91; *EJ*, vol. 16, p. 163; Rosenbloom, p. 150.

[1193]Ginsberg, p. 9.

[1194]Simonhoff, *Jewish Notables*, pp. 1-4; Feldstein, p. 13. See Leon Hühner, "Francis Salvador: A Prominent Patriot of the Revolutionary War," *Karp, JEA1*, pp. 276-91, as well as Hühner's, "The Jews of Georgia In Colonial Times," *PAJHS*, vol. 10 (1902), pp. 68-69; Albert M. Hyamson, *A History of the Jew in England* (London: Methuen & Company, 1908), p. 213; Rosenbloom, p. 151.

[1195]*JRM/Memoirs 2*, pp. 45, 51 and see quote on page 28.

[1196]Wolf and Whiteman, p. 190; *MCAJ2*, p. 580; *MEAJ2*, p. 328; Rosenbloom, p. 152.

Sasportas Family owned plantations in the South where many Black captives were held.[1197]

Wolf bar Schemuel (alias **Samuel**) was an overseer of "94 Negroes" on the plantation of **Stephen Boyd** (see entry). He complained in an 1820 letter that "I had to work in the water...with three Niggers, for a whole month." When he returned to the big house, he wrote: "my old master and mistress gave me black looks."[1198]

Henry Seessel (1822-1911) was a German Jewish immigrant migrated to New Orleans in about 1843. He went to Memphis as a businessman and bought four Africans "for our own use," for $3,100.[1199]

Abraham Mendes Seixas (1750 or 1751-1799). The brother of the famous colonial New York Jewish leader **Gershom Mendes Seixas**, he was typically reprobate in his attitude about the Black man and woman, evidenced by this poem he authored and published in the *South Carolina State Gazette*, September 6, 1794 (Seixas rhymes with gracious).[1200]

ABRAHAM SEIXAS,
All so gracious,
Once again does offer
His services pure
For to secure
Money in the coffer.

He has for sale
Some Negroes, male,
Will suit full well grooms.
He has likewise
Some of their wives
Can make clean, dirty rooms.

For planting too, He has a few
To sell, all for the cash,
Of various price,
To work the rice
Or bring them to the lash.

The young ones true,
If that will do
May some be had of him
To learn your trade
They may be made,
Or bring them to your trim.

The boatmen great,
Will you elate
They are so brisk and free;
What e'er you say,
They will obey,
If you buy them from me.

[1197]Wolf and Whiteman, p. 190; *EJ*, vol. 12, p. 1446; Rosenbloom, p. 153.

[1198]Blau and Baron, vol. 3, p. 800; Isaac M. Fein, *The Making of An American Jewish Community*, p. 11.

[1199]*MEAJ1*, p. 367; *JRM/Memoirs 1*, p. 367.

[1200]*MEAJ2*, p. 256; Golden, pp. 107-8; Libo and Howe, p. 61.

David G. Seixas and partner **Benjamin S. Spitzer** owned three slaves: "a woman who cooked their meals and kept house for them, and two males who worked in their store."[1201] Seixas is reported to have smuggled Africans into the United States after the government ban on the importation of slaves.[1202]

Eleanor Cohen Seixas, the daughter of **Philip Melvin Cohen** of Charleston, wrote in a diary about her resentment of the abolition of slavery:

> I believe deeply in the institution of slavery [and] regret deeply its being abolished. I am accustomed to have them wait on me, and I dislike white servants very much.[1203]

David and **Jacob Senior** were slave "entrepreneurs" who came to Curaçao from Amsterdam in 1685. Jacob and his wife **Esther** are recorded as having sold two slaves in Barbados on March 7, 1694 or 1695.[1204]

Dr. John de Sequeyra (1712-1795), a Williamsburg, Virginia, physician who treated the governor of that state, held at least 2 Africans as slaves. He was a leading physician for 50 years.[1205]

Simon Vaez de Sevilla was a seventeenth-century Jewish Mexican slave-shipper.[1206]

Shetfall Family was one of the most enterprising Jewish slave-dealing operations of Savannah, Georgia. At 27, **Benjamin Shetfall** (1692-1765) owned 1,000 acres and nine Africans. In 1756, he claimed to have 2 hostages for his 200 acres, though it is probable that he had dozens. In 1763, he claimed that 5 Black human beings slaved over an additional 50 acres. Benjamin also participated in the family's slave enterprise. His property was once attacked by the British, who carried off some of the Africans to Florida.[1207]

[1201]Korn, *Jews of New Orleans*, p. 93.

[1202]Sharfman, pp. 145-46.

[1203]Korn, "Jews and Negro Slavery," p. 212; "Acquisitions,"*AJA*, vol. 3 (1951), p. 43.

[1204]*EHJ*, p. 273; Stern, "Notes on the Jews of Nevis," p. 159.

[1205]Robert Shosteck, "Notes on an Early Virginia Physician,"*AJA*, vol. 23 (1971), p. 212.

[1206]*MCAJ1*, pp. 46-47.

[1207]*MEAJ2*, pp. 344-47; *MCAJ2*, p. 822; Simonhoff, *Jewish Notables*, p. 181; *JRM/Docs*, pp. 62-64, 80, 353; Korn, "Jews and Negro Slavery," p. 190; Rosenwaike, "Jewish Population in 1790," p. 67; David T. Morgan, "The Shetfalls of Savannah," *PAJHS*, vol. 62 (1973), p. 350; Rubin, p. 81; *EJ*, vol. 14, p. 1337; Rosenbloom, pp. 157-58.

In 1766, his brother **Levi** (d. 1775) reported 9 Black slaves for his 350 acres, and by 1769 he claimed to have 15 slaves and was granted another 300 acres. This is how Jacob Rader Marcus describes the "indefatigable industry" of Levi Shetfall:

> Taking the advice of Captain John Milledge of the Georgia Rangers, Sheftall — then about eighteen years of age — finally entered into the butcher business with a German Christian partner. In order to acquire capital, he saved every cent he made, never spending a shilling on himself except for the barest necessities, literally working day and night, and reducing his sleep to an absolute minimum. In the first year of his partnership he saved £150, working with a slave — and like a slave. By the early 1760's Levi owned a house, a lot, and six or eight Negroes, and could boast that in a period of six years he had never spent a penny on himself and had not tasted his first drink till he was twenty. Then he turned to another business, and the £1,500 he had saved disappeared. In 1768, after a couple of unhappy love affairs, he married and soon lost his second fortune — through no fault of his own, for he had forfeited it very likely by signing notes for the family or close friends. Once more he addressed himself to making money. He continued in the butcher business, opened a tanyard, acquired a wharf, a plantation, and forty-four slaves — all this in four years. Then came the Revolution and once more Levi lost everything, a fortune he valued at more than £10,000. He was then about thirty-five years of age.[1208]

The son of Benjamin, **Mordecai** (1735-1797), enslaved at least nine Blacks to work his 1000 acres. Three of those he named "Joe," "Anthony," and "Phillis" were disposed of in the following contract:

> And the said Modicai Sheftall (sic) for the considerations herein before mentioned, hath bargained, sold, and delivered, and by these presents doth bargain, sell, and deliver, unto the said Isaac Dacosta, his heirs, executors, administrators, and assigns, all those three negroe slaves known by the names of Joe, Anthony, and Phillis, together with the future issue and increase of Phillis; and also all his estate, right, title, and interest, whatsoever of, in, or to the before mentioned real estate and every part thereof, and of, in, and to the before named negroe slaves, to have and to hold the said parcel of six hundred and fifty acres of land, and two town lots hereinbefore mentioned, or intended to be hereby

[1208] *MCAJ2*, pp. 811-12.

> bargained and sold, and every part thereof, with the appurtenances and also the three before named negroe slaves, together with the future issue and increase of the female slave, unto the said Isaac Dacosta, his heirs, executors, administrators, and assigns.[1209]

Mordecai also issued warrants against runaway slaves. **Shetfall Shetfall**, while in custody of the British, received a letter from his wife Frances that read in part:

> ...I am obliged to take in needle work to make a living for my family, so I leave you to judge what a living that must be. Our Negroes have every one been at the point of death, so that they have been of no use to me for this six weeks past...[1210]

Esther Shetfall (b. 1771) directed the executors of her estate in her will of 1828:

> I order and direct that my Negro woman Caty be sold by my Executors at private or public sale, and the proceeds of the sale to go toward the payment of my debts and the erection of a stone over mine and my late sister Perla's grave. The surplus if any to be divided between my brothers Shetfall and Moses.[1211]

Elias Silva of New Amsterdam (New York) was charged in 1656 with "having a carnal conversation with a Negress slave."[1212]

J. Da Silva of Jamaica joined two other Jews, **J. Adolfus** and **L. Spyers**, in the 1812 attack on a Jamaican assemblyman's house because he advocated rights for Blacks.[1213]

Joseph De Silva, a merchant of the parish of St. Peter, Barbados, "knowing the uncertainty of Humane life," prepared his will dated April 17, 1725, which dispensed "my two niggers Peggy a woman & Gracy a girl."[1214]

Joseph Simon (1712-1804) was a wealthy shopkeeper operating as an Indian trader out of Lancaster, Pennsylvania. He was involved in no less than 12 partnerships in the regional trade

---

[1209]*JRM/Docs*, p. 353. Edmund H. Abrahams, "Some Notes on the Early History of the Shetfalls of Georgia," *PAJHS*, vol. 17 (1909), p. 183, states that Mordecai had "two negro servants." He apparently placed advertisements in the *Georgia Gazette* Nov. 22, 1764, for the return of runaway slaves Peter and Bosan or Boson. See Windley, vol. 4, p. 8.

[1210]*MEAJ2*, pp. 361-63; Marcus, *The American Jewish Woman*, p. 30.

[1211]Marcus, *The American Jewish Woman*, pp. 113-14; *MUSJ1*, p. 210.

[1212]Grollman, vol. 3, no. 1, p. 10; *MCAJ1*, p. 239; Rosenbloom, p. 159.

[1213]Hurwitz and Hurwitz, p. 46.

[1214]Samuel, p. 60.

and is considered to be one of the first white men to reach the Mississippi from the Pennsylvania area during the 1740s and 50s.

In 1759, Simon is listed as the owner of "a slave age 20, one horse and one cattle." By 1763, Simon had "three slaves aged 10, 15 and 20, one horse, two cattle and a tenant." Ten years later he owned three, ages 12, 30 and 40. He once owned a Black man named John "who had to be chained and thrown into jail after almost killing a man." Simon eventually sold him at a loss. There is a deed dated December 25, 1793, in which Simon sold to Christian Barr "a Negro boy named Cudago, age 15, weight 65 pounds, to be held until age 29." Among his correspondence there is a reference to Simon's sending slaves to Fort Pitt for various people. In 1776, a Philadelphia newspaper ran an ad seeking to locate "A Negro named John, slave of a Mr. Bogle, of Cumberland County, formerly belonging to Joseph Simon of the Borough of Lancaster."

Among his varied array of merchandise he sold drugs, and medicines, silk, wampum, tomahawks, lumber, white indentured servants, "Negroes" for sale or hire, ships, lottery tickets, and an item of uncertain description listed in one transaction called "Negroe knives." Simon himself is recorded as having claimed to have a monopoly on such trade in the region.

Simon came under suspicion for aiding the British war effort during the American Revolution by trading in banned British goods including tea. By the 1780s, Simon and fellow Jew **Michael Gratz** of Philadelphia became joint owners of vast tracks of land west of the Susquehanna.[1215]

Joseph Simon, described as a "Confederate veteran" from New Orleans, purchased a slave, according to a receipt. Slavery was presumed, however, to have ended in 1865.[1216]

Michael Simon helped his brother-in-law, **Simon Frank**, establish a dry goods store in Woodville, Louisiana, in 1850, under the name S. Frank & Company. By 1853, Michael Simon was "sufficiently well off to have bought a small plantation worked by about ten slaves."[1217]

[1215]Brener, pp. 8-20.

[1216]Isidore S. Meyer, "The American Jew in the Civil War," *PAJHS*, vol. 50 (1960-61), p. 287.

[1217]Ashkenazi, p. 149.

Benjamin Simons, of Charleston, placed several advertisements for runaway slaves in local papers. In the *South-Carolina Gazette and Country Journal*, April 19, 1774:

> RUN-AWAY from the subscriber about the 23d day of July last, a negro man named PRINCE, he is about 30 years of age, 5 feet 5 or 6 inches high, has a blemish in one eye, which was caused by the small-pox; he had on when he went away, a blue waistcoat, and a pair of light coloured breeches. He was brought up to the blacksmith's business in New-York. He was seen a few days after he absented himself, with a cart, about five miles from town. Whoever will deliver said negro man to me in Charles-Town, or to the warden of the work-house, shall receive FIVE POUNDS currency reward, and all reasonable charges, from Benjamin Simons.[1218]

Simons apparently sought "Abraham" in an advertisement in the *South-Carolina Gazette*, November 9 to November 16, 1767. The *South-Carolina and American General Gazette* of April 17 to May 1, 1776:

> RUN away about the first of April last, a stout, well made Negro Man named JUNE, formerly belonging to James Witter of James Island, and used to attend the Market, but was employed in the Ferryboat from Scott's Ferry in Town; he has been seen in Town, where he is harboured, and on James Island. Ten Pounds Reward will be paid to whoever will apprehend and deliver him to the Warden of the Workhouse.[1219]

Moses Simons was the nephew of Savannah's **Saul Simons**. In his will, the elder Simons stipulated that his executors were to hire out four Black slaves and the total annual income, $200, was to be used to keep young Moses at school.[1220]

Samuel Simons (d. 1824) of Charleston enslaved Africans named "Maria Chapman," "Pompey," and "Peggy." There is some evidence that "Maria," described as "a free woman of color," was sexually exploited by Simons.[1221]

[1218]Windley, vol. 3, pp. 692-93.

[1219]Windley, vol. 3, pp. 483, 627.

[1220]*MUSJ1*, p. 411.

[1221]Korn, "Jews and Negro Slavery," p. 202. Korn cites this case as one of "only five instances in which documentary evidence indicates [the] cohabitation of Jews and Negro women..." See herein "Jews and the Rape of Black Woman"; Blau and Baron, vol. 3, p. 797; Rosenbloom, p. 160.

Nathan Simson (d. 1725) was a New York merchant and shipper born in Germany. In 1717 and 1721, two of Simson's ships, the *Crown* and the *New York Postillion,*

> ...sailed into the northern harbor with a total load of 217 Negroes. The shipments came directly from the African coast, two of the largest slave cargoes to be brought into New York in the first half of the eighteenth century.[1222]

Sampson Simson "appears to [have been] the largest trader among New York Jews," and "one of the most prominent members of the New York Chamber of Commerce." He was one of the drafters of New York's constitution, served repeatedly as a member of the state's arbitration committee for grievances of New York merchants, was on its Committee on Regulation of Coinage and its Fishery Committee.[1223] According to historian Myer Isaacs, "He retained in his household several old family servants, some of whom had been slaves..."[1224]

Benjamin Solomon. In 1798, according to Richmond, Virginia, court records, Solomon accused an African woman named "Polly" of stealing two dollars worth of sugar. She was sentenced to five lashes on her bare back and the branding of her left hand.[1225]

Ezekiel Solomon participated in the 1776 sale of a Black female child in Montreal.[1226]

Haym M. Solomon (b. 1740) held as hostage a 10-year-old Black child named "Anna."[1227]

Henry E. Solomon. In 1825, Solomon used 6 Black people as collateral on a debt owed to Morton Waring.[1228]

[1222] *MEAJ1*, pp. 64-65; Hugh H. Smythe and Martin S. Price, "The American Jew and Negro Slavery," *The Midwest Journal*, vol. 7, no. 4 (1955-56), p. 316; Rosenbloom, p. 161.

[1223] Kohler, "New York," p. 83.

[1224] Myer S. Isaacs, "Sampson Simson," *PAJHS*, vol. 10 (1902), p. 112.

[1225] Ezekiel and Lichtenstein, p. 190.

[1226] Korn, "Jews and Negro Slavery," p. 190; "Acquisitions,"*AJA*, vol. 3 (1951), p. 44; *MCAJ3*, p. 1503.

[1227] Schappes, p. 599; Meyer, p. 285; and *PAJHS*, vol. 37 (1947), pp. 447-48.

[1228] A. S. Diamond, "Problems of the London Sephardic Community: 1720-1733," *Jewish Historical Society of New England*, vol. 21, p. 400.

Moses Solomon. In 1802, Moses Solomon was Charleston's constable whose job was to punish freedom-seeking Blacks.[1229]

Myer Solomon of Lancaster, Pennsylvania, "had two houses, two horses, one cattle and one slave."[1230]

Victor Souza of New Orleans skipped out on some debts in 1834, for which four of his African slaves were auctioned. He was caught, tried, convicted and sent to prison.[1231]

Benjamin Solomon Spitzer of St. Louis, along with **Gershom Mendes Seixas,** held three slaves who kept their house and ran their store. Spitzer also invested in the slave ships *Nancy* and *Jane.*[1232]

L. Spyers of Jamaica joined two other Jews, **J. Da Silva** and **J. Adolfus**, in the 1812 attack on a Jamaican assemblyman who advocated equal rights for Blacks.[1233]

Emanuel Stern (d. 1828), a Jew from New Orleans, ordered his 12-year-old Black child "Mathilda" to be auctioned off after his death. She was sold for $400 though valued at $250.[1234]

Louis Stix, according to Stanley Feldstein,

> expressed sympathy for the plight of blacks but did nothing to promote their liberation. Though he classified himself as an "outspoken" opponent of all involuntary servitude, he still advocated gradual emancipation and a government indemnity for "[his] southern neighbors" for their pecuniary losses in parting with their slaves.[1235]

A. F. Strauss of New Orleans was a major dealer in Black and white humans and would advertise the sale of as many as a hundred at a time.[1236]

[1229]Korn, "Jews and Negro Slavery," p. 190.

[1230]Brener, p. 8.

[1231]Korn, *Civil War,* p. 167.

[1232]Korn, *Jews of New Orleans,* pp. 93; *EJ,* vol. 15, p. 285 and vol. 14, p. 958.

[1233]Hurwitz and Hurwitz, p. 46.

[1234]Korn, "Jews and Negro Slavery," p. 184.

[1235]Feldstein, p. 98.

[1236]Korn, *Jews of New Orleans,* p. 163.

J. L. Tobias purchased a slave from David Derrick on January 26, 1857. The receipt reads, in part:

> I, David Derrick, for and in consideration of the sum of One Thousand and Fifty Dollars – to me – in hand paid, at and before the sealing and delivery of these Presents, by J. L. Tobias has bargained and sold, and by these Presents, do bargain, sell, and deliver to the said J. L. Tobias the Negro slave Stephen Warranted Sound to have and to hold the said Negro slave Stephen unto the said J. L. Tobias his Executors, Administrators, and Assigns, from and against all persons, shall and will Warrant and forever defend by these Presents.[1237]

Joseph Tobias (1745 or 1764-1810) of Charleston bought a Black woman named "Jenny" from Dr. James Cletherall for $500 on July 23, 1798.[1238]

Joseph Tobias (1684-1761) was a ship owner in Charlestown and president of *Beth Elohim* synagogue. He was the purchaser of six Black slaves—two men and four women—"probably all households servants."[1239]

Judica Torres, a Barbadian Jewess, owned two slaves.[1240]

Simja De Torres (d. 1746) was a New York slave trader, who imported seven Blacks from Jamaica on at least two recorded occasions in 1728 and 1742. One of the Africans was a three-year-old child. Another was named "Menasseh Perirei." She was also one of the leading benefactors of the Mill Street Synagogue (*Shearith Israel*) in New York City. She left to her nieces **Rachel**, **Rebecca**, and **Sinya** "one negro girl" each.[1241]

Judah Touro (1775-1854) was born in Newport and became the *hazzan* (minister) of *Yeshuat Israel* Synagogue, which he bought and renovated. Jewish historians claim that he was a humanitarian who abhorred slavery to such an extent that he bought slaves just to free them. On the contrary, wrote Leon Hühner, he bought slaves "to wait on him, or to work in his

---

[1237]Meyer, pp. 286-87.

[1238]Korn, "Jews and Negro Slavery," p. 187; Rosenwaike, "Jewish Population in 1790," p. 61; *EJ*, vol. 15, p. 1181; Rosenbloom, p. 168.

[1239]Thomas J. Tobias, "Joseph Tobias of Charles Town: 'Linguister'," *Karp, JEA1*, p. 118; Rosenbloom, p. 168.

[1240]Samuel, p. 43.

[1241]Hershkowitz, "Wills (1743-1774)," pp. 79-81; Pool, pp. 468-69; Friedman, "Wills," p. 153; Rosenbloom, p. 169.

various enterprises."[1242] In 1809, he profited from the auctioning of 12 African people, and in 1812 advertised rewards for the apprehension of seven Black runaways. He also did extensive business in merchandise, such as rag clothing, specifically to be used by slaves.[1243]

He was "one of the earliest of prominent American philanthropists," but Jewish historian Morris U. Schappes notes that "Negro institutions and causes, perhaps needing assistance most, were not among Touro's beneficiaries." As late as 1947, Blacks were not admitted to the hospital facilities of the Touro Infirmary in New Orleans.[1244]

Max Ullman of Mississippi was a private in the Confederate army who served all through the war, was twice wounded, and nearly thirty years later became rabbi of a congregation in Birmingham, Alabama.[1245]

Simon Valentine (full name: Simon Valentine Vander Wilden) "probably in the late 1680's...did business on [Jamaica]...handling chiefly indigo, flour, sugar, and Negroes." He owned a 500-acre plantation in 1699 on the outskirts of Charlestown worked by many African hostages.[1246] He was a respected and successful merchant in the year 1701.[1247]

Elias Valverde (c. 1691-1739 or 1740) was a Barbados merchant and slave owner who left money to his children expressly to buy still more African citizens. His last will and testament states that he left to his "Dear & Well Beloved Wife"

> ...the Negro Woman named Peggy & her two children called Santo & Rose girls, also a life interest only in my Negroes Primus, Sarah & Phillis. To son Jacob Valverde £450 as also a Negro Man named Cudjoe. To my grand-daughters on marriage or 18th birthday £50 to be layd out in purchasing Negroes for them or put out at interest or otherwise Employed for their best advantage....And I will that the Negro Punch shall serve and attend my said son during his life or till he shall have his Sight when I give and bequeath the said Negro to him and his heirs for ever But if he should not have his Sight then at his death I direct

---

[1242]Leon Hühner, *The Life of Judah Touro, 1775-1854* (Philadelphia: Jewish Publication Society of America, 1946), *passim.*

[1243]*EJ*, vol. 12, p. 1043; Korn, *Jews of New Orleans*, p. 89; Rosenbloom, pp. 69-70.

[1244]Schappes, pp. 333-41, 656-62.

[1245]Rufus Learsi, *The Jews in America: A History* (New York: KTAV Publishing House, 1972), p. 98.

[1246]Feldstein, p. 13; *MEAJ2*, p. 229; Rosenbloom, p. 171.

[1247]*MCAJ2*, p. 823.

> the said Negro to be sold and itts produce with the said sum of Six hundred pounds to be equally divided among my Residuary Legatees (sic).[1248]

Jacob Valverde, a 1680 resident of St. Michael, Barbados, doled out his "negros" in his will dated April 19, 1725:

> To well-beloved daughter Jael Valverde: "my negro woman called Rose also the negro wench call'd Mariba as also the negro wench called Great Quasiba."
>
> To well beloved daughter Lunah: "the negro woman Aba the negro girl Doegood & the negro woman Boss."
>
> To well beloved son Abraham: "my Pentateuchus or 5 books of Moses which I have in our synagogue as also the sylver ornaments or bells thereto belonging...(also)...the two negroes viz. Primus & August."
>
> To son Isaac: "the negro man nam'd London & the negro woman nam'd Diana."
>
> To son David: "the negro man call'd Manuel as also the negro boy call'd Antony."
>
> To daughter Esther: "the negro woman call'd Bella the young negro girl Bessy the said Bella's child & the negro woman Mall."
>
> To daughter Rebecca: "The Indian Wench Sary as also the negro wench Mainba."
>
> To daughter Simha: "the negro woman call'd Jenny & the negro girl call'd Quassiba the daughter of the said Jenny."
>
> To son Moses: "the negro woman called Nanny & her son call'd John Lopy as also the negroe boy call'd Purim."
>
> To son Aaron: "the negro woman called Esparansa as also the negroe boy call'd February."
>
> To daughter Lea: "the negroe girl call'd Peguey & alsoe the negro girl call'd Lilly...(also)...one gold spangle chain."[1249]

Daniel Warburg (1826-1859) of New Orleans had two "mulatto" sons named "Eugene" and "Daniel," as products of the rape of a Cuban Black woman named "Marie Rose."[1250]

[1248]Pool, pp. 464-65; Samuel, p. 89; Rosenbloom, p. 171.
[1249]Samuel, pp. 35, 61.
[1250]Korn, *Jews of New Orleans*, p. 181.

Moses Abraham Waterman sold whole gangs of African men, women, and children into slavery.[1251]

Judah Wechsler was a Jewish spiritual leader and vocal supporter of the African slave system.[1252]

Julius Weis of New Orleans was described by Jacob Rader Marcus as "probably the most distinguished Jew in New Orleans." He terrorized several Blacks in the period from 1853-1857 and purchased a Black barber in 1862.[1253] He "chase[d] after runaway Negroes, who were tracked down and brutally rounded up with the aid of bloodhounds."[1254]

Theodore Wiener proclaimed himself to be a "rank pro-slavery man."[1255]

Isaac Mayer Wise. The leader of the American Reform Movement viewed Blacks as "representing all that is debased and inferior in the hopeless barbarity and heathenism of six thousand years." He also said that "[t]he Negro was never free; and his bondage in Africa was simply duplicated in a milder form when he was imported here." He considered abolitionists to be "fanatics," "demagogues," "demons of hatred and destruction,"

> ...and habitual revolutionaries, who feed on excitement and delight in civil wars, German atheism coupled with American puritanism who know of no limits to their fanaticism, visionary philanthropists and wicked preachers who have that religion which is most suitable to their congregations.[1256]

Wise's biographer, James G. Heller, said of his subject: "Clearly the Abolitionists...were men whom he would detest and of whom he would disapprove with all the force of his soul. In his opinion they degraded religion, used it as a tool, and proved themselves unscrupulous and intemperate."[1257]

[1251]Bermon, p. 166.

[1252]Feingold, *Zion*, p. 90.

[1253]*JRM/Memoirs 2*, p. 47; Korn, "Jews and Negro Slavery," p. 213.

[1254]*JRM/Memoirs 1*, p. 20.

[1255]"Trail Blazers of the Trans-Mississippi West," *AJA*, vol. 8 (1956), p. 92.

[1256]Bertram W. Korn, *Eventful Years and Experiences* (Cincinnati: American Jewish Archives, 1954), p. 131.

[1257]James G. Heller, *Isaac M. Wise, His Life and Work and Thought* (New York: Union of American Hebrew Congregations, 1965), p. 340.

"Christian clergymen are the most violent abolitionists," charged Rabbi Wise, and further accused Protestant priests of causing Jefferson Davis' rebellion.[1258] "The whole host of priests would rather see this country crushed and crippled than discard their fanaticism or give up their political influence."[1259]

"Do you think the Israelites of the South must be your white slaves," he asked, "as you in your naturalization laws treat the foreigner, placing him below the negro?"[1260] During the Civil War he frequently intervened for the release of Confederate Jews from Union prisons and carried on a campaign for foodstuffs for Southern Jews.[1261]

When the issues of war and peace, freedom and slavery arose, Wise, as publisher of *The Israelite*, decided that "silence must henceforth be our policy, silence on all the questions of the day....But we shall be obliged to abstain entirely from all and every commentary on the odd occurrences of the day."[1262] Historian Bertram W. Korn wrote that "Peace and Union at any cost were his objectives in the weeks before the outbreak of war, even if the price involved the everlasting legalization of slavery."[1263]

Rabbi Wise wrote of the Abolitionist's reaction to General Grant's Order #11 expelling Jews from certain jurisdictions: "if so many Negroes had been injured as were Hebrews by the order of General Grant,...you would have cried as loudly as the people of Sodom and Gomorrah; but for the white Hebrew who gave you a God and a religion, you had not a word to say."[1264]

His rage against the Black man may have stemmed from his belief that "the Hyksos of Manetho, who oppressed the

---

[1258]Korn, *Eventful Years,* p. 149.

[1259]Korn, *Eventful Years,* p. 132.

[1260]Korn, *Eventful Years,* p. 132.

[1261]Segal, *Fascinating Facts,* p. 85.

[1262]Korn, *Eventful Years,* p. 126.

[1263]Korn, *Eventful Years,* p. 126. Heller, p. 344: "Certainly...it is true that Wise would have agreed to the continuation of slavery forever, if that would have called a halt to, or would have prevented, bloodshed."

[1264]Korn, *Eventful Years,* p. 133. It is interesting to note what Isaac M. Wise said of Lincoln in the *Cincinnati Commercial,* April 20, 1865: "Brethren, the lamented Abraham Lincoln, believed to be bone from our bone and flesh from our flesh. He was supposed to be a descendant of Hebrew parentage. He said so in my presence. And, indeed, he presented numerous features of the Hebrew race, both in countenance and character." See Sarna and Klein, *Jews of Cincinnati,* p. 53.

Israelites in Egypt, were Negroes."[1265] In June 1867, Wise visited Richmond and was bitter in his reaction to the Blacks, who seemed destined to assume control of the entire Southland. He wrote of their roaming the streets at will, while the whites remained in their homes. "Undoubtedly," wrote Dr. Korn, "he was absorbing the propaganda line of the defeated Confederates when he predicted that the whites would eventually be forced to leave the South; then the negroes would be in full command and would stimulate a flood of negro immigration from Africa."[1266]

Wise's beliefs about the Indian were somewhat more beneficent. Of the California Indians he wrote:

> ...though not total savages, [they] are very primitive and ignorant....[They do] nothing besides loafing and begging....They catch trout in the river, and then sell them to buy ammunition, shoot rabbits, birds, eat various roots and wild plants, also snakes, frogs, dogs, cats, and rats, and say, "Me work no." In conversation with several of them I found that they have no particular home and are heathens.[1267]

Benjamin Wolfe owned a store in Richmond, Virginia, which was burglarized in 1797, and about $500 in merchandise stolen. "Three negro slaves were tried for the offence. Isaac (lucky name) and Billy were acquitted, but on January 3, 1798, the day on which all three were brought to trial, Tom was found guilty and ordered to be hung, at the usual place, on the second Friday of February."[1268]

Jacob Woolf advertised for the return of his runaway slaves in the *South-Carolina Gazette*, July 7 to July 14, 1758:

> RUN AWAY from the Brig. Exbury, the subscriber master, a very likely negro fellow named [not shown], about 5 feet 7 inches high, and about 19 years of age, born in the West-Indies, and speaks very good English; had on black stockings, blue breeches,

---

[1265]Korn, *Eventful Years*, p. 148. More on Wise's attitude toward Blacks and slavery in Marcus, *Studies in American Jewish History*, pp. 189-93. See also Heller, p. 347, who quotes Wise:

> Negro slavery, if it could have been brought under the control of the Mosaic or similar laws, must have tended to the blessing of the Negro race by frequent emigration of civilized Negroes back to the interior of Africa; and even now that race might reap the benefit of its enslaved members, if the latter or the best instructed among them were sent back to the interior of Africa.

[1266]Korn, *Eventful Years*, p. 150.

[1267]William M. Kramer, ed., *The Western Journal of Isaac Mayer Wise, 1877* (Berkeley, California: Western Jewish History Center, 1974), pp. 19, 21.

[1268]Ezekiel and Lichtenstein, pp. 77-78; Korn, "Jews and Negro Slavery," p. 190; *EJ*, vol. 14, p. 160; Rosenbloom, p. 174.

white flannel jacket, and a blue cap bound with red bays. Whoever brings him to me, shall have 40 sh. reward.[1269]

The *South-Carolina Gazette*, November 10 to November 17, 1759:

> RUN AWAY from the subscriber, a negro man named GEORGE PRESTON, about 24 years of age, Jamaica born, speaks good English, and was brought up to the sea; he has a scar on his right eye-lash, and had on when he went away either a new pea blue jacket, or a blue coat with yellow lining, blue breeches or trowsers. Whoever apprehends the said negro and brings him to me, shall receive a reward of TEN POUNDS.[1270]

Solomon Woolf of No. 9 Broad Street in Charleston advertised in the *Gazette Extraordinary of the State of South Carolina* on July 15, 1784: RAN AWAY

> From the subscriber, the 8th instant, a Negro Wench named SUSANNA, 28 or 30 years of age, about 5 feet 2 inches high, thick lips, is coal black, speaks tolerable good English. Had on when she went away, a blue and white calico wrapper, red flannel and Huckaback coat. Whoever apprehends the above negro, and will deliver her to her master, or secure her in any [jail] or work house, so that he may get her again, shall receive Five Guineas Reward. All masters of vessels and others, are forbid to harbour or take her off on their peril.
>
> N.B. The said wench formerly belonged to Mrs. Russell, of Savannah, and has perhaps gone that way.[1271]

David Yulee (born Levy) had risen to political prominence and enjoyed the distinction of being the first Jew elected to the U.S. Senate. His strong oratory embraced the enslavement of Blacks for the use of whites and won him the first Senate seat from Florida. In February 1848, he offered a resolution in reference to New Mexico and Southern California, protesting against the abolition of slavery there on the ground that these territories belonged to all the citizens of *all* the states and that slave property could therefore rightfully be brought into them.[1272] In 1850, Yulee bitterly opposed an anti-slavery resolution of the legislature of Vermont on the grounds that its language was insulting to the South.

Florida passed her ordinance of secession on January 10, 1861, and on January 21 Yulee gave the first speech in the

---

[1269]Windley, vol. 3, p. 161.

[1270]Windley, vol. 3, p. 177.

[1271]Windley, vol. 3, p. 383.

[1272]He changed his name from Levy to Yulee to marry non-Jew Nancy Wickliffe. Leon Hühner, "David L. Yulee, Florida's First Senator," *PAJHS*, vol. 25 (1917), p. 22.

Senate to announce the secession of a Southern state.[1273] "What is advisable," he said,

> is the earliest possible organization of Southern Confederacy and of a Southern Army. The North is rapidly consolidating against us upon the plan of force. A strong government, as eight States will make, promptly organized, and a strong army with Jeff Davis for General in Chief, will bring them to a reasonable sense of the gravity of the crisis.
>
> Have a Southern government as soon as possible adopting the present Federal Constitution for the time, and a Southern army.[1274]

[1273]Hühner, "David L. Yulee, Florida's First Senator," p. 23; Mrs. Archibald Dixon, *The True History of the Missouri Compromise and its Repeal* (Cincinnati, 1899), p. 234; Learsi, p. 96. See also Simonhoff, *Jewish Participants in the Civil War,* pp. 266-68; Feingold, *Zion,* p. 89; Leonard Dinnerstein, "Neglected Aspects of Southern Jewish History," *AJHQ* (1971-72), p. 54; *EJ,* vol. 16, p. 894; Peter Wiernik, *The History of Jews in America: From the Period of the Discovery of the New World to the Present Time* (New York: Hermon Press, 1912, rev. 1931; reprint, Westport, Connecticut: Greenwood Press, 1972), pp. 207-8; G. Cohen, p. 87.

[1274]Hühner, "David L. Yulee, Florida's First Senator," p. 24.

Ode to a Black Man and Brother called "George"

The following letter was written to the Jewish owner of an African Black Man called "George." It exemplifies the courage, spirit, and dignity of the Black Man as he fought his Jewish oppressor.[1275]

> Reading, March 2, 1772
> Mr. Bernard Gratz, Merchant in Philadelphia
>
> Sir:
> I took your negroe George, some time ago, home, thinking I might be the better able to sell him, who, after being with me a night, behaved himself in such an insolent manner I immediately remanded back to the jail.
> About a week since, I put him up for sale at Christopher Witman's tavern, where there was a number of persons who inclined to purchase him. But he protested publickly that he would not be sold, and if anyone should purchase him, he would be the death of him, and words to the like purpose, which deterred the people from bidding.
> I then sent him back again with directions to the jailer to keep him at hard labour, which he refuses to do, and goes on in such an insolent manner that it is impossible to get a master for him here.
> I therefore request you'll send for him on sight hereof, or send me a line by Drinkhouse, or the first opportunity, what I shall do with him.
> He's now almost naked, and if not furnished soon with some clothes, I fear he'll perish.
> Pray let me hear from [you] and, in the mean time, I remain, with great regard, sir,
>
> Your humble servant,
> George Nagel
> N. B. He's now chained and handcuffed on account of his threats.

[1275] *JRM/Docs*, p. 419; Marcus, *Studies in American Jewish History*, p. 28. Some terms clarified from the colonial English spelling. Variant grammar in the original.

Selected Bibliography

Books

Abrahams, Israel. *Jewish Life in the Middle Ages.* New York: Atheneum, 1969.

Arkin, Marcus. *Aspects of Jewish Economic History.* Philadelphia: Jewish Publication Society of America, 1975.

Ashkenazi, Elliott. *The Business of Jew in New Orleans, 1840-1875.* Tuscaloosa: University of Alabama Press, 1988.

__________. *Pictorial History of the Jewish People.* New York: Crown Publications, 1984.

Baron, Salo W., and Arcadius Kahan, et al, eds. *Economic History of the Jews.* New York: Schocken Books, 1975.

Beller, Jacob. *Jews in Latin America.* New York: Jonathan David Publishers, 1969.

Berman, Myron. *Richmond's Jewry 1769-1976: Shabbat in Shockoe.* Charlottesville, Virginia: Jewish Community Federation of Richmond; University Press of Virginia, 1979.

Birnbaum, Philip. *A Book of Jewish Concepts.* New York: Hebrew Publishing, 1975.

Blau, Joseph L., and Salo W. Baron, eds. *The Jews of the United States, 1790-1840.* New York: Columbia University Press, 1963.

Bloom, Herbert I. *The Economic Activities of the Jews of Amsterdam in the Seventeenth and Eighteenth Centuries.* Port Washington, New York/London: Kennikat Press, 1937.

Broches, S. *Jews in New England.* New York: Bloch Publishing, 1942.

Cohen, George. *The Jews in the Making of America.* Boston: Knights of Columbus, Stratford Company, 1924.

Cohen, Henry. *Justice, Justice: A Jewish View of the Black Revolution.* New York: Union of American Hebrew Congregations, 1968.

Cohen, Robert. *The Jewish Nation in Surinam: Historical Essays.* Amsterdam: S. Emmering, 1982.

Davis-Dubois, Rachel, and Emma Schweppe, eds. *The Jews in American Life.* New York: Thomas Nelson and Sons, 1935.

Donnan, Elizabeth. *Documents Illustrative of the History of the Slave Trade in America*. 4 vols. Carnegie Institute of Washington, D.C., 1930-1935.

Elkin, Judith Laikin. *Jews of the Latin American Republics*. Chapel Hill: University of North Carolina Press, 1980.

Elkin, Judith Laikin, and Gilbert W. Merkx. *The Jewish Presence in Latin America*. Boston: Allen & Unwin, 1987.

Elzas, Barnett A. *Jews of South Carolina*. Philadelphia: Lippincott, 1905.

Emmanuel, Isaac S. *The Jews of Coro, Venezuela*. Cincinnati: American Jewish Archives, 1973.

Emmanuel, Isaac S., and Susan A. Emmanuel. *History of the Jews of the Netherland Antilles*. Cincinnati: American Jewish Archives, 1973.

Encyclopaedia Judaica. Jerusalem, Israel: Keter Publishing House, 1971.

Ezekiel, Herbert T., and Gaston Lichtenstein. *History of Jews of Richmond 1769-1917*. Richmond, 1917.

Fein, Isaac M. *The Making of an American Jewish Community: The History of Baltimore Jewry from 1773-1920*. Philadelphia: Jewish Publication Society of America, 1971.

Feingold, Henry L. *Zion in America: The Jewish Experience from Colonial Times to the Present*. New York: Twayne Publishing, 1974.

Feldstein, Stanley. *The Land That I Show You: Three Centuries of Jewish Life in America*. New York: Anchor Press/Doubleday, 1978.

Feuerlicht, Roberta Strauss. *The Fate of the Jews: A People Torn Between Israeli Power and Jewish Ethics*. New York: Times Books, 1983.

Fishman, Priscilla, ed. *Jews of the United States*. Jerusalem: Keter Publishing House, 1973.

Fortune, Stephen Alexander. *Merchants and Jews: The Struggle for the British West Indian Caribbean, 1650-1750*. Gainsville: University Presses of Florida, 1984.

Freyre, Gilberto. *Masters and Slaves: A Study in the Development of Brazilian Civilization*. New York: Alfred A. Knopf, 1946.

Freund, Miriam K. *Jewish Merchants in Colonial America*. New York: Behrman's Jewish Book House, 1939.

Golden, Harry L., and Martin Rywell. *Jews in American History: Their Contribution to the United States of America*. Charlotte, North Carolina: Henry Lewis Martin Co., 1950.

Goodman, Abram Vossen. *American Overture: Jewish Rights in Colonial Times*. Philadelphia: Jewish Publication Society of America, 1947.

Goslinga, Cornelis C. *A Short History of the Netherlands Antilles and Surinam*. The Hague: Martinus Nijhoff, 1979.

Grayzel, Solomon. *A History of the Jews*. Philadelphia: Jewish Publication Society of America, 1947.

Heller, James G. *Isaac M. Wise, His Life and Work and Thought*. New York: Union of American Hebrew Congregations, 1965.

Hershkowitz, Leo. *Wills of Early New York Jews (1704-1799)*. New York: American Jewish Historical Society, 1967.

Hirshler, Eric E., ed. *Jews From Germany in the United States*. New York: Farrar, Straus & Cudahy, 1955.

Hyamson, Albert M. *A History of the Jew in England*. London: Methuen & Co., 1908.

Karp, Abraham J. *Haven and Home: A History of the Jews in America*. New York: Schocken Books, 1985.

__________. *The Jewish Experience in America: Selected Studies from the Publications of the American Jewish Historical Society*. Waltham, Massachusetts, 1969.

Korn, Bertram Wallace. *American Jewry and the Civil War*. Philadelphia: Jewish Publication Society of America, 1951.

__________. *The Early Jews of New Orleans*. Waltham, Massachusetts: American Jewish Historical Society, 1969.

__________. *The Jews of Mobile, Alabama, 1763-1841*. Cincinnati: Hebrew Union College Press, 1970.

Learsi, Rufus. *The Jews in America: A History*. New York: KTAV Publishing House, 1972.

Lebeson, Anita Libman. *Jewish Pioneers in America: 1492-1848*. New York: Behrman's Jewish Book House, 1938.

Levitan, Tina. *Jews in American Life*. New York: Hebrew Publishing Co., 1969.

Marcus, Jacob Rader. *Early American Jewry*. 2 vols. Philadelphia: Jewish Publication Society of America, 1951.

__________. *American Jewry: Documents of the Eighteenth Century*. Cincinnati: Hebrew College Union Press, 1959.

__________. *The Colonial American Jew: 1492-1776.* Detroit, Michigan: Wayne State University Press, 1970.

__________. *Memoirs of American Jews 1775-1865.* 3 vols. New York: KTAV Publishing House, 1974.

__________. *The American Jewish Woman: A Documentary History.* New York: KTAV Publishing House, 1981.

__________. *United States Jewry, 1776-1985.* Detroit, Michigan: Wayne State University Press, 1989.

Pollins, Harold. *Economic History of the Jews in England.* East Brunswick, New Jersey: Associated University Presses, 1982.

Pool, David De Sola. *Portraits Etched in Stone: Early Jewish Settlers, 1682-1831.* New York: Columbia University Press, 1952.

Raphael, Marc Lee. *Jews and Judaism in the United States: A Documentary History.* New York: Behrman House, 1983.

Reznikoff, Charles, and Uriah Z. Engelman. *The Jews of Charleston.* Philadelphia: Jewish Publication Society of America, 1950.

Rischin, Moses, ed. *The Jews of North America.* Detroit: Wayne State University Press, 1987.

Rosenbloom, Joseph R. *A Biographical Dictionary of Early American Jews: Colonial Times through 1800.* University of Kentucky Press, 1960.

Rosenwaike, Ira. *On the Edge of Greatness: A Portrait of American Jewry in the Early National Period.* Cincinnati: American Jewish Archives, 1985.

Roth, Cecil. *Personalities and Events in Jewish History.* Philadelphia: The Jewish Publication Society of America, 1953.

Rywell, Martin. *Jews in American History: Their Contribution to the United States, 1492-1950.* Charlotte, North Carolina: Henry Lewis Martin Co., 1950.

Sarna, Jonathon D., ed. *The American Jewish Experience.* New York/London: Holmes and Meier Publishing, 1986.

__________. *Jacksonian Jew: The Two Worlds of Mordecai Noah.* New York: Holmes and Meir Publishing, 1981.

Schappes, Morris U. *Documentary History of the Jews in the United States.* New York: Citadel Press, 1950.

Sharfman, Harold. *Jews on the Frontier.* Chicago: Henry Regnery Co., 1977.

Shpall, Leo. *The Jews in Louisiana.* New Orleans: Steeg Printing & Publishing Co., 1956.

Siegel, Richard, and Carl Rheins, eds. *The Jewish Almanac*. New York: Bantam Books, 1980.

Simonhoff, Harry. *Jewish Notables in America: 1776-1865.* New York: Greenberg Publisher, 1956.

__________. *Jewish Participants in the Civil War.* New York: Arco Publishing Co., 1963.

Sloan, Irving J., ed. *The Jews in America: 1621-1970.* New York: Oceana Publications, Dobbs Ferry, 1971.

Turitz, Rabbi Leo E., and Evelyn Turitz. *Jews in Early Mississippi.* Jackson: University Press of Mississippi, 1983.

Vorspan, Max, and Lloyd P. Gartner. *History of the Jews of Los Angeles.* San Marino, California: Huntington Library, 1970.

Wiznitzer, Arnold. *Jews in Colonial Brazil.* Morningside Heights, New York: Columbia University Press, 1960.

Wolf, Edwin, II, and Maxwell Whiteman. *The History of the Jews of Philadelphia.* Philadelphia: The Jewish Publication Society of America, 1957.

Wolf, Simon. *The American Jew as Patriot, Soldier and Citizen.* Philadelphia: Levytype Co., 1895.

Articles

Bloom, Herbert I. "A Study of Brazilian Jewish History." *Publications of the American Jewish Historical Society*, vol. 33 (1934).

Glanz, Rudolf. "Notes on Early Jewish Peddling in America." *Jewish Social Studies*, vol. 7 (1945).

Grollman, Earl A. "Dictionary of American Jewish Biography in the 17th Century." *American Jewish Archives*, vol. 3 (1950).

Hershkowitz, Leo. "Some Aspects of the New York Jewish Merchant and Community, 1654 - 1820." *American Jewish Historical Quarterly*, vol. 66 (1976).

Hershkowitz, Leo. "Wills of Early New York Jews 1704-1799." *American Jewish Historical Quarterly*, vol. 56 (1967).

Hühner, Leon. "The Jews of Virginia from the Earliest Times to the Close of the Eighteenth Century." *Publications of the American Jewish Historical Society*, vol. 20 (1911).

Hurwitz, Samuel J., and Edith Hurwitz. "The New World Sets an Example for the Old: The Jews of Jamaica and Political Rights 1661-1831." *American Jewish Historical Quarterly*, vol. 55 (1965-66).

"The Jews of the Confederacy." *American Jewish Archives,* vol. 4 (1961).

Kohler, Max J. "Jewish Factors in Settlement of the West." *Publications of the American Jewish Historical Society*, vol. 16 (1907).

__________. "Phases of Jewish Life in New York before 1800." *Publications of the American Jewish Historical Society*, vol. 2 (1894).

Korn, Bertram W. "Jews and Negro Slavery in the Old South, 1789-1865," *Publications of the American Jewish Historical Society*, vol. 50 (1960).

Maslin, Simeon J. "1732 and 1982 in Curaçao." *American Jewish Historical Quarterly*, vol. 72 (1982).

Oppenheim, Samuel. "An Early Jewish Colony in Western Guiana, 1658-1666: And Its Relation to the Jews in Surinam, Cayenne and Tobago." *Publications of the American Jewish Historical Society*, vol. 16 (1907).

Platt, Virginia Bever. "And Don't Forget the Guinea Voyage: The Slave Trade of Aaron Lopez of Newport." *William and Mary Quarterly*, vol. 32, no. 4 (1975).

Smythe, Hugh H., and Martin S. Price. "The American Jew and Negro Slavery." *The Midwest Journal*, vol. 7, no. 4 (1955-56).

Supple, Barry E. "A Business Elite: German-Jewish Financiers in Nineteenth-Century New York." *Business History*, vol. 31 (1957).

Swetschinski, Daniel M. "Conflict and Opportunity in 'Europe's Other Sea': The Adventure of Caribbean Jewish Settlement." *American Jewish Historical Quarterly*, vol. 72 (1982).

Yerushaimi, Yosef Hayim. "Between Amsterdam and New Amsterdam: The Place of Curaçao and the Caribbean in Early Modern Jewish History." *American Jewish Historical Quarterly*, vol. 72 (1982).

Index

5535 W. Agatite
60630